ABA FUNDAMENTALS

Forensic Science

D. P. Lyle, MD

ABA FUNDAMENTALS

Forensic Science

D. P. Lyle, MD

AMERICAN BAR ASSOCIATION
Defending Liberty
Pursuing Justice

Cover design by Sonya Taylor/ABA Publishing.

Printed in the United States of America.

16 15 14 13 12 5 4 3 2 1

Library of Congress Cataloging-in-Publication Data

Lyle, D. P.
Fundamentals, forensic science / by D. P. Lyle. -- 1st ed.
p. cm.
ISBN 978-1-61438-352-9 (print : alk. paper)
1. Evidence, Expert--United States. 2. Forensic sciences--United States. I. Title.
KF8961.L95 2012
363.250973--dc23
2012010306

Discounts are available for books ordered in bulk. Special consideration is given to state bars, CLE programs, and other bar-related organizations. Inquire at Book Publishing, ABA Publishing, American Bar Association, 321 North Clark Street, Chicago, Illinois 60654-7598.

www.ShopABA.org

BOOKS BY DP LYLE, MD

NON-FICTION

Murder and Mayhem: A Doctor Answers Medical and Forensic Questions From Mystery Writers
Forensics For Dummies
Forensics and Fiction: Clever, Intriguing, and Downright Odd Questions From Crime Writers
Howdunnit: Forensics: A Guide For Writers
More Forensics and Fiction: Crime Writers Morbidly Curious Questions Expertly Answered

FICTION

The Dub Walker Series:
- Stress Fracture
- Hot Lights, Cold Steel
- Run To Ground

The Samantha Cody Series:
- Devil's Playground
- Double Blind

The Royal Pains Media Tie-In Series:
- Royal Pains: First, Do No Harm
- Royal Pains: Sick Rich

ANTHOLOGIES

Thrillers: 100 Must Reads
Essay: Jules Verne, *Mysterious Island*
Thriller 3: Love Is Murder
Short Story: "Even Steven"

DVD

Forensic Science For Writers

CONTENTS

ACKNOWLEDGMENTS

A special thanks to my wonderful agent Kimberley Cameron of Kimberley Cameron and Associates.

An equally special thank you to my excellent and professional editor Erin Nevius at ABA Publishing.

And a thanks to all who work in the criminal investigations arena, particularly the forensic scientists who toil away in often underfunded laboratories.

INTRODUCTION

For the practicing attorney, an understanding of forensic science is essential—and not just those involved in criminal cases, but also those who deal with civil litigation, contracts, dispute resolution, mediation, and virtually every other arena of legal practice.

If you don't practice criminal law, why would you need to know and understand forensic science? You've probably had a case that began as a simple contract dispute or divorce or inheritance but soon brushed up against criminal activity. Was this document forged? Is he the father of this child? Was this death indeed due to natural causes? The possible scenarios are endless.

Forensic science is a huge field, encompassing anatomy, histology, physiology, pharmacology, chemistry, physics, biology, bacteriology, entomology, anthropology, psychology, and other scientific disciplines. It is of course impossible to cover every aspect of forensics in this book. In fact, the subject matter covered in each chapter would require several textbooks to thoroughly explore.

Instead, I will attempt to open the doors to the world of forensic science and provide the reader with a broad understanding of its uses and limitations as well as an in-depth understanding of the most commonly employed forensic techniques—the ones you see on TV, read in the paper, and confront in your practice.

Do you need a background in the sciences to understand this material? No. In each chapter I will explain the concepts and techniques in easily understood language and keep technical jargon to a minimum. The hope is that you will gain a deeper understanding of forensic science and see new ways in which it can impact your practice.

Welcome aboard.

CHAPTER **1**

BASIC CONSIDERATIONS AND HISTORY

What is forensic science? What does the term "forensic science" mean?

One definition is "relating to the use of science in the investigation of criminal activity and the analysis and presentation of evidence before the court." Thus, forensic science is the interface of science and the law. Medico-legal, a term that is often substituted for forensic, makes clear this linkage between law and medical science. Forensic science is the application of various scientific methods to legal matters. It is the viewing of science, not through the glasses of a scientist, but rather through the lens of the law.

The word *forensic* is derived from the Latin word *forum*. In ancient Rome, the forum was where merchants, politicians, scholars, and citizens mingled and discussed issues of common interest. It also served as the place where public trials took place.

Today, the term "forensic" is applied to anything that relates to law, and forensic science is the application of scientific disciplines to the law. It is important to note that it differs from the term "clinical," which means "related to a medical clinic."

For example, clinical toxicology deals with medications and drugs in the care of medical patients. The clinical toxicologist will analyze samples taken from an intoxicated or deceased individual to determine what drugs might be present and if they played a role in the person's intoxication or death. He will determine if a patient's blood level of a certain drug is adequate to treat his condition without being high enough to cause side effects or other medical problems. In other words, the clinical toxicologist is concerned with patient care and treatment.

A forensic toxicologist uses similar testing procedures to help resolve legal issues. Did the victim die from a poison or a drug overdose? Was the erratic driver intoxicated? Was a suspect's aberrant behavior due to drug usage? Was a particular employee complying with her company's drug policies? Forensic toxicology deals with these types of questions.

A similar difference is seen between a clinical (hospital) pathologist and a forensic pathologist, who sits at the apex of the forensic (medico-legal) investigative system. A clinical pathologist is concerned with helping other physicians treat the ill. To do this, he might oversee the clinical lab, interpret lab tests, review biopsies and surgically removed tissues, and perform medical autopsies. A medical autopsy is designed to determine why someone died and to discover what complicating disease processes might also have been present.

The forensic pathologist is concerned with criminal harm and death. She might direct the crime lab (although not always, since more often than not the crime lab falls under the wing of the police or sheriff's department), interpret forensic tests, and perform forensic autopsies. A forensic autopsy is designed to explain why someone died or was injured, with the focus being to determine if a criminal act had taken place.

Similarly, a forensic (crime) lab is quite different from a medical (clinical) lab. Tests performed within the clinical or hospital lab are directed toward aiding the diagnosis and treatment of ill patients. A forensic lab is geared toward evidence testing in the hope of establishing a link between a suspect and a crime.

How did this marriage between law and science come about?

The Development of Forensic Science

How old is forensic investigation? When was science first used to solve a criminal case? No one knows for sure, but many feel that the origins can be traced to the famous Chinese investigator Sung T'zu, who published the first text on forensic science in 1247. It carried the rather poetic title *Xi Yuan Ji Lu*, or *The Washing Away of Wrongs*. It represented the first organized study of criminal investigation and touched on topics such as autopsies, causes of death, postmortem decay and insect activity, and poisoning. It soon enjoyed translation into other languages, including Japanese, German, French, Russian, and English.

The field of forensic science evolved in fits and spurts over the centuries that followed. Some techniques developed early and progressed rapidly, while others took a more leisurely pace, and still others are truly modern discoveries. No forensic science technique just magically appeared, but rather each followed its own unique evolutionary process.

Modern forensic science rests on a foundation of centuries of scientific discovery and, in fact, it could not have developed until sufficient knowledge of basic physical and biological principles was available. How could DNA testing become an accepted procedure until we knew DNA existed and understood how it worked? How could fingerprints be used for identification until we discovered their existence and their uniqueness?

The typical evolution of any scientific principle or technique is its initial postulation or discovery, followed by its testing and refinement by the scientific community. From there it usually enters the medical arena and then goes on to become a useful forensic tool. Virtually every forensic science technique, including procedures in ballistics, toxicology, and serology (the study of blood and body fluids), has followed a similar path.

For example, in 1901 Karl Landsteiner discovered that human blood contained certain proteins that could be grouped by types and from this devised the ABO blood groups that we still use today. His discovery opened the door for safe and effective blood transfusions without the danger of serious, even deadly, reactions. In 1915, Leone Lattes used Landsteiner's discovery to develop a simple method for determining the ABO type of a dried bloodstain and almost immediately applied his new technique to criminal investigations. Even today, ABO typing is used to identify suspects, exonerate the innocent, verify or refute paternity, and reconstruct crime scenes.

Throughout this book we will see similar evolutionary processes for many other forensic science techniques.

The First Forensic Scientists

This will probably surprise you: The first forensic scientists did not come from the world of science but rather from the world of fiction. (Proof that not only does art imitate life, but also that life imitates art.)

Sir Arthur Conan Doyle's Sherlock Holmes frequently used the sciences of fingerprinting, document examination, and blood analysis to solve crimes. In the first Sherlock Holmes novel, *A Study in Scarlet,* Holmes developed a chemical method to determine whether a stain was blood or not. Since this technique had yet to be used in a real-life criminal investigation, Sherlock was definitely ahead of the curve.

In his 1883 memoir *Life on the Mississippi,* Mark Twain talks of a thumbprint being used to identify a murderer. This predated both the groundbreaking work on fingerprints by Sir Francis Galton, who received knighthood for the "discovery" that he summarized in his 1892 book *Fingerprints,* and the famous Rojas case in Argentina (also 1892), which marked the first time that fingerprints had been used to gain a murder conviction. Later, Twain wrote of fingerprints being used in a trial in *The Tragedy of Pudd'nhead Wilson,* a work serialized in *Century Magazine* in 1893–1894 before appearing in novel form in 1894.

In each of these cases it is likely that the author was at least aware that testing for blood and fingerprint examinations was being studied rather than simply creating these techniques from whole cloth for their stories. Rumors and concepts often precede any true scientific discovery.

The first real-life forensic scientist was Hans Gross. His reasoned and methodic approach to criminal investigation and the mind of not only criminals but also their pursuers laid the foundation for modern criminology. In 1893, he published the first treatise on the use of scientific knowledge and procedures in criminal investigations. His classic 1910 work *Criminal Psychology* laid out the principles of criminal behavior and how evidence should be evaluated and used in criminal proceedings.

Others soon followed in Gross's footsteps, most notably Edmond Locard, a police officer and professor in Lyon, France. Locard made an extremely important observation that became known as Locard's Exchange Principle, which to this day remains the cornerstone of forensic investigation. It will be discussed in detail in Chapter 3.

An extensive timeline of forensic science achievements and milestones is included at the end of this book.

The Coroner and the Medical Examiner

You've probably seen the terms "coroner" and "medical examiner" used almost interchangeably. In truth they are quite different even though each can be the person in charge of "all things death." The title this person carries, whether coroner or medical examiner, depends upon which system is in place in the particular jurisdiction. In the United States, these are county-level positions, and the title afforded and the duties that follow vary from county to county.

The term "coroner" derives from the English office of the "crowner of the king" or the "keeper of the pleas of the Crown." It is unclear exactly when the office of coroner came into existence, but it might have predated the Norman Invasion since it was mentioned as early as 871, during the reign of Alfred the Great. However, it is believed that King Richard Plantagenet, also known as Richard the Lionheart, officially created the position in 1194. Then, in 1276 a legal document known as De Officio Coronatoris set out the coroner's duties and obligations. This was later replaced and refined by the Coroner's Act of 1887.

This "crowner" performed many functions that we associate with the modern coroner, including determining the cause of death. He also served as a judge in criminal proceedings. In this capacity he was considered an inquisitional judge in that he actually investigated crimes and actively pursued evidence and criminals rather than merely serving as "the trier of fact" for criminal cases. Inquisitional judges have their origin in ancient Roman law and serve as the basis for the judicial systems found in Russia, Spain, France, and other countries. Under English law, courtroom judges are non-inquisitional and are not actively involved in criminal investigation or evidence gathering. Rather, they hear the evidence provided by others and oversee the proceedings within the courtroom.

The English coroner is unique in that he is an inquisitional judge, who actively investigates crimes, in a non-inquisitional system. Early English settlers to the New World brought the office of the coroner with them so that in the United States we have a similar inquisitional coroner system.

The medical examiner (ME) is a more modern invention. Its origins can be traced to France and Scotland, and in the late 1800s this system was also brought to the United States. In almost all jurisdictions, the ME is a medical professional with at least an MD degree, and most modern MEs are trained in pathology, particularly forensic pathology.

In the United States, both of these forensic investigative systems exist. It varies from county to county so that one county might have a coroner while its neighbor has a medical examiner. For centuries in England, the king appointed the coroner. In the United States, since there was no king, the coroner became an appointed or elected position and this selection method, which also varies from county to county, continues today.

Who can be coroner? Almost anyone. Usually there are age and residency requirements, but often no special medical or forensic skills are part of the application process. The major skill required seems to be the ability to win an election or to secure an appointment from the county commission or whatever legal body is charged with the appointment. It is often more a popularity contest than anything else. The coroner might be the sheriff, newspaper publisher, neighborhood café owner, or local funeral director. As often as not he possesses little or no medical training or experience and thus might not be qualified to perform many of his duties. This deficiency led to the creation of the medical examiner system.

In 1877, Massachusetts mandated the replacement of coroners with medical examiners and required that medical examiners be licensed physicians. New York City adopted a similar system in 1915. In the 1940s, Congress established the Commission on Uniform State Laws and from this commission came the Medical Examiner's Act, which was adopted by most states. This led to the replacement of most coroners with medical examiners. However, with the exception of the District of Columbia, no federal program existed for investigating deaths until 1990, when Congress established the Federal Medical Examiner's Office in the Armed Forces Institute of Pathology.

Most medical examiner systems require the ME to be a pathologist, and some require that he be trained in forensic pathology. A forensic pathologist is a clinical (medical) pathologist with extra training in the field of forensics. He oversees all aspects of death and criminal injury, perhaps runs the crime lab, and performs "forensic autopsies."

In an ideal world, every jurisdiction would have a medical examiner, and that person would be a forensic pathologist. But that's not practical. Smaller and more rural jurisdictions simply do not have the population base nor the budget to justify the hiring of a qualified forensic pathologist as medical examiner. In this circumstance, the coroner has several options for acquiring specialized pathological services.

He might contract with a larger regional or state medical examiner's office for pathological and laboratory testing or hire a part-time forensic pathologist to serve as medical examiner. This individual would likely be given a title such as Deputy Assistant Coroner. Under the legal umbrella of the coroner's office, she would perform autopsies, testify in court, and perhaps oversee the crime lab. Also, in many areas where the coroner system is in place, the coroner will hire one or more full-time pathologists to serve as medical examiners or deputy assistant coroners. Each of these arrangements offers the (often unqualified) coroner a method to obtain the needed medical expertise so he can adequately investigate deaths and crimes.

The relationship of the coroner or ME to the crime lab varies from jurisdiction to jurisdiction. In some areas the ME oversees the forensic laboratory, while in others the lab might function under the auspices of law enforcement agencies such as the police or sheriff's department. And as with pathological services, many rural jurisdictions obtain lab services through contracts with major city or state crime labs.

NOTE: Since both systems exist in the United States, in this book I will use the terms coroner and medical examiner (ME) interchangeably.

Duties of the Coroner/Medical Examiner

The coroner or medical examiner wears many hats and often acts as judge, juror, investigator, and scientist. Her responsibilities cover virtually every aspect of death investigation and include the following:

- Determination of the cause and manner of death
- Determination of the time of death
- Supervision of evidence collection from the body
- Identification of unknown corpses and skeletal remains
- Determination of any contributory factors in the death

- Certification of the death certificate
- Presentation of expert testimony in court
- Oversight of the crime lab (in some areas)
- Examination of injuries in the living and determination of their cause and timing

In fulfilling her duties, she might interrogate witnesses, review witness statements and police or hospital files, visit crime scenes, examine collected evidence, study the results of crime lab procedures, perform autopsies, and gather any other evidence she feels she might need. To accomplish all this the coroner is typically given full subpoena power. She will often work with the police and homicide detectives to help guide their ongoing investigations by supplying them with the results of any forensic tests she or the crime lab has performed.

The Coroner/Medical Examiner in the Courtroom

One of the coroner's most important duties is to present evidence in the courtroom, for it is here that the world of science is brought to the law. His testimony can often make or break a case. In fact, his determination of the cause and manner of death will often determine whether a criminal case comes to court or not. If he states that the manner of death is natural or suicidal, it would less likely become a criminal proceeding. But, if the death is homicidal—and occasionally if it is accidental (as in an industrial setting)—the case might very well enter the courtroom.

He might be called to testify by either the prosecution or the defense. His sworn duty is to present the facts and offer an unbiased opinion based on these facts. He might be asked to discuss and explain the forensic evidence and to offer his expert opinion regarding this evidence to the judge and jury. In this regard he acts as an educator as well as a scientist. Often he is the only person the jury hears from who can make complex scientific information understandable. He might face experts with different opinions, so he must be able to pit his knowledge and communication skills against other experts in his field.

Each expert that appears before the court, including the coroner, should expect to be qualified before the jury. The attorneys will ask questions about his credentials, training, experience, areas of expertise, teaching positions, publications in the field in question, and anything else they deem will support or undermine his expertise. The side that called him will ask easy, supportive questions, while the other side will ask tougher questions in an attempt to "impeach" any testimony he might give. The coroner must be prepared for potentially unsettling questions.

Depending upon his own abilities and knowledge and depending upon the number and types of experts arrayed against or in support of him, the coroner might present all the evidence himself or he might ask members of his staff or the crime lab to present portions of the evidence. For example, he might give testimony regarding the autopsy, while a fingerprint expert might present that evidence. A toxicologist might discuss the results of the toxicological examinations. A firearms expert might reveal his findings. Or the coroner might present all this evidence himself.

With expert testimony, the judge typically allows a great deal more leeway as to how the information is presented to the jury than he does with most witnesses. Most witnesses are allowed only to answer questions, and if they stray too far afield the opposing attorney will object or the judge himself might rein them in. An expert is allowed to speak more broadly and to "teach" the jury. The reason for this latitude is that the expert is there to present and explain any evidence in his area of expertise. For example, it would be very difficult for the average juror to understand the impact of DNA evidence from a series of yes and no questions, but allowing the expert to explain what DNA is, how it is tested, and what the results of the testing mean gives the jurors the knowledge they need to understand and evaluate the evidence.

Because science is neither absolute nor static and because it is built on ever-changing theories, it is rare that an expert will say that something without doubt matches or that a particular result is absolute. Rather he will use phrases such as "similar to," "consistent with," "not dissimilar from," "compatible with," or "shares many characteristics with." Each of these terms speaks to the fact that forensic evidence is rarely, if ever, absolute but rather that it states probabilities. For example, no two people have the same DNA, but the testifying expert will not say that the DNA "absolutely matches" that of the defendant. Instead he will say that the probability that it matches is a billion to one. Almost, but not quite, absolute.

Crime Lab Origins

The first forensic laboratory in the United States was established in 1923 by the Los Angeles Police Chief August Vollmer. In 1929, the famous St. Valentine's Day Massacre (discussed in Chapter 17) prompted two Chicago businessmen to help establish the first independent crime lab, the Scientific Crime Detection Laboratory (SCDL) at Northwestern University. In 1932, the Federal Bureau of Investigation established a national forensic laboratory, which would offer services to law enforcement across the country. It served as the model for all future state and local labs so that now many states have networks of regional and local labs, which support law enforcement at all levels.

The CSI Effect

No discussion of forensic science would be complete without addressing the "CSI effect." It's a controversial topic in that there are widely differing opinions about its definition and even whether it exists or not.

The CSI effect derives from the many forensic science shows on TV, both fictional and documentary-style. Many point to the CBS series *CSI: Crime Scene Investigation* as the beginning of the phenomenon, which then expanded with the appearance of the "CSI clones" and other shows such as *Bones, NCIS, Cold Case,* and *Forensic Files.* It is almost impossible to turn on the TV without seeing a crime show, and forensic science is invariably part of the story. The same goes for virtually every case you see presented on national or local news.

The CSI effect could be defined as the impact of these shows, which reveal cool and clever forensic science techniques, on the public, criminals, law enforcement officials, juries, and courts. These shows have created a level of expectation that simply isn't realistic. They portray crime labs as being fully equipped with very expensive instruments and staffed with brilliant minds that magically uncover the most esoteric evidence. They make the very rare seem almost commonplace. They suggest that all these wonderful tools are widely available and frequently employed in criminal cases. The truth is vastly different. DNA testing is involved in perhaps 1 percent of cases, and it isn't available in 20 minutes. Crime labs are severely underfunded, and most have meager equipment, not the plasma screens and holographic generators seen on TV. The lab techs are indeed smart and dedicated individuals, but they aren't prescient. They can't magically solve complex crimes by simply "seeing" the solution in a microscope or within their minds. It doesn't work that way. (At least not often.)

So how does all this information—or misinformation—affect the public, criminals, and the police and courts? Simply put, they teach criminals how to avoid leaving behind evidence and unrealistically raise the expectations of the public.

Criminals watch these TV shows and learn to alter their behavior to avoid detection. They learn not to leave behind fingerprints and DNA evidence, to hide from surveillance cameras, to avoid using cell phones and computers in the planning and execution of their crimes, and a host of other things. Fortunately, these shows are not always accurate and don't cover all contingencies involved in the planning and execution of a crime, proving the old adage that a little knowledge is a dangerous thing. The criminal thinks he has thought of everything, but while he focuses on one bit of evidence he ignores others. An example would be the thief who planned a breaking and entering home robbery. He knew that shoe prints could be left in the soft dirt of the planter beneath his entry point window so he took off his shoes. He then realized he had not brought gloves, so to prevent leaving fingerprints, he removed his socks and used them as hand covers. The crime was interrupted by the homeowner, an altercation with bloodshed followed, and the thief left a bloody footprint on a piece of broken window glass. This proved to be his undoing. True story.

The public, who make up juries, come away from these shows believing that high-tech investigations are involved in every case, and if the police or prosecutors fail to make DNA or blood analysis part of the case they must have done something wrong. And in some cases defense attorneys latch on to this and use it to undermine the police investigation. During the famous Scott Peterson case, how many times did you hear news reports and pundits talk about the lack of DNA evidence—as if this made the case weak? In truth, finding Laci's blood or DNA on Scott or his clothing would be of little help. They were married and they lived together, so there were hundreds of innocent reasons for Laci's DNA to be found.

Back in the 1960s and 1970s, juries wanted confessions and eyewitnesses, both of which can be false and erroneous. Now, after the saturation of our psyche with forensic science, jurors expect DNA and other sophisticated evidence. This not only makes gaining a conviction more difficult but also gives prosecutors pause before filing charges in cases without such evidence.

So, it can be said that the CSI effect alters the criminal justice system in many ways. It helps criminals avoid detection, creates unrealistic expectations in the public and in juries, and makes prosecution of some crimes problematic. But there are positive aspects in that this increased interest in forensic science has led to more people choosing it as a career; indeed the number of colleges offering forensic science curricula and degrees has mushroomed.

Chapter 2

GENERAL ORGANIZATION OF FORENSIC SCIENCE

The world of forensic science involves many scientific disciplines that have been brought together under a single umbrella. This marriage was neither easy nor smooth. As mentioned earlier, the development of modern forensic science paralleled advances in science, particularly the physical and biological sciences. The invention of the microscope, the development of photography, the understanding of the biology and physics of blood spatter, and the discovery of blood typing and DNA analysis are examples of such advances. Before these scientific principles and procedures were applied to criminal investigations, they underwent years of refinement, often in the medical arena. Some techniques developed early and quickly, while others progressed more slowly, so that the various sciences entered the forensics arena in a more or less haphazard fashion.

Fingerprints and DNA, the two most individualizing techniques in forensics, are examples of this difference. Fingerprints, which require only visual inspection (perhaps with the help of a magnifying glass) and little scientific underpinnings, came along over 100 years ago. On the other hand, modern DNA techniques could not develop until we understood the biochemical world of the body's cells, a much more complex undertaking. This is the main reason it developed more slowly. The point is that the various disciplines of forensic science grew at different rates.

Similarly, the organization of these various scientific disciplines into a coherent field of study was neither smooth nor linear, and their use in criminal investigation varied greatly from country to country and even from area to area within the United States. This is still true today. Some jurisdictions have complete and sophisticated crime labs, while others are Spartan by comparison.

In large cities, such as Los Angeles, New York, Chicago, or Houston, the police, the crime lab, and the coroner's office employ hundreds, even thousands, of people and have budgets, though still woefully inadequate, in the millions. The crime lab is large and offers a wide array of services. On the other hand, a small rural town might have the police chief, a single deputy, and the local undertaker as the sum total of their forensic team.

This means that the types of scientific services offered by a particular crime lab and coroner's office depend upon its size and budget. State, regional, and larger reference labs might provide a wide array of forensic science services, while in smaller labs these services are typically more basic. To fill in these gaps, smaller labs outsource more sophisticated testing to larger regional labs. In addition, the FBI's National Crime Lab offers services to law enforcement throughout the country. Not only does the FBI lab perform virtually every type of test, it possesses or has access to databases on everything from fingerprints to tire track impressions to postage stamps.

Larger labs often have separate departments for each discipline, while smaller labs tend to combine services. For example, a large state lab might employ experts in firearms examination, tool marks, serology (blood examination), and DNA, while a local lab might combine firearms with tool marks and DNA with serology. In very small labs, a single technician might perform all of these duties. Obviously, in this circumstance a great deal of the work must be sent out to larger, more complete reference labs.

Regardless of the level of sophistication in a given jurisdiction, modern forensics integrates the varied scientific disciplines in an effort to solve crimes. This requires extensive coordination among law enforcement, the crime scene technicians, the crime lab, and the coroner.

Criminalistics and Criminalists

Two terms, **criminalistics** and **criminalists**, deserve attention since they often create confusion.

Criminalistics and forensic science are frequently confused but in fact the terms are often used interchangeably. The term criminalistics, which derives from the German word *kriminalistik* and can be traced back to Hans Gross, the first true forensic investigator, is defined as the science of analyzing and interpreting scientific evidence. The same definition could be applied to forensic science.

A criminalist is a forensic scientist who works in one or more of the various crime lab areas. Because of the wide range and sophistication of the scientific disciplines represented in the modern crime lab, many criminalists specialize in a single area of forensic science. They might work in toxicology (drugs and poisons), serology (blood), fingerprint analysis, chemistry, blood spatter analysis, document examination, or one of the other service areas of the crime lab.

Crime Lab Services

The forensic science services offered by the coroner's office and the crime lab can be divided into biological, physical, and ancillary arenas. We will visit each of these areas in considerable detail in later chapters, but first let's take a broad overview of these services.

Biological Forensic Science Services

Forensic pathology is the domain of the forensic pathologist, who is a medical doctor with subspecialty training in pathology and further training in forensic pathology. He might be the coroner, the medical examiner, or a subcontracted provider of pathological services. He is called upon to answer several crucial questions such as: Who is the victim? How did she die? What injuries did she suffer, and when and how were they inflicted?

The forensic pathologist will use the autopsy, police reports, medical records, suspect and witness interviews, the results of crime lab evidence evaluations, and much more in his pursuit of the answers. If he serves as the coroner or medical examiner, he must sign all official death certificates and is charged with determining the time, cause, and manner of death. Many natural as well as accidental, suicidal, and homicidal deaths come to his attention. He might also examine living victims to determine the cause and age of injuries, particularly in cases or assault, rape, or abuse.

Forensic anthropology is primarily concerned with the identification of skeletal remains. To do this, the forensic anthropologist will attempt to determine the age, sex, and race of the person, identify any illnesses or injuries the person might have suffered, and establish the time, cause, and manner of death as best he can. He might also be asked to identify victims of mass disasters or those interred in mass graves.

Forensic odontology is forensic dentistry. The forensic dentist helps identify unknown corpses by matching dental patterns with previous x-rays, dental casts, or photographs. Since tooth enamel is the hardest substance in the human body and often survives when nothing else of the deceased remains, the forensic dentist can often help with identifying skeletal remains and victims of mass disasters and mass graves. He might also be called upon to match a suspect's teeth to bite marks on the victim or on food and other products left at the crime scene.

Serology deals with blood and other bodily fluids such as saliva and semen. The forensic serologist will conduct blood typing, paternity testing, and often DNA profiling.

Toxicology is the study of drugs and poisons. The forensic toxicologist determines if drugs or poisons are present in both the living and the deceased and assesses their contribution to the person's aberrant behavior or death. He might also be asked to identify confiscated drugs, to determine if a driver was intoxicated, or to assess whether a worker has violated company drug use policies.

Botany, the examination of plant residue by a forensic botanist, can supply crucial crime scene evidence. Plant fragments, seeds, pollen, and soil can sometimes place a suspect at the crime scene or reveal that a corpse has been moved.

Forensic entomology is the study of insects that populate a corpse. The forensic entomologist studies the life cycles of flies and various other insects that feed on corpses and uses this knowledge to determine the approximate time of death. His understanding of insect habitats might also be useful in determining whether a body has been moved from one location to another.

Forensic psychiatry is the domain of the forensic psychiatrist, who deals with criminal and civil proceedings where the state of mind of the perpetrator is important in not only guilt and innocence but also in sentencing. He might be asked to address someone's sanity or competence to stand trial, sign documents, or give informed medical consent. In suicide cases he might be asked to do a "psychological autopsy" in order to determine the victim's possible motivations.

Physical Forensic Science Services

Trace evidence is any small item of evidence and includes hair, fiber, paint, glass, and soil. This evidence might place the suspect at the crime scene or in contact with the victim.

Firearms examination is commonly, but erroneously, referred to as **ballistics**. The forensic firearms examiner analyzes weapons, ammunition, fired bullets, shell casings, and shotgun and gunshot residue scatter patterns, and will often perform weapon serial number restorations.

Document examination is performed on documents whose age or authenticity is in doubt, as well as any document that might have been altered. To look for evidence of forgery, the document examiner uses handwriting analysis to match known exemplars to questioned documents and signatures. He might be asked to analyze the physical and chemical properties of paper and ink as well as to expose indented (second page) writing. Altered typewritten or photocopied documents also fall under his area of expertise.

Fingerprint examination uses finger, palm, and foot sole prints to identify unknown corpses and to match crime scene prints to a suspect or to those stored in databases such as the **AFIS (Automated Fingerprint Identification System)**.

Patterned evidence possesses a recognizable pattern that can be compared to other patterns. In addition to fingerprints, tire tracks, shoe impressions, and tool marks are considered patterned evidence.

Ancillary Forensic Services

The **evidence collection unit**, also called the crime scene investigation unit (CSIU) in many jurisdictions, is charged with collecting, preserving, and transporting crime scene evidence. The duties of the CSIU tech might include exposing and lifting latent fingerprints, collecting hair and fibers, sampling crime scene bloodstains, casting tire and shoe impressions, and gathering any other articles of evidence at the scene.

The **photography unit** photographically records the scene, all evidence, and the body (if one is present). These photos and/or videos are crucial to crime scene reconstruction and the presentation of evidence in the courtroom.

Evidence storage requires a secure place for storing and preserving the evidence. Often materials must be kept for years, even decades, and the chain of custody must remain unbroken throughout or the evidence could be compromised and lose its evidentiary value. Only authorized individuals can examine the evidence, and they must sign it in and out and account for it at all times.

Chapter 3

EVIDENCE

> Wherever he steps, whatever he touches, whatever he leaves, even unconsciously, will serve as a silent witness against him. Not only his fingerprints or his footprints, but his hair, the fibers from his clothes, the glass he breaks, the tool mark he leaves, the paint he scratches, the blood or semen he deposits or collects. All of these and more, bear mute witness against him. This is evidence that does not forget. It is not confused by the excitement of the moment. It is not absent because human witnesses are. It is factual evidence. Physical evidence cannot be wrong, it cannot perjure itself, it cannot be wholly absent. Only human failure to find it, study and understand it, can diminish its value.
>
> Paul L. Kirk, *Crime Investigation: Physical Evidence and the Police Laboratory,* Interscience Publishers, Inc., New York, 1953

Locard's Exchange Principle

Professor Edmond Locard (1877–1966) was a student of both medicine and law in Lyon, France, and served as an assistant to Alexandre Lacassagne, a well-known and respected criminal investigator and professor. Professor Locard developed the twelve-point fingerprint identification system, wrote the massive seven-volume *Traité de Criminalistique*, and in 1910, while working at the Lyon Police Department, developed the world's first crime lab. But despite all these accomplishments, he is best known for his Exchange Principle.

Locard's Exchange Principle is the basis, the heart and soul, of forensic science, and understanding this principle is critical to grasping the true workings of forensic investigation. As so elegantly stated above by Paul L. Kirk, the basic premise is that whenever a person comes into contact with another person, object, or place, an exchange of materials takes place. At any crime scene, blood and other bodily fluids, fibers, hair, fingerprints, and shoe prints are deposited or picked up and carried away by anyone present. If you own a pet, the hairs you find on your clothing are perfect examples of this exchange.

This **linkage** is the basic function of forensic science. Linked evidence proves that a person has come into contact with another person, place, or object. The analysis of fingerprints, blood, DNA, fibers, dirt, plant materials, paint, glass, shoe and tire impressions, and indeed every test performed by the crime lab is to create an association between the perpetrator and the crime scene or other elements of the crime (victim, weapon, etc.). In some cases, the simple fact that the suspect was at the scene implies guilt. A fingerprint on a broken window or pried-open filing cabinet, semen obtained from a rape victim, or blood shed at the scene by the perpetrator might link him to a location where he had no "innocent" reason to be.

Evidence linkage can also prove that two objects or substances share a common source. If a paint chip found in the clothing of a hit-and-run victim is matched to a particular car, this match shows that the car was the source of the paint. If blood, semen, or some other bodily fluid found at a crime scene matches the DNA profile of a suspect, it proves these materials shared a common source—the suspect.

Does this make either suspect guilty? Not necessarily. That determination will be made in a court of law. The linkage of the evidence simply puts the suspect at the scene. It will be up to the police and prosecutors to prove that this linkage is proof of guilt—or conversely, for the suspect and his defense attorney to offer an innocent reason for the evidence to be found where it was.

Let's say a woman is found murdered in her home and rape is suspected. DNA from semen found at the scene is matched to the man who lives next door. Does that make him the killer? When confronted, the one thing he can't deny is that the DNA found at the scene was his. But, he might have an innocent reason for it being there. What if the two were having an affair? What if he had visited her an hour or so before her murder? What if he says they had sex, but when he left she was alive and well? Forensic science can link him to the scene but it cannot always reveal why he was there and what transpired while he was there. It can't determine his ultimate guilt or innocence. Only a court can do that.

Besides making this linkage, forensic evidence also **identifies**. Is the white powder in the plastic bag cocaine or sugar? Is the carpet stain ketchup or blood? Is the drug in a victim's blood homemade methamphetamine or pharmaceutical pseudoephedrine? The forensic lab can identify each of these.

Simply put, evidence identifies or links, while courts convict or acquit.

If Locard's Exchange Principle is the cornerstone of forensic science, evidence is the raw material of the crime lab and is the sole reason the lab exists. Without evidence, what would the lab do?

Evidence can determine if a crime has been committed, link a suspect to a scene, corroborate or refute alibis and witness statements, identify a perpetrator or victim, exonerate the innocent, induce confessions, and help direct further investigation. A tall order for sure, but these problems confront forensic scientists on a daily basis.

This brings up a critical concept. You might think that evidence is used to point the finger at a particular individual, while the exact opposite is true. Evidence **eliminates** suspects until only one remains.

This isn't a modern concept. Again, we look to Sherlock Holmes, who stated in several of his stories that good evidence and clear reasoning eliminate all choices but one. For example, in *The Adventure of the Beryl Coronet,* Holmes states, "It is an old maxim of mine that when you have excluded the impossible, whatever remains, however improbable, must be the truth."

This is what forensic science does. It points the finger away from person after person until the perpetrator is left standing alone and exposed.

Using Evidence

Crime scene evidence serves several purposes in the arena of criminal investigation:

- **Corpus delicti**: This is a Latin term that means "the body of the crime" or the essential facts of the crime. Evidence will reveal exactly what type of crime was committed, such as robbery, murder, or a sexual assault.
- **Modus operandi (MO)**: This is the steps and methods the perpetrator employs to commit the crime. A criminal's MO tends to be repetitive, so that identification of his MO can help uncover the perpetrator.
- **Linkage**: The association or linkage of a suspect to a victim, a place, or other pieces of evidence is critical to solving the crime.
- **Verification**: Evidence can substantiate or refute suspect or witness statements.
- **Suspect identification**: Evidence such as fingerprints and DNA can often identify the perpetrator.
- **Crime scene reconstruction**: The evidence often allows investigators to reconstruct the sequence of events of the crime.
- **Investigative leads**: Evidence frequently directs the lines of further investigation.

As you can see, evidence serves many functions. Its true power lies in its ability to identify and compare evidence items, its inherent class and individual characteristics, its ability to reconstruct the events of the crime, and its capacity to associate or dissociate a suspect from the crime.

Evidence Classification

Evidence can be viewed or divided along several lines:

- Physical and biological evidence
- Direct and circumstantial evidence
- Identification and comparison
- Class versus individual characteristics
- Reconstructive and associative evidence

Physical and Biological Evidence

Physical evidence includes fingerprints, shoe and tire impressions, tool marks, fibers, paint, glass, drugs, firearms, bullets and shell casings, documents, explosives, and petroleum byproduct fire accelerants. Biological evidence includes a corpse, blood, saliva, semen, hair, and botanical materials, such as wood, plants, and pollens.

Direct and Circumstantial Evidence

Direct evidence, which is either eyewitness statements or confessions, directly establishes a fact. That sounds simple and straightforward, but direct evidence is by nature subjective, and this presents several problems. Eyewitnesses are notoriously incorrect in their identification of a suspect and their recall of events. This is because memory and recall are extremely subjective and are affected by the witness's mental and physical health, prejudices, experiences, and the emotion of the situation. It is easy to see that a witness with poor vision or hearing, with certain racial prejudices, or one that was highly emotional could easily, and often unintentionally, distort what he saw or heard. Previous studies of this phenomenon have shown that eyewitnesses are wrong as much as 50 percent of the time. Not a good track record.

On the other hand, circumstantial evidence is more objective and is subject to the laws of probability. This leads to the curious fact that circumstantial evidence is often much more reliable than direct evidence. Unlike an eyewitness account, accurate science is not altered by subjectivity. Its interpretation might be, but the result is the result.

What exactly is circumstantial evidence? Basically, it is any evidence that is not direct. Blood, hair, fibers, bullets, blood, DNA, and indeed all forensic science evidence are circumstantial in nature. This type of evidence requires that the judge and jury infer something from the presented evidentiary fact. For example, if a fingerprint found at the crime scene is matched to a suspect, the jury might infer that the print is indeed that of the defendant and that the fact that it was found at the crime scene links the defendant to the scene. Under most circumstances this is not absolute proof, but highly suggestive that he was involved in the crime. The jury must then unravel the circumstances under which the print was left. Is there an innocent explanation for it being there or does its presence indicate guilt?

Identification and Comparison

The forensic analysis of evidence items is done for two main purposes: **identification** and **comparison**.

Identification reveals exactly what a particular item or substance is. Is this white powder heroin, crystal methamphetamine, or sugar? Who manufactured the tire that left an impression at the crime scene? Are there petrochemical residues present in the debris of a suspicious fire? Identification in such circumstances is critical since if the powder is sugar and not heroin or the stain is indeed chocolate sauce and not blood, it is possible that no crime occurred. Conversely, if heroin or blood is identified, a criminal investigation might follow. After testing, the examiner might be able to state that the questioned substance is present or not present, or that the testing is inclusive and the presence of the substance can be neither ruled in nor ruled out.

Comparing evidence might reveal whether a known and a suspect item share a common origin or not. That is, did they come from the same person, place, or object? Did this fingerprint, hair, or blood come from the suspect? Does the bullet removed from a murder victim match the one test fired from the suspect's gun? Does the accelerant found at the fire scene match the gas found in the can in the suspect's garage? After testing two evidence items, the examiner might state that the two match or do not match, or that the comparison was inclusive.

Class Versus Individual Characteristics

Some types of evidence carry more weight than others. Hair and fibers can suggest, while DNA and fingerprints can absolutely make a connection. The difference is that some evidence shares **class characteristics** and others share **individual characteristics**.

Class characteristics are those that are not unique to a particular evidence item, but rather place the item into a specific class. If a .38 caliber bullet is removed from a murder victim at autopsy, then any and all .38 caliber guns are possible murder weapons. Other calibers do not belong to this class and would be excluded from consideration. The .45 caliber handgun found in the suspect's possession could not be the murder weapon, but the

.38 caliber handgun belonging to his wife must still be considered. More individualizing testing, such as matching the crime scene bullet to a bullet test fired by her .38, would then be needed to determine if this is the murder weapon or not.

Or let's say type A blood is found at a crime scene. This means that it could have come from any of the tens of millions of people who share this blood type. If the suspect also has type A blood, she remains a suspect, and DNA testing will be required to conclusively "match" the sample to the suspect. But, if she has type B blood, she is excluded and no DNA testing is needed.

Class evidence, though not as powerful as individualizing evidence, is both additive and cumulative. That is, each piece of class evidence alone is not strong enough to gain a conviction, but if multiple bits of class evidence are taken together, the overall weight of the evidence might make a strong case. A classic example is the Atlanta Child Murders case from a quarter century ago.

In Atlanta, Georgia, during the late 1970s and early 1980s, young black children began disappearing, their bodies turning up along and in nearby rivers. The situation created near hysteria and became racially charged with accusations and speculations about who might be killing the children. Evidence was developed that suggested the killer might be tossing the bodies into the rivers from bridges, so stakeouts were set up. Early in the morning of May 22, 1981, Atlanta police officers, while staking out a bridge over the Chattahoochee River, heard a splash and found a young black man on the bridge. His name was Wayne Williams. He was questioned and released. Five days later the body of 27-year-old Nathaniel Cater washed ashore downstream from the bridge, and Wayne Williams was arrested and ultimately tried for the Atlanta Child Murders.

The case largely rested on class fiber evidence. Twenty-eight different fiber types were found on several of the victims. These fibers chemically and optically matched blue, yellow, white, and yellow-green fibers of various synthetic types taken from Williams's kitchen and back room carpets, bedspread, throw rug, and car liner. Hairs matching those of his dog were also found. Williams was convicted.

The cumulative and additive nature of the class evidence against Wayne Williams made coincidence extremely unlikely. What are the odds that someone else left behind this combination of fibers and hair? Unlike individualizing evidence, class evidence is not absolute proof that a suspect is connected to a particular location, but when a large number of class evidence items are found, the likelihood that the suspect was present at the crime scene becomes overwhelming. One way to look at it is to say that a handful of class evidence is statistically equal to a single fingerprint, which possesses individual characteristics.

Individual characteristics are as close to absolute proof of the origin of the evidence item as is possible. The most individualizing types of evidence are fingerprints and DNA, since no two people possess the same prints or the same DNA (the exception being identical twins, who have the same DNA but different fingerprints). Impression evidence such as bullet ballistic markings, shoe and tire tracks, and tool marks are often unique enough to be considered individual evidence. Fracture or tear patterns as is seen in broken glass, torn paper, or duct tape ripped from a roll might possess edges that fit perfectly together like a jigsaw puzzle, thus indicating that the pieces shared a common source.

The overriding principal in the analysis of individual characteristics is that no two things are exactly alike. No two pieces of paper tear in exactly the same way. No two guns mark a bullet the same way. No two pieces of glass fracture in the same manner. No two pairs of shoes or sets of car tires wear in exactly the same way.

The real goal of the criminalist is to identify individualizing characteristics for it is those that truly "make the case," by positively identifying the source of the questioned evidence. If ballistics matched the markings on the .38 caliber bullet mentioned above to those from a bullet test fired by a suspect weapon, then these markings are individual evidence. They separate this particular gun from all other .38 caliber weapons and indicate that this particular .38 was the murder weapon. Similarly, in the type A blood example, DNA could be used to eliminate all of the people with type A blood except for the one person who actually left the blood at the crime scene.

The bottom line is that class evidence can considerably narrow the field of suspects and individual evidence can narrow it further, perhaps to a single person.

Reconstructive and Associative Evidence

Whether class or individual in quality, the evidence might allow investigators to reconstruct the events of the crime or to associate a suspect with the crime scene.

Reconstructive evidence helps in reconstructing the crime scene and determining the sequence of events that transpired during the crime. Broken glass or pried doors and windows might indicate the perpetrator's points of entry and exit. A window broken from the outside tells a different story than one broken from the inside. Shoe prints, blood spatters, and the trajectory of bullets might show where in the room everyone was and exactly how and in what sequence the crime occurred. Was the victim attacked from the front or from behind? Was the murder quick or did a struggle occur? Was the prime suspect at the scene at the time of the murder or did she, as she says, stumble into the scene later? Reconstructive evidence helps the ME determine who did what, where, when, and how, and helps determine who is being truthful and who might be lying. Crime scene reconstruction is part science, part art.

Associative evidence ties or links the suspect to another person, an object, or the crime scene itself. For example, the finding of a victim's hair or fibers from the victim's clothing on the suspect suggests that they had some degree of contact and thus that the two are linked to one another. A suspect's fingerprint, blood, or semen at the scene of a robbery, murder, or rape strongly links him to the crime scene. A murder weapon that holds a suspect's fingerprints will require a great deal of explaining. Each of these circumstances links elements (person, place, or object) of the crime to the suspect.

The Crime Scene

What constitutes a crime scene? What factors determine its size and boundaries? The crime scene not only encompasses the offense site but also entry and exit points and the routes of approach and escape. In a murder investigation the offense site would be the body location, while in a burglary it would include the cracked safe or pried-open cabinet. In an arson investigation it would be the torched structure. The routes of approach and escape might be pathways, streets, or a neighbor's yard. The complete crime scene might include an adjacent building, field, park, wooded area, or an entire street, even a neighborhood. Or there might be more than one scene—a primary scene and one of more secondary scenes.

Primary and Secondary Crime Scenes

Criminals don't tend to hang around the crime scene but rather move along fairly quickly. They might need to dump their tools, stolen getaway car, or a corpse. This means that important evidence might be found at a distance from the offense site. Investigators should avoid locking in on a single scene and must launch a diligent search for these other locations, or secondary crime scenes.

The **primary scene** is where the crime actually occurred, while any other associated scenes are deemed **secondary**. In a bank robbery, the bank would be the primary scene while the getaway car, the garage where it is secreted, and the thief's home or hideout would be secondary scenes. If a murder is committed in the victim's home, and the killer then transports the body to another location for disposal, the home would be the primary scene and the perpetrator's car and the "dump site" would be secondary scenes. Primary scenes typically yield more usable evidence than do secondary scenes, but not always.

Sometimes the primary scene is unknown and investigators have only a secondary scene to process. If the victim of a serial killer is found at a dump site, this would be a secondary scene. The primary scene, where the murder actually occurred, is not known. Investigators will try to use the evidence found at the secondary scene not only to help identify the killer but also to locate the primary scene, where other important evidence might be found. Let's say automobile carpet fibers from a special-order interior are found on the victim. This might lead investigators to a particular manufacturer and ultimately allow them to create a list of buyers or locations where that particular make, model, and interior was purchased. Such secondary scene evidence can help focus the investigation and might ultimately lead to the primary scene and the perpetrator.

Locating Unknown Crime Scenes

What if the investigators don't know where either the primary or the secondary scene is? They know that a crime has been committed but not where it happened or where the evidence, such as a corpse, might have been discarded. The Laci Peterson case is an example. When 8-month-pregnant Laci went missing, it soon became obvious that she had been murdered. A search of her neighborhood and the bay where her husband Scott had been fishing was launched. And of course months later her corpse, as well as that of her unborn son, Conner, washed up on the shore in San Francisco bay. Scott was later convicted of the double murder but had the two bodies not been found, he likely would have never been brought to trial. This is a classic example of knowing a crime occurred but not exactly where and underscores the importance of locating both primary and secondary crimes scenes.

When looking for evidence, such as a corpse, searchers use a number of low- and high-tech methods. Any and all evidence, such as the suspect's work and leisure habits as well as witness statements, is used to narrow the search area. For example, the person might work several miles from home, and searching along this route would be wise. Maybe he frequently ran or walked in a nearby wooded area. Maybe he owns a remote property, or perhaps his vehicle was spotted or some of the victim's clothing was found in a remote area. These bits of information can focus the search.

One basic rule is to "look downhill." Let's say it is believed that the body in question was buried near a remote roadway. In the area, the terrain rises above the road on one side and falls away on the other. Search downhill. Why? It is much easier to carry a body downhill than up. It's just that simple.

Once the area of search has been defined, a systematic approach rather than haphazard wandering is critical. Searchers should look for freshly turned dirt, trenches, and elevations or depressions in the terrain. Fresh graves tend to be elevated above the surrounding area, while older ones become depressed due to settling of the soil, decay of the body, and collapse of the skeleton. Interestingly, the depth of the depression is greater if the body is deeply buried. This is likely due to the larger amount of "turned" dirt, which is subject to a greater degree of settling as well as the increased weight of the dirt over the corpse, causing earlier and more complete skeletal collapse.

Tracking dogs, if provided with an article of the victim's clothing, might be able to follow a scent trail to the burial site. Specially trained cadaver dogs search for the scent of decaying flesh. They can often locate bodies in shallow graves or in water. "**Electronic noses**" might also be employed. These are gas chromatographic devices that sample the air and analyze it for the molecules of corpse decomposition, which are continually released from the soil and into the air. Such a device was recently employed in the famous Casey Anthony case. The trunk of her car, where investigators suggested she had kept her deceased daughter, Caylee, until she had an opportunity to bury her, tested positively for these chemicals. Casey was acquitted, but this evidence found its way into the courtroom for the first time, making this a landmark forensic science case.

Another important clue might come from changes in the vegetation near the grave site. The turning of the soil in the digging process and the presence of the body change the soil conditions. Alterations in compaction, moisture, aeration, and temperature might attract plant species that differ from those around the grave. Or, the plants typical for the area might grow more thickly or richly due to these soil changes. The body basically acts as fertilizer, and the decomposition process warms the soil. Alternatively, the freshly turned dirt might lose heat faster than normally compacted soil. These vegetative and thermal changes might be visible, particularly from the air, where reconnaissance, photography, and thermal imaging might prove crucial to locating the corpse. With thermal imaging the area might appear "colder" if the aerated soil loses heat rapidly or "warmer" if the decaying body releases enough heat to be detectable.

If a suspect area, such as a mound or depression, is found, special devices that locate sources of heat and nitrogen, both byproducts of the decay process, or that measure changes in the physical properties of the soil might be employed. Thermal and nitrogen probes as well as **ground-penetrating radar**, which can "see" into the ground, can often locate a buried body.

Buried bodies often add moisture to the soil, which in turn increases the soil's electrical conductivity. To measure these electrical changes, two metal probes are placed in the soil, an electrical current is passed between them, and the conductivity is measured. Changes in this current might reveal where the body is buried.

Magnetic devices such as simple metal detectors will sometimes locate the victim's jewelry or belt buckle. Or a **magnetometer**, which measures the magnetic properties of soil, might be helpful. Soil contains small amounts of iron, which gives it a low level of magnetic reaction. Since the area where the body is buried has proportionally less soil (the corpse takes up space), it will exhibit a lower level of magnetic reactivity. The magnetometer is passed above the soil and locates any areas that have low magnetic reactivity.

Regardless of which techniques are employed, if an area of interest is found, a more aggressive search is indicated.

Evidence Handling

Whether working at a primary or a secondary crime scene, the police, criminalists, and coroner's technicians must locate, protect, collect, and transport the evidence to the crime lab or the coroner's office for processing. Each of these steps must be properly completed or the evidence could be compromised and deemed inadmissible in court. In the case of a murder, the crime scene is under police jurisdiction while the corpse lies within the coroner's domain. The police might examine the deceased to be sure that he is indeed deceased and might remove a wallet for identification purposes, but the corpse should otherwise be unaltered until the coroner or technicians arrive.

Evidence Location

Evidence location is more often than not fairly straightforward. A person calls the police to report a burglary and then shows them the jimmied window, the open drawers and jewelry boxes, and the wide-open rear escape door. Or someone reports a body lying near a roadway. In these cases, the police and coroner know exactly where to begin their evidence search and can legally do so.

But what if the location of a possible evidence item is not associated with an active crime scene? Maybe stolen goods are believed to be in a suspect's garage or the documents that might reveal an embezzlement are locked in an office vault? In these cases the police have no right to simply walk in and search but rather will need a search warrant. We will look at that later in this chapter.

The best place to search for evidence is the focal point of the crime: the body in a murder case or the safe in a bank robbery. The route of approach, the entry point, the exit point, and the escape route are also fertile grounds for evidence location. The reason for this is our old friend Professor Locard and his Exchange Principle. The perpetrator of necessity will have closely contacted the body or the safe and will have passed through areas of approach, entry, exit, and escape. He might leave behind fingerprints, shoe prints, tire tracks, blood, hair, fiber, bits of broken glass, or paint chips. He might toss the murder weapon or the tool used to gain entrance along his escape route. He might accidentally drop a bloody glove.

Evidence Protection

Once the evidence is located, it must be protected until it can be collected and transported to the lab for analysis. This is of paramount importance since law enforcement's ability to successfully investigate and prosecute a crime can be lost at this critical point if the evidence is damaged, altered, or contaminated.

The initial protection of the evidence falls to the first responding officer, but that's not his only, or in many cases his primary, concern when he first approaches a crime scene. His personal safety comes first. What if the perpetrator is still present? What if she is armed? The officer must locate the perpetrator or perpetrators if they are present and attempt to neutralize any threat they might represent, including arresting and securing them while awaiting backup. Concurrent to this he should assist any victims, offer first aid as needed, and mobilize any necessary emergency medical services.

After these two important tasks are completed, he can turn his attention to the crime scene. At the heart of crime scene protection is Locard's Exchange Principle. Every person that enters the scene can leave behind evidence of their presence, take away crucial trace evidence on their shoes and clothes, or damage or alter any evidence that remains. With this in mind, the officer must keep everyone present, including the property owner, the person who called in the crime, and any suspects or witnesses, away from the scene. Since the officer has no way of knowing if any of these people are potential witnesses or suspects, he must prevent each of them from entering the scene or risk loss, damage, or contamination of evidence. This

PACKING SLIP

1 4 3 7 6 8 7

Via

Market ID: 738421165
Order ID: 1437687
Order Date: 09/14/2026
Shipping Method:

Ship To

ABE APTP Orders
0000000000
help@textbookrush.com
800 AVONDALE AVE
T3953PKJ
COLUMBUS, OH 43212, US

SKU	QTY	TITLE	TOTAL
BSM.1BZZF	1	Forensic Science	0.00

Order Total: $21.19

Your order has been packaged and created with great care. Enjoy! Bay State Books

#1437687

is underscored by the fact that some perpetrators report the crime or "witness" the crime themselves in an attempt to appear innocent. Some perpetrators even attempt to insert themselves into the investigation. That's not as rare as you might think. Since the officer might not initially know which witnesses will become suspects and which suspects might become useful witnesses, he should detain and separate (to avoid collusion) all potential suspects and witnesses. Of course, he might have no reason or legal right to detain some witnesses; if so he can only request that they remain and talk with the other investigators or at least obtain accurate identification and contact information from each.

Next, the crime scene must be cordoned off, using crime scene tape, barricades, automobiles, or other officers, and access must be limited to only the personnel absolutely needed to process the scene. This is often more difficult than it seems. The victim's family members and neighbors might be emotional, combative, or simply stubborn and refuse to leave the area. Members of the press are often clever in their methods to gain entry. Even members of the police force can prove difficult. How can a lowly patrol officer prevent the entrance of a captain or other high-ranking official who might wish to examine the scene? And of course never underestimate the meanderings of the curious bystander.

Once the perimeter is secured, a visitor log is created. Everyone who enters the scene must sign in, documenting his presence and the time he was there. This helps in many ways. For example, a stray fingerprint or footprint found at the scene can be compared to prints obtained from each of the investigators who signed in, and they can be easily identified or eliminated as the source of the print. If no match is found, the print might belong to the perpetrator.

Before the search for evidence commences, the scene is photographed so that it can be preserved in its unaltered condition. This must be done before any evidence or the body (if there is one) is moved or removed. This begins with several overview images, obtained from multiple angles. Close-ups of each item of evidence follow, as do photos of any injuries to the corpse, and any injured parties, including the suspect. Photos of injured persons might be done at the scene or at the hospital (even in the operating room), depending on the nature of the injuries.

The first step in processing the scene is a walk-through examination to get a "feel" of the crime and any possible evidence. This allows for a more organized approach to evidence collection. Specialized personnel, such as the coroner's techs, fingerprint and blood spatter experts, and crime scene reconstructionists, will then come in and do their jobs.

While processing the scene, everything that transpires is documented in notes, sketches, photographs, and perhaps on videotape. Crime scene sketches are extremely important because they show the spatial relationship of each evidence item to the other items or the body (Figure 3-1). The exact graphic coordinates for each piece of evidence must be indicated and located by its distance from two fixed points, such as a wall, doorway, tree, building, or sidewalk. These sketches are most often hand-drawn, but there are several computer programs available to help create this image.

Evidence Gathering

Once the crime scene has been defined and protected and the initial walk-through completed, the task of evidence collection begins. This is often a tedious and laborious process.

How and by whom the evidence is collected depends upon the size, budget, and organization of the crime lab or law enforcement agency charged with investigating the crime. In smaller, less well-funded jurisdictions, police officers will often perform this duty, while in larger, more sophisticated labs, specialized evidence collection units might be available. These are the CSI guys. Regardless of who gathers the evidence, they should be well schooled in proper techniques.

Evidence collection is not a haphazard process but rather follows a logical order. The first evidence collected is the most fragile or the most likely to be lost, damaged, or contaminated. Fragile evidence might include blood, fibers, hair, even fingerprints or shoe and tire tracks. It all depends on the situation. Outdoor scenes, where wind, rain, and other conditions can quickly damage or destroy evidence often present a special urgency.

The techniques for locating and collecting specific types of evidence is complex and beyond the scope of this text. We will look at some of these in later chapters but for now a general overview will give you a feel for how this is accomplished.

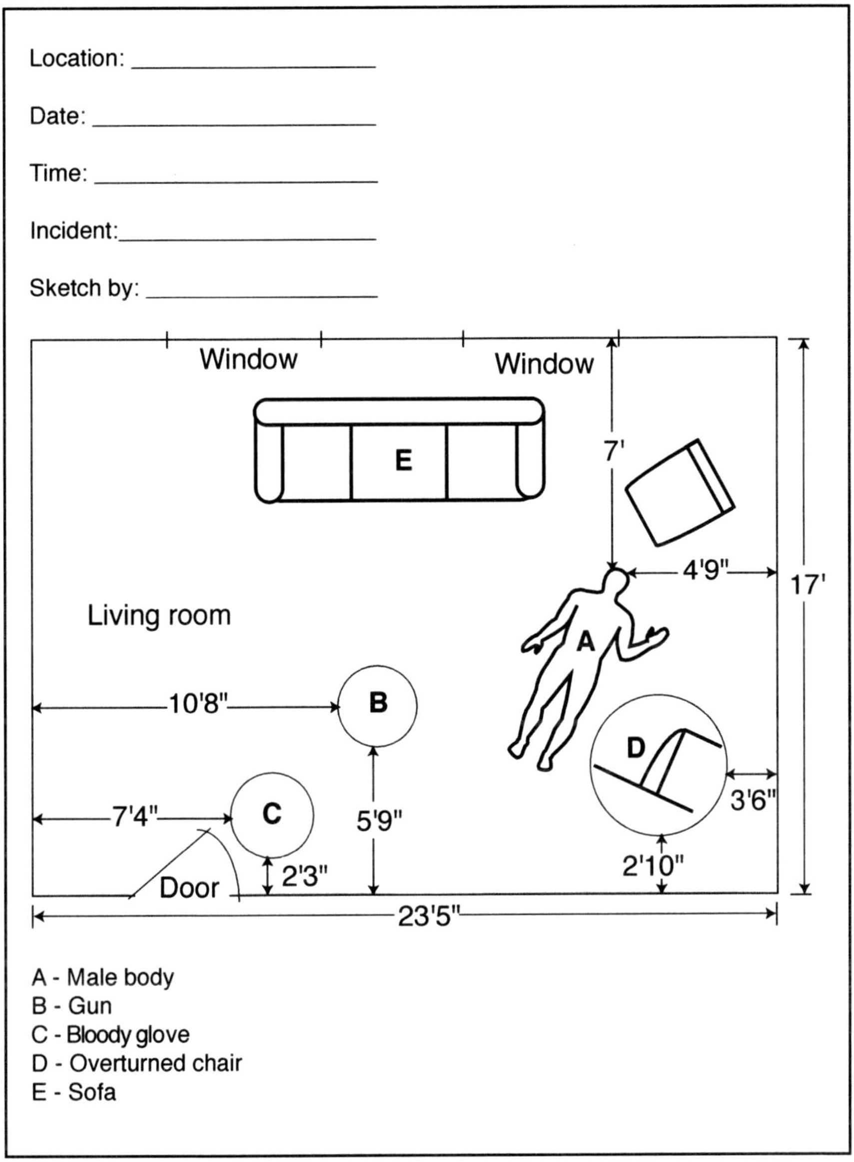

Figure 3-1

Crime scene sketch. The sketch shows the coordinate positions of each evidence item.

Obvious and exposed latent fingerprints should be photographed and then "lifted." The same is true for tool marks and shoe or tire impressions, which should be photographed before being lifted or cast. Fibers and hair should be searched for with alternative light sources and picked up with tweezers. Carpets and furniture should be vacuumed, using a fresh vacuum cleaner bag for each area. This often yields hair, fibers, and other trace material that might initially escape the technician's eye.

To avoid damage and cross-contamination, each piece of evidence must be packaged separately. Dry trace evidence can be placed in druggist's folds, which are small, folded papers. Envelopes, canisters, plastic pill bottles, and paper or plastic bags might also be used. Documents are sealed in plastic covers for transport.

Liquid evidence is put into unbreakable, airtight containers. This is also true for solids that might contain volatile evidence, such as fire remnants that are believed to contain accelerant residues (Chapter 18). Left unsealed, these chemicals might evaporate before testing can be done. Clean paint cans and tightly sealed jars work well for this type of evidence.

Moist or wet biological evidence must be placed in non-airtight containers so that it can air-dry. If not, the moisture can cause mold, mildew, and bacterial growth, which can lead to decay and destruction of the sample. Bloody clothing is often hung up and allowed to thoroughly dry before being packaged for transport.

Sometimes it's impossible to remove the evidence from the scene without damaging it. A tool mark on a pried window seal might be processed at the scene, or the entire window frame might be removed and taken to the lab. Bullet holes in drywall might likewise be processed on site, or a portion of the wall might be removed for later laboratory evaluation.

A very important aspect of evidence collection is the obtaining of proper control samples. These might come from the victim, the suspect, or items at the scene. An automobile carpet fiber found at the scene is most valuable if "control" fibers are available from the suspect's vehicle. This way, the "known" or control sample can be compared with the "unknown" crime scene sample. Control samples of blood taken from the victim and the suspect can be matched to an unknown bloodstain found at the scene to see which one, if either, shed the blood.

Sometimes these control samples take the form of **substrates** that are identical to the substrate of the evidence item in question. A substrate is any object, material, or environment on which something else acts, is placed, or is combined with. For example, a charred carpet that might contain accelerant residue such as gasoline is best compared against the exact same carpet that is free of any accelerant. A carpet sample taken in an area undamaged by the fire can provide the "known" sample. If the examiner finds a suspicious hydrocarbon chemical in the charred carpet that is not present in the known sample, he can be more certain that it is indeed a foreign chemical and not a component of the carpet or its adhesive.

Chain of Custody

Proof of **chain of custody** is essential in evidence collection since loss of this continuity of possession might render the evidence inadmissible in court. The defense could call into question the authenticity and integrity of the evidence since outside contamination could not be ruled out. For this reason, every person who handles the evidence must be accounted for and recorded, and this chain of custody must remain unbroken from crime scene to courtroom.

The person finding the evidence item must mark it for identification. If it is possible to do so without damaging the evidence or altering any of its specific identifying characteristics, the officer might simply write or scratch his initials onto the item itself. For example, he might scratch his initials on the side of a shell casing. Later in court, he can then positively identify this shell casing as the exact one he found at the scene. He could not do this with a bullet, since the striations on the side of the bullet would be altered, making a ballistic match more difficult if not impossible. The item is then placed into an evidence bag, which is initialed by the finder. The identifying information on the evidence bag should include the case number, the name and description of the item, the person finding it, witness to the discovery and recovery, and the date, time, and location of the find.

If the item itself cannot be safely marked, it is placed into the appropriate container or packaging and this in turn is placed into an evidence bag. Both the item container and the evidence bag must be clearly marked and initialed. For example, a DNA sample might be taken from a suspect's mouth using a moist cotton-tipped swab. After drying, the swab is placed into a sealed glass tube and the tube is marked with the collector's initials and date. The tube is then placed into an evidence bag, which is similarly marked. The collector can then testify that that is the sample he obtained by identifying his initials on the sample tube and the evidence bag.

Each person who accepts the evidence must initial or sign and date the evidence bag. He is then responsible for the integrity of the item until he passes it to someone else. Let's look at a shell casing found at a homicide scene. The finding officer will collect it, mark it, and place it into a marked evidence bag. He might then sign it over to the crime scene coordinator, who would transport it to the lab, where he would sign it over to the crime lab technician. After the tech's testing is completed, he might sign it over to the custodian of evidence, who will place it in a secured area until next needed. It could then be signed over to the prosecution for presentation in court. If this chain remains intact, each witness—the finding officer, the crime scene coordinator, the lab technician, and the custodian of evidence—could testify that the item presented in the courtroom is indeed the item collected at the scene and tested by the lab.

Crime Scene Reconstruction

As mentioned earlier, one of the functions of evidence is to reconstruct a crime scene, a process that is both science and art. The main goals of reconstruction are to determine the likely sequence of events and the locations and positions of everyone present during the crime—information that can be critical in determining suspect truthfulness and witness reliability.

Crime scenes can be considered **dynamic** (also called **active**) or **static** (also called **passive**). That is, was there a great deal of activity and movement involved during the crime's commission or not? Let's say someone suffers multiple fatal stab wounds. If the scene is relatively undisturbed, with the victim simply lying in a pool of blood, this would be a static scene. The person was stabbed and collapsed. That's it. But what if he put up a fight, moved from room to room, turned over furniture, broke objects such as lamps or glassware, or staggered outside, leaving a blood trail and bloody handprints and footprints along the way? This is a dynamic scene. The evidence would tell a different story in each case. If suspect or witness statements were in opposition to the evidence, suspicions would be raised.

As the investigator does her initial walk-through, she will begin to mentally formulate a hypothesis for the events of the crime. She will then measure each piece of evidence against this theory. She will consider not only what she observes at the scene but also crime lab test results, medical reports of any injured persons, and the autopsy findings. Anything that doesn't fit must be reconciled, or her theory must change. This means that the reconstruction of the scene is constantly in evolution as more evidence is gathered.

Logic and common sense play a role here, but the investigator must avoid making too many assumptions. Just because it seems logical that a perpetrator did a certain thing or that a piece of evidence ended up where it did because of some action by the perpetrator, if the evidence doesn't support this belief, the theory must be reevaluated. In the above scenarios, if a knife is found near the rear door of the house, logic would suggest that the assailant dropped it during his escape. But what if the ME examines the victim's wounds and determines that that particular weapon could not have been the murder weapon? Or what if it is the murder weapon, but the husband placed it near a broken window or jimmied rear door in an attempt to make it appear as though a breaking and entering homicide had occurred? The husband's fingerprints on the knife or tiny spatters of the victim's blood on the husband's pants or shoes might change things. In reconstruction, all evidence must be considered and explained.

Shoe prints might reveal the perpetrator's every step. Fingerprints might indicate the things he touched. Tool marks are often found at points of entry. Blood spatters, bullet trajectories, the angle of blows and stabs, and the nature of the victim's injuries as determined at autopsy might reveal the actual and relative positions of the assailant and the victim. Reading the pattern of post-mortem lividity might confirm that the body was moved several hours after death (Chapter 6). The discovery of attempts to clean up the scene might contradict a suspect's story.

Crime scene reconstruction must take all of this and much more into consideration. Skill and experience are required to create a "picture" of the crime. In later chapters we will look at how many types of evidence help in this endeavor.

Staged Crime Scenes

"Staging" refers to a situation in which a perpetrator alters evidence in an attempt to make the scene look like something it's not. The most common staging scenario occurs when the perpetrator tries to make a murder appear to be a suicide or accident. Let's say a husband strikes his wife in the head with a blunt object, killing her. He might then break a window or pry a lock to make it appear to have been a burglary gone bad. Or he might tear or remove part or all of her clothing to suggest a sexually motivated crime. Or he might place her in the bathtub and say she must have slipped and fell, striking her head. The evidence from blood spatter examination and from the autopsy might disprove each of these suggestions, leaving the husband with more explaining to do.

A "self-robbery" might be staged to look like a breaking and entering. Maybe jewelry is missing and a window is pried—and of course, the jewelry is insured.

Arson is often an attempt at staging. Perpetrators set fires to cover other crimes such as murder and embezzlement. The hope is that the fire will obscure any autopsy signs of murder or destroy the papers that reveal the theft.

The work of the investigators, the ME, and the crime lab often tells a different story than the perpetrator intended when he staged the scene. The pattern of a fatal head injury might not match the edge of the tub but rather the baseball bat in the closet, which also holds a faint bloodstain unnoticed by the husband. The forensic document examiner might quickly discover that a suicide note was not written by the victim but rather by the spouse (Chapter 19). The lack of carbon monoxide in the victim's blood and soot in his airways might reveal that he was dead before the fire started (Chapter 9). These findings, and many others, underscore why crime scene reconstruction is so valuable in determining that a crime scene has been staged.

Search Warrants

What if the location of a possible evidence item is not associated with an active crime scene? Maybe stolen goods are believed to be in a suspect's garage or the documents that might reveal an embezzlement are locked in an office vault? In these cases the police have no right to simply walk in and search. They need a search warrant.

Since the 4th Amendment to the United States Constitution protects citizens against "unreasonable searches and seizure," the police and crime scene investigators must usually obtain a warrant before any evidence search can begin. This warrant must be specific as to time, place, and items to be searched for and must be obtained based on "probable cause." Only a law enforcement officer can obtain a search warrant. Attorneys and private investigators cannot.

The steps in obtaining a valid search warrant are the preparation of a probable cause affidavit, preparation of the warrant, and obtaining the judge's signature. The affidavit must include the exact locations to be searched, the specific items to be searched for, and the reasons why the items might at the location in question. The affidavit and the warrant must be presented to the judge; if he feels that probable cause exists, he will sign the warrant, making it official.

This is usually fairly easy and straightforward, but not always. Several areas can trip up even seasoned investigators. The three issues that can make obtaining and executing a warrant problematic are probable cause, specificity of the search, and area to be searched. Let's look at each.

Probable cause means that the officer has a strong and concrete reason to believe that the items in question are at the location to be searched. A hunch or a mere suspicion will not work. Let's say a known drug dealer is believed to be selling from a suburban residence. The police have seen and photographed his street dealers coming and going at all hours. Maybe a couple of these dealers have been arrested and have told investigators that the house in question is where they obtain their supplies. This is more than a hunch. This is fairly solid evidence, and it is likely that a search warrant would be issued under these circumstances.

Another common scenario is for the police to possess information from an informant that the illegal activity under investigation frequently takes place at a certain location and at the hands of a certain group of individuals. In this circumstance the judge might require that the police demonstrate that the informant has been reliable in the past before he issues a warrant.

Search specificity means that the warrant must state exactly what evidence the police are looking for. They can't simply ask for a warrant to go look around and see what pops up. They must be looking for specific items. In the case of the drug dealer, they would be searching for drugs, sales records, maybe computers, and probably weapons, since these are often involved in drug trafficking. The warrant application should list all these items. Once granted, the police can then search any area covered by the warrant where these items might be found.

What if in the course of their search they find other evidence or illegal items that were not mentioned in the warrant application? Can these be seized? This is an interesting legal problem, and the answer is sometimes yes and sometimes no.

Let's say that someone has been selling bazookas and the police locate the house where they are being kept. They execute a warranted search for these weapons but in the process an officer opens a kitchen drawer and finds a bag of cocaine. Can this be seized and used in evidence? Probably not. Why? The warrant was for bazookas, which gives the right to search any place where a bazooka might be secreted such as attics, basements, closets, and crawl spaces, but not drawers and breadboxes, which are too small to conceal a bazooka.

On the other hand, if the search is for drugs but a bazooka is found in a closet, then this evidence is typically fair game. The reason is that drugs could have been hidden in the closet so searching there is covered by the warrant. For this reason, police attempt to include a number of small items in the warrant since this will allow for a more inclusive search.

Search area is a description of the area to be searched, and this must be explicitly stated. For example, if the warrant identifies a house, but not specifically the garage or a free-standing backyard storage shed, these areas are not covered by the warrant. Also, if the warrant specifies the garage but not any vehicles that might be inside, then only the garage can be searched. The vehicles are off limits.

Searching Without a Warrant

There are times when the police can conduct a search without a warrant. The Supreme Court has allowed warrantless searches in certain specific situations:

- **Emergent situations**: If someone's life or health is believed to be in danger, the police can enter the location without a warrant. Any evidence found during this emergent entry can be used. But, the police cannot make an emergency entrance, leave, and return at a later date to search for evidence. This second entry would require a warrant.

- **Immediate loss of evidence**: This exception would apply in cases where the suspect is destroying evidence or some outside agent, such as a structure fire, is threatening to do the same.
- **Lawful arrest**: If a suspect has been lawfully arrested, he and any property in his immediate control such as his home or vehicle can be searched.
- **Consented search**: No warrant is needed if the parties in question consent to a search of their person or property.

Evidence Standards of Acceptance

How do the judge and jury know that the science behind the presented evidence is real and not "junk science"? How do they know that the testing procedure has been properly confirmed and that the probabilities cited are real? What's to keep an expert from spouting personal beliefs, which have no scientific backing? The current standards for accepting evidence in the courtroom result from two landmark cases: *Frye v. United States* and *Daubert v. Merrell Dow Pharmaceutical, Inc.*

Frye v. United States

In 1923, the District of Columbia Circuit Court addressed the admissibility of polygraph (lie detector) evidence in the case of *Frye v. United States.* This landmark decision set the rules, now known as the **Frye standard**, for the presentation of scientific evidence before the court. This standard states that the court will accept expert testimony on "well-recognized scientific principle and discovery" if it has been "sufficiently established" and has achieved "general acceptance" in the scientific community. This allows for new scientific tests to be presented, but only after they have been thoroughly tested and accepted by the scientific community. *Frye* became the standard for many years and is still followed in many jurisdictions, but more recently it has been replace by *Daubert,* or Rule 702.

Daubert v. Merrell Dow Pharmaceutical, Inc.

Rule 702 of the Federal Rules of Evidence states that the "trier of fact," which means the judge, can allow expert testimony to help "understand the evidence" and to "determine a fact in issue" at his discretion. This was upheld and amplified in 1993 by the United States Supreme Court. In this ruling, the court said that the "general acceptance" clause in *Frye* was not absolute and handed the judge wider discretion as to what expert testimony he would allow in his court in any given case. To help judges in this regard, the court offered several guidelines.

For a new scientific technique or theory to be acceptable to the court it must:

- Be subject to testing and to peer review
- Be standardized with recognized maintenance of such standards
- Have a known and accepted error rate
- Attain widespread acceptance

This basically means that the technique or theory must be spelled out, tested, reviewed, accepted, and continually monitored for accuracy.

The admissibility of scientific evidence and testimony is often determined in pre-trial hearings and motions, which occur away from the jury. If in the eyes of the judge the evidence to be presented by the expert passes the *Frye* or *Daubert* standards, he will allow it before the jury. If not, he might exclude it from the trial. Another helpful reference: "The Admission of Forensic Science Evidence in Litigation" from *Strengthening Forensic Science in the United States: A Path Forward* by the Committee on Identifying the Needs of the Forensic Sciences Community of the National Research Council, available at http://www.nap.edu/openbook.php?record_id=12589&page=111.

Chapter 4

THE AUTOPSY

Autopsy, **necropsy**, and **post-mortem examination** are interchangeable terms that mean "examination of the dead." Autopsy, which has been with us for many centuries, actually means "to view oneself," so necropsy, which means "to look at death," is the more accurate term. However, "autopsy" has been the preferred term since the Middle Ages, and that continues today.

History of the Autopsy

Many ancient cultures performed autopsy-like procedures for religious and spiritual reasons, but not as an attempt to gain medical knowledge and certainly not for use in solving crimes. The evolution of the autopsy from a tool to study disease to a method for solving criminal cases took place in fits and spurts over many centuries.

As early as 3500 BC, the Mesopotamians, who believed that animal organs such as the liver carried messages from the gods, dissected corpses as part of religious ceremonies. The ancient Egyptians prepared corpses for the journey to the other side using techniques similar to the modern autopsy in that the internal organs (except for the heart) were removed and placed in ceremonial jars within the burial chamber and the body was treated with various preservative oils and salts.

The first autopsies to gain medical knowledge were performed by Erasistratus (c. 304–250 BC) and Herophilus (335–280 BC) during the third century BC. The renowned physician Galen (131–200 AD), surgeon to the gladiators, dissected human corpses in an attempt to prove that Hippocrates' "four humours" theory of disease was correct. Following Galen's example, Greek, Roman, Egyptian, and medieval European physicians performed autopsies in order to learn anatomy. This was not done in any organized fashion, and this knowledge was rarely shared across cultures since communication was rudimentary, medicine was poorly organized, and religious leaders weren't enthusiastic about opening up the human body.

The church's position changed with Pope Clement VI (1291–1352), during the Black Death that gripped Europe between 1348 and 1350 and killed 25 to 35 million people, or one-third to one-half of Europe's population. In the hopes of discovering the cause of this pandemic, Clement ordered that autopsies be done on plague victims. At that time, it was widely believed that the Black Death was due to supernatural causes and witchcraft or as punishment for mankind's evil, so it is curious that the Pope sought an anatomical reason for it. Of course, none was found since the tools and knowledge to uncover the true cause ere still centuries away.

In the late 1400s, the first medical schools appeared at Bologna and Padua, and Pope Sixtus IV (1414–1484), following Clements's lead, allowed human dissections as a part of medical and surgical training. Giovanni Morgagni (1682–1771), professor of anatomy in Padua, was the first to correlate autopsy findings with various diseases when he made the critical connection that disease was either caused by or resulted in anatomical changes in the human body, thus giving birth to the fields of gross anatomy and pathology. Around the same time, Anton van Leeuwenhoek (1632–1723) invented the microscope, which revealed the microscopic world to scientists. Still, it would be another two centuries before German pathologist Rudolph Virchow (1821–1902), using Leeuwenhoek's invention, established the roots of cellular biology and anatomy by showing that disease not only caused visible changes in organs, as Morgagni had pointed out, but also led to changes in the cells of the body. The work of these three medical giants changed our view of disease forever.

The first documented autopsies in North America were done by French colonists in 1604, during a harsh winter on the island of St. Croix, when nearly half of the 79 settlers died. Apparently these autopsies were performed in the hopes of uncovering what was killing off the community, which meant that these procedures were as much forensic as medical.

Forensic Autopsy Milestones

- Third century BC: Erasistratus and Herophilus performed the first post-mortem examinations in order to study diseases.
- 44 BC: An unknown Roman physician examined the body of Emperor Julius Caesar and determined that of his 23 stab wounds, only the one to his heart was fatal.
- Second century AD: Galen dissected corpses and wrote extensively on human anatomy.
- 1200s: First true forensic autopsies were performed at the University of Bologna.
- 1247: Chinese investigator Sung T'zu published *Xi Yuan Ji Lu,* a forensic manual, describing how to examine murder victims as an aid to solving the crime.
- 1500s: Ambroise Paré (1510–1590), a French military surgeon, described the anatomical features of war and homicidal wounds.
- 1642: The University of Leipzig began offering courses in forensic medicine.
- 1700s: Giovanni Morgagni performed and recorded autopsies on victims of murder.
- 1798: French physician Francois-Emmanuel Fodéré (1764–1835) published Traité de Médecine Légale, a landmark book in forensic medicine.
- 1813: James S. Stringham (1775–1817) became the first Professor of Medical Jurisprudence in the United States.

The Pathologist: Clinical Versus Forensic

The term "pathology "derives from the Greek words pathos, which means "disease," and logos, which means "the study of." Thus, pathology is the study of disease. The medical specialty of pathology began in the 1800s; by the beginning of the 20th century, gross and microscopic pathology were essential to our understanding of disease and death. By the mid-1900s, pathologists began to separate along subspecialty lines: the clinical pathologist and the forensic pathologist.

The **clinical pathologist** deals with disease states and uses lab tests and the autopsy to diagnose and study diseases. She will often oversee the hospital medical lab, interpret laboratory tests, and consult with treating physicians to help with the diagnosis and treatment of the living. The autopsies she performs are medical in nature in that they are designed to determine the cause of death and to search for the presence of disease.

A **forensic pathologist** is concerned with the interface of pathology and the law. He deals with injuries and death rather than disease in the living. He performs forensic autopsies and is often required to testify in court regarding his findings and opinions.

The training required for a clinical pathologist includes a college baccalaureate degree (4 years), a medical degree (4 years), internship (1 year), and a residency in pathology (4 years). A forensic pathologist typically must then serve an additional fellowship in forensic pathology or complete a period of practical training in a forensic pathology laboratory.

The Forensic Autopsy

The forensic autopsy varies from a medical autopsy in that it doesn't deal with disease but rather with potential criminal deaths or injuries. The forensic autopsy is asked to answer four basic questions:

- What is the cause of death? (What illness or injury led to the death?)
- What is the mechanism of death? (What physiological derangement actually resulted in death?)
- What is the manner of death? (Was the death natural, accidental, suicidal, or homicidal?)
- What was the time of death?

Each of these will be discussed in detail in later chapters.

Who Gets Autopsied?

Most deaths are natural and do not involve the coroner or medical examiner, who typically investigates deaths that are traumatic, unusual, sudden, or unexpected. The attending physician will sign the death certificate, the coroner will accept it, and nothing further is needed. But if the physician is uncomfortable with a particular situation or if she feels that the death is in any way suspicious, she might request the coroner or ME's involvement.

The coroner then might or might not perform an autopsy. He will review the medical records and if he is satisfied that no criminal activity is involved, he might do no further testing and sign the death certificate. If he needs an autopsy and other testing such as toxicological examinations to make this determination, he will complete those tests before certifying the death certificate. If he performs an autopsy it might be partial or complete. Let's say the person died from a head injury and the question is whether it was an accidental fall or a homicidal blow to the head. The coroner might only autopsy the victim's head or he might perform a complete forensic autopsy. It's his call.

The laws that govern situations in which the coroner will perform an autopsy vary among jurisdictions, though most operate under similar guidelines. The terms "reportable death" or "coroner's case" mean any death that must, by law, be reported to the coroner for his investigation. Common situations that might involve the coroner include the following:

- Violent deaths (accidents, homicides, suicides)
- Deaths at the workplace, either traumatic or from toxin exposure
- Deaths that are suspicious, sudden, or unexpected
- Deaths that occur during incarceration or police custody
- Deaths that are unattended by a physician, that occur within 24 hours of admission to a hospital, that occur in any situation in which the victim is admitted while unconscious and never regains consciousness prior to death, or that occur during medical or surgical procedures
- A found body, whether known or unidentified
- Before a body can be cremated or buried at sea
- At the request of the court

But even cases that fall into one of these categories might not be autopsied. As stated above, the ME has the final say. If the cause and manner of death are obvious and the circumstances not truly suspicious, he might not need an autopsy before signing the death certificate.

The Autopsy Procedure

A forensic autopsy is a scientific procedure that is performed in order to gather evidence of the cause and manner of death. It employees gross and microscopic examination of the body as well as toxicological (drugs and poisons), serological (blood), and any other ancillary testing the ME deems necessary.

The timing of the autopsy depends upon many factors, and might be done immediately or several days after the death. Weekends and holidays, excessive workload, and the need to ship the body to a larger lab can each cause delay. In the interim the corpse is stored in a refrigerated vault, which if only for 4 or 5 days results in little corpse deterioration.

Obviously, each pathologist has his own method of doing things, but in general the forensic autopsy follows a standard protocol. Many of the steps overlap and might be performed in a different order, depending upon the nature of the situation, but they typically include the following:

- Identifying the deceased
- Photographing the body, clothed and unclothed
- Removing of any trace evidence
- Measuring and weighing the body
- X-raying all or parts of the body
- Conducting an external examination of the body
- Dissecting the body
- Conducting a microscopic examination of any tissues removed during the external examination or dissection
- Performing toxicological and other laboratory examinations

Let's look at each of these steps in greater detail.

Identification of the deceased is critical, particularly if the death becomes the subject of a criminal proceeding. There must be no doubt as to who the deceased was. In homicides this helps focus the investigation, since in the overwhelming majority of murders the perpetrator and the victim have some connection—often a close connection. Usually, the identity of the person is not in question because family members or friends offer this information. If not, photos, fingerprints, dental records, and DNA might prove useful.

Photography should be done with the body both clothed and unclothed. Frontal and profile facial images are followed by photographs of each injury, scar, birthmark, tattoo, and unusual physical feature.

Trace evidence such as hair, fibers, fluid or soil stains, and other bits of small evidence should be searched for and gathered from the corpse and the clothing before the body is moved for weighing and measuring. A magnifying glass and alternative light sources such as laser, ultraviolet, or infrared light are often helpful. The clothing should then be carefully removed, packaged, and taken to a clean environment for further examination and a more diligent search for trace evidence.

Measuring and weighing is the first step in the actual post-mortem examination. The ME will record height, weight, estimated age, sex, race, and hair and eye color.

X-rays of the corpse are often extremely useful and can reveal injuries to bones and some soft tissues as well as foreign bodies such as bullets, fractured knife blades, and other embedded objects. Post-mortem x-rays are extremely useful in gunshot wounds (GSWs) since bullets are unpredictable and move in unusual paths through the body, particularly if they strike bones. X-rays can locate the bullet's final resting place so that it can be retrieved for ballistic examination. Bullets often deform and break up, leaving behind chips and fragments, which reveal their path through the body. Since knowing the bullet's path might indicate the relative positions of the assailant and the victim, this information can prove useful in crime scene reconstruction.

External examination of the corpse, if possible, should commence at the crime scene, though this is not always practical. The advantage is that this will give the ME an overall view of the crime scene, the body, and the body's position relative to other evidence such as weapons, shoe impressions, fingerprints, and blood spatters. Photographs help, but being there gives a clearer picture. When the body is removed from the scene, it must be done carefully to protect any trace evidence associated with the victim. The corpse is typically wrapped in clean plastic sheets and then placed in a clean body bag, as each of these will collect any trace evidence that falls from the body and will prevent the accumulation of any foreign materials during transport, which could confuse or contaminate the evidence.

Once in the lab, the body is removed from the transport wrappings and placed on the autopsy table. The plastic sheet and the body bag are then taken to the crime lab where a search for trace evidence is done. The pathologist will focus on the clothed corpse and search for trace evidence. Any findings will be photographed and collected. He will carefully inspect the victim's clothing for damage. Why is this important? Let's say the victim had been stabbed. If the defects in his shirt don't match the stab wounds found on his body it is possible the victim was re-dressed after death in an attempt to stage the crime scene.

Next, the ME will remove the victim's clothing and send it to the crime lab for processing. He will then measure the body temperature, determine the state of rigor mortis, and document the presence and location of any livor mortis (lividity). As we will see in Chapter 6, each of these will help him estimate the time of death and might also indicate whether the body was moved after death. He will then search the corpse for trace evidence as well as blood, semen, or other stains. In traumatic deaths, the victim's fingernails will be clipped or scraped in case the victim managed to scratch his attacker. In sexual assault cases, the pubic hair will be combed to search for hair from the rapist, and vaginal and anal swabs for semen will be obtained. The ME will also take samples of the victim's head, eyebrow, eyelash, and pubic hair for comparison with any foreign hair found on or around the body. Fingerprints will then be taken, followed by photographs of each injury.

Dissection is the opening of the body for internal examination. This is accomplished by making the classic "Y" or "T" incision, which has three arms. Two extend from each shoulder down to the lower end of the sternum (breast bone). The third continues down the midline of the abdomen to the pubis. The ribs and clavicles (collar bones) are then cut or sawed through and the breastplate is removed, exposing the heart and lungs. Blood is often taken from the heart for later analysis. The heart, lungs, and other internal organs are then removed, examined, and weighed. Tissue samples are taken from each for later microscopic examination. Stomach contents are examined and samples are taken for toxicological examinations.

The ME will then examine the brain. To do this, the scalp is incised and peeled from the skull, which is then opened with a saw. The brain is examined in situ (in place) and then removed. As with the other organs, it is weighed and examined and tissue samples are taken.

After the exam is completed, the organs are returned to the body and the incisions are sutured closed. The body might then be released to the family for burial.

Microscopic examinations require that the removed tissue samples are "fixed" in a formalin solution, imbedded in blocks of paraffin, and then thinly sliced. The slices are placed on a glass slide and stained with biological stains such as hematoxylin and eosin (H&E) for viewing under a microscope.

Toxicological examinations of blood, urine, bile, stomach contents, and any other collected body fluid are performed by the toxicology lab.

The Official Autopsy Report

Only after the ME has completed the autopsy exam and reviewed all the tests will he file a report. This report consists of the anatomical and microscopic findings along with attachments that contain the results of any ancillary tests such as toxicological, serological, or DNA analyses. Using this information, the ME will then offer his opinion as to the cause and manner of death. These will be discussed in Chapter 7.

If no ancillary tests are needed, the report might be filed immediately, but if the results of these tests are crucial to the ME's determinations, the report might not be released for days or weeks, sometimes months. At times, the ME might file a preliminary statement and await the return of these reports before filing his final report. Since his findings and opinions can impact the police, prosecutors, suspects, and the families of all involved, the ME is typically cautious in both preliminary and final reporting.

It is important to note that even his final report is not "written in stone"; if new evidence that changes his opinion is uncovered, he can revise his report at any time. For example, if a chronically ill, elderly woman dies in a nursing home, the ME might decide that an autopsy is not necessary and file his report stating that the manner of death was natural. But what if a large inheritance or insurance policy is at stake and someone comes forward with evidence that suggests that a murder might have occurred?

The ME might exhume the body (if already buried) and search for signs of injury or poisons. If he finds trauma or toxins that could have caused the death, he might amend his report to reflect that the manner of death is homicidal rather than natural. A police investigation would then ensue.

Each pathologist has his own method and style of preparing the final report, but certain information must be included. A typical format would be as follows:

- External examination
- Evidence of injury
- Central nervous system (brain and spinal cord)
- Internal examination of chest, abdomen, and pelvis
- Toxicological examinations
- Other laboratory tests
- Opinion, which should include an assessment of the cause and manner of death

CHAPTER 5

CORPSE IDENTIFICATION

Criminal investigators are often confronted with an unidentified corpse. The victim might have been dead for hours, days, months, years, or many decades. Identifying these corpses might take only minutes or might take many months or years, and in some cases the corpse is never identified. This can be a very complex process that involves many different forensic disciplines and techniques.

If the body is more or less intact, size, sex, race, scars and tattoos, facial photographs, fingerprints, and DNA examination as well as the victim's clothing might help with identification. But if the body is significantly decayed, much of this identifying information is not available, and if the remains are skeletal, the problem is further magnified. In this situation the expertise of a forensic anthropologist, a forensic odontologist (dentist), and a forensic artist might be needed. Whether the investigation centers on a single body, victims of a mass disaster such as a plane crash or hurricane, or a collection of corpses found in a mass grave, the skills of these experts are crucial.

Why Is Identification Important?

The desire to reunite the deceased with his family and friends and to allow a proper burial are, of course, central concerns, but for the criminal investigator corpse identification is critical. The identity of a homicide victim is perhaps the single most important factor in solving the crime, since 90 percent of the time, people are killed by people they know. This relationship might be spouse, family, friend, lover, neighbor, or business associate. One of the factors that make serial killers so difficult to track is that these are usually "stranger killings" in that the killer and the victim had no prior relationship. But most killers and victims do, so identification of the corpse allows investigators to dig into the victim's relationships and ultimately reveal the killer. They might discover that the wife had a motive to kill her husband, or a business partner wanted the entire business for himself, or the spurned lover wanted revenge. Without identifying the corpse, these paths of investigation would go unexplored.

The opposite is also true—and for the same reasons. Identifying the killer might help identify the victim, because the relationship goes both ways.

Basic Considerations

Mother Nature is not kind to the dead. From the moment of death, bacteria, insects, predators, and environmental conditions begin to destroy the body. When discovered, the condition of the body depends upon the time since death and whether the body has been exposed to the elements or predators. Regardless of the time frame and the conditions, ultimately most, but not all, corpses decay until only the skeleton remains.

An unburied corpse is directly exposed to the elements, predatory animals, and insects. In warm, moist climates, bacteria and insects can reduce a corpse to bones in short order, while in colder, drier areas, this might take many months, even years. Animal predators might completely or partially consume the corpse or scatter bones and body parts far and wide.

But even burial doesn't offer complete protection. The most important factors in the destruction of a buried body are the time since burial, the burial container, and the depth of the grave. A body buried with no coffin or similar enclosure will deteriorate much faster than one in a metal coffin. A shallow grave will attract more insects and predators than will one that is six feet deep.

A body tossed into water presents similar problems. Whether weighted down or not, corpses almost always sink and will remain submerged until enough decomposition gas collects within the tissues and body cavities to make it buoyant, at which time it will become a "floater." As we will see in a later chapter, the time required for this depends mostly on the water temperature. Though bodies in water are protected from insect activity, they are subject to attack by various marine creatures, and the corpse might be consumed or dismantled and scattered by these predators.

As you can see, what happens to a corpse and the time it takes for a corpse to decay completely vary with its location. The general rule for corpse decomposition is that one week in the open equals two weeks in water equals eight weeks in the ground.

But, as stated above, not all bodies decay and become skeletal. Certain environmental conditions can lead to incredible degrees of preservation, even after many years. Soil high in acid or alkali content, as is found in some boggy areas, can delay or prevent bacterial growth and thus putrefaction (decay). These "bog people" can remain in remarkably good condition for many decades. Frozen bodies are often very well preserved, as are those that undergo mummification. Mummification occurs when a body is exposed to very dry conditions, which desiccate (dry out) the body, removing the water that bacteria need to grow and putrefy the corpse. What remains is a dark-colored corpse that looks as though leathery skin has been shrunk over a skeleton. (This is similar to the process for making beef jerky.)

One interesting scenario is that sometimes the victim of poisoning with toxins such as arsenic can be very well preserved. It seems that the arsenic actually kills the bacteria that cause decay so that a corpse that is many years old might appear as if the victim had been dead only weeks.

Getting Rid of the Body

Since the victim's body is the primary piece of evidence in a homicide, and without it proving guilt is much more difficult, murderers often attempt to get rid of the corpse. Most simply bury the body or dump it in water or in an isolated area, while others go to extremes. Some are very clever, while others, such as John George Haigh—known as the "Acid Bath Murderer"—are not so smart.

In 1949, John George Haigh confessed to multiple murders. He also said he drank his victims' blood and destroyed their corpses with sulfuric acid, which he kept in a vat in his workshop. He took the victims' money and, through forgery, their property and businesses. Haigh laughed at the police, believing they could not prosecute him without a corpse. Imagine his surprise when, even with no intact bodies but rather based on forged documents he used to steal from his victims' estates and dentures belonging to victim Olive Durand-Deacon recovered from the acid sludge found in his basement, he was convicted and hanged at London's Wandsworth Prison on August 16, 1949.

Like Haigh, other criminals have attempted to destroy corpses with acid—most famously, the serial killer Jeffrey Dahmer. Indeed, powerful acids can destroy a corpse, bones and all, if enough acid is used over a sufficient period of time. The problem is that acids will not only destroy the corpse, but also the bathtub and the plumbing. Acid fumes will peel the wallpaper, burn the killer's skin, eyes, and lungs, and alert the neighbors that something next door is amiss.

Though attempting to destroy a corpse with acid is not common, using fire is. Fortunately, this is rarely successful. Short of a crematorium, where temperatures of 1500 degrees or more are used for over two hours, a house or vehicle fire rarely burns hot enough or long enough to destroy a human corpse. The body might be severely charred on the surface but the inner tissues, internal organs, and bones are often surprisingly well preserved.

Another favorite is quicklime (calcium oxide). Murderers use this because they have seen it in the movies and because they don't typically have degrees in chemistry. If they did, they might think twice about this one. Not that quicklime won't destroy a corpse, it just takes a long time. Most killers who use this method simply dump some on the corpse and bury it, thinking the lime will do its work and nothing will remain. But when quicklime contacts water, as it often does in burial sites, it reacts to create calcium hydroxide (slaked lime). This corrosive material might damage the corpse, but the heat produced during its creation will kill many of the putrefying bacteria and dehydrate the body, thus slowing decay and promoting mummification. So quicklime might actually help preserve the body.

Whether it's Mother Nature or the perpetrator that conspires to destroy the corpse, something almost always remains. It might be an intact body, a partially destroyed corpse, or a single bone. The ME will use whatever he has available to begin the identification process.

Identifying the Corpse

An intact or a partially decayed body gives the coroner a great deal to work with, since age, race, sex, and stature are usually obvious. If the victim's face is intact, facial photographs are of course very helpful, since they can be compared with photos or descriptions of reported missing persons; once a presumptive match has been made, family or friends will often make the final identification. If no missing person matches the general characteristics of the corpse, photos can be circulated to law enforcement and the media and then hopefully someone will recognize the deceased.

It's not always this easy, though, and the ME must often resort to other means.

Burial Artifacts

Corpses are often buried with their clothing, jewelry, and other items. A wallet, ID card, or military dog tags are of course helpful, as are Medic Alert medallions or bracelets, lockets that contain a picture of a loved one, and rings and bracelets that are inscribed with names, initials, or dates. Clothing might be distinctive in style or manufacturer and this can lead investigators to where and when the items were purchased, and sometimes even by whom. Laundry marks can often be traced to a particular cleaner and then to the owner of the item.

If the victim is buried in a coffin or wrapped in a blanket or some other material, these might prove helpful. Coffins often bear the manufacturer's name, and often a serial number, but only rarely are unidentified homicide victims placed in expensive coffins. The construction materials used to manufacture makeshift wooden coffins might be traceable to the manufacturer or retail seller, or perhaps similar materials can be found at a suspect's home. Blankets or sheets often have manufacturer or seller tags. Examination of plastic bags and wrappings might reveal the manufacturer or seller, and often the perpetrator's fingerprints or bits of trace evidence remain on such materials.

Body Marks, Diseases, and Scars

Body marks such as birthmarks and tattoos are often so distinctive that they supply strong identifying evidence.

Birthmarks come in many varieties and some, such as former Soviet President Mikhail Gorbachev's purplish port-wine stain (nevus flammeus), are very distinctive. In fact, no two of these are identical, so old photos revealing the mark could be used to make a positive identification.

Tattoos are often just as distinctive. Family members or friends might recognize the design. Some tattoos can be traced to the artist, particularly today since tattoos are considered body art and some tattoo artists have very individual styles. Followers of such art can often identify a particular artist's work. Tattoos and other body marks on those who have been arrested are often sketched or photographed as part of the booking process. If such sketches or photos exist from a previous arrest, they can be compared to those on the corpse.

Gang tattoos, which identify a person as a member of a particular gang, can greatly narrow the search, since many jurisdictions maintain files of the tattoos associated with the gangs that operate in the area. An example would be California's Cal/Gang. Established in 1987, it is a database of information on known gang members throughout the state, including descriptions and/or photos of members' tattoos. Many states use the similar GangNet. A search of one of these databases might yield a "hit" and supply the needed identification.

The forensic chemist might also prove helpful. Many tattooists use black pigments that contain carbon, reds that contain mercuric chloride, and greens with potassium dichromate. Others use aniline-based dyes. It is possible to sample and analyze the pigment from the corpse's skin and help confirm that a particular artist did the work.

The usefulness of tattoos is underlined in a famous Australian case that became known as the "Shark Arm Murder." In April 1935, two fisherman caught a large tiger shark off the coast of Sydney, Australia, and donated the creature to a local aquarium. A few days later the shark regurgitated a well-preserved, muscular, Caucasian human arm. The shark was sacrificed and opened but no other human remains were found.

The arm, which appeared to have been removed post-mortem by a knife and not by the shark's teeth, bore a distinctive tattoo of two boxers squaring off. The wife of Jim Smith recognized the tattoo, and fingerprints obtained from the remains confirmed her identification.

Police then discovered that Patrick Brady, a known forger and drug trafficker, had gone on a fishing trip with Smith just before his disappearance. Police theorized that Brady killed Smith, hacked him to pieces, and stuffed his remains into a trunk that was missing from the fishing shack the two men had shared. His arm must have slipped free in the water and been swallowed by the unfortunate shark. Under questioning, Brady implicated another man named Reginald Holmes, who was shot to death the day before the inquest into Smith's death was to begin. Brady's attorneys obtained an injunction from the Australian Supreme Court, halting the inquest on the grounds that an arm was not sufficient evidence to bring murder charges. The police charged Brady with murder anyway, but a jury, likely influenced by the Supreme Court ruling, acquitted him.

Certain medical conditions or evidence of previous surgical procedures uncovered at autopsy might also help the ME make the identification. Acromegaly, neurofibromatosis, scleroderma, and other uncommon medical conditions might lead to a quick identification. National registries and support groups, such as the Scleroderma Society and the Neurofibromatosis Society, maintain databases of membership and if the deceased was a member, this might prove useful.

If the victim has had an appendectomy or a gall bladder removal, a search of missing persons' reports of the same age and sex who also had these procedures might help. This is particularly true if the surgery was fairly recent, since the ME can often determine the approximate age of surgical wounds.

A surgical appliance is any artificial, manufactured device used in surgical treatment, and these often bear serial numbers. The manufacturer can then supply the hospital where the replacement was done, the surgeon who performed it, and the person who received it. Artificial joints, pacemakers, heart valves, and many other devices have traceable serial numbers.

Fingerprints

Unless the corpse is severely deteriorated, fingerprints (Chapter 13) can usually be obtained and matched against those of a known missing person and those in national fingerprint databases such as the FBI's Automated Fingerprint Identification System (AFIS). A match here would lead to a quick identification. Fingerprints can sometimes be obtained from mummified bodies. The finger pads of such corpses are shriveled and have the texture of old leather, but soaking them in water or glycerin might swell them enough for fingerprints to be obtained. Other methods include the injection of saline into the tips of the fingers, which swells the pads and reveals the prints, or carefully slicing away the finger pad skin, which is then placed between two microscopic slides for viewing and photographing.

Dental Comparisons

Forensic odontologists (dentists) are frequently involved in the identification of corpses, whether individuals, victims of mass disasters, or those found in mass graves. The value of dental comparisons stems from their being almost as individual as fingerprints and DNA. Everyone's teeth are different. Most people have the same number and types of teeth, but the length, width, and shape of each tooth shows great variability. Add to this missing, misaligned, chipped, furrowed, worn, and reconstructed (fillings, crowns, and bridges) teeth, and this individuality becomes even stronger.

When faced with an unidentified corpse, the ME will make a set of dental x-rays, and sometimes dental impressions, which can then be compared with the dental x-rays or charts of a missing person who fits the corpse's general description. With a match, the identity of the corpse is confirmed. The main deficiency of dental comparisons (fingerprints and DNA, too) is the need for something to compare the corpse's dental pattern against. The police must have some idea who the person might be if they are to obtain that person's dental records for comparison.

Chemical analysis of filling materials can be helpful by leading investigators to the manufacturer of the material or to the dentist who uses it. Let's say only a few local dentists used the type of filling material found in a corpse or that the material had been used in only a handful of local patients. A comparison of those patients' dental records with the dental pattern of the corpse might lead to a positive identification.

At times the forensic dentist might see changes that relate to the person's occupation or hobbies and use this information to narrow the list of possibilities. For example, the mouthpiece of certain wind instruments can alter the teeth of those who frequently play them and nails can chip the teeth of the carpenter who holds them in his mouth as he works.

Using teeth as a method of identity is not a modern endeavor. In the first century AD, the Roman Emperor Claudius demanded to see the teeth of his beheaded mistress, who apparently had a distinctively discolored front tooth. William the Conqueror used his crooked teeth to bite, and thus identify, the wax seal on his letters. Paul Revere not only alerted the colonists of the approach of British forces, but he was also a gifted metal smith and engraver and had been schooled in the art of dentistry. In 1775, he made a set of dentures for his friend, Dr. Joseph Warren. In June of that year, Dr. Warren fell in the Battle of Bunker Hill and was buried in a mass grave for those killed in action. Warren's family wanted his body disinterred for a private burial. To do this Dr. Warren's corpse had to be distinguished from the others. A positive identification came when Paul Revere recognized the dentures he had made for his friend.

Blood Type and DNA

Blood typing will be discussed in great detail in Chapter 10, but this technique can help with corpse identification if only by excluding certain possible identities. This is based on the fact that a person's blood type is determined by the blood type of his parents, and certain pairings cannot produce children of certain types. For example, if a corpse that is thought to be John Smith is found to have type B blood and John's parents are type O and type A, the corpse is not John since these two parents could not bear a type B child. So, blood typing excludes John. But if the corpse had type A or type O blood, then John remains a possibility. This does not confirm that the corpse is John, but it doesn't exclude that possibility either.

Like fingerprints and dental comparisons, the usefulness of DNA (Chapter 11) in identifying an unknown corpse is limited by the need for DNA from the person suspected of being the corpse. Let's say the police and the ME suspect that the unidentified corpse is John Smith, who has been missing for a few months. The corpse is severely decayed, so visual identification is impossible, fingerprints cannot be obtained, and John has no dental records. If John's family can produce his hairbrush or toothbrush or perhaps envelopes or stamps he had licked, the ME might be able to extract DNA from these to compare with that taken from the corpse. With the newer DNA techniques (Chapter 11) of Polymerase Chain Reaction (PCR) and Short Tandem Repeats (STR), this type of identification is becoming increasingly common.

On December 19, 1999, Antoinette Robinson of Vallejo, California, reported that her 7-year-old daughter Xiana Fairchild was missing. An extensive search of the area revealed nothing. In January 2001 a construction worker found a partial skull and jaw bone near a mountainous road some 60 miles south of Xiana's home. The bones were from a child around

Xiana's age. DNA from one of the molars in the jawbone was compared with DNA obtained from Xiana's toothbrush and the remains were identified as those of Xiana. Ultimately, Curtis Dean Anderson, a cab driver who had been fired a few days before Xiana's abduction, was charged with the crime. When charged, he was in prison serving a 251-year sentence for the abduction and molestation of an 8-year-old girl, who managed to escape from him just days before Xiana's disappearance. Investigators discovered that Anderson had been to Xiana's house a few weeks before her disappearance, visiting Robert Turnbough, a fellow cab driver and boyfriend of Xiana's mother.

As with fingerprints, a national databank known as the Combined DNA Index System (CODIS) can be helpful. Though still not universally used, it is growing rapidly. If the victim's DNA profile is in CODIS, a match can be made.

Cause of Death

The ME's determination of the cause and manner of death, if he is able to make one, might help identify the victim. A drug overdose would lead to canvassing local dealers and users. A distinctive knife wound might instigate a search for where such a weapon could be purchased and ultimately who bought it. The bullet removed from the victim of a gunshot wound could lead to the murder weapon and the shooter. The point of these types of investigations is that identifying the perpetrator might allow identification of the victim since, as stated earlier, most murders occur between people who know each other.

If none of the above information leads to identification of the corpse, the coroner must resort to more creative methods. The case of Abraham Becker and Reuben Norkin illustrates just how clever an astute ME can be.

Abraham Becker and his wife, Jennie, had a rocky marriage at best. On April 6, 1922, they attended a party at a friend's home in New York City. Jennie ate canapés, almonds, grapes, and figs. After they left the party, Jennie was never seen alive again. Becker said that she had run off with another man. The police investigation led to Reuben Norkin, a business associate of Becker's. Under pressure, Norkin admitted that he had helped Becker bury the missing woman's body. He said that Becker had killed her with a wrench and buried her body in a shallow grave, sprinkling it with lime in the hopes of hastening its destruction. He led police to the shallow grave.

When confronted, Becker said that the corpse was not that of his wife. He said that his wife was larger than the corpse and that the clothes were not the ones she had been wearing when last seen. Medical examiner Dr. Karl Kennard performed an autopsy and found that the victim's stomach was very well preserved. Within he found almonds, grapes, figs, and meat-spread canapés. Becker countered that any woman could have eaten these foods, but when the meat-spread was tested, its ingredients were identical to the spread served at the party. It was an old family recipe. Both men were convicted of murder.

Skeletal Remains

Sometimes the forensic team doesn't have a body to work with but rather only skeletal remains. These might be in the form of an intact skeleton, a partial skeleton, a handful of bones, or a single bone. They might be scattered on the ground, buried, or within a structure, such as a house or barn.

Unknown skeletal remains present special problems for the ME. With no tissues to work with, she might call on the expertise of a forensic anthropologist and a forensic odontologist to help with the identification process. As with a corpse, the investigators will follow a logical sequence in attempting to identify the remains. The first questions that must be answered are the following:

- Are the bones human?
- What are the victim's biological characteristics (size, age, sex, and race)?
- How long has the person been dead?
- What is the cause and manner of death?

Are the Bones Human?

Most of the time, particularly if an intact skeleton is available, this determination is easy. But sometimes, the effects of nature and the activities of various animal predators can scatter and destroy portions of the skeleton and this can lead to difficulties. For example, the front paw bones of a bear are similar to those of a human hand, shell fragments from some turtles often resemble skull fragments, and the ribs of sheep and deer appear similar to human ribs.

If the victim is an infant or young child, determining that the bones are human is even more difficult. Infant bones and teeth are much smaller and easier to confuse with those from small animals. An infant's skull is not completely fused (joined together into a single structure) so that an intact skull will not be found. Still a skilled forensic anthropologist can usually distinguish human bones from those of other animals. This is a highly technical endeavor and requires great experience, so it is beyond the scope of this text.

Biological Characteristics

If the bones are human, the anthropologist will next evaluate the corpse's biological characteristics, such as age, stature, sex, and race. Simply determining the sex of the deceased will cut the possibilities in half. If the bones are those of a 60-something, five-foot-tall Caucasian female, these findings would exclude any persons not fitting this profile. Once these characteristics are determined, the search can turn toward individualizing characteristics such as bony evidence of disease, congenital defects, or skeletal trauma.

With an intact adult skeleton, the determination of sex can be made 100 percent of the time, age to within 5–10 years, height to within 1.5 inches, and race most of the time. With only a partial skeleton or just a few bones, the accuracy of each of these determinations diminishes.

Age is best determined by looking at the teeth and skull, as well as the maturity of the bone growth centers and the normal age-related changes in the bones and joints. Each of these gives only an estimate of age, so the examiner must in the end make her "best guess." Age can be more accurately estimated in the young because the teeth and bones in children and adolescents follow a predictable growth and maturation pattern. By assessing the stage of this development, a fairly narrow age range can be determined. Later in life, changes in the teeth and the skeleton occur at a much slower rate, and this broadens the range of age assessment.

Humans have two sets of teeth: 20 **deciduous** (baby) and 32 **permanent** (adult). The formation, eruption, and loss of baby teeth and the appearance of permanent teeth occur in a known sequence. The shedding of deciduous teeth and the appearance of the permanent teeth are completed by about age 12, except for the final teeth to appear, the third molars or wisdom teeth, which typically erupt by age 18. This knowledge can help assess the age of any individual who was 18 or younger at the time of death.

In adults, the skull is of little use for age estimation, but in infants it can be helpful. An infant's skull is actually in several pieces that with time fuse or meld together along jagged lines of separation known as **suture lines**. It would seem logical that the pattern of the closure of these sutures would be useful, and in the very young child they can be, but unfortunately this fusion occurs in a widely variable pattern, so that age estimation is not that accurate.

The body's long bones (arm and leg bones) consist of three parts: the **diaphysis** (shaft) and the **epiphyses** at each end (Figure 5-1). The growth plates (epiphyseal plates or ossification centers) are located near each end where the diaphysis and the epiphyses come together. Bones can continue to grow only as long as these epiphyseal plates are "open." When they "close," or ossify, growth is no longer possible. The timing of this varies, but is typically completed by the mid 20s, and tends to occur slightly earlier in females than in males. If the skeleton in question is small, with no fusion of the epiphyses, the person was likely a child. If the bones are that of a nearly grown individual and if these growth plates are partially fused, the person

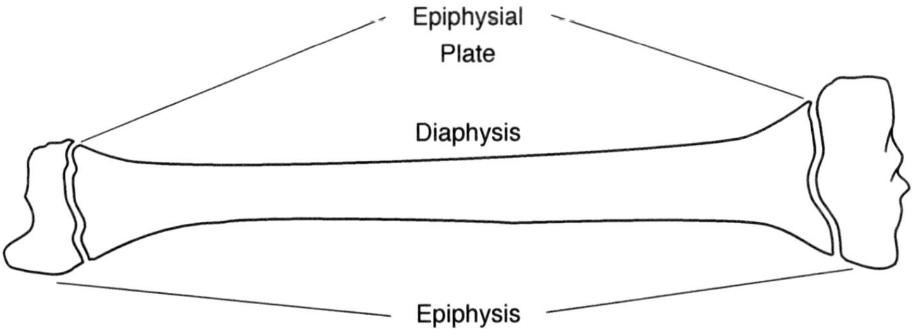

Figure 5-1

Human long bones consist of the diaphysis (shaft) and two epiphyseal end pieces. The two epiphyses (growth plates) bind these segments and are the location of bone growth. When these plates fuse, growth ceases.

would have been a teenager or in his early 20s at death. If the growth plates are fully fused, the person was probably over 25 years of age.

In addition, the complete closure of the epiphyses in the various bones of the body occurs at more or less predictable times. The plates near the elbow close between age 12 and 14, those of the hip and ankle around 15, and those of the shoulder between 18 and 20. This allows for fairly accurate age determination between the ages of about 13 and 20.

Another marker of age is the **pubic symphysis** (Figure 5-2). The right and left pelvic bones join to the spinal column in back at the sacroiliac joints and in the front to each other at the pubic symphysis. This union is a thin band of cartilage that is slightly scalloped. With age, this cartilage band evolves toward a thinner and straighter line so that the "straightening" of this line is a rough indicator of age that is useful only up to about age 50.

Another important area to examine is the sternal (breastbone) ends of the ribs. Early in life, these are smooth and rounded, but with age become pitted with sharper edges. Evaluating these changes can narrow age predication to 1.5 years up to age 30 and within 5 years up to age 70. After that, these changes are of little use. Arthritis and other joint abnormalities are not common before age 40, so if significant arthritis is seen, the person was probably beyond 40 and more likely 60 or so at the time of death.

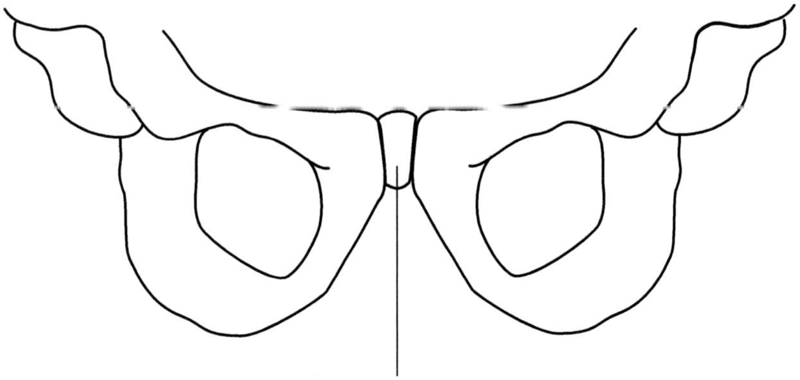

Figure 5-2

Pubic symphysis. The pubic symphysis is the frontal union of the right and left halves of the pelvis. Straightening and narrowing of the junction occurs with aging.

Stature is easily determined by simple measurement if a complete skeleton is available, but even if not it can be estimated if one or more of the long bones are available by a technique called **allometry**. Long bones include the femur (upper leg bone), the tibia (larger of the two lower leg bones), the humerus (the upper arm bone), and the radius (the larger of the two forearm bones). The most accurate bones to use are the femur and the tibia. There are rules of thumb such as height is equal to five times the length of the humerus, but the use of one of the many tables and formulas for each of the long bones allows a more accurate estimate. For example, the formulas developed by Genoves in 1967 indicate that for males, height can be determined using either the femur or the tibia and using these equations:

Femur length in centimeters $\times$ 2.26 + 66.38 = Height in centimeters

Tibia length in centimeters $\times$ 1.96 + 93.75 = Height in centimeters

But what if the examiner has only fragments of these bones? Fortunately, other formulas have been worked out that allow the estimation of the bone length from fragments; once this is determined, the estimated length can be used to calculate the height.

After the height is estimated, the examiner will examine the bones in detail and make a best guess as to the person's build. There are no formulas here, just educated guesses. For example, if the bones are thick, particularly in the areas where muscles attach to the skeleton, the person likely had a muscular physique; if not, a slighter build. Similarly handedness can be estimated since the dominant side tends to have thicker, stronger bones.

Sex is not always easy to determine from skeletal remains, and the accuracy with which it can be done mostly depends on which bones are available. Even though males tend to have larger and thicker bones than do females, this is far from universal, so bone size and thickness are only marginally useful. Things such as overall size, nutrition, and level of physical activity play important roles. For example, a large female who was well fed and worked at manual labor might have a more "male" skeleton than would a male who was small, malnourished, or sedentary. Still, the thickness of certain bones can prove useful. In general, the diameters of the heads of the humerus, the radius, and the femur are almost always larger in males.

The **pelvic bones** are the most reliable for sex determination. The male pelvis is designed only for support and movement, while the female pelvis is adapted for childbirth (Figure 5-3 A and B). The female pelvis is wider and with a larger pelvic outlet, which allows passage of the infant during childbirth. Also, the **sciatic notch** (where the sciatic and other nerves pass through on their way to the leg) is wider in females than in males (Figure 5-3 C and D).

The skull is also useful since male skulls have thicker and more prominent ridges and crests, particularly in areas where facial and jaw muscles attach. In addition, the posterior ramus of the **mandible** (jaw bone) in males is slightly curved, while in females it tends to be straight (Figure 5-4).

Determining sex from skeletal remains of infants and children is more difficult since the gender-specific changes described above aren't prominent until after puberty.

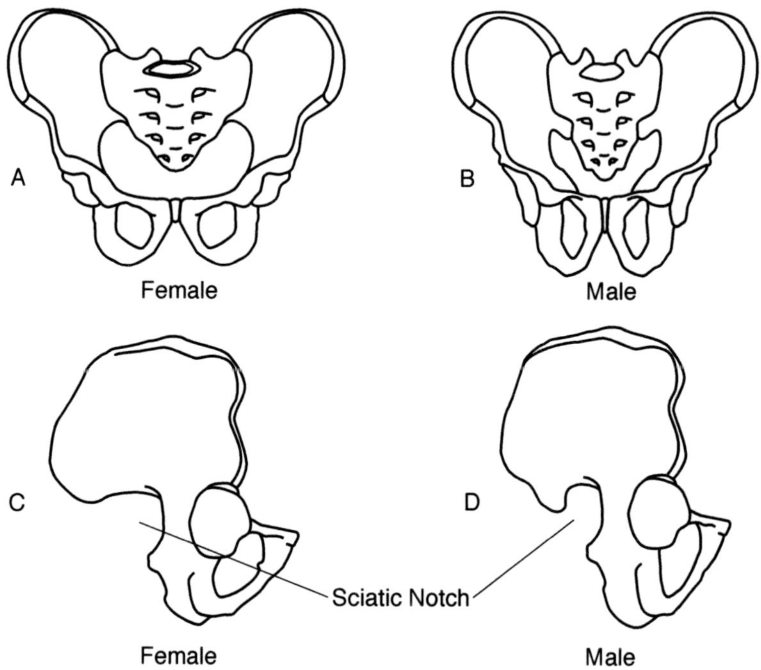

Figure 5-3

Pelvic bones. The female pelvis (A) is wider than the male (B). In addition the sciatic notch is broader in females (C) than in males (D).

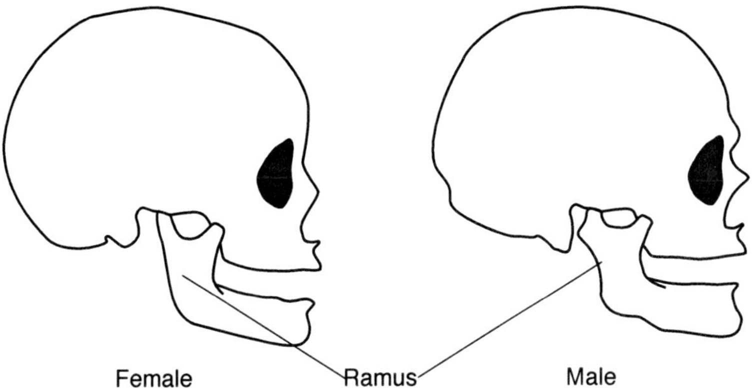

Figure 5-4
The mandible. The posterior ramus of the mandible is curved in males, but straight in females.

Racial classification is very difficult, if not impossible, since no single skeletal trait is racially distinct. Any classification is rough at best. There are only three groups to which a given skeleton can be assigned: **Caucasoid**, **Negroid**, or **Mongoloid**.

Caucasoid individuals tend to have high, rounded or square skulls, straight faces, and narrow, protruding noses, while those of Negroid or Mongoloid descent tend toward lower and narrower skulls and wider, flatter noses. Negroids tend to have proportionally longer arms and legs than do Caucasoids, while in Mongoloids the limbs are shorter. Caucasoid individuals have a forward curve to their femurs, while in Negroid persons this bone is straighter.

It should be obvious that the skeleton of an individual of mixed racial origin would share characteristics of the individual races in his ancestry. Often this racial admixture makes racial assignment impossible.

Individual characteristics include not only DNA and dental patterns, but also bony evidence of disease or trauma. DNA can often be extracted from bones, and skeletal remains often have at least some of the teeth still in place; each of these, as we saw above with an unidentified corpse, can be useful for identification. Also, primary bone cancers and those that metastasize (spread) to bone and infectious diseases such as tuberculosis, syphilis, and osteomyelitis (bone infection) usually leave behind characteristic findings. Bone disorders, such as Paget's disease and rickets, and old fractures are easily identified. The finding of any of these injuries or diseases would further narrow the possibilities to persons known to have had the disease or injury indicated. As mentioned earlier, finding an artificial hip, pacemaker, or other device among the skeletal remains would be very helpful, since the serial numbers etched on these devices can be easily traced to the recipient.

Time Since Death

Taphonomy is the study of what happens to the human body after death. The term comes from the Greek words *taphos,* which means grave or burial, and *nomos,* which means rules or laws, so taphonomy literally means the "rules of burial." How the body decays, if it does, and how it becomes skeletonized or mummified are the domain of taphonomy. We will dig deeper into this in Chapter 6.

When the forensic anthropologist examines skeletal remains, one of the first questions he must answer is: How old are these bones? This is critical since bones that are hundreds of years old have no forensic use, while those that are 2 years, 20 years, or even 50 years old might very well have forensic use. For the forensic anthropologist, estimating the time since death is never easy and becomes increasingly more difficult with each passing month. However, he does have a few techniques that will help him.

Artifacts of the burial site such as clothing, jewelry, and casket materials might indicate the period of the burial. For example, arrowheads or musket balls would suggest a different time frame than would synthetic materials and plastic objects. Pages from a newspaper or a magazine would set the outside range for the time of death. It could be later, but not earlier.

Chemical analyses of the bones might help. Proteins and their amino acid building blocks contain **nitrogen**. Bones consist of a protein matrix to which calcium is attached. As bones slowly deteriorate, the protein, and thus the nitrogen, level decreases. Measuring the nitrogen level offers an estimate of how many years or decades the bones have been interred. This is inexact since the rate of protein and nitrogen loss is highly variable. But the various amino acids that make up the bone's protein matrix disappear at different rates. Analysis of fresh bones might yield as many as 15 different amino acids, while those that are 100 or more years old might have only seven. Two of the longest surviving amino acids are **proline** and **hydroxyproline**. Their absence would suggest that the bones had been buried many hundreds of years.

Ultraviolet (UV) light is another useful tool. Fresh bones fluoresce (glow) a pale blue color under UV light. If the bone is cut crosswise, this glow can be seen across the full thickness of the bone. This fluorescence is lost over time from surface to inside. Since the long bones are hollow, this loss of fluorescence occurs from the outside surface and the inside (marrow) surface toward the middle of the bone. A bone that is less than 100 years old might glow across its full thickness, but with time this fluorescent band becomes progressively thinner until after several hundred years it disappears.

Radioactive isotopes can help age bones. **Carbon 14** (C14) dating is of little use in forensics since its half-life (time it takes to decay by 50 percent) is 5700 years. It is useful for dating something that is many hundreds or thousands of years old, but not for shorter time periods. But, other radioactive materials can be helpful. With the testing and use of nuclear devices in World War II and throughout the 1950s and 1960s, the global environment saw an increase in **C14, strontium 90**, **cesium 137**, and **tritium** (a radioisotope of hydrogen). The finding of increased amounts of one or more of these in bones means that the victim died after about 1950. Those who died earlier were not exposed to these environmental increases so would show no such elevation.

Cause and Manner of Death

As we will see in Chapter 7, determining the cause and manner of death is critical as to whether a criminal investigation will follow. If the death is natural, there will be no investigation; if the ME determines that the death was a homicide, a vigorous investigation would follow. With skeletal remains this determination is difficult and often impossible, but occasionally clues to the cause and manner of death can be uncovered. Of course blunt-force trauma, knives, and bullets can lead to death without impacting the skeleton, but sometimes evidence is left behind.

With blunt-force injuries, such as falls or blows from a blunt object, the injured bone might show fractures, fragmentation, and impact marks (dents and depressions). Sometimes these injuries will suggest what type of object was used. A baseball bat, a tire iron, and a hammer will each leave behind different depressions in a skull. With sharp-force injuries, such as with an axe or knife, cut surfaces, nicks, and chips where the blade struck the bone might be visible. Occasionally, metallic remnants from the weapon can be seen along the cut surface.

In gunshot deaths, finding a bullet or two with the remains is helpful, but even if not, gunshots often leave behind evidence such as entry and exit holes in the skull and gouges and other defects in other bones. Sometimes, measuring the entrance hole will estimate the caliber of the bullet, which can narrow the search for the weapon.

One of the problems facing the examiner is whether the bony injuries occurred around the time of death or many years earlier. A skull fracture that occurred years before death and one that occurred at the time of death mean two entirely different things. Fractured bones heal by way of **callus** (scar) formation, a process that takes months. No healing occurs after death, so a fracture with callus formation must have occurred months before death. On the other hand, peri-mortem fractures show no signs of callus formation, suggesting that they occurred around the time of death and might indeed be the cause of death.

What about fractures that occur years after death, after the skeleton has been exposed to nature or predators for many months or years? Can the examiner determine that fractures occurred long after death and have no bearing on the cause of death? Often, he can. Living bones contain moisture and proteins, which makes them less brittle. They tend to fracture in a spiral or "greenstick" fashion. Bones that have dessicated (dried out) are more brittle and tend to crumble more readily and fracture more cleanly, usually parallel or at a cross-section to the long axis of the bone. By examining the nature of any fractures the forensic anthropologist might be able to distinguish pre-mortem from distant post-mortem fractures.

Based on the timing and nature of skeletal injuries, the forensic anthropologist and the ME might be able to determine the cause of death, but determining the manner of death (Chapter 7) is more problematic. What if the findings suggest that the individual died as a result of a skull fracture? Was this from a blow to the head (homicidal), a fall (accidental), or a fall after a heart attack or stroke (natural)?

Facial Reconstruction

Facial reconstruction is part science and mostly art. It can be extremely useful in skeletal identification if a likeness of the individual can be created and circulated, with the hope being that someone will recognize the person. It is a fascinating process that often involves a forensic anthropologist, dentist, and artist or sculptor. The goal is to use a complete or partial skull to recreate either a two-dimensional image on paper or a computer screen or a three-dimensional sculpting. The freehand or computer artist will use an image of the skull as a framework and then overlay it with an image that best represents what the person must have looked like in life. This takes a bit of guesswork and a great deal of experience and talent.

For the sculptor, the skull, or more likely a cast of the skull, serves as the framework, and a clay model is created one layer at a time. Studies have determined the average skin thickness over certain boney landmarks of the skull. Small spacers that reflect these various thicknesses are placed in these areas and are then connected by strips of clay. This latticework is then filled in and contoured. As with drawn renderings, this requires the hand and eye of an artist.

However, many problems plague each of these techniques. Hair and eye color, hairstyle, and the presence or absence of facial hair are not known. Features such as the nose and ears are made of cartilage and are often absent. To draw or sculpt these features requires a "best guess." Similarly, the thickness of the skin and the amount of body fat must also be estimated, and errors in this estimation may greatly affect the final model.

If a missing individual who fits the general characteristics of the remains is identified and if a photograph of this person is available, a technique called **skull-to-photo superimposition** might help confirm the identification. In this process the photo is superimposed over a similar sized photo of the skull and the bony landmarks are compared. This can rarely provide a conclusive match but it can eliminate certain candidates. If the photo reveals that the eyes are too widely spaced, the cheekbones too broad, or the chin of a different contour, the skull is not that of the suspect individual. On the other hand, if all these features match, the suspect individual cannot be excluded. This technique was used to help solve one of the greatest mysteries of the 20th century: Was Josef Mengele really dead?

Josef Mengele, the Nazi "Angel of Death," conducted an array of unspeakable human experiments on prisoners of Hitler's Third Reich and alone oversaw the deaths of perhaps 400,000 people. Yet, when the Russians took the concentration camps at Auschwitz, few people knew the name Mengele. In fact, it was not until many years later, with the capture of Adolf Eichmann, that Mengele became the prime target of Nazi hunters.

From the 1960s and into the 1980s, sightings and rumors placed Mengele at various times in Argentina, Brazil, and Paraguay, and he became the world's single most sought-after war criminal. In 1985, Wolfram and Liselotte Bossert, a German couple living in Brazil, showed authorities what they believed to be Mengele's grave near the village of Embu.

Scientists from the United States and Germany as well as experts from the Simon Wiesenthal Center in Vienna, Austria, took part in the examination of the skeletal remains. They determined that the bones were that of a Caucasian male, whose size and age matched that of Mengele. Unfortunately, Mengele's SS file was sketchy at best, and in particular his hand-drawn 1938 dental chart was inexact. It revealed that Mengele had 12 fillings but did not pinpoint their locations. Also, it made no mention of his gap-toothed smile.

German forensic anthropologist Richard Helmer had been working with photographic superimposition. He took a photograph of the skull, marked over thirty identifying points, and then superimposed it over a known photo of Mengele. The match was perfect. Final confirmation came in 1992 with DNA matching of materials obtained from the bones with samples taken from Mengele's relatives.

Photographic Comparisons and Age Progressions

Occasionally the forensic anthropologist is asked to determine if two photos are of the same person, sometimes with photos taken years or decades apart and of variable quality and technique. Sometimes one photo is from a surveillance camera, while another is a candid snapshot. The key to such comparisons is that, though everyone's face undergoes age-related changes, there are certain features that do not change. The examiner will superimpose one photo over the other and compare fixed structures such as orbital ridges (eyebrow area), nasal openings, and chin contour. A match would suggest, but not prove, that the photos were of the same individual.

Sometimes the forensic anthropologist, working with a forensic artist, must "age" a photograph. That is, estimate how the person's facial features might have changed over the years. Using an old photograph of the individual, these scientists make a "best guess" as to what the individual might look like years later. There are even computer programs to aid the process.

To help make this "best guess," the examiners will often perform a psychiatric profile on the missing person. This is a look into the type of person he was, what type of work he did, what his dietary and exercise habits were, whether he is likely to have undergone cosmetic surgery or not, and many other things. This information helps them estimate what facial changes have likely occurred in the individual over the years. A major triumph of this technique was realized in the case of John List.

In 1971, neighbors noticed that they had not seen John List and his family for some time and that their large home in Westfield, New Jersey, seemed deserted except for the lights that blazed throughout the house every night. The police investigated and found the bodies of Helen List and the three List children neatly placed on sleeping bags in a room near the back of the house. In an upstairs bedroom they found the body of John's mother, Alma. Each had been shot. John List was nowhere to be found.

Five addressed envelopes were taped to a filing cabinet, each containing a letter that explained his rationale for committing the multiple murders.

Apparently he was on the brink of bankruptcy and did not want his family humiliated by a life on welfare, so he spared them this by killing them. Two days later, his car turned up in the long-term parking at New York's JFK Airport.

Thirteen years later, Bernard Tracey, who was still investigating the cold case attempted to rekindle interest in the case by approaching *Weekly World*, a supermarket tabloid. They ran a story on the John List case on February 17, 1986. Wanda Flanery of Aurora, Colorado, thought the photograph that accompanied the story resembled her neighbor, Bob Clark. She mentioned this to Bob's wife, Delores, who scoffed at the idea that her church-going husband could ever be a murderer. Shortly thereafter the Clarks ran into financial difficulty due to Bob's poor handling of their money and relocated to Richmond, Virginia.

Still frustrated by his inability to crack the case, Bernard Tracey approached the television show *America's Most Wanted*. They hired forensic sculptor Frank A. Bender to fashion a bust of what John List might look like some 18 years after his last known photograph. Dr. Richard Walter of the Michigan Department of Corrections was brought in to offer a profile of John List as an aid to the reconstruction. He felt that List's religious background would make it unlikely that he had undergone any plastic surgery and that his lifestyle would not be one of diet and exercise. This was valuable information since either could alter List's pattern of aging.

FBI specialist Gene O'Donnell, using the latest computer technology and the photograph of John List, was able to "age" the photo by adding gray, receding hair and fleshly jowls. He also included thick-rimmed glasses similar to those List wore in the photo. On May 21, 1989, *America's Most Wanted* aired the John List case along with the "aged" photo. Over 250 calls came in, one from an anonymous caller in Colorado who said that John List was living in Richmond, Virginia, under the name of Bob Clark. The caller later turned out to be a relative of Wanda Flanery. Fingerprints proved that Bob Clark and John List were the same individual. On April 20, 1990, nearly two decades after murdering his family, John List received a life sentence.

Multiple Corpses

If identifying a single skeletal corpse is difficult, mass graves and scenes of major catastrophic events present special problems for the forensic anthropologist. This is particularly difficult in mass graves where only a jumble of skeletal remains is found. The examiner might never be able to ascertain the exact number of victims, but he can at least determine the minimum number. If he finds 60 skulls, jaw bones, or hip girdles he can conclude that a minimum of 60 people were interred in the site. There could be more, but not less.

Then each bone must be analyzed using whichever of the above techniques is deemed appropriate. More recently, DNA has helped greatly, but it is still a long and arduous process.

CHAPTER 6

TIME OF DEATH

In homicide cases, the three most important things the ME must determine are the **cause**, **manner**, and **time** of death. In this chapter we will consider the time of death and in the next chapter the cause and manner.

Why do the ME and the police invest so much time and effort in determining the time of death? Why is the time of death often vigorously debated in court, each side trying to tweak the timeline to its advantage? The reason is that this alone can exonerate or focus suspicion on a suspect, can substantiate or refute witness and suspect statements, and can literally make or break the case.

Before we look at why this estimation is so important, let's first define the term "time of death." Time of death seems to be a simple and straightforward term that obviously means the exact time that the victim drew her last breath. It's not quite that simple. It might surprise you to learn that there are actually three different times of death, and they aren't always in sync:

- The **physiological** time of death: When the victim's vital functions actually ceased.
- The **legal** time of death: The time recorded on the death certificate.
- The **estimated** time of death: The time the ME estimates that death occurred.

The only absolutely accurate determination of the time of death is when the person dies with a physician or other skilled medical professional present. Here the physiological, legal, and estimated time of death are the time the physician marks in the medical record. Otherwise, it's impossible to determine the exact time of death.

You might ask, what about the circumstance where someone witnesses the fatal blow or gunshot, or what if the event is recorded on a timed surveillance camera? Wouldn't that be accurate? Maybe, maybe not. If the witnessed event led to immediate death, then the witness would have seen the actual death. But if the witnessed event is simply the trauma that led to death, but not the actual moment of death, then the witness's estimate is not accurate. People can survive massive and apparently lethal injuries for hours, even days.

But most deaths are not witnessed. Natural death might come during sleep, accidental and suicidal deaths often occur when the victim is alone, and in homicides, the perpetrator is typically the only witness. This means the ME must estimate the time of death using the various techniques available to him.

These three times of death can differ by days, weeks, even months, if the body is not found until well after physiological death has occurred. For example, if a serial killer kills a victim in July, but the body is not discovered until October, the physiological death took place in July, but the legal death is marked as October since that is when the corpse was discovered and the death was legally noted. The ME's estimated time of death could be July, or it could be June or August. It is an estimate, and as we will see, many factors conspire to confuse this determination. But, it is critically important for the ME to be as accurate as possible.

The Importance of the Time of Death

Why is the time of death important? Isn't it more crucial to determine who did it than guessing when it happened? The fact is that an accurate estimation of the time of death can eliminate some suspects while focusing attention on others. Let's say a husband tells investigators that he left for a business meeting at 2 p.m. and returned at 8 p.m. to find his wife dead. He says that he was home all morning and that she was alive and well when he left. If the ME determines the time of death was between 10 a.m. and noon, the husband has some explaining to do, but if the estimation suggests that the death occurred between 4 p.m. and 6 p.m., he has an alibi for that time period. This will move the investigation in a different direction.

Notice that in the above example the ME gave a range rather than an exact time for his estimated time of death. He didn't say 4:30 but rather said between 4 and 6 p.m. Simply put, that's the best he can do and that's why it's called the estimated time of death. It's a best guess.

The time of death is not confined to criminal investigations and can also play a role in civil situations. Insurance payments might depend upon whether the insured individual was alive at the time the policy went into effect or if he died before the policy expired. Even a single day can be important. Likewise, property inheritance can hinge on when the deceased actually died. Suppose two business partners die near the same time. Their contract might state that the company assets go to the survivor if one of them dies. In this case, the heirs of the one that died last would own the company assets. Similarly, the dispersal of property under a will might be affected by which spouse died first.

Determining the Time of Death

Determining the time of death is both art and science and requires that the ME use several techniques and observations to make his estimate. As a general rule, the sooner after death the body is examined, the more accurate this estimate will be. Difficulties arise because the rate of post-mortem changes varies widely from corpse to corpse. There is no single factor that will accurately indicate the time of physiological death, but rather several factors must be considered together to reach a "best guess." But when the principles are properly applied, the ME can often estimate the physiological time of death with some degree of accuracy.

The principle observations and tests he will employ include the following:

- Body temperature
- Rigor mortis
- Livor mortis (lividity)
- Degree of putrefaction

- Stomach contents
- Corneal cloudiness
- Vitreous potassium level
- Insect activity
- Scene markers

Let's look at each of these.

Body Temperature

Normal body temperature is 98.6° Fahrenheit. After death, the body progressively loses (or gains) heat until it equilibrates with that of the surrounding medium. The formula or "rule of thumb" for heat loss is 1.5°/hour.

Hours since death = 98.6 − Corpse core temperature/1.5

Let's say a body is found in an office where the temperature is a steady 72°. The ME determines that the core temperature is 92.6°. The above formula would reveal:

Hours since death = 98.6 − 92.6/1.5 = 6/1.5 or
approximately 4 hours

This approximate rate of heat loss continues until the environmental temperature is attained, after which it remains stable. After this equilibration is reached, corpse temperature is no longer useful for estimating the time of death. This sounds simple but unfortunately it's not quite that straightforward.

The 1.5°-per-hour rule varies greatly, depending on the environment surrounding the body, the size of the corpse, clothing, and other factors. For example, a body in a temperate room will lose heat much more slowly than will one in an icy, flowing stream. A body that is fully clothed and lying in the sun will lose heat more slowly than will an unclothed corpse exposed to a chilling rain or a cool breeze. And a body in a hot environment such as an enclosed garage in Phoenix in August where the ambient temperature could be 125° or more will actually gain heat. The key is that the corpse will lose or gain heat until it reaches equilibrium with its environment.

The coroner or his technician should obtain a body temperature and measure the temperature of the surrounding medium—air, water, snow, or soil (if the body is buried). The body temperature should be taken either rectally or by measuring the liver temperature, which more accurately reflects the true core body temperature. This is done through a small incision in the upper right abdomen through which the thermometer is passed into the tissue of the liver. This should be done only by a trained individual and under the direction of the ME. Care should be taken not to alter or destroy any existing wounds on the body. Some people have stated that measuring the core temperature by inserting the thermometer into a wound such as a knife or gunshot injury would yield an accurate number and negate the need to make a new incision. This should never be done since the introduction of any foreign object might contaminate or alter the wound, which could be key evidence in the case. A rectal temperature is usually more practical.

But even under the best of circumstances, body temperature determination has several inherent sources of inaccuracy. One of the assumptions made in this process is that the initial body temperature was the normal 98.6°. Contrary to what is taught in grammar school health classes, this number is an average and actually varies from person to person. Some people have higher normal temperatures than do others. Women tend toward higher temperatures than do men. Febrile illnesses of course elevate the body temperature, while certain chronic illness, dehydration, or the presence of prolonged shock prior to death will lower initial body temperature. There is also some diurnal (morning versus evening) variation in body temperature in most people. So any calculation of corpse temperature change begins with some degree of error.

A corpse loses heat passively by three distinct mechanisms: **radiation** (heat lost as infrared heat rays), **conduction** (heat passed on to any object that contacts the body), and **convection** (heat lost into the moving air). Obesity, heavy clothing, warm still air, exposure to direct sunlight, and an enclosed environment slow heat loss, while if the body is in contact with cold surfaces such as marble or cool concrete, or is exposed to cold water or wind, heat loss will be greater. Children and the elderly tend to lose heat faster, as do those who are chronically ill or emaciated.

As you can see, and as we will see with all other methods for determining the time of death, heat loss is fraught with inaccuracies. Still, with early and careful measurement of the core body temperature and with consideration for the conditions surrounding the corpse, a reasonably accurate estimate can often be made.

Rigor Mortis

Rigor mortis is the post-mortem stiffening of a corpse. It is due to a chemical reaction that involves **adenosine diphosphate (ADP)** and **adenosine triphosphate (ATP)**. When we move a muscle, any muscle, there is a conversion of ATP to ADP that releases the energy needed to cause muscular contraction. Then the body reconverts the ADP to ATP as it readies for the next contraction. This process requires oxygen and nutrients. At death, the heart stops, blood flow ceases, and the muscles no longer receive the needed oxygen and nutrients. ATP will gradually break down and convert to ADP and the muscles will begin to contract. This is what causes the rigidity of rigor mortis. Later, as the muscles begin to decompose as part of the putrefaction process, they become flaccid (relax) and the rigor resolves.

This process occurs in each of the body's muscles at the same time, but the appearance of the actual rigidity doesn't. Rigor typically follows a predictable pattern, being detectable first in the small muscles of the face, neck, and hands before progressing to the larger muscles. The reason for this progression from smaller to larger muscles is simply that smaller muscles possess less ATP so the loss is relatively more rapid. Thus, smaller muscles will exhibit stiffening more readily than will larger ones. The relaxation of rigor follows a similar pattern in that it also begins in the smaller muscles and progresses to the larger ones. The reason is again due to size. Smaller muscles will decay more rapidly than will larger ones. So if the ME finds a body with stiffening in the hands and jaw but flaccidity in the shoulders and hips, the rigor is beginning; if the opposite is true—the small muscles are flaccid and the larger muscles still rigid—rigor is waning. This is a gradual process, so that there is some overlap and these determinations are not always easy.

In general, rigor begins approximately 2 hours after death and the entire contraction process is completed by about 12 hours. At that time, the body is completely stiff and fixed in the position of death. This is called the **rigid stage** of rigor mortis and lasts about 12 hours. Then the decay process takes over and the corpse will relax into what is termed the **flaccid stage** of rigor mortis.

The general rule is 12-12-12. Under normal conditions, rigor begins in about 2 hours, maximizes at about 12 hours, remains unchanged for 12 hours (rigor stage), and resolves over the next 12 hours (flaccid stage). So, rigor is useful only in the first 36 hours or so after death. Under normal conditions, that is. There are wide variations from corpse to corpse and from situation to situation and it is these variations that make rigor an unreliable method for determining the time of death.

Let's look at a few of these variations.

In any situation where most of the ATP is already converted to ADP at the moment of death, rigor can occur very quickly. Extreme muscular activity such as someone drowning, fighting, or running would be examples as each of these activities would consume most, if not all, of the muscular ATP and rigor could come on within minutes of death. Interestingly, a victim who was chased prior to death might show the first signs of rigor in the legs, which is where the ATP depletion would be greatest.

Persons who die with violent seizure activity might also show rigor very quickly since the muscular contractions associated with seizure activity would deplete muscular ATP. The same is true for victims of strychnine poisoning. This drug causes violent convulsions and muscular spasms, conditions that mimic severe physical or seizure activity, and can often trigger almost instantaneous rigor.

Elevated body temperature also increases ATP consumption. Victims of sepsis (infection throughout the blood stream), pneumonia, or any other febrile process as well as those that succumb to heat stroke might develop rigor very rapidly.

The opposite is also true. Cold conditions slow the process of ATP loss considerably and will delay the onset and development of rigor. A victim who dies from exposure in a cold clime or one that is frozen immediately after death might not develop rigor for days, perhaps not until the body is warmed or thawed.

Rigor can be broken by bending and stretching the corpse, which breaks up the muscle fibers. Once broken, rigor will not return.

Cadaveric spasm is a term applied to the situation where rigor occurs instantaneously throughout the body, locking the corpse in the exact posture it was in at the moment of death. The corpse could be frozen sitting, kneeling, reaching, or in virtually any position. Cadaveric spasm occurs under extremely violent physical and emotional situations. Though controversial, cadaveric spasm is best viewed as simply instantaneous rigor, since the conditions that cause cadaveric spasm are similar to those that cause early onset of rigor.

Livor Mortis

Livor mortis (also called **lividity** or **post-mortem hypostasis**) is a dark discoloration of portions of the body due to the settling of blood within the corpse as dictated by gravity. It not only helps determine the time of death but also might indicate whether a body was moved after death.

Lividity is a purplish hue of the tissues that can easily be mistaken for bruising. At death, the heart stops beating and the blood ceases to move. Gravity then causes the stagnant blood to settle into the dependent (lower) areas of the body. In a supine corpse lividity will occur along the back and buttocks, while a corpse lying on its left side will show lividity along the downside of the left shoulder, arm, hip, and leg.

However, any dependent area that presses against a firm surface will appear pale and will be surrounded by the lividity. For example, a corpse lying on its back will show lividity along its entire lower surface except where the body actually contacts the hard floor. The back of the head, shoulder blades, buttocks, and calves will show pale points of contact. The reason for this is that the weight of the body compresses the blood vessels in these support areas and prevents the accumulation of stagnant blood. Tight clothing can sometimes do the same thing. A belt, waistband, or brassiere might leave a pale track through an area of lividity.

Why is the lividity this dark bluish-purple color? Where arterial blood is rich in oxygen (O_2) and thus bright red, venous and capillary blood are depleted of O_2 and are more purple in hue. Also, at death, when the heart and circulation cease, no fresh blood reaches the cells of the body. In a futile attempt to survive, the cells of the body extract all the O_2 they can, leaving the blood depleted of O_2. This oxygen-poor blood is dark purple; when it settles it produces purple lividity.

But, not all lividity is so dusky.

In carbon monoxide (CO) and cyanide (CN) poisoning, the lividity can take on a cherry-red or pinkish coloration. CO combines with hemoglobin creating **carboxyhemoglobin**, which is bright red in color. Similarly, CN combines with hemoglobin to produce **cyanohemoglobin**, also bright red in color. So, blood that is rich in carboxyhemoglobin or cyanohemoglobin is bright red and the resulting lividity will reflect this.

Another situation that might produce pinkish lividity is where the victim is exposed to very cold conditions at or around the time of death, as in deaths from hypothermia. The extreme cold slows all cellular activities, including the post-mortem removal of O_2 from the blood. This leaves the blood rich in oxygen, red in color, and causes red or pink lividity.

Lividity typically appears between 30 minutes and 2 hours after death and reaches its maximum by 8 to 12 hours. Initially, this discoloration can be shifted by rolling the body to a different position. If a body is supine for a couple of hours and then rolled to its left side, the lividity that had begun accumulating along the back will shift and begin accumulating along the left side. This shifting is possible because the blood remains within the vascular system and is still able to move. But, after 6 to 8 hours, the lividity becomes fixed and rolling the body to another position will not result in a shifting of the discoloration. The reason for this is that after about 6 to 8 hours the blood vessels in the area begin to break down and the blood seeps from the vessels and stains the surrounding tissues. As opposed to the blood that remains within the vascular system, this blood in the tissue is fixed in position. The ME can use shifting and fixed lividity to estimate time of death and to determine if the body has been moved or repositioned, something the dead do not do without assistance.

If a body is found face down with fixed lividity along the chest, abdomen, and front of the legs, the ME can conclude that the death was at least 6 to 8 hours earlier. It might be longer but it is not likely earlier. If the lividity can still be shifted, death likely occurred less than 4 hours or so earlier. On the other hand, if a body is found face down, but with fixed lividity along the back, then the body was moved at least 6 hours after death, but not earlier or the lividity would have shifted to the newly dependent area. This means the body lay on its back for at least 6 hours after death, long enough for the lividity to become fixed, and was then rolled to its stomach or moved to an entirely different location and deposited on its stomach.

This fixing process occurs gradually so is not an all-or-nothing phenomena. This means that around 3 to 6 hours after death some of the lividity might be fixed and some still able to shift. If the ME finds that the corpse has some faint areas of fixed lividity along the back and true fixed lividity along the front, he might conclude that the body lay on its back for 3 or 4 hours and was then moved and placed face down, where it laid for 6 or more hours.

So, a careful examination of the lividity pattern can help determine the time of death and can often help reconstruct the sequence of events after death in cases where the corpse has been moved or repositioned. If the patterns and the body position don't match, it suggests that someone had reason to move the body. That someone is often, but not always, the killer. Sometimes a family member who finds the corpse of a loved one will reposition them to a more acceptable position or place before calling the police.

As you might suspect the appearance and the fixing of lividity varies with the circumstances. Since the rate of body decay depends primarily on the ambient temperature and since the fixing of the lividity is due to breakdown of the blood vessels and the seepage of the released blood into the tissues, anything that hastens or slows the decay process will do the same for the fixation of lividity. In hot and humid environments this fixation might occur in as little as 3 or 4 hours, while in colder climes it might take as long as 36 hours.

Degree of Putrefaction

Putrefaction means decay or decomposition of a body. Under normal circumstances it follows a predictable pattern, which the ME can use to help estimate the time of death.

Decomposition begins immediately after death and involves two distinct processes: autolysis and putrefaction. **Autolysis** is the process of self-digestion by the enzymes within the body's cells. As with most chemical reactions it is hastened by heat and slowed by a cooler environment. Putrefaction is the bacteria-mediated destruction of body's tissues. The responsible bacteria mostly come from the intestinal tract of the deceased, though environmental bacteria and yeasts contribute to some degree. Bacteria thrive in warm, moist environments, become sluggish in colder climes, and cease their activities if frozen, so that warmth increases the rate of decay, cold slows it, and a frozen body will not undergo putrefaction until it thaws. Regardless of how long it takes, the decomposition process will eventually result in skeletonization of the corpse. But the process is not always uniform, and decomposition can be spotty so that portions of a body might decay while others are left more or less intact.

Besides environmental temperature and moisture, other conditions alter the rate of decay. Obesity and excess clothing, which trap heat within the corpse, increase the rate of putrefaction, while a thin, unclothed corpse lying on a cold surface would decay much more slowly. Sepsis (blood infection) is particularly destructive to the body and might accelerate the decay process so much that after only 24 hours the corpse could appear as if 5 or 6 days had passed. The reason is that not only would the body temperature be higher at death in this circumstance, but also the septic process would have spread bacteria throughout the body. This allows the decay process to begin quickly and in a widespread fashion.

Another important factor in the rate of decay is the location of the body. If exposed, the process will proceed much faster than if the corpse is buried or in water. The general rule is that one week exposed above ground equals two weeks in water and eight weeks in the ground.

Exposed corpses or those buried in shallow graves attract various predators, such as dogs, cats, bears, and rats, that feed on the flesh and carry away portions of the corpse. Any remaining bones can often reveal claw and tooth marks that in turn can reveal the predatory species. For example, dogs and cats tend to remove V-shaped wedges of tissue, while rodents tend to leave shallower, smooth-edged wounds and their incisors (front teeth) leave parallel grooves on the surface of gnawed bones. The ME will look for evidence of predator activity since their activities might bear on his estimated time of death.

Decomposition is not the only way a body can change after death. Under certain circumstances **mummification** or **adipocere formation** might occur.

A dry environment, such as when a corpse is left in a desert or at high altitude, locations usually associated with a very low relative humidity, can cause a corpse to dessicate (dry out), resulting in mummification. The low humidity removes moisture from the tissues, inhibiting bacterial growth and putrefaction. In ancient Egypt, spices and salts were rubbed on the corpse to hasten the drying process so that the corpse would mummify rather than decay. A leathery, dark-colored corpse that looks as if the skin has been "shrink-wrapped" over the bones results. Mummified corpses often remain intact for long periods of time.

Adipocere is the result of a chemical process called **saponification**, which is basically soap making. In this case the reaction is between the body's adipose (fatty) tissues and bacteria such as Clostridia perfringens, the bacterium that causes gas gangrene. Body fat is converted into oleic, stearic, and palmitic acids, which are the primary constitutes of adipocere. The result is a gray or brownish, greasy or waxy substance, which can cast the body so that at first glance it might appear to be a mannequin or as if it had been carved from a large bar of soap. Adipocere most often occurs in bodies found in water or warm, damp areas and usually takes several months to form so that it is a broad indicator of time of death. A corpse that has significant adipocere formation would not likely have been dead only a couple of weeks.

If conditions are just right, each of these processes can occur in the same corpse so that it might be partially skeletonized, partially mummified, and partially converted to adipocere.

You've probably heard the term **floaters**. These are bodies that either die in water or are dumped into water shortly after death. Initially the body will sink, but as putrefaction occurs and gases accumulate in the tissues and body cavities, the body will rise to the surface and float. Since the production of these gases depends upon the action of bacteria, it is greatly affected by the temperature of the water. In the warm waters of the Gulf of Mexico a body might float after only a week or two, while in cold waters it can take many weeks or months.

One of the most difficult tasks for the ME is determining the approximate time of death in a corpse that is weeks or months old. In this situation, body temperature, rigor mortis, and lividity are no longer useful, so this is where the expected stages of post-mortem decay come into play.

To accurately use this technique, the ME must examine the local conditions where the body was found. For example, a corpse dumped in a cold Colorado mine will decay much more slowly than one deposited in a sunny field in Georgia. The average temperature and humidity are key to his assessment, and the ME might consult a **forensic climatologist** to assess recent daily highs and nightly lows and use this to refine his time estimate. For example, a corpse left in a wooded area would decompose much faster if the average daily high and low was 85 and 65, respectively, as compared to

65 and 45. A corpse exposed to a heat wave for 4 or 5 days might look like one exposed to a more normal temperatures for 10 to 14 days.

In buried corpses, the moisture in the soil is critical, with more moisture translating to more rapid decay. Burial site soil moisture depends on the relative humidity, the amount of rainfall, and the degree to which the soil drains. Graves in moist, rainy, and low-lying areas would contain more water than would one on a hillside in a drier area. The ME must consider these variables in his estimation.

To further complicate things, the body's location and degree of exposure might change at any point after death. Murder victims are not infrequently stored for a few days prior to burial or dumping and are sometimes moved from one site to another. The killer simply might not have been able to get rid of the body at the time of the murder and might return later after developing a plan for disposal. Or the corpse might be moved because the police are getting too close to locating it. It might even be moved by nonhuman agents such as water or landslides.

The passage of several days between the death and the burial of the victim presents the ME with changing exposure conditions, which can introduce errors into his time of death estimation. He will look for evidence that the body has been moved and attempt to analyze each place where the body lay and estimate how long it lay there in order to make an educated guess of time of death. This is no simple task and is often impossible.

Our meager knowledge about how corpses decompose led Dr. William Bass to develop the University of Tennessee Forensic Anthropology Facility (**The Body Farm**) in 1971. Here he could study the rate and pattern of decomposition of bodies under various environmental conditions. He basically created an outdoor taphonomy laboratory. At any one time the facility might have a hundred or more bodies decomposing in the sun or shade, buried at various depths and in varying soils conditions, in water, in the trunks of cars, stuffed in trash bags, rolled in carpeting, interred beneath concrete slabs, or hanging from scaffoldings. His contributions to the field of taphonomy are immeasurable.

Stomach Contents

Contents of the victim's stomach can often be very helpful in determining the time of death. After a meal, the stomach empties in approximately two to three hours, depending on the type and amount of food ingested. If a victim's stomach contains largely undigested food material, then the death likely occurred within an hour or two of the meal. If the stomach is empty, the death likely occurred more than four hours after eating. Additionally, if the small intestine is also empty, death probably occurred 12 hours or more after the last meal.

The actual time required for stomach emptying depends on a number of factors. Heavy meals and those rich in protein and fat digest more slowly than do smaller meals and those high in carbohydrates, sugars, and liquids. Alcohol and many sedative and narcotic drugs slow digestion and gastric emptying, while other drugs and some medical conditions hasten these processes. Also, there is great individual variation in rate of digestion. As we have seen with the other methods for estimating time of death, examining gastric contents has some drawbacks. Still, it can prove useful.

Let's say a businessman is found dead in his hotel room and the ME determines that his stomach is full of undigested food materials. If he had dinner with a business associate from 8 until 10 p.m., then returned to his room, his full stomach would indicate that the death occurred shortly after he returned to his room. The ME might place the time of death between 10:00 p.m. and midnight—unless his blood alcohol level was high and he had had a very fatty meal, in which case the death might have occurred slightly later.

Corneal Cloudiness

The clear covering over our pupils are called **corneas**. At death they become cloudy and opaque. This can occur in a very few hours if the eyes are open or might take up to 24 hours if closed.

Vitreous Potassium

The vitreous humor is the clear, thick liquid that fills our eyeballs. After death, the concentration of potassium within the vitreous increases at a constant rate over the first few days. This increase is due to release of potassium from red blood cells into the vitreous. This can be useful for three or four days after death and has the advantage of being independent of ambient temperature.

Insect Activity

A dead body attracts numerous insects, typically flies and beetles. Each species tends to appear at predictable times and in a predictable sequence, and the ME will use this to aid in his determination of the time of death. Unfortunately, these patterns vary greatly, depending upon geographic region, specific locale, time of day, and season. Because of the complex nature of the bug world, the ME will often request the assistance of a forensic entomologist. **Entomology** is the study of insects and **forensic entomology** is the study of the insects that populate a dead body.

Insects help with predicting the time of death in two basic ways. The first method uses the predictable developmental stages of insects, most notably the blowfly, and the second addresses the succession of insect species that populate the corpse. Blowflies appear early and other species later in the decay process.

The field of forensic entomology is too complex to consider in any great detail, but a look at the most common species, the blowfly, will give you a glimpse at the problems the forensic entomologist faces.

When a body is left exposed, blowflies often appear within the first hour after death. They seek out the moist areas such as the nose, mouth, armpit, groin, and any open wounds to lay their eggs. The eggs hatch to **larvae** (maggots) within hours. Over the next 10 days the larvae feed, grow, and repeatedly molt. There are tables that show the growth rate of these larvae so that the entomologist can compare those found at the scene with these length tables and estimate the age of the larvae. This will indicate whether the larvae are three days or nine days old. After the larval stage the outer covering of the maturing flies harden and they become **pupae**. Approximately 12 days later adult flies emerge. So, this entire cycle takes 18 to 22 days.

So, under normal circumstances, if the entomologist finds only eggs, the death likely occurred less than 48 hours earlier. If he finds larvae, but no pupae, the death occurred between 2 and 10 days earlier, and the size of the larvae can narrow this further. The finding of pupae indicates that 10 or more days have passed, while the presence of mature hatchlings would indicate that death occurred two to three weeks earlier.

As you might suspect, it's not really that easy. Fly activity will be delayed if the corpse is inside a closed house or other structure and might not occur at all if the corpse is in a container such as a car trunk, barrel, or tightly closed plastic sheeting. Blowflies do not deposit eggs at night and are less plentiful and even absent in winter. Rain and wind might keep them away. So, if the victim was murdered at midnight, the blowflies might not appear until dawn and if it is cold, rainy, and windy out, they might not appear at all. Also, if conditions become unfavorable, the maggots might go dormant for extended periods of time. If the body is in an area where it is warm during the day and very cold at night, they might be dormant half of each 24-hour period. If it turns cold for several days, the developmental process might be put on hold. As with the putrefaction timeline, a forensic climatologist can be helpful in these situations.

It is important to understand that insect studies can give only a minimum time since death occurred. If pupae are found, the corpse must be at least eight to ten days old. It can't be less since the pupae would not have had time to appear, but if the weather is inhospitable it could be much longer. Another compounding factor is that the insects appear in waves and new generations appear all the time. The adults produced after two weeks will themselves lay eggs and these eggs will follow a similar cycle. So a three-week-old corpse might show eggs, maggots, pupae, and adults. Sorting all this out is no easy task.

Insects might also show that the corpse has been moved. A corpse populated with insects that are not found in the area of its discovery would suggest that the corpse had at one time been where these species of insects live, and therefore must have been moved.

In some cases, insects can help with toxicological examinations. As the insects feed on the corpse, they will ingest whatever chemicals are contained within the tissues. If the corpse is too decayed for adequate toxicological testing, the insect larvae might reveal the toxin. In addition, some chemicals retard while others accelerate the maturation rate of the larvae and might alter the estimation of time of death. Just another factor the ME and the forensic entomologist must consider.

Scene Markers

Scene markers are nonscientific findings and include any information found at the scene or gleaned from witnesses, family, or friends. If someone saw the victim alive at some point in time, the death must have occurred after that. If that sighting is accurate, that is. Family and friends can reveal the person's habits and any changes they have observed. Missed appointments or work, missed daily walks or visits to the coffee shop, uncollected mail or newspapers, and dated sales receipts can be useful.

The victim's clothing and position might be helpful. For example, if the victim missed a tennis date and is found near the door that led out to his garage, dressed in his tennis gear, racket nearby, it would be logical that he died as he was leaving for his game.

Putting It All Together

Time of death determination is no easy matter since no single test or observation will give an exact time. The ME will use all available information and his own experience to formulate a reasonable range for the time of physiological death. Sometimes he is faced with information that is conflicting. Let's say a body is found at 6 a.m. The body temperature is 90°, lividity is fixed, rigor is full, and no appreciable insect activity is noted. How would the ME use this to determine the time of death? The body temperature would suggest that death occurred 6 or so hours earlier, and the lividity would give a range of 6 to 8 hours. Typically, full rigor would take 8 to 12 hours to occur. The lack of insect activity would be expected since the death likely took place near or after sunset. Since none of these are absolute times, the ME will combine them for a best guess. He might conclude the most likely range would be 6 to 9 hours and place the time of death at between 9 p.m. and midnight the previous day. That's about the best he could do, but this might be enough if the prime suspect has no alibi for that time period.

Chapter 7

CAUSE, MECHANISM, AND MANNER OF DEATH

Somewhere death occurs every minute of every day, but only a small portion of these involve the criminal investigative system. Though the coroner or ME has the ultimate responsibility for signing and recording all death certificates, it is in cases where criminal activity is suspected or civil litigation is involved that he brings his expertise to bear. And when he does, his determination of the cause, mechanism, and manner of death are of paramount importance. Let's define these terms:

- **Cause of death**: Why the individual died.
- **Mechanism of death**: The physiological derangement that lead to death.
- **Manner of death**: The reason and by whose hand the death occurred.

The Cause and Mechanism of Death

Causes of death are things such as heart attacks (myocardial infarctions, or MIs), gunshot wounds, and traumatic brain injuries. These are the diseases or injuries that lead to death.

The mechanism of death is the actual physiological derangement that caused the victim to die. In an MI, the mechanism could be a lethal change in heart rhythm (cardiac arrhythmia), or the heart could be so severely damaged that it can no longer pump adequate amounts of blood to sustain life (cardiogenic shock), or, rarely, the MI can lead to rupture of the heart muscle (ventricular rupture). Each of these mechanisms of death results from the same cause—an MI.

A gunshot victim can also die by different mechanisms. The bullet could damage the heart or the brain so that the mechanism would be direct trauma to the heart or brain. The bullet could cause extensive bleeding so that the mechanism of death would be exsanguination (bleeding to death). Or, the wound could become infected, leading to sepsis (infection of the blood stream) and septic shock, and this would then be the mechanism of death.

Similarly, the victim of a blow to the head could die from direct trauma to the brain (cerebral contusion), bleeding into the brain itself (intracerebral bleed), or bleeding around the brain (subdural or epidural hematoma), which could lead to compression of the brain and result in the stoppage of breathing (asphyxia). Again, one cause can lead to death by several mechanisms.

Conversely, one mechanism can result from several different causes. Exsanguination (the mechanism of death) can occur with gunshots, stab wounds, bleeding ulcers, or excessive ingestion of blood-thinning medications such as warfarin. In each case, blood loss and shock are the physiological derangements.

From these examples you can see that a single cause might result in death by varying mechanisms and a single mechanism can result from several different causes. The coroner must make these determinations and his conclusions can greatly impact any criminal proceedings.

Let's say a man is struck and killed by a car driven by an intoxicated driver. If the ME determines that the blunt trauma from the car caused severe and lethal brain injuries, the driver might be charged in the man's death. But, what if the ME determines that the injuries were not that severe and that the victim died from internal bleeding, which the paramedical and hospital personnel failed to recognize and treat appropriately? Who's responsible for the man's death? In each of these scenarios the cause of death is blunt trauma, but the mechanism is either a brain contusion or exsanguination. The ME's assessment of the mechanism will determine what legal actions might follow. One could lead to a charge of vehicular manslaughter and the other to a medical malpractice suit.

To further cloud the issue, what if investigators discover that the man had been depressed and suicidal and actually threw himself in front of the car? Would the death then be a suicide?

This is where the manner of death, the reason, and by whose hand the death occurred, enter the picture.

The Five Manners of Death

The ME's determination of the manner of death must consider the root cause of the sequence of events that led to death and assess by whose hand and for what purpose this cascade began. In other words, how and why did these events take place? Who initiated the events and with what intention? Was the death caused by the victim, another person, an unfortunate occurrence, or Mother Nature?

The five manners of death are as follows:

- **Natural** deaths are due to natural disease processes such as heart attacks, cancers, pneumonias, and strokes. This is by far the most common manner of death.
- **Accidental** deaths result from unplanned and unforeseeable events such as falls, automobile accidents, and in-home electrocutions.
- **Suicidal** deaths are by the person's own hand and include self-inflicted gunshots, drug overdoses, and self-hangings.
- **Homicidal** deaths are brought about by the hand of another.
- **Undetermined** or **unclassified** is an extra category that is applied in situations where the coroner can't accurately determine the appropriate category.

Just as causes of deaths can lead to many different mechanisms of death, many causes of death can have several different manners of death. For example, a gunshot wound to the head can't be natural, but it could be deemed homicidal, suicidal, or accidental, depending on by whose hand and for what purpose the gunshot occurred. Regardless of the circumstance, it is imperative that the ME accurately classifies the manner of death, as this determination will decide what happens next.

The ME's Determination

When faced with a sudden and unexplained death, the ME will take a series of logical steps to evaluate the case. He will gather information from police reports, medical records, witness statements, and interviews with family, law enforcement, and medical personnel. He might perform an autopsy and any needed ancillary tests (toxicological examinations, firearms examinations, blood spatter analysis, etc.) he deems necessary. It is important to note that what he does or does not do is up to him. If he feels he can assign a manner of death with no interviews or testing and with no autopsy, he will do so. If he feels he needs this information he will proceed along that path. To help him in this process he has full subpoena power (in most jurisdictions) and usually the blessing of the court.

In the case of an unexplained death, such as one with no overt trauma or readily apparent cause, the ME will first look for natural causes. He might review medical records, perhaps discuss the situation with the deceased person's physician, and perform an autopsy if he feels it is necessary. These investigations might reveal that the person died from an MI, an infection, the failure of organs such as the liver or kidneys, diabetes, or any number of other diseases. In this case the manner of death would be natural.

If no natural cause is present, the ME will look for less obvious trauma, poisons or drugs, and other signs of accidental, suicidal, or homicidal death. We will take a closer look at some of these signs in later chapters.

What about undetermined or unclassified deaths? Why would a trained and experienced ME have trouble assigning a manner of death?

Let's say a drug abuser dies from a heroin overdose. Heroin, and other narcotics, when taken in excess can lead to coma, cessation of breathing, and death from asphyxia (Chapter 9). Here the cause of death is a drug overdose and the mechanism is asphyxia. But what is the manner?

What if the victim has a history of overdoses, both accidental and as previous unsuccessful suicide attempts? If he dies from a drug overdose (cause), was it an accident or suicide (manner)? To the ME, the autopsy and laboratory findings would be the same, regardless of the victim's intent. To help him with his estimate, the ME might order a **psychological autopsy** in which a forensic psychiatrist delves into the person's personal history and attempts to uncover any motives for suicide. Even after this, the intent, or lack of intent, of the deceased might not be apparent and the manner of death might be listed as undetermined or unclassified. Simply put, there is no way to know for certain whether the person overdosed accidentally or purposefully.

But it gets even muddier. What if the victim was a police informant or was due to testify against a local dealer? What if the dealer knew this and sold him powder that was 90 percent heroin, rather than the usual 15 percent? How would the user know? Not being a chemist, he would simply shoot up as usual, completely unaware that he was actually taking six times his usual dose. Here the manner of death would be homicide yet to the ME and the forensic toxicologist, this death would appear identical to one due to an accident or a suicide.

The key point: It's the intent and by whose hand the event occurred that determines the manner of death, and this is not always apparent.

The ME's Report

Once the ME completes his analysis, he will file a report in which he lays out the essentials of the case and comes to some conclusion regarding the cause, mechanism, and manner of death. The manner of death is an opinion expressed by the ME after he has looked into the circumstances leading to and surrounding the death as well as any testing he has performed or ordered. His opinion might or might not be accepted by the courts, law enforcement, attorneys, or the victim's family. Even if he concludes that a death was a homicide, prosecutors might not agree and might not file criminal charges. A family might sue to change the manner of death, particularly in situations where the manner of death has been ruled a suicide.

Changing the manner of death to accidental might help them accept the loss or perhaps effect any insurance payments.

The ME's manner of death determination has no time limit. For example, a victim who was shot by a perpetrator during a robbery and admitted to a hospital could have a very long hospitalization. During the course of his treatment he could develop pneumonia and die as a result. The cause of death would be pneumonia, but the manner of death might be homicide. How can this be? Isn't pneumonia a natural cause of death? After all, the perpetrator might have shot him, but he didn't cause the pneumonia that killed him. Actually he did, just not directly. The event that began the "cascade of events" that led to death was the gunshot. If not for that, the victim would not be in the hospital and would not have developed the pneumonia that led to his death. The time lag between the inciting event and the actual death, which could be days, months, years, or decades, might have little bearing on the final determination of the manner of death.

The ME's opinion is not "written in stone" and can be changed if new evidence comes to light. Let's say an elderly man dies in a nursing home of an apparent stroke or MI and the ME signs the death off as a natural event. Later a conflict over an inheritance or an insurance policy rears its head, and a family member or insurance investigator comes forward with information that the death might not have been so natural. The body is exhumed and high levels of arsenic are found in the remains. With a natural death ruled out, the question then becomes, was this death a suicide, a homicide, or the result of an accidental ingestion? The ME would then share this information with law enforcement and an investigation would begin. Once further information was uncovered, the ME might be able to reclassify the death. If the family uncovered a suicide note, suicide might be favored. If a family member suddenly has a pocketful of insurance money and a bottle of arsenic-containing pesticide hidden in his closet, homicide might be the ruling. Or, and this is not as strange as it might seem, what if family members state that the victim possessed the odd belief that a little arsenic taken each day was good for arthritis? Would an accidental death be more likely?

Tackling these types of complex problems is common for the ME. How effective he is depends upon his training, skill, and experience.

CHAPTER 8

TRAUMATIC INJURIES

Trauma to the human body comes in many forms: gunshots, stabbings, blunt-force injuries, thermal and electrical burns, and bite marks. Rape and abuse, traumatic events themselves, often involve various types of traumatic injury.

Guns and Bullets

Gunshots wounds (GSWs) are a common cause of death in accidental, suicidal, and homicidal shootings. The mechanism of death depends upon the location and the severity of the injury. For a gunshot to be immediately fatal, extensive trauma to the brain, the heart, or the upper spinal cord must occur. Otherwise death is slower, typically from exsanguination (bleeding to death) or a secondary wound infection. The manner of death depends upon the intent of the person discharging the weapon. The intentional shooting of oneself would be a suicide, while if the shooter did not intend to harm himself or others, it would be accidental. If someone else fires the weapon it could be accidental or homicidal, depending on the shooter's intention.

As we saw earlier when discussing the autopsy (Chapter 4), bullets that enter the human body often behave in odd ways. They can strike bones and change direction. They can do more or less harm than would seem apparent by the nature of the wound. For example, even a GSW to the head will not always result in brain damage. The bullet can flatten against the skull and never penetrate the bone or enter the brain. It can ricochet off the skull and leave the body entirely. It can burrow beneath the scalp and be found at some distance from the entrance wound. Anything is possible.

The same thing can occur with a GSW to the chest. The bullet might strike the sternum or a rib and flatten against the bone, or ricochet in any direction. It might leave the body or burrow beneath the skin, never entering the chest, or be deflected upward into the neck or downward into the abdomen. It's very unpredictable, as most emergency room physicians will attest.

For this reason, whether the victim is among the living in a hospital emergency department or on the coroner's autopsy table, if the bullet or bullets cannot be readily located, x-rays of the chest, abdomen, and sometimes the entire body will be taken. Since lead bullets are readily visible under x-rays, the surgeon or the ME can locate them in this manner.

When the coroner examines a gunshot victim, he must locate all entrance wounds and exit wounds (if any) and trace the path of each bullet through the victim's body if possible. Only with this information can he determine which bullet, if any, led to the victim's death. This information might be critical to the prosecution of the crime.

Let's say a woman is shot several times: once in the arm, twice in the chest, and once in the head. The shooter claims it was self-defense, but crime scene analysis and the autopsy reveal that the limb and chest wounds occurred while the victim was standing and the shot to the head came after she was on the floor. Here the arm and chest shots could indeed be self-defense, but the headshot less so, since the "attacker" was down and the shooter could have fled or called for help.

But, which was the fatal shot? If one of the bullets to the chest severely damaged the heart and led to death, the subsequent shot to the head would be of less consequence since the victim would have died anyway. In this case, a first-degree murder conviction might be difficult. But, if neither of the chest wounds was immediately fatal, the shooter could be facing a murder charge.

This becomes even more important if two shooters are involved. If one assailant fired the shots to the victim's limbs and chest and the other the single shot to her head, the ME's opinion as to which was the fatal shot would be crucial to the prosecution. The shooter that fired the lethal shot would face the more serious charges. To make this determination, the ME must evaluate the characteristics of each entry and exit wound, follow the path of the bullets through the body, and determine the damage done by each.

Entry Wounds

The characteristics of gunshot entry wounds depend on several factors, including the distance between the victim and the gun's muzzle, the caliber and velocity of the bullet, the angle at which the bullet enters, and whether the bullet remains within the victim or passes completely through and exits the body—called a "through-and-through" gunshot wound.

When a gun is fired, the smokeless powder explodes, forcing the bullet from the cartridge and down the gun's barrel. Along with the bullet, hot gases and particles of burned and unburned gunpowder are also ejected from the muzzle. The gases are predominantly carbon monoxide, carbon dioxide, and nitrogen oxide, while the particulate matter contains lead, bismuth, and antimony, which are useful when testing for gunshot residue (more on this later).

Each of these ejected materials travels a different distance from the muzzle (Figure 8-1). The hot gases travel only a few inches, the particulate matter a foot or two, and, of course, the bullet a considerable distance. The character of the entry wound will depend upon which of these components actually contact the skin, and the ME can use this information to determine the distance between the gun's muzzle and the victim the moment the gun discharged.

The anatomy of an entrance wound depends on the muzzle to skin distance (Figure 8-2). Though it can vary from weapon to weapon, in general, if the muzzle is two or more feet away from the victim, the entrance wound will be a small hole, smaller than the bullet due to the elastic quality of skin, surrounded by a blue-black halo called an **abrasion collar**. This comes from the skin literally wiping away the burned powder, grime, and

Figure 8-1

Gun muzzle output. A discharged firearm expels the bullet, burned and unburned powder, and hot gases. Which of these marks the entry wound depends upon the distance between the muzzle and the victim.

oil residue the bullet collects as it passes through the barrel. This "smudging" is often easily wiped away with a wet cloth.

If the muzzle to skin gap is between six inches and two feet, there might also be **tattooing** or **stippling** of the skin. This is due to the burned and unburned powder embedding in the skin and/or causing tiny hemorrhages (red dots of blood within the skin) in a speckled pattern around the wound. These cannot be wiped away because the particles are actually embedded (tattooed) into the skin. The diameter of this circle of stippling increases as the distance between the muzzle and the entry point increases (Figure 8-2 B). The tattooing resulting from a gunshot inflicted from a distance of 10 or 12 inches will be compact and dense, while that from a shot delivered from 18 to 24 inches will be broader and less dense.

If the muzzle is only a few inches away (Figure 8-2 C), the stippling will be very compact and partially obliterated by charring from the hot gases. Here, the skin around the entry wound is burned and blackened by the heat from the expelled gases. In addition, the carbon monoxide in the gases combines with hemoglobin and myoglobin (iron containing compounds that reside in the blood and muscle tissues, respectively). This reac-

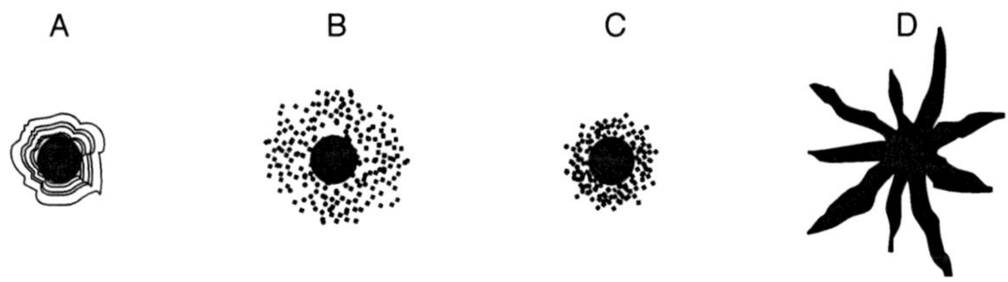

Figure 8-2

Gunshot entry wounds. The anatomy of an entry wound depends upon the distance between the muzzle and the entry point. If far away (A), the wound will be a simple hole with a faint abrasion collar. If closer (B), there might be stippling or tattooing, which becomes more dense the shorter the distance is (C). With contact wounds, the skin is torn by the hot gases into a stellate pattern (D).

tion produces **carboxyhemoglobin** and **carboxymyoglobin**, compounds that are bright red and impart this hue to the surrounding tissues. Thus, a gunshot from a very close distance will produce a hole, a compact area of stippling, a surrounding area of charring, and a bright red hue to the above compounds.

A **contact** GSW (Figure 8-2 D) occurs when the gun's muzzle is pressed against the skin at the time of discharge. Here, skin charring and the above mentioned bright red hue will be prominent. More importantly, since the rapidly expanding gases can neither expand the gun's metal barrel nor force their way very deeply into the tissues, they will rip the skin in a star-shaped or **stellate pattern.** This is particularly true if the contact wound is over a bone such as the skull. Thus, a contact wound will rip the skin in a classic stellate pattern, char the skin severely, and produce the bright red tissue color as described above.

How might the ME use this information? Let's say a victim is found shot in the head, a gun lying on the bed beside him, and a suicide note spread open on the dresser. Looks like a simple suicide, if there is such a thing. But, what if the ME's examination of the entry wound indicates that the muzzle was not held against the victim's head but rather was at least 2 feet away. Go ahead. Try it. Your index finger is the barrel. Try holding your hand such that the tip of your finger is 2 feet from the side of your head. If not impossible, it is at least awkward and not the position someone would likely hold a gun. Further, what if the bullet's entry angle indicates that it came from behind the victim? It simply isn't possible for the victim to have held the weapon in that position. This means that someone else did. The simple suicide might now be a homicide.

What if the victim is shot through clothing such as a shirt or jacket? If so, the hot gases and unburned powder that would normally cause tattooing and charring of the victim's skin are intercepted by the clothing. Here the ME and the forensic firearms examiner (Chapter 17) will analyze the residue pattern on the garment to estimate the firing distance. In general, the farther the distance, the wider the spread of the residue. To accurately estimate this distance, the examiner will use the suspect weapon and similar ammunition and perform a series of test firings into similar fabric from several distances. He will then compare the residue pattern on the test shots with those on the crime scene garment and estimate the firing distance.

Exit Wounds

Obviously, if the bullet remains within the victim, there is no exit wound, but if it does exit, the ME must decide which wound is the entry and which is the exit. This is usually easy but not always, particularly if there are multiple GSWs. Exit wounds tend to be larger and more ragged than entry wounds because the bullet is damaged and deformed during its passage through the body, which results in the bullet ripping or tearing the tissues as it forces its way out through the skin. The anatomy of the wound depends upon the size, speed, and shape of the bullet. A soft lead bullet is easily deformed, particularly if it strikes any bony structures during its passage, and produces more extensive tissue damage and often a gaping, irregular exit wound. Similarly, hollow-point bullets, which have a depression or hollowed area in their nose, suffer greater deformation, cause more tissue damage, and create larger exit wounds.

The opposite is true with **jacketed** bullets. These bullets are completely or partially covered with metal, Teflon, or other hard material and are typically high-velocity bullets with extraordinary penetrating power. They will often pass directly through the victim with little if any deformation so that the exit wound might be small and resemble a typical entry wound. In some cases it isn't possible for the ME to distinguish between entry and exit wounds. This can complicate his ability to reconstruct the crime.

Another situation that might give the ME problems is a **shored exit wound**. This occurs when the tissues at the exit point are supported, such as when the victim is leaning against a wall or some other structure or is wearing tight, tough clothing such as those made of leather or woven fabrics. Here, supported skin is less likely to tear, so the exit wound will be smaller, less ragged, and might look like an entry wound.

Shotgun Wound Patterns

A shotgun expels a cluster of shot (small round beads) rather than a single bullet. As with other guns, it might be critical that the ME determine the distance between the muzzle and the victim, since this alone might distinguish between a murder and a suicidal or accidental shooting. It might also support or refute a suspect or witness statement. For example, if the ME determines that the muzzle had been approximately six feet from the victim, then a suicidal and, most likely, an accidental shooting, is ruled out, and homicide must be considered.

Rather than the characteristics of the wounds, the most important factor in making this determination is the spread pattern of the shot. A general rule is that the shot spreads an inch for every three feet it travels. This depends greatly upon the choke applied to the barrel. The choke is an alteration in the diameter of the end of the barrel, which concentrates the shot pattern. The four degrees of choke, from narrowest to widest, are full, modified, improved cylinder, and cylinder-bore. The latter is no narrowing or choking of the barrel at all. If the barrel is sawed-off, the scatter is greatly increased.

The easiest way to determine the muzzle-to-victim distance is to fire the suspect weapon, using the same ammunition type, from several distances until you recreate the shot pattern found at the crime scene. This will approximate the distance from which the murder weapon was fired.

Sharp-Force Injuries

Sharp-force or penetrating injuries come from pointed or sharp-edged weapons such as knives, scissors, axes, swords, ice picks, forks, wooden stakes, and other similar objects. Only sharp-force injuries to the heart, brain, or the upper part of the spinal cord would be immediately fatal. Otherwise, death comes from excessive bleeding, or much later from secondary wound infections.

Just as we saw with GSWs, when faced with fatal penetrating injuries, the ME must determine the cause and manner of death. He will examine each and every wound, attempt to determine what types of weapons were likely used, and then assess which wounds were potentially lethal. With a single stab wound to the heart, this is easy, but with multiple wounds it becomes more difficult.

With multiple wounds, the goal is to determine the sequence of the injuries and to estimate which wound or wounds were fatal. If there were multiple assailants, this becomes critical, since the one that delivered the fatal wound could face the more serious charges.

Sharp-force wounds can be divided into three general types: stab wounds, incised (cutting) wounds, and chopping wounds.

Stab Wounds

Stab wounds are caused by pointed instruments such as knives (the most common), ice picks, scissors, swords, and even screwdrivers. Deaths from stab wounds are most often homicidal, but might also be accidental if the victim slips and falls on the instrument. They are rarely suicidal since it is difficult to self-inflict a stab wound with enough force to be fatal. In cases of suicide, the deeper, lethal punctures are typically associated with smaller, shallower wounds called **hesitation wounds**. These vary greatly in size and depth as the individual musters the courage to make the final stab. When the ME encounters hesitation wounds, suicide must be considered.

The main characteristics of stab wounds are that they are deeper than they are wide. When analyzing such injuries the ME will measure the depth and width of the wound and from this estimate the type and size of the instrument used. It is important to note that the depth might not reflect the actual length of the blade, but rather only the minimal length. A four-inch-deep wound could have been made by a four-inch blade, or by a longer one, such as an eight-inch blade, but it could not result from a three-inch blade. So the depth gives only the minimum length of the weapon. An exception would be where the knife has been thrust to-the-hilt, and the hand guard has left a patterned abrasion around the wound. The hand guard is the piece of metal between the handle and the blade that keeps the user's hand from sliding down onto the blade. If this impacts the skin with enough force, it can leave a bruise or abrasion that matches the guard in shape and size. In this situation, the ME would know that the measured depth of the wound reflects the actual length of the blade. This also gives him the shape and size of the hand guard, which might in turn help determine the type of knife used.

Measuring the width of the blade is more difficult. Human skin is elastic and contracts around the wound once the weapon is removed, making the wound appear smaller than it actually is. On the other hand, some people, particularly the elderly, have poor skin elasticity, and the wound might actually gape open and appear larger than it is. Or the blade might be twisted or removed at an angle that varies from its entry angle, or the victim might withdraw or turn away from the attacker. Each of these can distort the wound. The ME must consider each of these as he analyzes stab wounds.

With clean wounds, the ME can often determine if the blade was straight, curved, or serrated on one edge. A double-edged blade tends to create wounds that are pointed on each end, whereas with a single-edged blade, one end might be pointed and the other squared.

Some stabbing instruments leave behind distinctive wounds. An ice pick leaves small round wounds, a barbecue fork leaves paired, uniformly spaced wounds, and a kitchen fork leaves four evenly spaced punctures. The wounds left by scissors would depend on whether the two blades were separated at the time of use or not.

Analyzing wound characteristics requires skill, attention to detail, and experience. If properly done, the ME can often determine the type of instrument used, but identifying the exact weapon is virtually impossible. That is, he can say that the wounds are consistent with a certain weapon but can't say that it was a particular weapon to the exclusion of all others. However, there are two notable exceptions.

If the tip of the knife blade broke off and remained in the wound, the crime lab might be able to jigsaw match the broken edge to that of a suspect weapon. This is powerful individualizing evidence since no two things fracture in the same way. Such matches are conclusive on the order of fingerprints (Chapter 13) and DNA (Chapter 11). Blood found on the suspect weapon might also provide the link. Murderers often overlook small flecks of blood on the blade or handle or blood that has seeped into the groove between the blade and the hand guard. Wiping down or rinsing the knife will not always remove such traces. If found, DNA matching to a victim is strong evidence that this knife was the actual murder weapon.

The ME will also look for defensive wounds. These are the wounds inflicted by the attacker on a victim who is attempting to defend himself. Punctures, cuts, and slices on the victim's hands and arms indicate that he tried to avoid or block the stabs. These effectively rule out an accidental or suicidal manner of death.

In determining the sequence of multiple injuries and which wounds were potentially fatal, the blood spatter pattern (Chapter 14) can be helpful. The ME will use these patterns to reconstruct the sequence of events surrounding the murder as best he can. This is very complex and not always easy. For example, a stab wound to a carotid artery in the neck could spray blood a great distance and be quickly lethal, while one to the muscle of the thigh would bleed less and be much less deadly. Furthermore, post-mortem wounds don't bleed, so any wounds associated with a large amount of blood loss must have occurred while the victim was alive, and any that show no bleeding would have been delivered post-mortem.

Incised Wounds

Incised wounds result when a sharp instrument is drawn across the skin. Unlike stab wounds, they have no characteristic width or depth and thus reveal little of the nature of the weapon. Still the ME must determine the manner of death in anyone who dies after an incised wound.

Accidental incised wounds typically involve the hands and are rarely fatal. To be lethal, an accidental cut would have to involve the neck or a major artery, which can happen with falls onto sharp instruments or edges, injuries suffered in a car accident or other such trauma, with the use of power tools such as band, circular, or chain saws, or from falling or flying glass fragments.

Suicidal wounds are usually found on the victim's wrists and rarely on the neck. As with stab wounds, suicidal incised wounds are frequently accompanied by hesitation marks. Right-handed individuals typically cut their left wrist and left-handers their right. If not, the ME might consider that the death was a homicide staged to appear as if it were a suicide.

Homicidal incised wounds are typically seen on the neck. If the assailant is behind the victim, the cut usually extends from high up on one side near the ear, sweeps downward across the front of the throat, and then back up on the opposite side (Figure 8-3). It tends to end up lower than it began. The path of this sweep is left to right in a right-handed assailant and the opposite for a left-handed one.

If the attacker is facing his victim, the cut is usually shorter and horizontal (Figure 8-4). Defensive wounds on the hands and arms are more common in frontal assaults.

As you can see, accidental, suicidal, and homicidal incised wounds typically involve different areas of the body and reveal different cut patterns. Knowing these locations and patterns helps the ME reconstruct the scene and determine the manner of death.

Chop Wounds

Heavier, sharp-edged implements such as axes and meat cleavers produce chop wounds, which tend to be deep and wedge-shaped, and are often accom-

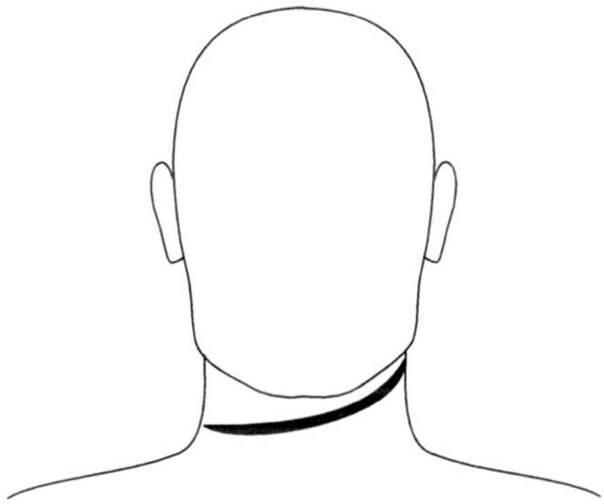

Figure 8-3

Rear assault, incised neck wound. The path on the blade is from high on one side of the neck, down and across the throat, and slightly upward again. Here the assailant would be right handed, since the wound begins high on the left side of the neck. With a left-handed attacker, the path would be opposite.

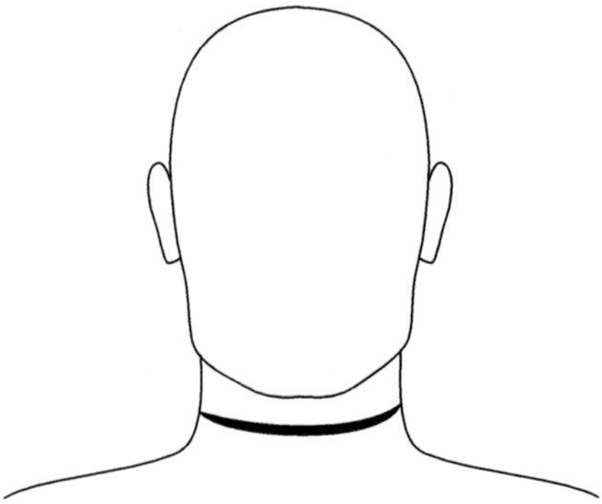

Figure 8-4
Frontal assault, incised neck wound. When an assailant faces his victim, the slashing wound is typically horizontal.

panied by fractures, grooves, and chips in underlying bones. Lethal chop wounds are usually accidental or homicidal and rarely suicidal in nature. It's not uncommon for accidental injuries to occur during wood chopping, where the blow severs a major artery and death follows from extensive blood loss. Homicidal chop wounds are typically to the head or neck, and of course defensive wounds can be present. The location and angle of delivery of the wound can usually help the ME determine that the death was homicidal rather than accidental.

Blunt-Force Trauma

Everyone has experienced blunt-force trauma. Bumping into a table, hitting your head on a cabinet, or catching a baseball with your face are examples. Football is a game built on blunt-force trauma, as is professional boxing. Childhood is a marathon of trauma, beginning with learning to walk.

Blunt-force trauma occurs whenever someone is struck with a blunt object such as in an assault, a fall, or an automobile accident. The resulting injuries depend on the location, the force, and the number of blows inflicted. In general, the greater the force of the blow, the greater the injury, while the greater the surface area struck, the less the injury. This means that a board or boat oar will produce less injury than would a baseball bat swung with the same force. The board's greater surface area spreads out and lessens the degree of injury.

The ME is often asked to determine what object caused a blunt-force injury. This alone might lead to identifying the assailant. For example, if the ME determines that a ball-peen hammer caused the victim's skull fracture and the prime suspect just happens to have one in his possession, this could be useful information.

The ME is also often asked to determine the age of an injury. If a victim's cuts, bruises, and abrasions are two days old, they could not have occurred at the time of the lethal assault. This might greatly affect the charges filed against the assailant.

Just as we saw with victims of sharp instrument attacks, the victim of a blunt trauma assault will attempt to block the blows with his hands and arms. This can result in abrasions, contusions, lacerations, and even broken bones.

Blunt force injuries are of four types: abrasions, contusions, lacerations, and fractures.

Abrasions

Abrasions (scrapes) result when the superficial layer of the skin is removed. They are classified as scrape abrasions, impact abrasions, and patterned abrasions, and each comes from a different mechanism.

Scrape abrasions occur when an object scrapes or brushes away the skin. Common examples are scratches from thorns or fingernails and slides across pavement as occurs when a vehicle strikes a pedestrian. Rope nooses and various types of strangulation ligatures can also cause neck scrape abrasions.

Impact abrasions occur when a blunt object strikes the skin, crushing it, and leaving behind a raw area. These occur with blows from baseball bats and other objects and tend to be small and discrete.

Patterned abrasions are a special type of impact abrasion. Sometimes the pattern of the object is reflected in the abrasion. The abrasions left by a chain might reveal the link pattern. The grill pattern of a car in a hit-and-run might be seen on the victim. A rope used for strangulation (Chapter 9) might leave an abrasion where the braid pattern is readily visible. Or punches from an assailant who wore a ring with a large initial or unusual pattern might leave a distinctive patterned abrasion.

Sometimes the ME is asked to age an abrasion. This is a difficult process and rests on the typical healing pattern of such injuries. Normally the healing process can be divided into five stages: scab formation, cell regeneration, cell growth, remodeling, and finally a return to normal. Scab formation begins almost immediately but is not visible for about 6 hours. The area appears dark red and under the microscope large numbers of specialized white blood cells called polymorphonuclear cells (polys, for short) are seen. This is followed by evidence of cell regeneration, which is the reappearance of lost epithelial (skin) cells. This stage begins around 1.5 days after the injury but is not clearly visible until about three days. Epithelial cell growth continues over the next 5 to 10 days, and by about day 12 the skin is remodeled. This remodeling is a thinning of the skin, which takes on a slightly pale appearance. Over the next week or two, the skin completes its repair and all remnants of the wound disappear. Rarely do abrasions leave permanent scars. The ME will analyze injuries in both the living and the deceased with these stages in mind and make his best guess as to the general age of an abrasion.

Let's say a suspect in an assault that occurred the previous night is found to have scrape abrasions that appear to be from fingernails on his face and arms. He says the injuries are from thorns he encountered while hunting a week earlier. If the ME finds that the scratches could not be more than 24 hours old, the suspect has some explaining to do.

Contusions

Contusions (bruises) result from traumatic damage to small blood vessels, which then leak blood and impart a blue-black color to the injured tissues. If the blood collects in a pocket beneath the skin (known informally as a "goose egg") it is called a **hematoma**, whose literal translation means a "blood tumor."

Not all trauma causes a visible contusion, since sometimes the trauma isn't powerful enough to damage the blood vessels and at other times the bruise is deep and not visible on the surface. Conversely, the presence of bruises doesn't necessarily mean that the person was intentionally injured. Some people, particularly children and the elderly, bruise from even minor or unnoticed trauma, as do those who have bleeding disorders or liver cirrhosis, or who take aspirin or other blood-thinning medications.

Some contusions reflect the object that caused it. A chain, rope, or ring might leave behind a contusion that reveals its pattern. A board might cause a broad bruise with straight parallel edges. A car grill pattern on the victim of a hit-and-run and finger-shaped neck bruises in cases of manual strangulation deaths are other examples. The ME can often use these patterns to determine the type of object used in the crime.

As we saw with abrasions, the dating of bruises depends upon the sequence of color changes that a contusion goes through as it heals. You've seen this many times on your own body. A bruise changes from faint blue-black to a darker blue-black to greenish-yellow and finally to brownish-yellow before it fades. What causes these changes? Initially the blood stains the tissues, but very quickly tissue enzymes begin to break down the hemoglobin in the blood, and these breakdown products cause the other changes in color. Finally, scavenger cells called macrophages remove these remnants and the contusion fades. This process follows a more or less predictable pattern and takes about two weeks to complete. By assessing these color changes the ME can estimate the time that the bruising occurred. Again, if a suspect in a 24-hour-old assault says that the bruises on his arms are a week old, the ME's findings that they are of more recent vintage will damage his credibility.

The age of bruises can be critical in cases of child and elder abuse. Such abuse tends to be repetitive, so that the victims will often show multiple contusions of varying ages. Physicians must always be alert to the possibility of abuse when a child shows such an array of injuries. Similarly, when evaluating the accidental death of a child, the ME must diligently search for signs of repeated injury since this might mean that the death was not truly accidental, but rather was the final insult in a series of abusive acts.

Another aspect of contusion analysis is determining whether the injuries occurred before or after death. If before or around the time of death, they might be part of the assault but if they occurred after death it's possible they are the result of handling or transporting the corpse, and the perpetrator might not be responsible for them. This can be critical in some cases.

Pre-mortem means before death, **post-mortem** after death, and **peri-mortem** around the time of death, which can be further defined as the seconds or very few minutes immediately before or after death. Trauma administered during each of these time frames causes differing results, and the ME can use these changes as a general guideline for dating contusions.

If the victim suffers a contusing blow many minutes or hours before death, the bruise will be fairly diffuse and widespread around the area of impact. If the blow is struck in the peri-mortem period, the bruise will be smaller and with more distinct edges. In the former, the blood has time to seep into and spread through the tissues while in the latter it doesn't.

What about post-mortem contusions? Is it possible to bruise a corpse? Yes, but it's difficult. Contusions require a leakage of blood from injured vessels, and this in turn requires that blood flows into the injured vessel. At death, the heart stops, the blood ceases to circulate and clots, and no new blood reaches the injured area. So post-mortem injuries don't produce bruises. Most of the time, anyway.

If a blow is delivered to a corpse with sufficient force, vessels might be damaged and any blood stagnated within them might leak into the tissues. With no blood flow, the bruise will be smaller than would one that formed before death, but this can still make the ME's job of dating bruises more difficult. A skilled and experienced ME can usually tell the difference.

Sometimes a body suspected of having suffered blunt-force trauma shows no evidence of bruising. Here, the victim might have died quickly, before there was sufficient time for the blood to seep to the surface and become visible. But the bruising might have occurred deeply within the tissues and muscles or within various internal organs. In this situation, during the autopsy, the ME might make a series of deep cuts into the muscles along the back, arms, and legs and slice into the organs to search for this deep bruising. If he found contusions or hematomas in these areas, he would know that the victim had indeed suffered blunt-force trauma.

As we saw with GSWs and sharp force wounds, the ME must determine which if any of the contusing blows were potentially lethal. This can directly impact the cause and manner of death as well as substantiate or refute a suspect's or witness's account of events. In cases where there are multiple assailants, his evaluation might determine what charges are filed against which defendants.

Lacerations

Lacerations are often caused by sharp instruments but can also follow blunt trauma if the skin is crushed, sheared, torn, or ripped by the impact. This is more common in areas where the skin lies close to the bone, such as the scalp. An **avulsion**, a severe laceration where a section of the skin is actually torn away from the underlying tissues, most often occurs when the blow strikes at an oblique or tangential angle.

Sometimes the nature of the laceration and any associated contusions will give the ME a clue as to type of instrument that caused the injury. A board or a baseball bat would leave a broader area of skin disruption than would a thinner metal rod or a thicker car bumper.

Fractures

Bone fractures come in many varieties. A **simple** fracture is a single break, a **comminuted** fracture is one in which the bone breaks in two or more places, and a **compound** fracture is one in which the bone protrudes through the skin. Each can follow either **direct** or **indirect** trauma.

Direct fractures occur when an object directly strikes a bone and can be considered either **transverse** or **crush** in nature (Figure 8-5). A transverse fracture is one that is perpendicular to the long axis of the bone, and a crush fracture is one in which the bone is broken into pieces. A crush fracture often produces a **compression wedge**, which can indicate the direction of the blow in that the point of the wedge "points" in the direction of the force. This can help the ME reconstruct the events of the crime or accident. In automobile versus pedestrian accidents, this type of fracture is often termed a **bumper fracture** since it results from the impact of the vehicle's bumper against the victim's legs.

Indirect fractures are not due to a direct trauma, but rather occur when some other force is applied to the bone with sufficient force to cause it to break. Traumatic indirect fractures can be divided into four basic types (Figure 8-6): **angulation**, **rotational**, **compression**, or a **combination** of these types.

Angulation fractures (Figure 8-6 A) tend to be simple transverse breaks and occur when a bone is bent to the point of breaking. **Rotational fractures** (Figure 8-6 B) follow the twisting of a bone, as when an arm or leg

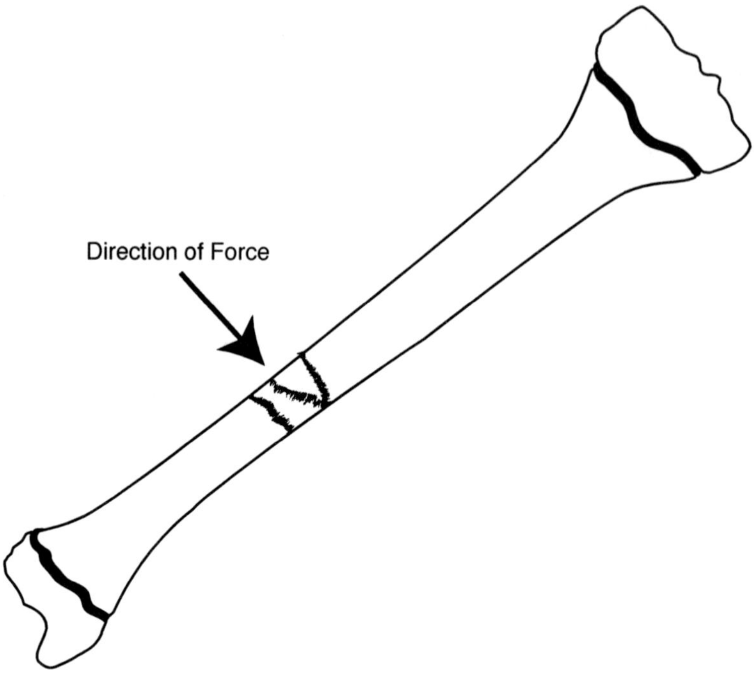

Figure 8-5
Direct fractures. Direct fractures can be either a simple transverse break or a crush fracture. The latter often produces a compression wedge that indicates the direction of the applied force.

is violently rotated. These tend to be **spiral** fractures, which literally spiral down the long axis of the bone. The path of the spiral indicates the direction of the twisting force. These types of fractures are frequently seen in sports injuries as well as in abused children. **Compression fractures** (Figure 8-6 C) result when a force is applied along the long axis of the bone and drives the bone into its end such as happens in automobile accidents where the knee is slammed into the dashboard or when someone falling from a height lands on his feet. These can cause T- or Y-shaped breaks. Sometimes a bone is subjected to many types of forces, resulting in fractures of all three types. This is not uncommon in automobile accidents and falls from high places.

A fracture heals with the formation of scar called a **callus**. The callus, which takes two to three weeks to form, is a fibrous capsule-like structure that surrounds the fracture. Bone formation and the closing of the fracture

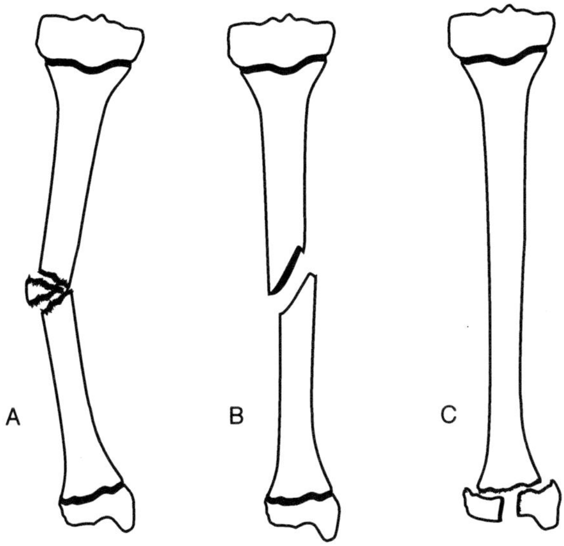

Figure 8-6
Indirect fractures. Indirect trauma may result in fractures that are angulation (A), rotational (B), compression (C), or a combination of these types.

follow, a process that requires another three or four weeks. Complete healing might take five or six months. This process is faster in the young and slower in the old and varies from person to person.

As with other injuries, determining the age of fractures can be important to the ME, particularly in cases of child or elder abuse where fractures of varying ages are often seen. In these situations, x-rays might show fractures that are years old, others that are weeks old, and still others that are fresh, indicating the ongoing nature of the abuse. As with bruises, whenever a physician sees a child or elderly person with fractures of varying ages, the likelihood of repeated abuse must be considered.

Trauma to Internal Organs

Evaluating injuries to internal organs is a broad and complex subject, which is beyond the scope of this book, but in general when confronted with a death from multiple trauma, the ME will attempt to determine the cause and mechanism of each injury, estimate the sequence of the injuries, and determine which injuries, if any, were the proximate cause of death. For example, did death result from the ruptured spleen or from the contused heart and lungs? This determination can implicate or exonerate a suspect, confirm or repudiate suspect or witness statements, and assign blame for the death in any situation in which there were multiple attackers.

Head Injuries

The head is the single most dangerous location for blunt-force trauma. Brain injuries and skull fractures are most often accidental, usually from falls or motor vehicle accidents, but they also occur in assaults or in suicide attempts where the individual jumps from an elevation or purposefully crashes his car. In head injury deaths, it falls to the ME to determine what instrument caused the trauma and whether the injury was accidental, suicidal, or homicidal in nature.

Blunt head trauma can result in anything from a simple bump on the head (**contusion**) to loss of consciousness (**concussion**) to death. Death usually requires bleeding somewhere inside the **cranium** (skull). **Intracranial bleeding** can result from the rupture of an artery, a vein, or multiple small capillaries, any one of which can follow trauma.

Several different membranes (thin sheets of tissue) cover the brain. The most important is the **dura mater**, which separates the brain from the skull. The space between the dura mater and the skull is called the **epidural space**, while the space between the dura mater and the brain is the **subdural space**.

Intracranial bleeds are of three basic types (Figure 8-7):

- **Intracerebral bleeds**: Bleeding within the brain tissue itself
- **Epidural bleeds**: Bleeding between the dura and the skull
- **Subdural bleeds**: Bleeding between the dura and the brain

Intracerebral bleeds typically result from strokes, ruptured aneurysms (swelling in the arteries that are prone to rupture), and blunt or penetrating head trauma. Epidural bleeds typically follow skull fractures, which result in injury to or laceration of the epidural arteries that course over the surface of the brain. Traumatic subdural bleeds are due to torn veins in the subdu-

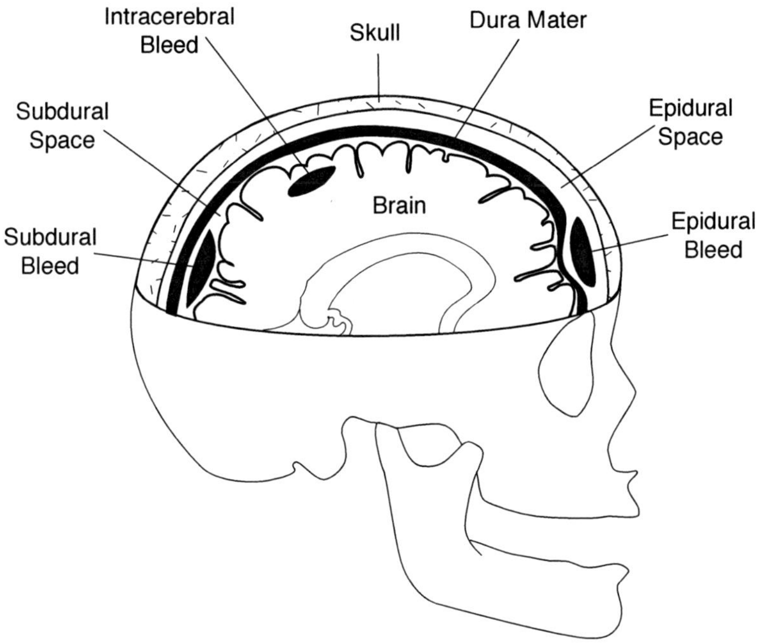

Figure 8-7

Intracranial bleeds. Any bleeding within the skull is called intracranial bleeding. Subcategories include intracerebral bleeds (within the brain), subdural bleeds (between the brain and the dura mater), and epidural bleeds (between the dura mater and the skull). All are potentially deadly.

ral space. They can occur with or without fracture of the skull. Each of these bleeds is potentially lethal without immediate and effective medical care.

The skull is a rigid capsule. It's designed that way to protect the brain. But, in traumatic injuries this rigidity is a double-edged sword. When bleeding occurs anywhere within the skull, the bony skull cannot expand and the pressure inside rises rapidly, squeezing the brain. The only outlet is the hole (***foramen magnum***) at the posterior (back) base of the skull where the spinal cord exits (Figure 8-8). The mounting pressure shuts down all brain function and ultimately pushes brain material into the foramen magnum and down along the spinal cord. This is called **brain stem herniation**. The brain stem controls breathing; when it is compressed in this fashion, breathing shuts down and death from asphyxia follows. This process can occur over minutes, hours, or days.

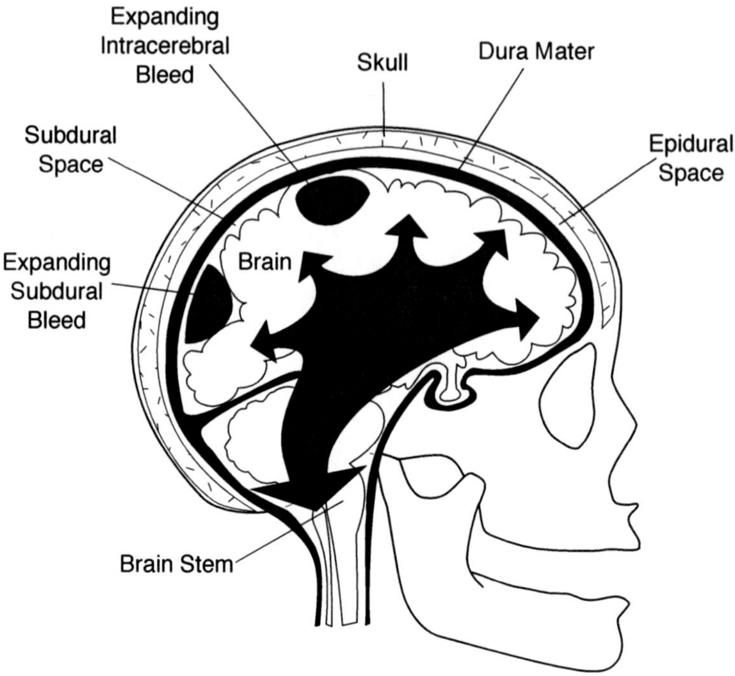

Figure 8-8

Brain stem herniation. Bleeding within the rigid skull can elevate the pressure and force the brain downward into the foramen magnum.

At autopsy, the ME would easily determine that a blow to the head had occurred and could locate bleeding into and around the brain. He might then conclude that the cause of death was blunt-force injury with intracranial bleeding. The manner of death would depend upon whether the blow was accidental or intentional.

It is important to note that significant brain injury can occur with or without a fracture of the skull. Alternatively, a skull fracture might or might not be associated with injury to the brain. Skull fractures can be simple linear, circular, stellate, or depressed (Figure 8-9).

Simple linear fractures occur with low-impact injuries such as falls or a blow to the head. **Circular** fractures require more force such as a blow from a pipe, hammer, or similar object. Depending on the angle and the force of the blow, a circular fracture might be a complete or incomplete cir-

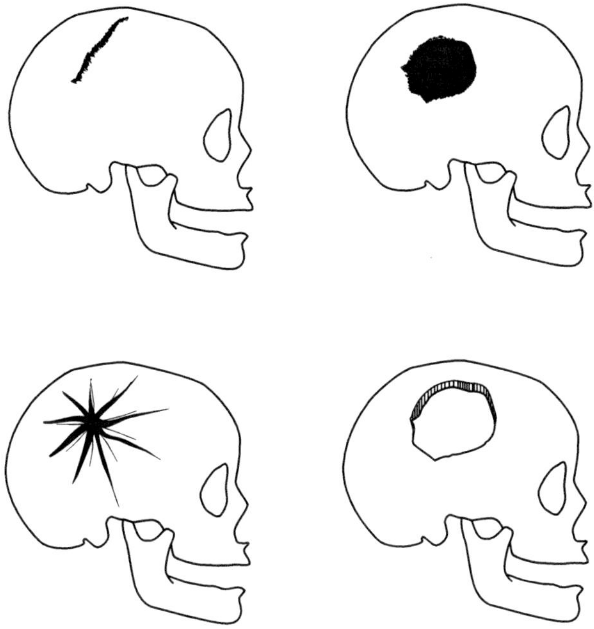

Figure 8-9

Skull fracture types. Skull fractures may be simple linear, circular, stellate, or depressed. The type of fracture seen reflects the weapon or injury that caused it.

cle. With an even more powerful blow, the fracture might take on a **stellate** or star-like shape. This results when the force of the blow bends the skull inward, causing it to fracture along multiple lines of stress. A **depressed** skull fracture occurs when a section of the skull is pushed inward against the brain. A hammer, for example, can produce such a fracture by forcing a circular segment of the skull inward.

The ME will analyze any skull fractures and estimate what instrument likely caused them. This might help him establish the manner of death. Let's say a man is found dead at the bottom of some stairs and his wife says he fell. At autopsy the ME finds a depressed skull fracture that suggests the fatal blow came from a hammer and not from the stairs or the floor. If a hammer is found at the scene he might be able to determine that the shape and size of the hammer's head matches the depressed portion of the skull exactly. He would then likely state that the manner of death was homicidal and not accidental.

Coup and Countercoup Brain Injuries

Coup and **countercoup** injuries constitute special types of brain trauma and are often called **acceleration-deceleration injuries**. These occur in situations characterized by rapid acceleration or deceleration. This means that the brain either collides with a stationary or slower-moving structure or a faster-moving structure collides with a stationary or slower-moving brain. How does that work?

The brain sits within the skull and is surrounded by **cerebrospinal fluid**. Like an egg yolk within the shell, the brain is suspended to some degree and can move a little. If someone is struck in the head or if his head is moving and strikes an object (the dashboard in an auto accident or the ground in a fall), two types of injuries can occur. The first is called a coup injury and is at the site of the impact. The second injury is a countercoup injury and involves the side of the brain opposite the blow. The mechanism for this is controversial and complicated, but a simple way to look at it is that the blow to the skull imparts some motion to the brain, which then collides with the opposite side of the skull, causing injury to that area.

If a blow is applied to one side of the head, the brain will absorb some of the blow's energy and might be injured (a coup injury). The blow will also cause the brain to move and bounce off the other side of the skull (the countercoup injury). In an auto accident, the brain is moving (along with the person) and when the forehead strikes the dashboard, a coup injury might occur at the site of impact (Figure 8-10). The brain will then bounce backward and strike the back of the skull, causing a countercoup injury.

This type of injury is also seen in **shaken baby syndrome**. The violent back and forth movement of the infant's head repeatedly bangs the brain against the skull and can lead to severe brain damage and death.

At autopsy, the ME might find a brain injury at the site of the traumatic blow as well as contusions, lacerations, and bleeding of the brain on the side opposite the blow. Sometimes the coup injury is not evident and the ME finds only the countercoup damage. In these situations, the countercoup injury might be mistaken for a direct injury, which could lead to an erroneous conclusion about how the injury occurred. He might say that the

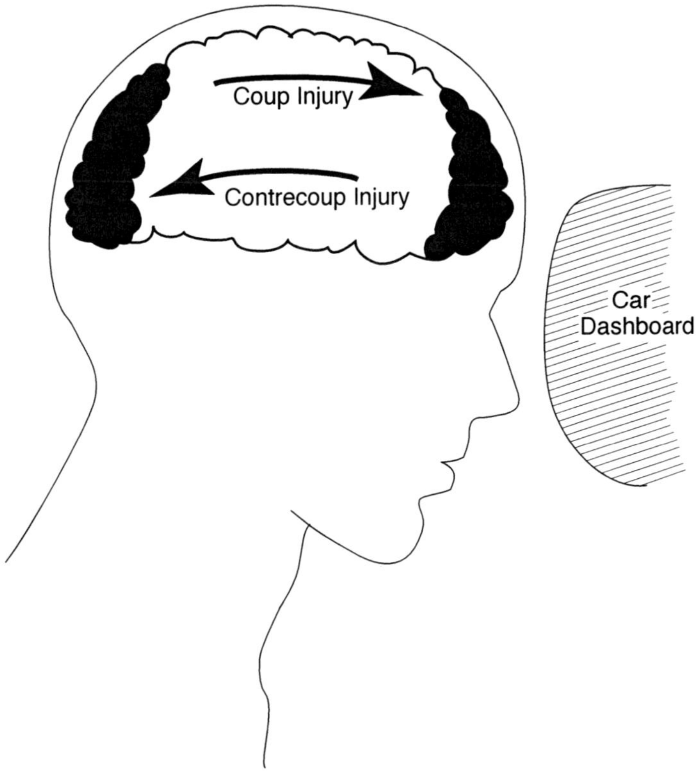

Figure 8-10
Coup and countercoup injuries. When the head strikes the dashboard the brain in the area of impact is injured (coup). The brain might then bounce backward and strike the back of the skull (countercoup).

victim was struck from behind when in fact the blow came from the front, and this could confuse the reconstruction of the crime scene.

Electrical Injuries

Electrical current can be considered either low- or high-voltage. Low-voltage currents, found in residential settings, are between 600 and 1000 volts. High-voltage currents, found in industrial situations, are in the 1000- to 8000-volt range. Virtually all deaths from electrical current are accidental, since it is rarely used for suicide or homicide.

When electricity enters the body, it takes the shortest path from the point of entry to the point of grounding and can kill by several different mechanisms. Whether it is deadly or not depends upon its voltage and the duration of contact. A low-voltage current can take several minutes to do harm, while a high-voltage one can kill instantly.

Low-Voltage Shocks

Residential alternating current (AC) is low-voltage and will cause only minor burns if the exposure is brief. With longer exposures, severe skin burns and extensive internal organ damage (particularly the liver and bone marrow) can occur and can ultimately cause death. But the greatest danger of a low-voltage shock is its effect on the heart.

The normal heartbeat is due to a rhythmic pulse of electrical current that originates in the heart's internal pacemaker and flows through the heart muscle in a well-organized pattern. A low-voltage AC shock can interfere with this rhythmicity and lead to deadly cardiac arrhythmias (changes in heart rhythm), such as ventricular tachycardia and fibrillation, and instantaneous death.

High-Voltage Shocks

High-voltage electrocutions occur in industrial settings and from contact with high-tension lines when they fall to the ground in storms or in vehicle accidents. Direct contact with these is not necessary since the current can arc or "jump" from the line to a person standing nearby.

High-voltage shocks can cause severe internal and external burning with even very brief exposures, but they are less likely to cause dangerous cardiac rhythm changes. The reason is that higher-voltage currents are **defibrillatory** rather than **fibrillatory**. Defibrillatory means that they convert an abnormal rhythm back to a normal rhythm rather than the other way around. In a cardiac arrest, the external shock that a physician gives to the patient is higher voltage, intended to restore a normal rhythm where a deadly, abnormal rhythm exists. Even though high-voltage shocks are less likely to cause deadly cardiac rhythm changes, they can paralyze the respiratory center in the brain and death can follow from asphyxia.

At autopsy, the signs of electrical injury include charred skin at the point of contact, the point of grounding, or both. If the victim grabs an electrical cable with his right hand, the current might flow through his body and exit into the ground through his left foot. Here the ME would expect to see burning or charring of the right hand and left foot. Sometimes in low-voltage electrocutions there is no charring but rather redness and blistering at the contact point. Depending on the voltage, internal organ damage can be extensive.

One interesting phenomenon of electrocution deaths is the appearance of localized rigor mortis. The spasm of rigor mortis results when the adenosine triphosphate (ATP) in the muscles drops after death (Chapter 6). With electrocution, the muscular spasm caused by the electrical current might consume the ATP and cause a more sudden onset of rigor in the affected area. In the above example, the victim's right arm and left leg could show signs of rigor long before the rest of the body.

Lightning

Lightning is a direct current (DC) and is extremely high-voltage (3 million to 200 million volts). Fortunately, the current is very brief, averaging from 1 to 100 milliseconds (thousandths of a second). This is why some people survive lightning strikes.

Lightning strikes come in four varieties:

- **Direct strike**: The lightning hits the victim directly. This is the most serious type and more likely if the victim is holding a metal object such as a golf club or umbrella.
- **Flashover**: The lightning travels over the outside of the body. This is more likely if the victim is wearing wet clothing or is covered with sweat.
- **Side flash**: The current splashes onto the victim from a nearby building, tree, or other person.
- **Stride potential**: This happens when the lightning strikes the ground near a victim where one foot is closer to the strike than the other. This causes a potential electrical difference, called a **stride potential**, and the current can enter through one leg, spread through the body, and exit via the other leg.

Lightning injuries are primarily due to the body's conversion of electrical energy to heat, which can char the skin, scorch the clothing, fry various internal organs, and even fuse or melt metal objects in the victim's pockets, buttons on her shirt, belt buckles, and the metal fillings in her teeth. Significant damage to the heart, liver, kidneys, bone marrow, brain, spinal cord, and muscles are common.

One rare but interesting sign of lightning strikes are **Lichtenberg figures** (Figure 8-11). First described by German physicist Georg Christoph Lichtenberg in 1777, this is a painless, red, fern-like pattern over the back, shoulders, buttocks, or legs. It appears quickly and tends to fade over 12 to 48 hours, leaving behind no scars or discolorations. Their cause is unclear, but when they are seen they are **pathognomonic** (absolutely indicative) of lightning strikes.

Bite Wounds

Bite injuries occur in cases of murder, rape, torture, assault, and child or spousal abuse. They also might be used for self-defense, so they can be either offensive or defensive. Offensive bite wounds are inflicted on the victim by the perpetrator and tend to be well-defined. They can be single or multiple. Defensive bite wounds are inflicted by the victim on the attacker and tend to be more diffuse, irregular, and associated with tearing and ripping of the skin.

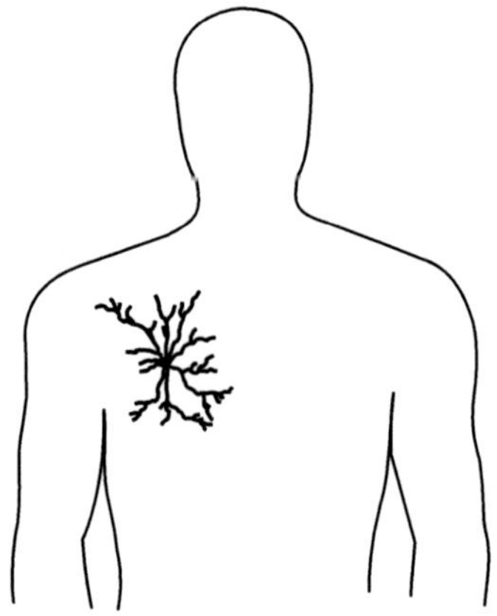

Figure 8-11

Lichtenberg figures. This arboresque pattern of skin discoloration is seen only in lightning strikes.

It's disturbing that we must even discuss the art of bite mark analysis, but bite mark comparison is an important forensic tool. It involves not only marks left on human victims but also bite patterns left on food and other objects. For example, if a perpetrator bites into an apple or a piece of cheese, or uses his teeth to tear a piece of tape, the ME might be able to use these to match against the dental pattern of a suspect.

Bite marks on human flesh are similar, except that flesh, unlike an apple, is elastic and recoils somewhat, so that the details are less clear. Still, a match between the punctures and bruises left on the skin and the dental pattern of a suspect can often be made. If, as in the case of serial killer Ted Bundy (see below), the individual's teeth are damaged, chipped, or in an unusual pattern, an individualizing match can sometimes be made. For many serial killers, pre- or post-mortem biting is part of their "signature" (Chapter 20).

As with blunt-force contusions, the ME can often use the degree and pattern of bruising to distinguish among pre-mortem, peri-mortem, and post-mortem bite marks. As discussed earlier, contusions (bruises) are due to bleeding within damaged tissues and occur only in the living. Bites that are inflicted many minutes before death tend to leave behind a diffuse bruising pattern since the blood has sufficient time to spread away from the injury site. Peri-mortem bite marks, where the bleeding has less time to spread, possess a more distinct or well-defined bruise pattern. Post-mortem bites might show punctures or indentations, but since there is no blood flow, bruising doesn't occur.

All bite marks should be carefully photographed and then swabbed for saliva so that amylase testing (Chapter 10), ABO typing (Chapter 10), and DNA analysis (Chapter 11) can be done. Once a suspect is identified, a mold of his teeth can be compared with the victim's bite marks. The lack of a match can exclude the suspect, while a match, though suggestive, cannot confirm that the suspect is the perpetrator. Further testing, particularly DNA profiling, can offer more conclusive evidence.

Using bite mark patterns to solve crimes is not new, as witnessed by the famous Gordon Hay case. On August 7, 1967 the body of missing 15-year-old Linda Peacock of Biggar, Scotland, was found in a cemetery. She had been beaten and strangled with a rope, but there was no evidence of rape. A bite mark near her right breast revealed that one of the killer's teeth was unusually jagged. The investigation led the police to a nearby low-security detention center for juvenile offenders. Dental impressions were taken from the center's 29 residents and a match to Gordon Hay, who had a rare disorder called hypocalcination, which causes pits and craters in the teeth, was made.

Bite mark evidence was first allowed into a United States courtroom in 1954 in *Doyle v. Texas*. Since then many cases have revolved around bite patterns, including the case of the infamous serial killer Ted Bundy, where bite mark evidence ultimately led to his conviction.

Between 1969 and 1975 a series of brutal sexual homicides swept through the Pacific Northwest, Utah, and Colorado. The female victims each possessed dark hair, parted in the middle. The killer used various ruses to entrap his victims, often wearing a fake cast or feigning some injury to elicit the victim's help with some task. The killer would then overpower the victim and take her to a remote area where she would be tortured, raped, and murdered.

As police in various jurisdictions worked the cases, one name kept cropping up: Theodore Bundy. On November 8, 1974, 18-year-old Carol DaRonch managed to escape from Bundy. Nearly a year later, on August 16, 1975, police stopped a driver for suspicious behavior and found handcuffs and a crowbar in the car. The driver was Ted Bundy. Carol DaRonch identified him as her attacker, and he was convicted of kidnapping and sentenced to 1 to 15 years in prison. But Ted proved slippery. In June 1977, he was extradited to Colorado to face a murder charge. He escaped but was recaptured eight days later. A few months later, on December 30, he escaped again and made his way to Florida.

On the night of January 15, 1978, Bundy entered the Chi Omega sorority house on the campus of Florida State University in Tallahassee, where he assaulted and raped four students, killing Lisa Levy and Margaret Bowman. Less than two hours later another student was attacked. She survived.

One month later, police arrested Chris Hagen for driving a stolen vehicle and quickly discovered that Chris was actually Ted Bundy, who was wanted for murder in several states. He would first be tried in Florida for the Tallahassee murders.

Bundy had left little evidence (no fingerprints, blood, or semen) at the Chi Omega house and neither of the two surviving victims could identify him as the attacker. However, investigators found a bite mark on Lisa Levy's buttocks. Bundy's teeth were misaligned and chipped and matched these bite mark bruises. On July 23, 1978, Bundy was convicted. He was executed in the electric chair on January 24, 1989.

Rape Investigation

Unfortunately, rape is not a rare crime. In order for rape to be charged, three things must have occurred: actual penetration, the use of force, and the lack of consent. Penetration does not need to be complete, and force might be applied through violence, the threat of violence, or coercion. Sometimes rape is accompanied by homicide, either as part of the violent act or afterward to prevent the victim from identifying the assailant.

In a living rape victim, it is critical that a complete rape exam be done as soon as possible after the act. Unfortunately, and for many reasons, victims often wait days, if not months or years, before reporting the crime. Or the victim will shower or bathe before going to authorities or to a hospital. On the surface this might seem to be odd behavior, but rape is not like a punch in the face. It carries with it an array of emotions and social baggage in that the victim often feels ashamed, even guilty, and wants to avoid the inappropriate, but real, feeling of social stigmatization, not to mention fear of a court system that all too often puts the victim "on trial."

The physician should take a complete medical history, examine the victim's entire body, including the genitalia, for evidence of trauma such as bruises, abrasions, or lacerations, and note and photograph each injury. Guided by what the victim says transpired during the assault, vaginal, anal, and oral swabs for DNA should be obtained. The victim's pubic hair should be combed for foreign hairs and fibers and her clothing examined for stains. If any are found, samples are taken and the clothing is packaged and taken to the crime lab for evaluation. All evidence collected is turned over to law enforcement for transport to the crime lab for study.

Once the physician's examination is completed, the victim's injuries are treated and she is given medications to prevent pregnancy and to treat any possible venereal disease. A wait and see attitude is not adopted in this situation, but rather the philosophy is to treat these possibilities as soon as possible. A test for HIV is obtained and repeated over the next several months. A rape counselor usually becomes involved immediately to help the victim with the psychological fallout from the assault.

At the crime lab a search for spermatozoa in the swab samples will be undertaken. In living victims, motile sperm can be seen up to about 12 hours after intercourse and in rare cases up to 24 hours. Non-motile sperm can persist for two or three days. As sperm die off, they initially lose their tails, leaving behind only **sperm heads**. These can be seen up to 7 days after intercourse. So if the victim states that she last had consensual intercourse three days earlier, the finding of non-motile sperm or sperm heads is of little help, but any motile sperm could not have come from that episode and must be related to the rape.

Even if no sperm are found, rape cannot be ruled out since the assailant might have used a condom, had a previous vasectomy, failed to ejaculate, or be azoospermic. **Azoospermia** is a condition in which no sperm is produced.

Fatal Assaults

In rape-homicides, many of the same examinations are performed by the ME rather than a physician. He will initially examine the victim while clothed and search for trace evidence and stains. The clothes are then removed and sent to the crime lab for further processing while the ME turns his attention to the body.

He will search for foreign hair, fibers, or other trace evidence. Stains will be examined and swabbed and nail clippings and scrapings are obtained in case the victim managed to scratch her attacker. He will examine and photograph each injury as well as search for evidence of penetration. Vaginal, anal, and oral swabs will be obtained.

Even if no overt genital trauma is found, the ME will look for signs that sexual intercourse took place. Vaginal fluids will be examined, both chemically and microscopically, for semen. Chemical tests for acid phosphatase, an enzyme found in abundant quantities in semen, and P30, a semen-specific glycoprotein, will be done (Chapter 10). Acid phosphatase can be present up to 72 hours after intercourse. A problem arises when the victim has had consensual sex during the two or three days before the assault. There is no method for determining if elevated levels of acid phosphatase are remnants of this consensual act or of the rape itself.

As in the living victim, a microscopic search for sperm will be done. Sperm survive longer in a corpse than in a living victim because in a living woman the vagina produces certain chemicals that destroy sperm, while in a corpse sperm are destroyed only through decomposition, which requires many days. Sperm can sometimes be found for up to two weeks in a corpse.

CHAPTER 9

ASPHYXIA

Under normal circumstances, oxygen (O_2) is inhaled into the lungs' air sacs, where it crosses into the blood, combines with the hemoglobin of the red blood cells (RBCs), and is transported throughout the body. The cells then extract the O_2 from the hemoglobin. An interruption at any step in this O_2 supply chain can lead to **asphyxia**, which can best be defined as the deprivation of O_2 to the cells of the body, resulting in cellular dysfunction and ultimately death.

Asphyxia occurs by several mechanisms. The air might be oxygen-poor or some airway obstruction might prevent it from entering the lungs. The lungs might be damaged or filled with water so that the O_2 can't reach the blood. Certain toxins interfere with the uptake of O_2 by the blood or its utilization by the cells of the body. Asphyxia can also follow obstruction of the arteries in the neck, as occurs during strangulation, which prevents oxygen-filled blood from reaching the brain. Each of these defects can lead to death from asphyxia.

Asphyxia can result from suffocation, strangulation, toxic gases, and drowning.

Suffocation

Suffocation occurs whenever sufficient oxygen is unable to reach the blood stream, whether from air poor in oxygen or from some impediment to it reaching the lungs or the bloodstream. There are five general categories of suffocation: **environmental suffocation**, **smothering**, **choking**, **mechanical asphyxia**, and **suffocating gases**.

Environmental suffocation occurs whenever the inhaled air is low in O_2. Even if the lungs and circulatory system function normally, if the O_2 content of the air is deficient, it is of little use to the body. Normal air contains 21 percent oxygen. If this percentage drops to 10 to 15 percent, judgment and coordination suffer, while below 10 percent consciousness is lost, with death occurring at around 8 percent. This is the reason adults are warned as part of the pre-flight routine on commercial airlines that if the cabin pressure fails, they should put on their oxygen mask before helping children with their masks. If the adult can't coordinate—or worse, loses consciousness—there might be no one to help either of them.

Deaths from an oxygen-poor environment are almost always accidental, though homicide is a possibility. A child might accidentally lock himself into an old refrigerator where once the oxygen is consumed, death from asphyxia follows. The same occurs whenever a victim enters an underground chamber or mine that is poor in oxygen. Deaths in structure fires are most often due to asphyxia as the flames consume oxygen.

There are no specific autopsy findings in most cases of environmental suffocation, so the determination of the cause and manner of death relies more on the circumstances surrounding the death. If the victim is found in an oxygen-poor environment or an airtight enclosure and there is no evidence of trauma, toxin exposure, or natural causes, the ME would likely determine that the death was due to accidental suffocation.

Smothering occurs when some external device prevents air from entering the nose or mouth. This is distinguished from choking (see below), in which the obstructing material is within the mouth or throat. Smothering deaths can be accidental, homicidal, or suicidal.

Suicidal and accidental smothering usually involves a plastic bag. The suicidal individual will place the bag over his head, often securing it with tape or a rope, and occasionally binding his own hands. This is particularly true in cases of "suicide pacts," where two or more people commit the act together. Trash bags, dry cleaner bags, and similar products can lead to accidental smothering in children.

Homicidal smothering usually employs a pillow, bedding, plastic bag, or the killer's hands. When a pillow or a plastic bag is used, marks on the victim are typically not present unless the victim puts up a struggle. If so, abrasions or bruises are often left on the victim's face or arms by the killer's attempts to control the victim. Furthermore, if the victim struggles, rigor mortis can appear early. Just as with deaths that occur during exercise, the struggle consumes the muscular adenosine triphosphate (ATP), and this often leads to earlier onset of rigor (Chapter 6).

The major pathological finding of suffocation was first described in the 19th century by Ambrose Tardieu when he identified small blood spots called **microhemorrhages** in the lung tissues of suffocation victims. He named them Tardieu spots, a moniker that is still used today. Though not present in all cases of smothering, when present they help the ME assess the cause of death. If there are no external bruises and no microhemorrhages in the lungs, and if the pillow or bag is removed before the body is found, the ME might not be able to determine the true cause of death.

Choking, as opposed to smothering, occurs when the blockage is within the mouth or airways. Choking deaths might be natural, homicidal, or accidental.

Natural choking can result from acute fulminating **epiglottitis** or **diphtheria**. The former is an acute inflammation of the epiglottis, which is the flap at the upper end of the trachea (main airway) that closes to prevent the aspiration of food and water when we swallow. When inflamed, it can rapidly swell and block the airway. Thanks to childhood immunization programs, diphtheria is now rare in the United States, but 100 years ago it claimed thousands of lives every year. It is a bacterial infection of the throat, caused by the bacterium *Corynebacterium diphtheriae*, that leads to the formation of a thick, tenacious scab-like sheet called a pseudomembrane. This membrane can peel away from the throat and obstruct the airway, causing death from asphyxia.

Homicidal choking, though not common, occurs when a sock, cloth, ball, or other object is placed in the victim's mouth before a gag is applied. As with deaths from smothering, if the choking device is removed before the body is found, the ME might not be able to determine the exact cause of death.

Most choking deaths are accidental. Children inhale small objects such as pieces of balloons, parts of toys, and food materials, while in adults the culprit is almost always food. This is so common that it has been given the moniker "café coronary." Typically, the victim is eating, suddenly stops talking, perhaps grabs his throat, and collapses. On the surface it looks like a heart attack or "coronary." In reality, the airway is obstructed, the victim cannot breathe or speak, the oxygen level in his blood drops dramatically, and he collapses and dies. Cardiopulmonary resuscitation (CPR) is not effective in this situation because mouth-to-mouth respiration is ineffective if the airway is blocked. The **Heimlich maneuver** was designed for this situation.

Mechanical asphyxia occurs when some external force is applied to the body, preventing the expansion of the chest and thus respiration. Examples include a person trapped beneath a heavy object such as a car or a collapsed wall or crushed by a stampeding crowd. In these situations, the external pressure is so great that the victim literally can't take a breath. Boa constrictors kill exactly this way. Once the snake wraps itself around its prey, it tightens its coil with each exhalation until the prey is trapped permanently in the position of exhalation and is unable to take another breath. Death follows quickly.

Tragically, infants may die from mechanical asphyxia when a parent rolls onto them during sleep. Such deaths are often erroneously deemed to be from **sudden infant death syndrome (SIDS)**.

A bizarre form of mechanical suffocation is known as **burking**. The name comes from the nefarious activities of killers William Burke and William Hare. William Burke was a merchant in Edinburgh, Scotland, in the early 1800s, who collected, repaired, and sold old shoes as well as trafficked in old clothes, skins, and human hair. In 1827, he hooked up with William Hare, who ran a beggars hotel in the village of Tanners Close. In December of that year, a resident of the hotel died, and Burke arranged to sell his body to a Dr. Knox, who needed corpses for his dissection demonstrations at Surgeon's Square.

Burke and Hare loaded the man's coffin with bark, buried it in front of many witnesses, and then delivered the body to Dr. Knox, receiving

7 pounds and 10 shillings in return. Wanting to continue this profitable enterprise, the pair became grave robbers, supplying corpses to the doctor for 8 pounds in summer and 10 in winter. (It must have been more difficult to dig them up when the ground was cold.)

But when locals refused to die fast enough, they resorted to kidnapping and killing people who were not likely to be missed. Burke would sit on them and hold their mouth and nose closed until they suffocated. Burking was born. Ultimately, a lodger at the hotel notified authorities when she discovered their sixteenth and final victim beneath a bed, where Burke and Hare had stashed the body while awaiting an opportunity to transport it to Surgeon's Square. The two men were arrested, Hare turning "King's evidence" and testifying against Burke. Burke was convicted and hanged before 40,000 witnesses on January 28, 1829.

Suffocating gases are not poisonous but rather diminish the O_2 percentage of inspired air. Normal room air is approximately 78 percent nitrogen, 21 percent oxygen, and 1 percent other gases. If some other gas is added to the mixture, the percentage of O_2 declines and inhaling this new mixture can lead to hypoxia (low blood O_2 levels) and death. Deaths from suffocating gases are usually accidental but can be suicidal or homicidal.

Carbon dioxide (CO_2) and **methane** are common suffocating gases. Each is odorless and thus undetectable to the person exposed. Methane is the principal component of natural gas. For home use another chemical is added to give it an odor so that leaks can be detected. Otherwise deaths from home gas leaks would be even more common than they are.

Let's say an equal amount of methane and room air are mixed, resulting in a 50 percent decline of O_2 in the air. In this case the percentage of O_2 would drop from 21 percent to 10.5 percent, a lethal level. Anyone who inhaled such a mixture would very quickly develop lethargy, confusion, disorientation, loss of consciousness, and ultimately coma and death. Mines and sewers, where high levels of both methane and CO_2 can accumulate, are particularly treacherous. Anyone who entered could become hypoxic and confused, fall into unconsciousness, and die.

There are no specific autopsy findings in deaths from suffocating gases, but in methane-related deaths high levels of methane might be found in the victim's blood. Since CO_2 is a normal constituent of blood and its level often rises around the time of death, it may be difficult or impossible to determine the cause of death when this is the culprit. Here the circumstances of the death might be the only thing that allows the ME to make the proper determination of the cause of death.

A particularly tragic case of mass CO_2 poisoning occurred at Lake Nyos in Cameroon in 1986 when an odd geological event known as a **limnic eruption** occurred. This eruption caused a large amount of CO_2-laden water to rise up from the depths of the lake and the CO_2 escaped into the surrounding air. Since CO_2 is slightly heavier than air, it settled like an invisible and odorless fog over a wide area, asphyxiating nearly 1,800 people and 3,500 livestock.

Strangulation

Strangulation is a form of asphyxia in which some outside force compresses the airways and blood vessels of the neck, preventing blood from reaching the brain and air from entering the lungs. The neck is a vital link between brain and body for several reasons: Neurological communication occurs by way of the spinal cord, which extends downward from the base of the brain; the brain's blood supply must pass through the two carotid arteries that lie on either side of the larynx (voice box or Adam's apple); and air enters the lungs through the trachea (windpipe). This vital conduit is exposed and vulnerable to injury, both accidental and intentional.

There are three basic types of strangulation: manual strangulation, ligature strangulation, and hanging.

Manual strangulation is performed by hand, while **ligature strangulation** employs a rope, cord, wire, or other flexible material. **Hanging** is basically ligature strangulation in which the body weight is used to tighten the noose. Manual and ligature strangulation are almost always homicide, while hangings are predominantly suicidal.

Each of these strangulation types results in **cerebral hypoxia**, a low level of oxygen in the brain. This occurs because strangulation blocks the airway, preventing the victim from breathing, and occludes the carotid arteries, preventing the flow of blood to the brain. Of these two, the occlusion of the arteries is the predominant cause of unconsciousness and death. We can remain awake and alive for several minutes without breathing, but if the blood supply to the brain is interrupted or severely limited, loss of consciousness can follow in a few seconds, and death in a minute or so.

As we will see later, the unexpected rapidity with which consciousness is lost during carotid compression is an important factor in deaths and brain injury from choke holds and during autoerotic asphyxiation.

A common, though not universal, finding in all types of strangulation is **petechial hemorrhages**, also called **petechiae**, in the conjunctivae (the pink parts around the eyeball) and the sclerae (the white part) of the eyes. These are small red dots or streaks that result from blood leaking into these tissues as the pressure within the neck veins, and thus in the small capillaries of the conjunctivae and sclerae, dramatically rises during the strangulation process.

Manual strangulation often leaves contusions and abrasions on the victim's neck. The contusions can mimic the shape of the assailant's fingers and the abrasions can result from the assailant's fingernails. The latter often appear as linear scratches or as thin, semicircular marks where the nails dug in. The victim's face is typically congested and petechial hemorrhages are commonly seen. Bleeding into the neck muscles is sometimes seen at autopsy, as are fractures of the **cornu** (horn) of the thyroid cartilage (Adam's apple) and the tiny **hyoid bone** (Figure 9-1).

Another form of manual strangulation is the **choke hold**, which is at times employed by law enforcement to subdue a combative subject. There are two basic types: the **bar arm hold** and the **carotid hold**. The purpose of each is to collapse the carotid arteries and render the individual unconscious. In the former, the officer will place his forearm across the front of the subject's throat and, using his other hand, will grasp his wrist and pull back, applying pressure to the neck. In the carotid hold, the officer will place the crook of his elbow against the center of the subject's neck and again grasp his wrist and pull back. This produces a scissors effect, which occludes the two carotid arteries. Unconsciousness and brain damage or death can occur if either of these is applied too aggressively or for too long.

Ligature strangulation deaths are most often homicidal, though some are accidental, even suicidal. Devices used for homicidal ligature strangulations are ropes, wires, electrical cords, and clothing such as neckties, belts, bras, and stockings. If the ligature is soft, such as a towel or silk scarf, it might not leave visible bruises, and if the device is removed before the victim is found, the ME will have a more difficult time determining the exact cause of death. If the ligature is thin, such as an electrical cord, a

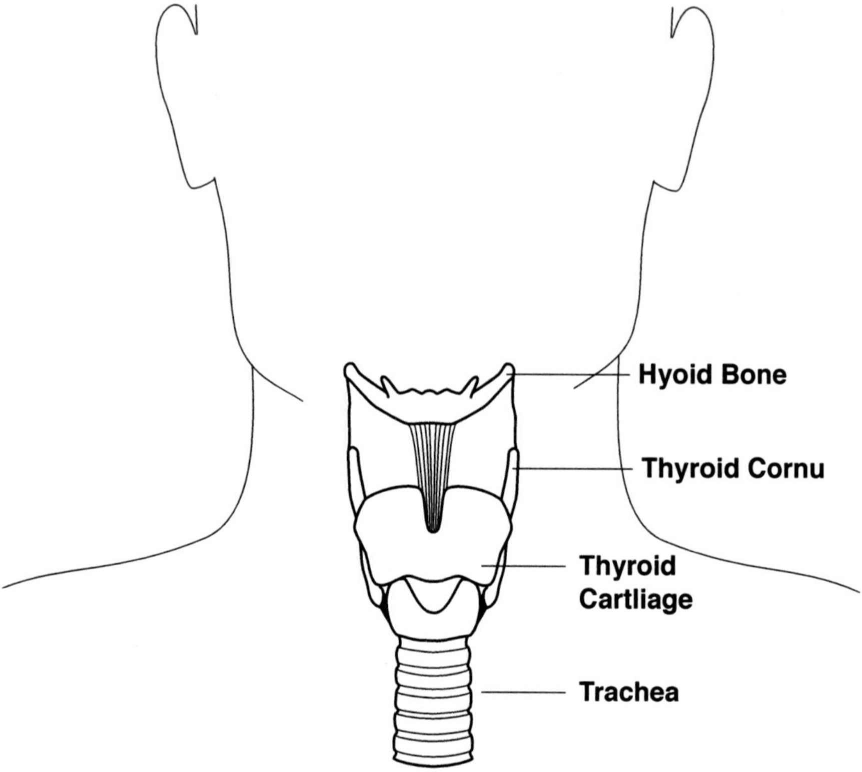

Figure 9-1

The thyroid cornu and the hyoid bone. These delicate structures are often fractured during manual strangulation, but less often in ligature strangulation and hanging.

groove or **furrow** will often remain. This furrow is a deep impression that matches the width of the ligature used. With thicker devices like ropes, the groove is wide and shallow and the associated bruising might reveal the pattern of the ligature used such as the braid pattern of a rope or the link pattern of a chain. With thinner devices, the groove is deep and narrow.

As with manual strangulation, the victim's face is typically congested and scleral and conjunctival petechial hemorrhages are seen. However, bleeding into the neck muscles and fractures of the thyroid cartilage and the hyoid bone are much less common. This difference is probably due to the thickness of fingers and the diffuse pressure they apply as opposed to the thinner area of compression with a ligature.

Even in severely decomposed corpses, the ligature mark can be preserved. Apparently the compression of the tissues within the furrow collapses the underlying capillary blood vessels so that the bacteria that cause putrefaction, which tend to disseminate throughout the body by way of the blood vessels, can't reach the furrow in any great number and as a result the decay process is slowed.

As opposed to hangings (see below), the furrow in ligature strangulation tends to be horizontal (Figure 9-2 A). The reason for this is that whether the assailant is facing the victim or approaching from behind, he will tighten the ligature by pulling laterally on its ends.

Suicide by ligature strangulation is rare, but it does occur. Since it takes approximately fifteen seconds or so to lose consciousness, the victim has time to secure the ligature in place by either tying a knot or by wrapping the cord around his neck several times. Once the victim loses consciousness, he can't loosen the ligature and death from asphyxia follows. Accidental ligature strangulation, also rare, typically occurs when a scarf, tie, or other article of clothing becomes entangled in a piece of machinery or a moving apparatus such as a ski lift, elevator, motorcycle, or car. Perhaps the most famous victim of accidental ligature strangulation was Isadora Duncan.

The iconic Isadora Duncan was born May 27, 1878, in Oakland, California, where her pianist mother introduced her to music and to many of the

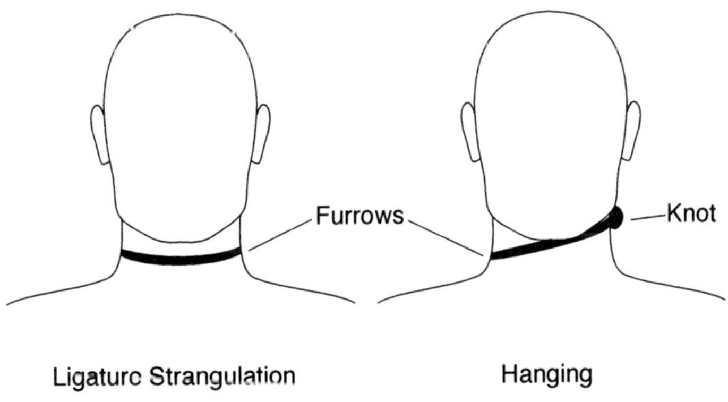

Figure 9-2

Ligature strangulation and hanging marks. With ligature strangulation the furrow tends to be horizontal (A), while with hanging, it angles across the neck with the higher end toward the knot (B).

world's great composers. At an early age Isadora began to experiment with new forms of dance that drew on elements of music, poetry, and nature. For this she became known as the "mother of modern dance." She lived a flamboyant lifestyle and dressed the part, developing a fondness for very long scarves that flowed along behind her. This fashion statement led to her death when, on September 14, 1927, in Nice, France, her scarf became entangled in the wheels of a moving Bugatti, strangling her.

Hangings result when a noose or other ligature is pulled tight by the body weight of a person who is either completely or partially suspended. Though the airway can be compressed and breathing interrupted, the true cause of death in most hangings is compression of the carotid arteries. Hangings are almost always suicidal; homicidal hangings, though they do occur, are rare. Accidental hangings, also uncommon, most often involve children who become entangled in a rope or clothing. Except for judicial (legally directed) hangings, fractures of the cervical vertebrae (neck spinal bones) are uncommon because these fractures require that the body drop a sufficient distance, and this is very unusual in suicidal and accidental hangings.

Though there are seven cervical vertebrae, it is the second, or C2 (also called the **axis**), that is typically fractured in judicial hangings. The first, or C1 (the **atlas**) is melded with the base of the skull, and it is C2 that takes the brunt of the force of the fall (Figure 9-3). In fact, a fracture of C2, regardless of its cause, is called the "hangman's fracture." Death is usually immediate, though it might take 15 minutes or so for the heart to stop.

In suicidal hangings, the victim tends to use whatever is handy. Ropes, belts, bed sheets, clothing, and electrical cords are common. You might think that if the victim's hands are bound, someone else must have facilitated the hanging, either as a homicide or an aided suicide. However, this is simply not the case. Suicide victims not infrequently bind their own hands to prevent a change of heart. In this circumstance, the ME will examine the knots and might even employ the expertise of a **forensic knot expert** to determine whether the knot was self-tied or not. If not, then homicide becomes a real possibility.

In addition, the knot expert might be able to characterize the knot and narrow the suspect list. People tie knots based on their knowledge, skill, and habits. Certain knots indicate certain professions or hobbies. For

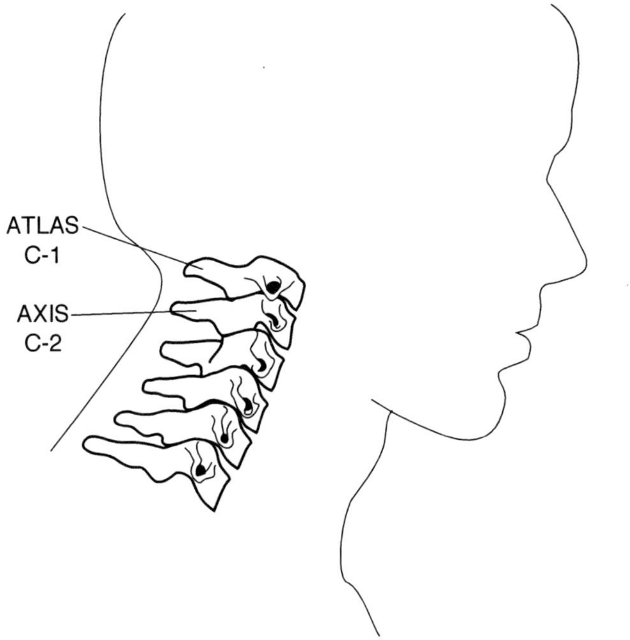

Figure 9-3
Hangman's fracture. A fracture of the second vertebral vertebra (C2), which occurs during judicial hangings, is called the "hangman's fracture."

example, knots used in nautical situations are very different from those used on a farm or cattle ranch and would vary widely from the common "bow" or "granny" knot the average person uses on shoes and packages. Also, if the binding ligature is of an unusual or distinct material, this might offer useful leads. If the ends have been cut, examining these cuts might provide valuable tool mark evidence (Chapter 15).

The neck markings seen after hanging depend on the nature of the noose used. Soft nooses such as sheets might leave little or no markings, while a rope or cord might imprint a deep and distinct furrow. The longer the body hangs, the deeper the furrow. Occasionally the furrow and any associated bruising will reveal the braid pattern of a rope or the link configuration of a chain.

The furrow in hanging victims is typically an inverted V and tends to be diagonal across the neck with its high end toward the knot (Figure 9-2

B). Since the corpse hangs by the "bottom" of the noose, if the knot is to the victim's left side, the furrow will be lower and much deeper on the right side of the neck and will angle upward toward the left ear, where near the knot it shallows and disappears. This differs from the furrow found in ligature strangulation, which is typically horizontal.

If the victim is found several hours after the hanging and lividity has appeared, it will be in the dependent areas, which in this situation would be the legs, forearms, and hands. Facial congestion and petechial hemorrhages can be seen, but bleeding into the neck muscles and fractures of the thyroid cartilage or the hyoid bone are less likely to occur in hangings than in manual strangulation. In a suicidal hanging where the victim has not tied his hands, fingernail abrasions and claw marks might be found on the neck.

Another factor to consider is that the victim could have been subdued with drugs or alcohol and then hanged as part of an elaborate homicide and an attempt to stage the death to look like a suicide. For this reason, a toxicological analysis should be performed on all victims of hanging. Clouding the issue is the fact that the victim might have taken alcohol or drugs in order to "get the courage" to do himself in. Here the ME might be able to determine whether the level of drugs and alcohol found in the victim were enough to "knock him out" or merely enough to impair his judgment. If the victim had enough drugs in his system to render him unconscious, he could not have hanged himself. This is an easy call in most cases, though not in all (Chapter 12).

Autoerotic and **sexual asphyxia** are unique types of strangulation death. Autoerotic asphyxia is most often seen in males involved in some masturbation ritual, while sexual asphyxiation is part of partner sexual activities. The concept is that partial asphyxia accentuates sexual enjoyment. One of the first symptoms of cerebral hypoxia (low oxygen in the brain) is giddiness, and this sensation is believed to enhance sexual arousal. It is also a very dangerous game.

The most common methods employed are partial hanging, self-release ligatures, and plastic bags. The solo victim will rig up a device or situation where the rope or chosen ligature will compress the neck "on demand." It might be an elaborate setup or something as simple as leaning one way or the other while restrained by a rope around the neck. Some form of "self-rescue device," such as the victim being able to move a certain way to relieve pressure or a sharp instrument to cut a ligature or slice open a bag, is often involved. Unfortunately, miscalculations can lead to tragedy. Cerebral hypoxia can lead to poor judgment, erroneous assessment of the level of hypoxia, and sudden loss of consciousness. Once unconscious, the victim is unable to save himself. In partner sex, a miscalculation by one can lead to death of the other.

Sometimes the ritual involves the inhalation of various gases, which lead to hypoxia and other physiological derangements. Nitrous oxide and amyl nitrate, both commonly used in sex play, can cause a sudden and profound drop in blood pressure, which can lead to loss of consciousness and death. When coupled with partial asphyxia, these inhaled gases can be particularly treacherous.

The typical scene is a male victim, partially suspended by a hanging noose, surrounded by erotic magazines, photos, or paraphernalia. At times, his hands will be bound, which might suggest a homicide staged to look like an accidental death. But, such binding might be part of the ritual. As discussed above, an examination of the bindings might reveal whether the victim could have bound himself or not.

Toxic Chemicals

As opposed to suffocating gases, which simply replace oxygen in the breathed air, toxic gases interact with the blood or tissues of the body in a manner that prevents oxygen transport or utilization. The most common toxic gases encountered by the ME are **carbon monoxide (CO), hydrogen cyanide**, and **hydrogen sulfide**. Deaths due to CO might be suicidal, accidental, or homicidal; those due to cyanide are usually suicides, and those involving hydrogen sulfide are typically accidental.

Carbon monoxide is treacherous, deadly, and common. It is tasteless, odorless, colorless, and undetectable by humans. It results from the incomplete combustion of carbon-containing fuels such as paper, wood, and gasoline. Complete combustion of these fuels yields carbon dioxide (CO_2), but when there is a deficiency of oxygen or if the fire is smoldering and doesn't produce enough heat to drive the reaction to completion, incomplete combustion occurs and results in the production of CO. Faulty stoves, heaters, and fireplaces as well as the exhaust from a car engine are common sources, and charcoal briquettes, which are designed to smolder rather than burst into flame, are particularly dangerous. Using a charcoal grill in an enclosed space such as a garage or tent leads to rapid CO accumulation, as can faulty butane and propane camp stoves and heaters.

Carbon monoxide's treachery lies in its great affinity for hemoglobin, the oxygen-carrying molecule within our red blood cells (RBCs). When inhaled, CO binds to hemoglobin, producing **carboxyhemoglobin**. It does so 300 times more readily than does oxygen and thus displaces oxygen. In other words, if the hemoglobin is presented with both oxygen and carbon monoxide, it is 300 times more likely to combine with the CO. The result is that the blood that leaves the lungs and heads toward the body is rich in CO (carboxyhemoglobin) and poor in O_2 (**oxyhemaglobin**). This strong attraction between hemoglobin and CO means that even breathing air that contains only small amounts of CO can lead to big problems. For example, breathing air that contains a CO level as low as 0.2 percent might lead to blood CO saturations greater than 60 percent after only 30 to 45 minutes. So, a faulty heater or smoldering fire that produces only a small amount of CO becomes increasingly deadly with each passing minute.

This powerful attraction also explains how some people succumb to CO poisoning in open areas such as working on a car in a driveway. Typically the victim is found lying near the car's exhaust. Similarly, swimmers and water skiers who loiter near a dive platform on the back of a powerboat with an idling engine can die from CO poisoning.

The degree of exposure to CO is measured by determining the percent of the hemoglobin that is carboxyhemoglobin. The signs and symptoms of CO toxicity parallel these levels. The normal level is 1 to 3 percent but might be as high as 7 to 10 percent in smokers. At levels of 10 to 20 percent, headache and inability to concentrate occur. Between 30 and 40 percent, headaches increase, as do pulse and breathing rates, and nausea, vomiting, dizziness, and lethargy appear. Between 40 and 60 percent the victim becomes confused, disoriented, weak, and poorly coordinated. Above 60 percent coma and death are likely. These are general ranges since the actual effect of rising CO levels varies from person to person. In the elderly and those with heart or lung disease, levels as low as 20 percent can be lethal.

A running car engine in an enclosed garage is a common method for suicide but could also be used for homicide. If the killer subdues the victim by force or by way of intoxication, he could place the victim in his car and let the CO actually do him in. When determining the manner of death in such cases, the ME will look for evidence of trauma to the victim as well as perform a toxicology screen. Finding trauma, such as a blow to the head, might change the manner of death from suicide to homicide, but finding drugs might not. Some people use multiple suicide methods to assure success, and a drug overdose combined with CO inhalation is not rare.

When more than one person is found dead in a house or a car and there is no evidence of trauma, CO toxicity must be considered since the odds that two or more people died from natural causes at the same time and in the same place are extremely small.

Carboxyhemoglobin is bright red in color and imparts this hue to the blood, organs, and tissues. When the ME performs an autopsy and sees bright cherry-red blood and organs, he will suspect CO poisoning as the cause of death. This finding is not absolutely conclusive since cyanide exposure (see below) can also result in cherry-red blood and tissues. Livor mortis in these situations might be red or pink rather than the usual blue-gray color (Chapter 6).

Those who survive CO intoxication can have serious long-term health problems. The brain is particularly vulnerable since it is extremely sensitive to lack of oxygen. Symptoms and signs of brain injury can begin immediately or be delayed for several days or weeks. The most common aftereffects include chronic headaches, memory loss, blindness, confusion, disorientation, poor coordination, and hallucinations. The ME might be asked to evaluate a living victim in this situation if the exposure was due to a criminal act or if a civil suit is involved.

Cyanide, contrary to what is seen in movies and novels, is rarely used for murder but is occasionally used for suicide, particularly mass suicides, such as the Jonestown tragedy (see below). Accidental poisoning of individuals or groups is usually seen in industrial settings. Cyanide salts are used in metal electroplating, jewelry making, and x-ray recovery industries. The plastic manufacturing industry uses solvents called nitriles, which contain cyanide. When burned, these nitriles can release hydrogen cyanide gas, the most deadly from of this substance. The most common cyanide salts are sodium and potassium cyanide, which are white powders. When ingested, these powders react with the acids in the stomach to produce hydrogen cyanide gas. Hydrogen cyanide is also the agent used in gas chamber executions.

Cyanide is a metabolic poison, meaning that it works on a cellular level. It reacts with the iron in **cytochrome oxidase**, an enzyme necessary for the cell to use oxygen, resulting in cellular asphyxia and death. It's as if all the oxygen in the body had been suddenly removed. It's still there but the body's cells can no longer use it. Since the cells are no longer able to remove oxygen from the blood, the blood remains very well oxygenated (rich in oxyhemoglobin) and thus bright red. Also the reaction of cyanide with the blood's hemoglobin produces **cyanohemoglobin**, a bright red compound. This combination tints the cyanide victim's blood bright red, similar to what is seen in CO poisoning. The ME would see the reddish hue of the blood and internal organs and the pinkish lividity and would suspect the presence of cyanide or CO and would test for both. In addition, he might be able to detect the typical bitter almond odor of hydrogen cyanide. Curiously, though, the ability to detect this odor is genetically determined—about 50 percent of people can and 50 percent can't.

Fundamentalist Christian pastor Jim Jones established his Peoples Temple in the 1950s in Indianapolis, Indiana, where his outlandish claims that he could cure cancer, heart disease, and other maladies, drew criticism. In the 1970s he moved his congregation to Ukiah, California, and from there to San Francisco and Los Angeles, where he warned his congregation of the coming end of the world. Suspicions arose about many of Jones's financial dealings, and when an exposé appeared in a California magazine, he moved his followers to the makeshift town of Jonestown, Guyana.

Rumors of human rights abuses followed, and this attracted the attention of some members of the Congress. In 1978, Congressman Leo Ryan and members of the press visited Jonestown, and after talking with many of the Peoples Temple members, sixteen members requested to leave with the congressman and return to the United States. As they awaited a plane at Port Kiatuma Airport, they were ambushed by several of the Temple's security guards. Congressman Ryan and four others were killed and eleven were wounded. Fear of retribution led Jones and the Temple leaders to arrange a mass suicide where they fed the congregation a fruit drink laced with cyanide and the sedatives valium and chloral hydrate. Over 900 people perished, including more than 250 children.

Sewer gas, often found in sewers and cesspools, is composed of carbon monoxide, methane, and **hydrogen sulfide**, a byproduct of fermentation. When inhaled, hydrogen sulfide converts oxyhemoglobin into **methemoglobin**, which does not release O_2 to the tissues, thus effectively suffocating the cells of the body. Methemoglobin imparts a dark purple color to the blood, which can be seen at autopsy. In addition, the ME would find high levels of sulfide in the blood of sewer gas victims. These deaths are almost always accidental and occur when the victim enters an area rich in sewer gas.

Drowning

Drowning is a form of asphyxia since the victim dies from lack of oxygen. As the lungs' bronchial tubes (airways) and alveoli (air sacs) fill with water, the ability to oxygenate the blood is lost. With this loss of air supply and the elevated oxygen consumption by the muscles in the struggle to survive, the oxygen level in the blood rapidly falls, and loss of consciousness and death follow very quickly.

Drowning is almost always accidental but can be suicidal or homicidal. For the ME, the determination of the manner of death is often difficult. Whether the victim fell, jumped, or was pushed into the water, drowning is drowning. It looks the same regardless of how it came about.

Even determining that the person actually drowned is difficult and is mostly a **diagnosis of exclusion**. The circumstances of the death are often more important than any autopsy findings. If there is no evidence of trauma or natural disease to explain the death and if the victim is found in water, the ME might determine that the death was from drowning. The reason for this confusion is that there are few pathological findings at autopsy that can definitely indicate that the person drowned.

Common sense would suggest that if the lungs are full of water, the victim must have drowned. Unfortunately, it's not that simple. The lungs and airways of any corpse submerged in water for several hours will passively fill with water. For this reason, the ME might not be able to determine if the victim was dead or alive when he entered the water and can't say whether the victim drowned or not. This can be critical to determining the cause of death and can impact what charges are filed against which suspect when multiple assailants are involved. Let's say two men attack a woman. One beats her severely and the other tosses her in the water. Whether she died from blunt trauma or from drowning would affect how the crimes were charged.

Further confusing the issue are several medical conditions, such as heart attacks and certain drug overdoses, that cause pulmonary edema (water-filled lungs). This means that if a victim suffered a heart attack and developed severe secondary pulmonary edema before falling into the water or died from certain types of drug overdose and was dumped into water, the autopsy findings might be similar to those of someone who truly drowned. For this reason, a complete toxicological analysis should be performed on all suspected drowning victims.

To add even more confusion, 15 percent of drownings are "dry drownings." In this situation, the intake of water into the throat causes **laryngeal spasm**. This means that the larynx reacts to the water by constricting or closing in spasms. This shuts down the passage of air into the lungs and the victim asphyxiates. This closing of the airway also prevents water from entering the lungs so that they are dry at autopsy. Some believe that this is more common in salt water than in fresh water drowning, but this is controversial.

When dealing with a potential drowning victim, the ME has his hands full. But he does have a few tricks that might help.

If the victim is alive when he enters the water, the struggles to breathe will cause a great deal of pressure trauma to the sinuses and the lungs, and if so the ME might find hemorrhaging (bleeding) into the sinuses and airways. Also, when the victim inhales water, he takes in any floating debris the water might contain and the ME might see this in the sinuses, airways, and lungs. This debris consists of dirt, gravel, plant materials, sand, and microscopic animals and plants. The ME might employ a forensic chemist, botanist, or geologist to help identify and determine the site of origin of these materials. For example, the finding of pine pollen and bits of pine needles within the lungs would suggest that the victim drowned in a nearby pine-shaded pond and not the backyard swimming pool. Or the absence of these and the finding of high chlorine levels in the water taken from the victim's lungs would suggest the opposite.

An analysis of the sand in a victim's mouth might be traceable to a particular beach. It could be the chemical nature of the sand itself or any associated insects or bits of leaves, animal fur, or bird feathers that pinpoints the location of the drowning. This can be extremely important in cases where the body has been moved.

Other clues that the victim was alive when he entered the water can be found by examining the bone marrow. What could the bone marrow possibly have to do with drowning? The key lies with finding tiny creatures called **diatoms** within the marrow. Diatoms are single-celled organisms that inhabit both salt and fresh water. They have silica in their cell walls and are very resistant to degradation. If the victim's heart is still beating, any diatoms in the inhaled water will pass through the lungs, enter the blood stream, and be pumped throughout the body, where they tend to collect in the bone marrow. This means that if a microscopic analysis of the marrow reveals diatoms, the victim must have been alive at the time of water entry. Since diatoms are so resistant to degradation, this technique might be useful in severely degraded and even skeletal remains, where no lungs or sinus tissues are available for examination. Unfortunately, diatom testing is not that straightforward and is controversial.

As you can see the determination of whether a victim drowned is often a "best guess" situation. The ME might depend more on the circumstances of the death than on any autopsy or laboratory findings.

CHAPTER 10

BLOOD AND OTHER BODILY FLUIDS

Serology is the analysis of blood and other bodily fluids, such as semen, saliva, and tears. Since many crimes, from assaults to homicides, result in the spillage of blood, blood is the most common biological fluid left at a crime scene. It is also the most useful since it offers the forensic team several investigative avenues, some of which depend on blood's physical properties (how it behaves as a liquid), while others depend upon its chemical and biological behaviors.

We delve into the physical properties of blood in Chapter 14, where we will see how blood spatter analysis is used to reconstruct crime scenes, determine the sequence of events surrounding the crime, and follow the actions of the perpetrator, the victim, and often the witnesses. In this chapter we will look at the work of the **forensic serologist**, who comes in after the blood spatter analysis is completed to conduct chemical and biological tests of any crime scene or suspect blood samples.

It is worth noting that since the advent of DNA testing (Chapter 11), the serological evaluation of blood and other bodily fluids has diminished as a forensics tool. Simply put, DNA testing offers much greater individualization than does serology, yet serology remains a useful tool for the forensic scientist.

The Characteristics of Blood

Blood is a complex substance. Its liquid portion, called **plasma**, contains proteins, enzymes, clotting factors, and electrolytes, as well as three basic types of cells: **leucocytes** (white blood cells, or WBCs), **erythrocytes** (red blood cells, or RBCs), and **platelets** (tiny cells involved in blood clotting). If whole blood is allowed to clot and the clot is removed, the yellowish liquid remaining is called **serum**. It contains most of the proteins and enzymes of plasma, but none of the cells or clotting factors, which have been consumed by the clotting process.

For years, blood transfusions from one person to another weren't possible. Too often the blood would clot within the recipient's veins and death wasn't uncommon. Then, in 1901, Karl Landsteiner made one of the most important discoveries in medical history when he observed that this transfusion reaction wasn't universal. Sometimes it would occur and at other times it wouldn't. His extensive research into this phenomenon led to his discovery that human blood could be classified into 4 types, which he designated A, B, AB, and O. Landsteiner called his classification scheme the **ABO system**.

He showed that if a person received blood from a donor with the same type of blood, he was much less likely to have a reaction than if he received blood from a donor of a different type. Landsteiner's ABO system is still in use today and serves not only as the basis for all blood transfusions but also for matching blood samples in the forensic lab.

The ABO System

From a forensic point of view, the two most important components of blood are the RBCs and the serum, since these alone can determine the ABO type of a blood sample or bloodstain. On the surface of the RBCs, the cells that transport oxygen from the lungs to the tissues, are molecules called **antigens**, and it is these antigens that determine the blood type. There are only two types of antigens, designated either A or B. Type A blood has only A antigens on its RBCs, type B only B antigens, type AB both A and B antigens, and type O neither antigen.

Landsteiner also discovered another antigen in the blood, which he called the **Rhesus** or **Rh factor** because his studies were performed in Rhesus monkeys. RBCs that possess this factor are designated Rh positive and if not Rh negative. So A-positive blood possesses the A antigen and the Rh factor, while O-negative possesses neither the A nor the B antigens and no Rh factor.

The serum also contains specialized proteins called **antibodies**, termed either **anti-A** or **anti-B**, depending upon which antigen they recognize. These antibodies are highly specific in that they recognize and react with only their specific antigen and not with any other. That is, if an anti-A antibody comes into contact with an A antigen, a reaction will occur, but since it is highly specific for the A antigen it will not react with a B antigen. This reaction forms an **antigen-antibody complex**, the root cause of transfusion reactions and the basis for the blood typing procedure.

These anti-A and anti-B antibodies are found in the blood serum, but which one, if any, depends on the blood type. It would make no sense for a type A person to possess anti-A antibodies, since this would lead to an antigen-antibody reaction that could be deadly. So, the serum contains antibodies that are directed against the blood antigens that differ from the ones on its own RBCs. Blood with A antigens on its RBCs (type A blood) has anti-B antibodies in the serum (Figure 10-1), while blood with B antigens on its RBCs (type B blood) has anti-A antibodies in the serum. Blood with both A and B antigens (type AB blood) has neither anti-A nor anti-B serum antibodies, and blood with neither A nor B antigens (type O blood) has both anti-A and anti-B antibodies in the serum.

Type	Antigens on RBCs	Antibodies in Serum
A	A	Anti-B
B	B	Anti-A
AB	AB	None
O	None	Anti-A and Anti-B

Transfusion reactions occur when the recipient's serum antibodies react with the red blood cell antigens of the donor's blood. For this reason, a type A person can't receive type B blood without risking a reaction. A type A recipient has anti-B antibodies in his serum, so if he is given type B blood,

Figure 10-1

Blood type antigens and antibodies. In a person with type A blood, A antigens cover the surface of red blood cells (RBCs), while the serum contains anti-B antibodies, which would not react with the A antigens but would react with B antigens found on type B or type AB blood.

these anti-B antibodies will immediately react with the B antigens on the type B RBCs of the donor's blood. This reaction results in **agglutination**, or "clumping," of the blood cells, which in turn leads to skin rashes, kidney damage, and death.

Agglutination occurs because the serum antibodies are **bivalent**, meaning they have two reactive ends. If each end of the antibody reacts with an RBC surface antigen, it forms a dumbbell-like complex of two RBCs and one antibody. As the reaction continues, the RBCs are bound into a latticework and clump together (Figure 10-2).

Blood typing utilizes this reaction. Serum that contains antibodies is called **anti-serum** (plural is **antisera**). Serum that contains anti-A antibodies is called **anti-A serum**, and serum that contains anti-B antibodies is called **anti-B serum**. Employing these two types of antisera, blood type can be quickly determined. For example, if a given blood sample agglutinates when exposed to anti-A serum but not with anti-B serum, then the sample's RBCs contain only antigen-A and the blood type is A. If the sample reacts only to anti-B serum and not anti-A serum, it is type B. If it reacts

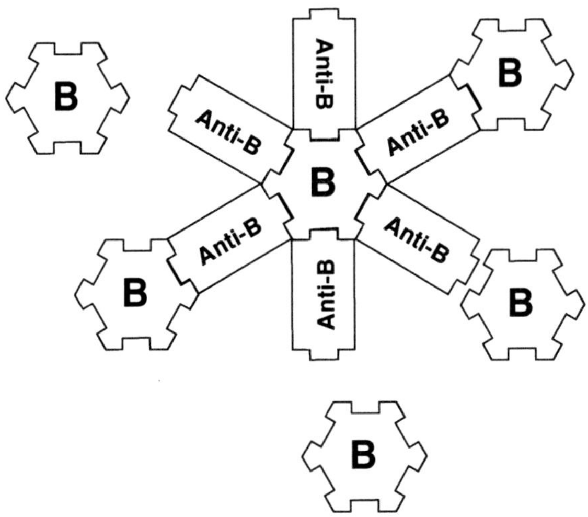

Figure 10-2
Antigen-antibody agglutination reaction. If type B blood is transfused into a type A individual, the anti-B antibodies in the recipient's serum will react with the B antigens on the surface of the donor's RBCs, causing the cells to agglutinate, or clump together.

to both, it is type AB, since this would mean that the RBCs possess both A and the B antigens. If it reacts to neither, the RBCs possess neither antigen and the type is O.

Reacts to Antisera	Blood Type
A Only	A
B Only	B
Both A and B	AB
Neither A nor B	O

Thus, the antisera contain antibodies that "test for" or react with antigens on the RBCs, and it is the antigen (or antigens) on the RBCs that determine the blood type.

This means that which antisera react with a particular blood sample will reveal which antigens are present and thus the blood type of the sample. The serologist will determine the type of each submitted crime scene and suspect sample. In situations where more than one person shed blood, this information might help with crime scene reconstruction. Such blood typing was critical to crime scene reconstruction in the famous Jeffrey MacDonald case.

At 3:40 a.m. on February 17, 1970, U.S. Army Captain Dr. Jeffrey MacDonald called the military police (MPs) to his home in Fort Bragg, North Carolina. They found MacDonald lying on his bedroom floor next to the body of his wife Colette. He wore only blue pajama bottoms, its matching top spread across Colette's chest. She had suffered multiple stab wounds. The word "pig" had been written in blood on the bed's headboard. In another room, the bodies of the two MacDonald children, five-year-old Kimberley and two-year-old Kristen, lay in pools of blood. Jeffrey MacDonald had suffered a single knife wound to his chest.

MacDonald stated that he was asleep on the living room sofa when he heard Colette screaming. He was immediately attacked by three men and a woman, who he described as hippies and who chanted, "Acid is groovy" and "Kill the pigs," while they slashed him with a knife. They tore his pajama top, which he then wrapped around his hands, using it to parry the thrusts from the knives. He was ultimately knocked unconscious and later awoke to find his family dead. He attempted mouth-to-mouth resuscitation on each of his daughters and then found Colette with a knife protruding from her chest. He removed the knife, covered her with his pajama top, and phoned the MPs.

The MPs had many concerns. Why were MacDonald's injuries minimal while his family had been slaughtered? Colette had been stabbed 21 times; Kristen and Kimberley over two dozen each. Why was the living room, where MacDonald had allegedly been attacked by four people, so neat? Only an up-ended coffee table and a turned-over flowerpot were out of place. How could MacDonald provide detailed descriptions of four assailants whom he saw only in the dark and without the glasses he typically wore? Why was the torn fingertip of a latex surgical glove found in the couple's blood-stained bed? Interestingly, the MPs found a copy of *Esquire* magazine with an article on the recent Manson family murders in the living room. In these murders, messages, including the word "pig," were also written in blood at the crime scenes.

Unfortunately, the investigation was less than perfect and evidence was lost, so charges against MacDonald were dropped. The story might have ended there, except that on December 15, 1970, MacDonald went on the

Dick Cavett Show, where he berated the military, accusing them of gross incompetence. This led to a renewed interest in Captain MacDonald.

The FBI entered the investigation and uncovered some interesting evidence. In an odds-defying coincidence, each family member had a different blood type, which allowed investigators to track their movements, particularly those of Jeffrey MacDonald. His blood was found in small quantities in only three places: on his glasses in the living room, on a cabinet where a box of surgical gloves were stored, and on the bathroom sink, where investigators believe he inflicted his own minor wound. There was neither blood nor fingerprints on the two phones MacDonald used to call for help, on the knife MacDonald said he removed from his wife's chest, or on the knife and ice pick found outside near the back door. Had they been wiped clean?

Blue fibers from MacDonald's pajamas were found everywhere. Almost. They were in the two girls' rooms and all over, around, and even beneath Colette's body. Yet, none were found in the living room where MacDonald was allegedly attacked and the shirt was ripped.

Perhaps the most damning evidence came from the FBI's crime lab. Analysts showed that the 48 holes in the blue pajama top exactly matched the 21 wounds to Colette when the garment was folded over her chest. More importantly, each of the punctures was round and smooth, indicating that the garment was stationary when the blows were struck. Had the top been in motion, as it would have been if MacDonald were using it for defense, it would have shown ragged and irregular holes.

Lastly, Colette's blood stained both halves of the torn top. When the two pieces were placed side by side, like adjacent pieces of a jigsaw puzzle, the stain pattern matched, suggesting that the stain occurred before the top was torn. This directly contradicted Captain MacDonald's statement that he had placed the top over his wife's body after it was torn.

In July 1979, nearly a decade after the murders, Jeffrey MacDonald went to trial for the triple murder and received three consecutive life terms.

Blood and the Serologist

Fresh blood is usually red, but bloodstains tend toward purple or brown and can be confused with grease, paint, chocolate, and many other materials. The color of a bloodstain depends upon its age and what conditions it has been exposed to. When the serologist analyzes a liquid sample or a stain that could be blood, she must answer three questions:

- Is it blood?
- Is it human blood?
- Whose blood is it?

If the stain isn't blood, no further testing is required. If it is blood, the serologist will then determine if it is human and, if so, will work to match it to a suspect. For blood to be useful, it must be found in sufficient amounts and in good enough condition to allow testing. If it is severely degraded by decay or damaged by heat or chemical exposure, typing and DNA profiling (Chapter 11) might be impossible.

Testing liquids and stains to determine if they are blood is not new. For centuries, the microscope has been used to visually identify blood cells, which would prove that the substance is blood. But this required liquid blood and not the typical crime scene clotted or dried blood, neither of which contains identifiable cells. Several other tests appeared in the 1800s, including the **hematin test**, developed by Polish scientist Ludwig Teichmann in 1853. This also required liquid blood since in this test the blood was mixed with acetic acid and salt crystals, heated, and then viewed under a microscope. The presence of the characteristic rhomboid crystals proved the sample was blood. This test is similar to the present-day Teichmann and Takayama tests (see below).

The **guaiacum test**, developed in 1862 by Dutch scientist Izaak Van Deen, used the guaiac resin of a West Indian shrub and is the precursor of the present-day phenolphthalein test (see below). In the guaiacum test, the blood sample was mixed with hydrogen peroxide and guaiacum and, if it was indeed blood, a blue color would appear. In 1887, a similar test was used by Sherlock Holmes to identify a bloodstain in the very first Holmes story, *A Study in Scarlet.*

Is It Blood?

When analyzing a stain, the modern serologist takes a two-tiered approach, using **presumptive** and **confirmatory** tests. Presumptive tests are cheaper and faster, and when they are negative, more expensive testing is not necessary. When positive, they indicate that blood is likely present and confirmatory testing will follow.

Presumptive blood tests yield either a **color** change (benzidine, o-tolidine, phenolphthalein, tetramethylbenzidine, and leucomalachite green) or a **fluorescent** (glowing) reaction (fluorescein and luminol).

Benzidine and o-tolidine (3.3'-dimethylybenzidine), though at one time popular, are no longed used, since in the mid-1970s each was found to be potentially carcinogenic (cancer producing). Phenolphthalein is the active compound in popular the **Kastle-Meyer color test**. The major advantage of this test is that the reaction is very quick, with the color change appearing in a minute or two. The major disadvantage is that certain vegetable products, such as potatoes and horseradish, might also cause the reaction to occur. Tetramethylbenzidine (TMB) is found in **Hemastix**, a dipstick that turns blue-green in the presence of blood. Leucomalachite green (LMG), available since the early 1900s, produces a green color when blood is present.

Fluorescent tests include fluorescein and luminol. Each reacts with the RBC's hemoglobin and will then fluoresce (glow) when exposed to ultraviolet (UV) light. At a crime scene, either is sprayed where blood is believed to be, the lights are lowered, and an ultraviolet light source is directed over the area. The glowing bloodstains that result not only suggest the presence of blood, but also define its area of distribution. Spurts, spatters, drag marks, and foot and handprints appear almost as if by magic.

Fluorescein, also available since the early 1900s, has two advantages over luminol, in that it is thicker and doesn't drip and run as readily and will more readily stick to walls and other vertical surfaces, and it does not react with household bleach (as does luminol), which makes it better suited for stains that have been cleaned up. Perpetrators often scrub away bloodstains, assuming that if the blood can't be seen it can't be found. Fortunately, that's not true.

The major advantage of luminol is its extreme sensitivity. It can reveal blood that is present in extremely small amounts, as little as one part per million. With luminol, the fluorescence appears immediately and fades quickly, so photographs or videos are used to capture the images of the blood patterns.

Once one of the presumptive tests indicates that blood is likely present, a confirmatory test is used to confirm or deny that fact. **Confirmatory blood tests** include the **Teichmann test** and the **Takayama test**. Each relies on a reaction between a chemical and the hemoglobin of the RBCs, which results in the formation of crystals that are visible under a microscope. These tests work well with fresh blood as well as very old stains. The Teichmann test uses acetic acid and a chloride compound, which produce brown, rhomboid-shaped crystals in the presence of blood. The Takayama test (also called the pyridine test) results in the formation of pyridine ferriprotoporphyrin or hemochromogen crystals.

Once confirmatory testing has proven that the sample is blood, the next question is whether it is human blood or that of another species.

Is It Human Blood?

Crime scene bloodstains are most often of human origin, but not always, so the forensic serologist must determine if the blood is human or from a dog, cat, or some other animal. The technique for making this distinction dates to February 1901, when German professor Paul Uhlenhuth published a paper on his **precipitin method**. In that same year he was called on to use his new test in a famous double murder case known as the Werewolf Murders (see below).

Similar to what we saw with blood typing, the tests used for species determination are antigen-antibody reactions. The difference is that an antiserum that reacts with antigens specific to humans rather than with the A and B red blood cell antigens must be created. The resulting reaction, or lack of reaction, will determine whether the blood is human.

This process requires the creation of an antihuman serum that reacts only with uniquely human antigens. To do this, a human antigen (human blood) is injected into a rabbit or other animal, which will then manufacture antibodies against the antigen. The animal's blood, now rich in antihuman antibodies, is removed and the antiserum is isolated. This antiserum is then used to test blood samples and determine if they are from humans.

In the laboratory, if a solution containing the antihuman antiserum is brought into contact with a sample of human blood, an antigen-antibody complex is formed. This complex precipitates (falls out) of the solution and is visible along the line of contact between the two solutions. If the blood is not human, no reaction occurs and no line of precipitation is seen. The modern crime lab contains antisera to a variety of common animals such as dogs, cats, deer, cows, and sheep. Using these, the serologist can determine the species that shed the blood. The most commonly used tests are the **ring precipitin test**, the **Ouchterlony double diffusion test**, **crossover electrophoresis**, and **antihuman hemoglobin**.

In 1901, the dismembered bodies of two young boys were found on the German coastal island of Rugen. The victims had literally been ripped apart, their body parts scattered over a wide area. Their skulls had been crushed and the heart of one of the boys was missing. A bloodstained stone, believed to be the murder weapon, was found nearby. Witnesses had earlier seen Ludwig Tessnow with the boys. A search of his home turned up clothing with suspicious dark stains. Tessnow said the stains were from wood dyes that he had been using. Interestingly, he had offered the same explanation three years earlier when he was suspected in the murder and dismemberment of two young girls in Osnabruck, Germany. Even more bizarre, a local farmer said he had seen a man who looked like Tessnow fleeing from his fields after ripping the limbs from several of his sheep. At the time, these types of savage killings of humans and animals were often believed to be the work of werewolves, so they were often referred to as werewolf killings.

The police investigating the deaths of the two young boys knew of Professor Uhlenhuth's new test and asked for his help. He did indeed find wood dye on Tessnow's clothing, but he also found human and sheep blood. Tessnow was convicted and executed.

Whose Blood Is It?

Once the blood has been identified as human, the question becomes: Whose blood is it? The goal of the forensics team is to associate, or dissociate, the crime scene blood sample with a particular person. Blood typing can narrow the possibilities, but DNA is required for true discrimination (Chapter 11).

The first step in this process is to determine the sample's blood type. The technique for doing this is similar to, but slightly more complex than, the typing protocol described earlier in this chapter. Simply determining the sample's ABO blood type can narrow the suspect list and completely exonerate some suspects.

The population distribution of the four ABO types is:

O	43 percent
A	42 percent
B	12 percent
AB	3 percent

If the blood is AB, it will narrow the focus to 3 percent of the population and will exonerate any suspects with types A, B, or O. Everyone with type AB blood would remain in the suspect pool. But by adding in the Rh factor, the serologist can narrow the list further. The approximate percentages of people with the various ABO-Rh combinations are:

O-Pos.	33 percent
O-negative	8 percent
A-positive	33 percent
A-negative	7 percent
B-positive	10 percent
B-negative	3 percent
AB-positive	5 percent
AB-negative	1 percent

If the crime scene blood is AB-negative, 99 percent of the population has been eliminated as its source. But that's not the last trick the serologist has at his disposal. In addition to the A and B antigens, RBCs contain other proteins, enzymes, and antigens with such catchy names as Duffy, Kell, and Kidd, as well as the very useful **phosphoglucomutase**, or **PGM**. Each of these also has a known distribution in the population and can serve to further narrow the suspect list.

Many enzymes are **polymorphic**, meaning they come in varying forms. These polymorphic types are called **isoenzymes**. PGM comes in many different isoenzymes with at least ten of them being common. As with ABO antigens, these enzymes are inherited independently, which means that regardless of ABO type, a particular individual could have any combination of the isoenzymes of PGM. The serologist can use this fact to further narrow the list of suspects that could have left a particular bloodstain.

Let's say a stain has been found to be AB-negative and to possess PGM 2. The AB-negative blood type is found in only 1 percent of the population, and PGM 2 is found in only 6 percent of the population. Since these two factors are inherited independently, the probability of a particular individual being type AB-negative, PGM 2, is only 0.06 percent, or about 6 per 10,000, or 1 per 1,667 people. Not perfect, but better than ABO typing alone. There are several other blood enzymes and proteins that can further whittle at the suspect list, but the modern lab uses DNA analysis to make, or not make, the final match.

Paternity Testing

Paternity testing often enters the courtroom as part of civil and criminal cases. Maybe an inheritance is in question, or perhaps the murder of a pregnant female is an attempt to hide an affair, rape, or incest. Though DNA is a more definitive paternity test, quick and cheap ABO blood typing can exclude a suspect father.

Let's look at how this works, beginning with a few genetic basics. The cells of our body contain genetic material, which we call DNA. Some of this DNA is packed into units called genes, which are the basic units of inheritance. The genes are arranged on thread-like structures called **chromosomes**. Humans have 46 chromosomes that are arranged into 23 pairs. On each chromosome, each gene has its own specific location, which we call a **locus** (plural is **loci**). When the chromosomes pair up, so do these loci. This means that our genes pair up in what is called an **allelic pair**.

Each of the genes in an allelic pair can be, and usually are, different. They also often possess different "strengths." That is, one will have a greater say in the particular trait governed by the pair than will the other. We call the stronger of the two **dominant** and the weaker **recessive**. So in any gene pair, one gene might be dominant and the other recessive. Some genes are of equal strength and are termed co-dominant, meaning that they are equally powerful in their expression.

There are two other important terms to consider. **Phenotype** is how we physically appear, or how a gene is expressed. **Genotype** is what our genes are like. In blood grouping, the phenotype is simply the blood type, but this does not tell us the genotype, or what gene alleles the person actually possesses.

Our ABO blood groups (phenotypes) come in only four types: A, B, AB, O. But, for some of these types there are two possible gene pairings (genotypes). It is important to know that in this system, A and B are co-dominant while O is recessive. This means that a person who receives an A gene from one parent and an O gene from the other will have type A blood, but not type O, since the A gene is dominant.

At conception, we receive one ABO gene from each parent, and this allelic pairing of genes (genotype) determines what blood type (phenotype) we will express. The possibilities are as follows:

Phenotype	**Possible Genotypes**
A	AA or AO
B	BB or BO
AB	AB
O	OO

As you can see, individuals with type O blood must have an OO genotype. They can't possess either an A or a B gene since this would "dominate" the O gene and produce either type A or type B blood, respectively. This means that type O individuals must receive an O gene from each parent.

A type A person could have received an A gene from each parent (AA genotype) or an A gene from one and an O gene from the other (AO genotype). Since A is the dominate allele, when paired with the recessive O gene the A gene is the one that is expressed. Outwardly, AA and AO individuals would each have type A blood but genetically they would be different. One would have an AA allelic pairing and the other an AO.

From this you can see that a type A parent who is AA can give only an A gene to their offspring, since all their eggs or sperm have an A gene. But, a type A parent who is AO could give either an A or an O gene, since half their eggs or sperm would be A and the other half O. If both parents are type A, there are several possibilities for the genotype, and thus the phenotype, of their offspring:

Both parents AA:	Child must be AA
One parent AA and other AO:	Child can be either AA or AO
Both parents AO:	Child can be AA, AO, or OO

The same situation exists if both parents are type B. Simply substitute B for A in the above pairings.

If both parents are type O (genotype by definition OO), they can have only type O (genotype OO) children, since neither has an A nor a B gene to donate. For a child to be type AB, one parent must donate an A gene (AA, AO, or AB) and the other a B gene (BB, BO, or AB). If either parent is type O, they could not have an AB offspring since that parent could not pass on an A or a B gene.

Blood typing cannot verify paternity, but rather can exclude a particular individual. For example, a man with type AB blood could not father a child with type O blood. If the child in question possessed type O blood (genotype OO), the type AB man (genotype AB) would be excluded from consideration. A type A (genotype AA or AO) man could be the father, but only if he were an AO genotype. If he were AA, he would also be excluded. But, even if he is AO, he still might not be the father. He simply cannot be excluded. This is where DNA matching (Chapter 11) is employed.

In order to perform paternity testing using DNA, samples must be available from the mother, the child, and the suspected father. Two of the three won't work, but if all three are available, paternity can be established with 99 percent accuracy.

Other Bodily Fluids

Though blood is the most common biological fluid found at the crime scene, semen, saliva, and rarely vaginal fluid are also seen. During sexual assaults, the attacker's semen and saliva are commonly transferred to the victim, the victim's clothing, or nearby surfaces. Saliva can be obtained from the stamp and envelope of a threatening letter or an extortion or ransom note. Cigarette butts and food items found at crime scenes can yield saliva from which DNA can be extracted.

Of course all this requires that these stains be found and sampled. Sometimes stains are apparent; other times they are invisible. The simplest method for locating these fluid stains is with an **alternative light source** (or **ALS**), which is any light source that isn't standard ambient sun or room light. With laser, ultraviolet, and other alternative lights, these fluids will often fluoresce (glow), but if not, there are other methods available.

Let's look at how each of these biological fluids are located, identified, and analyzed.

Semen is exclusively male and consists of fluids from the seminal vesicles and the prostate gland and in most cases contains spermatozoa. The semen of men who suffer from **oligospermia** (low sperm count) or **azoospermia** (no sperm) possesses little or no sperm, as is also the case after a successful vasectomy.

At the scene of a sexual assault (Chapter 8), a search for semen should include the corpse (in cases of murder), the victim (if alive), underwear, condoms, bed sheets, mattresses, carpeting, flooring, and anywhere else the semen might have been deposited. Once the samples are collected, analysis can begin. This two-step process involves presumptive and confirmatory testing. Presumptive testing is based on the fact that semen contains a very high level of the enzyme **acid phosphatase (AP)**, while confirmatory testing relies on the presence of **spermatozoa** or **prostate-specific antigen** (**PSA** or **P30**).

Acid phosphatase, produced by the seminal vesicles and a major constituent of semen, is also found in other animals and some plants, which can at times create confusion and false positive results. Certain fruit and vegetable juices such as watermelon and cauliflower, some fungi, contraceptive creams, and even vaginal fluid itself can give a false-positive acid phosphatase test.

The most widely used presumptive test is the **Brentamine Fast Blue test**. Here the sample is collected on a moist cotton swab or piece of filter paper and then treated with a combination of alpha-naphthyl phosphate and Brentamine Fast Blue. A bright purple color that appears within two minutes is a positive result and means that semen could be present but does not absolutely prove that fact. If this test is negative, further testing isn't required, but if it is positive, confirmatory testing should follow. The two most commonly used tests are microscopic examination and PSA analysis.

Since spermatozoa are present only in semen, finding them is absolute proof that semen is present. The sample is placed on a microscope slide and treated with one of several stains, such as the combination of Nuclear Fast Red and picroindigocarmine (PIC), which stains the spermatozoa red, making them readily visible.

If no spermatozoa are seen, the examiner will then test for PSA, which is highly concentrated in semen. This test is quick and simple and, when positive, confirms the presence of semen. Though vasectomy and one of the low-sperm-count syndromes mentioned above might markedly reduce or eliminate spermatozoa from the semen, the PSA level will remain unchanged. This is because PSA is produced in the prostate gland, which lies "downstream" from where the vasectomy procedure is done. This highly specific and very sensitive procedure allows for testing of even very old semen stains, and in many cases, PSA can be detected on clothing and bedding that has been washed.

Once the presence of semen has been confirmed, the serologist will attempt to match the semen to a particular individual with ABO typing and DNA analysis. Usable DNA depends upon whether the sample is damaged or degraded, and ABO typing requires that the perpetrator be a **secretor**.

A secretor is someone who secretes his ABO proteins in other bodily fluids such as seminal fluid, saliva, vaginal fluid, and tears, while a **non-secretor** does not. This means that blood type can be determined from these fluids in secretors but not in non-secretors. Approximately 80 to 85 percent of individuals are secretors.

A secretor with type A blood will secrete type A antigens in his or her bodily fluids. Blood type B persons secrete type B antigens, blood type AB individuals secrete both A and B antigens, and persons with type O blood as well as all non-secretors secrete neither. So the finding of neither A nor B antigens means the person was either type O or a non-secretor. It is important to note that secretor status has no bearing on DNA testing, since DNA can be obtained from these fluids in both secretors and non-secretors.

Let's suppose that a rape victim is a secretor of type B, while the prime suspect is a secretor of type A. If testing of the victim's vaginal swab shows only type B antigens, these could have come from the victim, the perpetrator, or both. The prime suspect, who is a type A secretor, is not the perpetrator, as he would have left behind type A antigens. The police must now search for a suspect that is type B, type O, or a non-secretor since the perpetrator must have left behind either B antigens (type B) or no antigens at all (type O or non-secretor status). In the latter case, the B antigens found would be from the victim.

Similarly, if the victim is a type A secretor and the vaginal swab reveals types A and B, the perpetrator must be either type B or type AB. He cannot be type O or a non-secretor, since the type B antigen could not have come from the victim and must have come from the attacker. If the victim is type O and no antigens are found in the vaginal smears, then the perpetrator must be either type O or a non-secretor. If he were a secretor of type A, type B, or type AB, he would have left antigens behind.

Thus, secretor antigen matching is similar to blood typing. It can eliminate someone but cannot conclusively identify a particular person as the assailant. This requires DNA testing (Chapter 11).

Time Since Intercourse

The timing of sexual intercourse or rape is often critical in criminal proceedings since this determination can implicate or exonerate a suspect. But, can the time lapse since intercourse be accurately determined? Only in the broadest sense and only in some situations.

In living victims, sperm remains motile for 4 to 6 hours, and only rarely up to 12 to 24 hours, so if motile sperm are found in vaginal swabs, the sexual act likely occurred less than 6 hours earlier. After that, the sperm die and begin to fragment. First the tails are lost, leaving behind **sperm heads**, followed by further fragmentation and destruction. The survival of sperm heads and sperm remnants is extremely variable, but in general these remain in the vagina for up to 6 or 7 days, the rectum for 2 to 3 days, and the mouth less than 24 hours. In cases of rape-homicide, sperm fragments might remain in the vagina of the corpse for one to two weeks. The ME can use this information to make a "best guess" of when the act occurred.

Why is the timing of intercourse so important? Suppose a woman accuses a man she had been dating of rape. She goes to the police and states that he came to her house and forced her to have sex just two hours earlier. The man states they last had sex two days earlier and that it was consensual. If the rape exam reveals motile sperm, her story holds, but if only heads and fragments are found, her story comes into question and his story is confirmed. Mostly. What if he raped her but did not ejaculate or used a condom? There would be no fresh sperm, only that left from two days earlier. Rape or no rape? Forensic science can't resolve this. Only a judge and jury can.

Vaginal fluid detection is difficult but might be important in non-ejaculatory rapes and penetrations with foreign objects. Swabs taken from the suspect's penis or from any suspected foreign object can be tested for evidence of vaginal fluid. The epithelial cells that line the vagina are rich in the starch **glycogen**, which when stained with **periodic acid-Schiff (PAS)** reagent take on a bright magenta color. If such cells are found on the suspect's penis or on the rape object, vaginal fluid could be present.

A major problem with this test is that it can be falsely negative. The reason is that not all vaginal epithelial cells contain glycogen. Cells from young girls before menarche contain none and those from post-menopausal women rarely do. Also, the amount of glycogen found in these cells varies with the stage of the woman's menstrual cycle. This means that a positive test is very helpful but a negative one does not necessarily mean that vaginal fluids aren't present.

Saliva has been recovered from everything from stamps to food to bite marks. It can often reveal ABO blood type in secretors as well as DNA for profiling. Saliva is rich in the digestive enzyme **amylase**, and this enzyme is the basis for testing for saliva at a crime scene. There is no confirmatory test for saliva, but the two most common presumptive tests employ iodine and the Phadebas reagent.

The **Phadebas reagent** is an insoluble complex composed of a starch bound to a dye molecule. This complex is not soluble so that when placed in a liquid it will not dissolve and will not impart any color to the liquid. Amylase breaks down the complex and releases the dye, which is soluble and will add color to the liquid. The more amylase that is present, the more dye that is released, and the darker the liquid medium will become. The degree of color change is measured by a **spectrophotometer**, which is an instrument that accurately measures color changes in liquids. The greater the color change, the higher the concentration of amylase in the sample and the more likely that it is saliva.

CHAPTER 11

DNA

To say that DNA profiling has altered the landscape of criminal investigation would grossly understate its importance. Its usefulness stems from its ubiquitous nature and unique structure. It is found in many materials commonly shed at crime scenes: blood, semen, saliva, sweat, tears, skin cells, hair follicles, and many other human tissues. Other than fingerprints (Chapter 13), it is the only evidence that allows for absolute individualization, since no two people, except identical twins, share the same DNA. Identical twins possess the same DNA but different fingerprints.

Our understanding of DNA and its uses in both medicine and forensics is an evolving field. It is a complex subject, but in this chapter I will attempt to simplify it and hopefully give you some degree of understanding of its impact on the world of forensics.

The Structure of DNA

DNA (deoxyribonucleic acid) is the body's instruction manual. Within it lie the genes that determine height, size, eye and hair color, intelligence level, musical ability, and virtually everything else that makes each of us individual. DNA itself is inert, in that it does nothing except store information.

Translating this information into action depends on other molecules, such as various RNAs (ribonucleic acids) and protein enzymes.

The body is made up of approximately 60 trillion cells, a big number that looks like this: 60,000,000,000,000. Each of these cells, except for the red blood cells (RBCs) in the blood, contains a nucleus, and it is within the nucleus that the DNA resides. Some of this DNA is packaged into units called **genes**, the basic units of heredity. The genes are in turn arranged along a long structure called a **chromosome**.

Humans possess 46 chromosomes arranged into 23 pairs. These pairs are numbered 1 through 22, with the final two being the sex chromosomes, termed X and Y.

The DNA molecule is a **polymer** (long string of repeating components) of smaller molecules we call **purine bases**. Though there are many different purine bases, only four are involved in the production of DNA. These are **guanine**, **cytosine**, **thymine**, and **adenine**, which are typically referred to by their first letter: G, C, T, and A. All life is based on these four molecules.

The number of bases strung together in any given DNA strand can be in the millions and they can hook up in any conceivable order. Like a typewritten message, where letters are strung together into meaningful words and sentences, the order in which these bases are linked determine the message contained within the DNA. The highly variable nature of this pattern is what makes DNA so useful for identification.

Our DNA is **double-stranded**, meaning that it consists of paired strands of these bases that are wound together in a **double helix**, a spiral-like structure that looks like a twisted ladder (Figure 11-1). It is important to note that when these bases pair up to form a double strand, each strand is a "mirror image" of its mate. The reason is that the **rules of base pairing** dictate that C binds only with G and A only with T. It has to do with the size and shape of these bases, but digging deeper into that is not necessary for you to understand how DNA is used in the forensic world.

Using these rules, a section of double-stranded DNA might look like this:

G-C-T-T-A-C-T-A-A
C-G-A-A-T-G-A-T-T

You can see that A always lines up with T and C always with G.

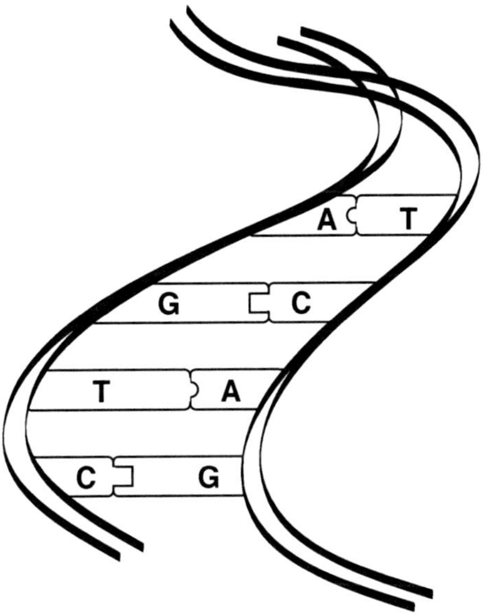

Figure 11-1
DNA double helix. The rules of base pairing dictate that cytosine (C) must pair with guanine (G), and adenine (A) must pair with thymine (T). This pairing holds the "twisted ladder" together.

The term **genome** refers to the total DNA within a cell. Each of us has approximately 6 billion bases, or 3 billion base pairs, in our DNA. Since these bases can be put together in any order, the possible base sequences for any given DNA strand is literally astronomical. This is the reason each of us is unique and the reason DNA typing (fingerprinting) in the forensics lab is so accurate.

Each DNA strand contains two different types of DNA: **genes**, which make up about 5 percent of our DNA and determine our genetic characteristics and inheritance, and what is called **non-encoded DNA**, also called **junk DNA**. Junk DNA does not directly produce any of our characteristics but it does support and affect certain gene functions. And, important to our discussion, it is the junk DNA that is of most interest to the forensic scientist.

Our genetic individuality is fixed at conception, when we receive half of our chromosomes, and thus our DNA, from each parent. Each egg and each sperm contains 23 **unpaired** chromosomes so that when they join during egg fertilization, the resulting zygote will have 23 **paired** chromosomes. This zygote then grows into the fetus. If we receive half our DNA from each parent, why aren't all siblings identical? Each child only has two parents, so how different could they be? Let's do the math.

The mother will donate one chromosome from each of her 23 pairs to each egg she produces. Which member of each pair she donates is independent of which member of every other pair she donates. If we consider each member of the 23 pairs as either A or B, she would have a chromosome 1A and 1B, chromosome 2A and 2B, and so on. Think of it as a Chinese restaurant menu with a column A and a column B. You can select from either column but you must order 23 items to fill you plate.

If all the selections came from column A, the egg would possess 23 A's. The same can be said if they all came from column B. Or half could be from each column, and these could be chosen randomly. This means that one egg could be BBAABABBBAAABBAABABABBA, while another could be BBAABBABABBBABAAABBABAA. Since each chromosome has two choices (A or B) and since they are independent of one another, the possible combinations are 2 multiplied by itself 23 times. That is, $2 \times 2 = 4$; $4 \times 2 = 8$; $8 \times 2 = 16$, etc. Do this 23 times and you'll see that the mother can produce 8,388,608 different types of eggs.

Of course, the father can produce the same number of different types of sperm. Add to this that any of these 8 million sperm types can combine with any of the mother's 8 million egg types to produce a fertilized egg, and the possibilities for the chromosomes any individual might receive become staggering. In fact, there are over 8 trillion possible combinations.

It's this diversity that allows the forensic scientist to identify a perpetrator or exonerate a suspect with such a high degree of accuracy. This discriminatory power is underlined by the famous Colin Pitchfork case.

In 1983, 15-year-old Lynda Mann was brutally raped and murdered near the rural English town of Narborough. In 1986, Dawn Ashworth, also 15, met a similar fate. Panic spread through the community, but the police investigation quickly hit a wall. In 1987, as a more or less last-ditch effort, the investigators decided to try the new technique of DNA matching, which had just been developed by Dr. Alec Jeffreys at the University of Leicester. The police believed that the killer lived and worked in the area, so they asked that all males in the area submit a blood sample for testing. After screening several thousand samples, no match was made. Then a man came forward saying that a co-worker named Colin Pitchfork had persuaded him to give a blood sample in his place. A sample was then taken from Pitchfork and it matched. He confessed and was sentenced to life in prison. This was the first time that mass DNA screening had been used to solve a criminal case and is the subject of Joseph Wambaugh's book *The Blooding*.

DNA and Forensic Science

How did DNA become such a powerful forensic science tool?

DNA was discovered by Swiss biologist Friedrich Miescher in 1868, but many years passed before its purpose was revealed. In 1943, while working with bacteria, Oswald Avery, Colin MacLeod, and Maclyn McCarty discovered that DNA carried genetic information, and then in 1953, James Watson, Francis Crick, and Maurice Wilkins discovered the double-helical structure of the DNA molecule. Further study revealed that all humans, and indeed all primates, share approximately 98 percent of the genome. This means that 98 percent of your DNA is the same as everyone else's as well as that of the chimpanzees in your local zoo. If this is the case, how can DNA be used to distinguish one person from another? The key is the other 2 percent.

In 1984, Alec Jeffreys and his associates at the University of Leicester discovered that portions of each person's DNA were unique. By using special **restriction enzymes**, which cut DNA into shorter pieces, they found that certain areas of this long DNA molecule exhibited **polymorphism** (many different forms). This DNA polymorphism is found in our non-encoded "junk" DNA. These areas are highly variable in length and base sequence and are unique in each of us. It is the analysis of these areas that allows discrimination of one individual from another. Shortly after discovering this polymorphism, Jeffreys developed a process for isolating and analyzing these areas of human DNA. He termed this analysis **DNA fingerprinting**.

Jeffreys employed restriction enzymes to cut out certain sections of this DNA. These segments are called **loci** (singular is **locus**). Within these loci he found that certain base sequences constantly repeated. Since these are of variable length and repeat along the length of the DNA strand a variable number of times, they are called **variable number tandem**

repeats (VNTRs). To analyze these VNTRs he developed a process called **restriction fragment length polymorphism (RFLP)**. This is the oldest method for DNA fingerprinting and yields the familiar "bar code" DNA pattern (Figure 11-2). The major problem with RFLP is that it requires a rather large DNA sample that is of good quality.

DNA analysis dramatically changed in the early 1990s with the introduction of the **polymerase chain reaction (PCR)** and **short tandem repeats (STRs)**. PCR takes advantage of the method by which double-stranded DNA replicates (copies) itself in nature through a technique called **amplification**. This allows for repeated copying of the DNA in a sample so that a larger quantity of identical DNA can be made. It requires as little as a billionth of a gram of DNA to produce an essentially unlimited amount. This solved the problem of very small crime scene samples. In fact, by employing the PCR technique, only a single cell is needed to supply enough DNA for analysis. This means that usable DNA can often be obtained from a licked stamp, the rim of a cup or can, a bitten food item, a cigarette butt, a tear, and even a fingerprint, which consists of grime, skin oils, and cellular debris. The person's DNA is found among this cellular debris.

STRs are very short repeating sequences of DNA that are three to seven bases long, as opposed to the very long sequences of VNTRs, which

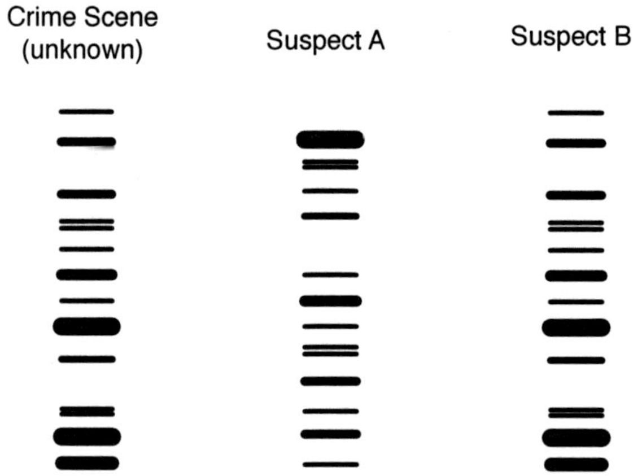

Figure 11-2

DNA fingerprint. The RFLP method results in columns of bands that can be compared with other samples. In this case Suspect B matches the crime scene sample, while Suspect A does not.

can be hundreds of bases long. Their short sequence, multiple polymorphic types, and frequent repetition make them highly discriminatory and useful when the DNA sample is partially degraded or fragmented.

For this reason, VNTR and the RFLP testing method have been supplanted by the combination of PCR and STR, which has become the standard in most labs. The advantages are many. It requires much smaller samples and is much faster and more reliable than RFLP. It can more easily be automated so that many samples can be processed in a very short period of time. Using PCR and STR analysis allows samples to be analyzed in a few hours in some cases, as opposed to a month or more using RFLP. Also, there are many more known STRs than there are VNTRs, which gives the forensic scientist more repeats to analyze.

Though the old bar code profile can be generated by the PCR-STR method, this more automated analytic system displays the STR peaks on a graph. The process of comparison is similar in that if all the peaks of the graph obtained from the analysis of two different DNA samples are identical, then the two samples share a common source (Figure 11-3).

The future of DNA testing might lie in **single nucleotide polymorphism (SNP)**, where the level of differentiation falls to a single base. We saw that RFLP fragments were fairly long, a drawback that lessens their value in degraded or damaged samples (see below). This problem was circumvented by the discovery of STRs, which are very short fragments. But, what if the DNA examiner could use single nucleotide bases as the standard

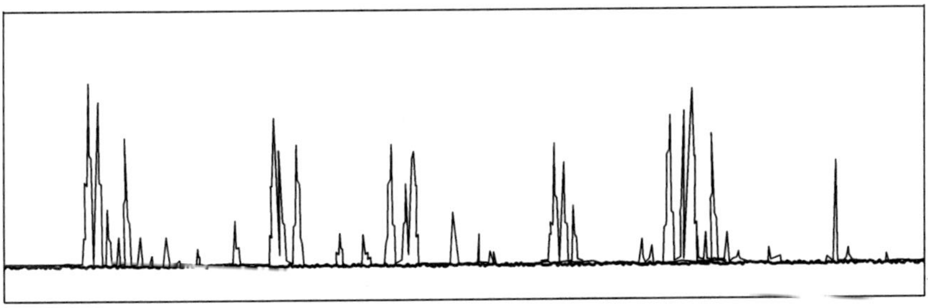

Figure 11-3
DNA graph. STR graph obtained with combination of PCR and STR analysis.

for matching? This would increase the discriminatory power of DNA even further. This is what SNP does.

Let's say that two sequenced DNA strands looked like this:

CGATTACAGGATTA

CGATTACAAGATTA

If we searched for an STR repeat that was ATTA, these two strands would be indistinguishable, since both have two ATTA repeats. But, with single nucleotide analysis the strands differ by a single base: the ninth base in the first sequence is guanine (G), while it is adenine (A) in the second one.

SNP can be used with PCR amplification and can be easily automated, theoretically allowing for discriminating two DNA samples based on a single nucleotide difference. The major problem at present is that it is expensive and most labs are not equipped for this analysis.

DNA Matching: A Numbers Game

Since the current standard is STR analysis, exactly how do STRs work?

We each possess our own unique DNA and we receive half of this DNA from each of our parents in the form of paired chromosomes, one coming from each parent. Our DNA, which makes up our chromosomes, is also paired. And since each of these DNA strands possesses STRs, we receive STRs from both parents. Earlier we saw that there were over 8 trillion possible chromosomal combinations for the child of any two parents. The same goes for STR patterns.

This means that each of us will have a variable number of STRs in any given locus on each of our DNA. Since the number of any given STR at any given locus can be determined, and since the number of STRs at that locus varies from person to person, we can use these facts to determine whether any two DNA samples share a common source. That is, did they come from the same person?

In addition, if we know how often a given number of STR repeats is found at a locus in the general population, we can use this information to calculate the odds that the two DNA samples came from the same person. This is similar to what we saw with ABO blood typing (Chapter 10), where blood type AB eliminated 97 percent of the population. A single locus of STR analysis can work similarly.

How conclusive is a match from a single locus? Not very, but if the test is repeated from several locations, the odds add up quickly.

Let's say we examine a single locus on two DNA samples for a 4 base-long STR such as ATTA. The crime scene sample shows that this STR repeats 6 times on one chromosome (one DNA strand received from one parent) and 11 times on its paired chromosome (the other DNA strand received from the other parent). On the suspect sample, we see this STR repeat 5 times on one chromosome and 21 times on the other. Based on this single locus we can conclude that these two samples came from different people and thus that the suspect is not the one who left that DNA sample at the crime scene. No further testing is needed to exclude him.

But what if the two samples matched? What if each had STR repeats of 6 and 11? What would that tell us? Not much, since this would be only one locus. Let's say that that pattern, 6 and 11, was found in 2 percent of the population. This locus would eliminate 98 percent of all people but would not eliminate the suspect since he possessed this pattern. But what if we then looked at a dozen loci and they all matched? What are the odds that two people would have received the exact number of repeats from each parent at each of these loci? That would happen in only 1 of literally trillions of conceptions. This means that no two people have the same pattern of STR repeats and thus no two people possess identical DNA.

For example, let's say we analyzed the STRs of a crime scene sample at 5 different loci and found these repeats at these loci:

Locus 1	14 and 3
Locus 2	7 and 11
Locus 3	2 and 16
Locus 4	15 and 8
Locus 5	1 and 13

Now let's say we know that the occurrence of each of these STR repeat patterns at these loci in the general population is 1 percent, 3 percent, 2 percent, 1 percent, and 2 percent, respectively. This means that 1 in 100 people share this same repeat pattern at locus 1, 3 in 100 share this same repeat pattern at locus 2, and so on. If a suspect's DNA and DNA obtained at the crime scene show the exact same repeat patterns at all 5 loci, what are the odds that the DNA found at the scene came from someone other than the suspect? Since the inheritance of the STR patterns at each locus is independent of any other locus, the percentages (fractions) must be multiplied by each other:

$$1/100 \times 3/100 \times 2/100 \times 1/100 \times 2/100 = 12/10{,}000{,}000{,}000$$
or 12 out of 10 billion

This means that there are only 12 chances out of 10 billion, or roughly one in a billion, that the DNA found at the crime scene came from someone other than the suspect. And this was using only 5 loci. The FBI database currently uses 13 loci, and they are exploring expanding this to more. Now, imagine if the suspect's DNA matched the crime scene sample at 13 loci. We would be looking at odds in the one per trillions. Or put another way, if the STR count at all 13 loci in a crime scene sample match the count at the same 13 loci of the suspect sample, what are the odds that the crime scene sample came from someone other than the suspect? Astronomical would be the word.

So, DNA is a numbers game. The more loci used, the greater the odds that two matched samples share the same source becomes.

Degraded DNA

All this clever testing requires a good DNA sample. If it is degraded (damaged and broken by heat, chemicals, decay, or some other process), it might prove worthless for testing. Since DNA fingerprinting depends on counting the number of repeated sequences in a given locus of the DNA strand, it should be obvious that if the DNA is already broken up, such a count becomes impossible. You can't simply put the strand back together and then count. Severely degraded DNA, which has been broken into small fragments, is of little value, but what if it is only partially degraded and the surviving fragments are fairly long?

STR analysis can still be used in many such situations. Since STRs are much shorter than VNTRs and require less lengthy DNA segments for their location and counting, the likelihood that the pattern will be disrupted is much less when STRs are used. It is for this reason that STR analysis is the norm for DNA fingerprinting. And why SNP analysis, which looks at individual bases, might someday become the standard.

Still, if the sample is severely degraded and the lab has only a pile of very short fragments or single bases to work with, no typing can be done. Not even STR. It would be like trying to read a book in which all the sentences had been reduced to fragments and single words—*For Whom the Bell Tolls* might be indistinguishable from *The Cat in the Hat*. However, if the book were only torn into chapters, we would have little trouble distinguishing between the two. A partially degraded DNA sample would be the latter situation, while a severely degraded sample would be the former.

But, you can also see that with good-quality DNA samples, DNA typing is highly accurate, and when analyzed properly, its discriminatory power is absolute. It will not give false results. It will give either a match or no match, but it will not point the finger of suspicion in the wrong direction.

Locating DNA

Of course to use DNA as a forensic tool it must be located. Without a usable sample the crime lab will have nothing to work with. DNA is found in virtually every tissue and fluid in the human body, many of which are shed at crime scenes. Things like blood, semen, urine, saliva, tears, hair, bone, teeth, and tissues such as skin can yield usable DNA. Let's look at these common sources in more detail.

Blood: The red blood cells (RBCs) of the blood have no nuclei, so they have no DNA, but the white blood cells (WBCs) do. When the lab extracts DNA from blood, it is the WBC DNA that is isolated for testing.

Semen: Semen has DNA within the spermatozoa. But what if the person is azoospermic (produces no sperm) or has had a vasectomy? No sperm, no DNA. But, the epithelial cells that line the urethra have nuclei that contain DNA. The urethra is the channel that connects the bladder with the outside world and as the ejaculate moves along it, it collects some of the urethral cells. The DNA in these can often be used to develop a DNA fingerprint.

Urine: Urine contains no DNA, but it often contains WBCs and other cell types such as the urethral cells described above that do have DNA.

Saliva: Saliva also contains no DNA, but, as we saw above, it collects the DNA-containing epithelial cells of the salivary ducts as it passes from the salivary glands to the mouth. It also collects cells from the lining of the mouth, called the **buccal mucosa**. When a DNA mouth swab is taken from a person, these cells are collected and tested.

Tears: Like saliva and urine, tears contain no cells, but the epithelial cells that line the tear ducts do. These cells are carried out with the tears and can be a source of DNA.

Hair: Hair itself contains no nuclear DNA, but the follicle cells do. Hair that has been cut or has fallen out naturally does not typically have follicular material attached and is not likely to possess nuclear DNA. But, hair that has been yanked out will often carry follicular material with it, and this will serve as a source for nuclear DNA. Still, the hair shaft itself contains a useful, special type of DNA called **mitochondrial DNA** (discussed later in this chapter).

Bone: Bones are not just the body's inert framework, but rather are living and active tissues. They grow and repair themselves when necessary. This is possible because bones have cells called osteocytes, and these cells contain DNA. DNA can be extracted from bones, sometimes those that are thousands of years old.

Teeth: Teeth are very hardy and are typically the last part of the body to dissolve away. The hard enamel contains no cells, but it protects the pulp cells, allowing them to survive for many years, even under adverse conditions. Drilling into the teeth of even very old skeletal remains can sometimes yield usable DNA.

Skin and other tissues: The cells of our skin and other tissues contain DNA within their nuclei.

Since DNA resides within biological materials, it is subject to the same bacterially mediated putrefaction process that eventually destroys an entire corpse. For this reason, DNA-containing materials found at a crime scene must be properly handled. They should be air-dried before packaging, since failure to do so leaves behind moisture, which promotes bacterial growth. If air-drying is not possible or practical, the sample should be frozen. If not properly collected and protected, DNA can degrade and become unusable.

How much DNA is needed? Obviously the more the better, but by employing the PCR technique, even very small samples can yield enough DNA for analysis. A single hair with a follicle from an old hairbrush; a single tear or drop of blood; saliva in a bite mark or on a toothbrush, postage stamp, or envelope, or on food materials from hamburgers to chicken bones to cola cans; the face-side of the perpetrator's mask, telephones, pens and pencils; a single fingerprint (known as **Touch DNA**, discussed in Chapter 13); or even a tooth from a 1000-year-old mummy have each yielded usable DNA. Human DNA has even been extracted from maggots found on a decaying corpse up to 4 months after death.

Two famous cases show how very small and very old samples of DNA can be used to reach a conviction: the Brown's Chicken Massacre and the Green River Killer. Each case also parallels the advancements in DNA testing over the past 20 years.

On the evening of January 8, 1993, two assailants robbed Brown's Chicken and Pasta Restaurant in Palatine, Illinois. They got away with around $2,000, but before they left they herded the seven employees into a walk-in cooler and executed them. The police had no suspects and the case went cold for nine years until 2002, when a girlfriend of one of the killers implicated him. During the original investigation, a partially eaten piece of chicken had been found in a trash bin and police theorized that the killers had had a meal while waiting for the restaurant to empty of customers at closing time. The chicken remained frozen in the cooler so that in 2002 it was tested. DNA obtained from saliva found on the chicken matched Juan Luna. Ultimately Luna and his partner James Degorski were convicted and given life sentences.

The Green River Killer received this moniker because he dumped his mostly prostitute victims along the Green River near Seattle, Washington. Between 1982 and 1991, nearly 50 murders were attributed to this killer. The suspect list developed by the task force assigned to the cases was nearly as long.

On April 8, 1987, police executed a search warrant on the premises of one of the suspects, Gary Ridgeway. After obtaining several bags of evidence from his house they requested that he undergo a polygraph, but Ridgeway refused. They then asked for a saliva sample and Ridgeway complied by biting on a small square of surgical gauze.

Unfortunately, most of the victims weren't found until they had severely decayed or been reduced to skeletons, so semen samples were available from only a very few of the victims. These samples were very small, and if the then current RFLP testing procedure had been employed it would have consumed the entire sample, leaving nothing to test against future suspects if no match to Ridgeway was found. So the samples, as well as Ridgeway's saliva, were stored. In the mid-1990s, the combination of STR and PCR analysis appeared and by 2000 these became the accepted standard.

In 2001, this technique was used to test Ridgeway's saliva sample, obtained in 1987, with the PCR-amplified semen samples taken from Opal Mills, Marcia Chapman, and Carol Christensen, each killed in 1982 or 1983. A match was made and Gary Ridgeway was arrested and charged with four of the Green River killings. However, this case took a dramatic and controversial turn on November 5, 2003, when Ridgeway pleaded guilty to 48 murders in exchange for a sentence of life without the possibility of parole, thus sparing himself a possible death sentence.

These cases show that if DNA samples are properly collected and stored, they can remain useful for decades. It also emphasizes the fact that science progresses. Without the discovery of the PCR-STR technique and its replacing the old RFLP method, Luna, Degorski, and Ridgeway might never have been convicted of their crimes.

Also, without these advances, many cold cases might never have been solved and many erroneous convictions might never have been overturned. It seems that hardly a week goes by that some case from 30 years earlier is solved or that someone previously convicted of a rape or murder is freed when modern DNA testing enters the picture.

And it works both ways. Some criminals attempt to use DNA testing to cast doubt on their deserved conviction. Anthony Harold Turner of Milwaukee is an interesting example.

In 1999, Turner was convicted of rape after DNA obtained from three victims matched his DNA with a probability of 3 trillion to 1. Turner claimed he was a self-educated DNA expert and denied that the DNA was his, suggesting that the crime scene samples must have come from someone with the exact same DNA. Since Turner had no twin brother, he was convicted. But, as he was awaiting sentencing a woman came forward saying that she had been raped. Imagine the prosecutors' surprise when the DNA obtained from this victim also matched Turner, who was safely tucked away in jail. How could this be?

It turned out that some members of Turner's family had paid the woman $50 to claim that she had been raped. Where did the semen used to stage the fake rape come from? Through a family member, Turner managed to smuggle it from jail in a small ketchup packet.

Never underestimate the cleverness of criminals.

But even without such shenanigans, DNA testing can become confusing in some medical entities. **Bone marrow transplants** and **chimerism** are examples.

As odd as it might sound, there are some people walking around with another person's DNA in their blood. This was pointed out in a case worked by Abirami Chidambaram of the Alaska State Scientific Crime Detection Laboratory in Anchorage. Semen obtained from a rape victim matched that of a man who was in jail on another charge at the time of the alleged rape. The investigation revealed that years earlier the man had received a bone marrow transplant from his brother. This meant that he and his brother, who was not an identical twin, now shared the same DNA in their blood. This also meant that the finger of suspicion for the rape was now directed at the brother. Of course, identical twins share the same DNA pattern, but how is it possible that these two non-identical (fraternal) twin brothers shared the same DNA in their blood cells?

Bone marrow transplants are typically done in patients suffering from certain types of leukemia or some other blood disease. The patient is given chemotherapeutic agents that completely wipe out all his native bone marrow cells, and then bone marrow from a compatible donor is infused into the patient's vein. The bone marrow material migrates to the patient's bone marrow, sets up shop, and begins cranking out blood cells. This means that the circulating blood cells now have the DNA of the donor's marrow and not that of the patient.

This confusion can be resolved if the forensic DNA examiner tests other cells from the patient. Buccal cells, or cells from any other tissue in his body, will reflect his native DNA and will not match the DNA profile of his own blood. A bone marrow transplant does not change the DNA in all the recipient's cells, only those of his bone marrow and blood. So a person who has had a bone marrow transplant will have two different DNAs: the DNA in his blood will match that of the donor and the DNA everywhere else will be his own native DNA.

Chimerism is a rare genetic condition that can cause similar confusion. In Greek mythology, the Chimera was composed of parts from various animals. Descriptions of this creature vary but an example would be one with a lion's head, goat's body, and a snake's tail. In humans, a **chimera** results from the abnormal combination of two or more fertilized (and at times unfertilized) eggs. A little basic genetics will explain this.

Fraternal twins come from two separate eggs and sperm cells. They are as different as if they had been born years apart and are twins only because they share the same womb at the same time. **Identical twins** come from a single egg and sperm. After the egg is fertilized, it begins to divide to produce more identical cells. After the first division, if the two **daughter cells** separate and each then goes on to develop a separate fetus, the two fetuses will have the exact same DNA and will be identical twins.

A chimera is formed when two fertilized eggs (each egg different and each fertilized by a different sperm cell as in fraternal twins) join together and then go on to produce a single fetus. Here, since the fetus is the result of two eggs and two sperm cells, the child will have two different types of DNA. It's as if two fraternal twins were blended together into one person, which is essentially what happens. As you might guess, the chimeric individual would have two distinct DNA patterns. Some tissues might have one DNA, other tissues might have the other, and still others might exhibit a combination of the two DNAs. For example, the blood could have one DNA, the liver the other, and the buccal mucosa both.

This could greatly confuse DNA testing.

Testing Paternity

We saw in Chapter 10 how ABO blood typing can be used to exclude paternity but cannot absolutely state that the man in question is the father of the child. To establish paternity, DNA is used. This technique requires DNA from the mother, the child, and the suspected father. Two of three won't work.

As explained earlier, we get all of our DNA from our parents and no DNA from any other source. This means that a child possesses a DNA pattern that is a combination of that from its mother and its father. This doesn't mean that the child will have every DNA band or peak that each parent possesses, but it does mean that the child cannot have a band or peak that neither parent has. Where would it come from?

In paternity testing, a DNA profile of the mother and the child are created and then compared to the profile of the suspected father. If the child possesses a DNA fragment that is not present in either the mother or the suspected father, then the man is not the child's parent. This fragment must have come from someone else (the real father), and paternity for the suspect father is excluded (Figure 11-4).

Sometimes paternity testing can help solve murders, as in the Ian Simms and A. J. Kelly cases.

On February 9, 1988, Helen McCourt, a 22-year-old insurance clerk in the small village of Billinge in northwest England, disappeared. She had stopped at the George and Dragon, a local pub owned by Ian Simms, to whom she might have had a romantic link. Witnesses reported hearing screams from the pub and when police confronted Simms he had several scratches on his face.

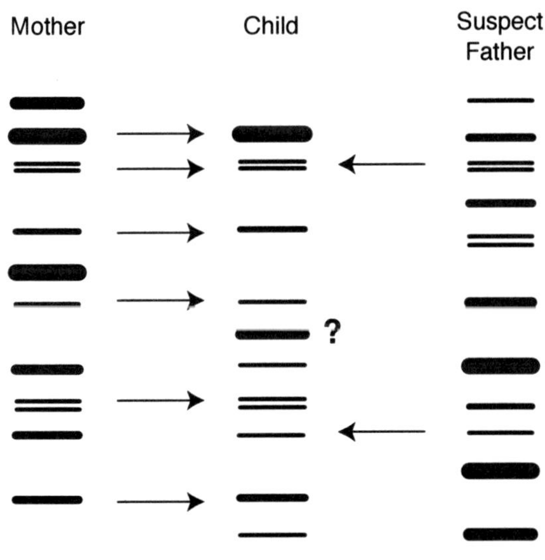

Figure 11-4

DNA paternity testing. Every band in the child's DNA fingerprint must match a band from one or the other parent. If the child possesses bands that did not come from either the mother or the suspect father, the suspect father cannot be the child's parent and paternity is excluded. In this example, the child possesses a band that is not found in either the mother or the suspect father so the suspect did not father the child.

Investigators uncovered a great deal of evidence: hair matching McCourt's and one of her bloody earrings in Simms's car; bloodstains on the stairway and the bedroom floor of Simms's home; and, in various areas of the county, McCourt's blood-stained coat and clothing, which also held hairs from Simms's dog and fibers from his carpet. They also found a length of electrical cord that bore strands of McCourt's hair. But McCourt's body was never found.

The problem the investigators faced was proving that the blood in Simms's apartment was McCourt's. With no body, they turned to the girl's parents. Samples taken from her mother and father were matched against the blood found at Simms's home. At trial, Dr. Alec Jeffreys, the father of DNA fingerprinting, testified that the odds the blood from Simms's apartment came from someone other than the daughter of the two parents was 14,500 to one. Simms was convicted and received a life sentence.

A. J. Kelly almost got away with it. He apparently repeatedly molested the 11-year-old daughter of his girlfriend and then terrorized her into silence. When the child became pregnant, A. J. denied involvement despite suspicions to the contrary.

Then A. J. got lucky. The child was stillborn and cremated. A. J. was off the hook. Until he and his girlfriend got into a domestic altercation that involved the police. In the heat of the moment the woman shouted that A. J. had had sex with and impregnated her daughter, who was now thirteen. This got the attention of the police. But what could they do? The stillborn child had been cremated, so DNA wasn't available and without it paternity could not be proven.

Then A. J. got very unlucky. The University of Nebraska Medical Center, where the young victim had gone when she suffered the stillbirth, always kept tissue samples for stillbirths in case they might offer some clue as to why the fetal death occurred. Testing this retained tissue, along with DNA samples from A. J. and the girl proved that A. J. was the father. He was convicted of first-degree sexual assault.

Familial DNA

Though each person possesses his own DNA pattern, there are many commonalities among close relatives, such as between siblings and between parents and their children. This closeness can't make an exact ID, but if a crime scene sample is very similar to a given suspect, it might mean that the person who left behind the DNA is a close relative of the suspect—maybe a brother or sister, or a parent, or a first cousin. So even though the suspect is exonerated as the sample donor, his close relatives will come under greater scrutiny.

This is a controversial technique, since many feel that it is an invasion of privacy to test relatives based on "similar" DNA. Others feel that this is simply another tool to find and bring to justice the perpetrator of a crime. Let's say that a man is accused in a rape-murder, and when the semen sample obtained from the victim is tested, it reveals that the crime scene DNA is similar but not identical to the suspect's DNA profile. He is exonerated but his brother, or father, or first cousin, will enter the suspect pool. Testing each of these individuals might turn up an exact match and the crime might be solved.

This technique recently resulted in the conviction of the serial killer known as the Grim Sleeper. It was the first time familial DNA was employed to solve a homicide in the United States.

The Grim Sleeper was the moniker attached to a serial killer who operated in the 1980s, took a 13-year break from his killings, and then resurfaced in 2002. The name came from his often-long periods of inactivity between killings, as if he were asleep. Then in 2010, Christopher Franklin was arrested on a felony weapons charge and his DNA entered the system. His profile was found to be similar to but did not exactly match DNA obtained in some of the Grim Sleeper's murders. This led police to focus their investigation on Christopher's close relatives, including his father, Lonnie. They followed him until they were able to collect a discarded, partially eaten slice of pizza. DNA found on the pizza matched the crime scene DNA. Lonnie was arrested and convicted, bringing an end to the Grim Sleeper.

Mitochondrial and Y-Chromosomal DNA

So far, we have discussed the uses of nuclear DNA, that is, the DNA that resides within the nuclei of our cells. But, the body also has non-nuclear forms of DNA that are useful to the forensic scientist: mitochondrial and Y-chromosomal DNA.

The DNA used for standard DNA testing is nuclear DNA, and it can be extracted from any nucleated cell. But, cells also contain non-nuclear DNA within the **mitochondria**, which are small organelles that reside within the cytoplasm of the cell and supply energy for cellular functions. Each cell contains many mitochondria.

Mitochondrial DNA (mtDNA) has several characteristics that make it unique. It is passed from generation to generation by the maternal lineage, mutates rarely, is found in places where nuclear DNA doesn't exist, and is exceptionally hardy.

Your mtDNA is inherited unchanged from your mother and only from your mother. And she received hers from her mother, and her mother from her mother, and so on. How does this happen?

At fertilization, the egg supplies the cell and half the DNA while the sperm supplies only half the DNA (Figure 11-5). The sperm cell itself breaks down and disappears after passing along its genetic material. This means that the actual cell and all the cell components (including the mitochondria) of the developing zygote come from the mother. As the cell divides and multiplies, these mitochondria are also copied and passed on with each cellular division, so that all the cells of the body contain identical mtDNA.

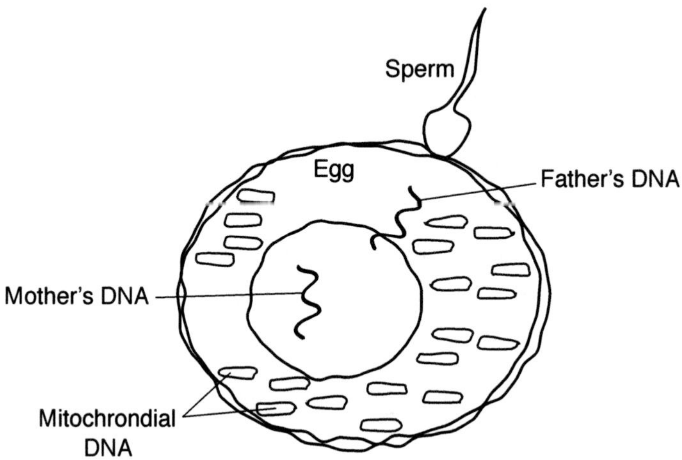

Figure 11-5

The fertilization process. At fertilization, the egg supplies half of the DNA, the cell, and all the cellular structures to the fertilized zygote, while the sperm supplies only half the DNA.

Since mtDNA undergoes a significant mutation only once every 6,500 years or so, it is unchanged over many generations. Your mtDNA is identical to that of your mother, your great-great grandmother, and your maternal ancestors from 1,000 years ago. Thus, anyone's maternal lineage can be accurately traced over many generations, and this fact can be used to prove that two people share the same maternal linage. For this reason, mtDNA is an extremely useful tool in ancestry studies. It is also useful to the forensic scientist.

Mitochondrial DNA is very hardy and can often be extracted from older tissues and from the bones and teeth of very old skeletons. It is found in some tissues, like hair, whereas nuclear DNA is not.

Hair is composed of dead cellular debris, with its only "living" part being the follicle. The cells of the follicles contain nuclear DNA, which can be used for DNA profiling, but the dead cells of the hair have no nuclei and thus no DNA. This means that hair that has been yanked out or shed with a follicular bulb attached can provide nuclear DNA, while hair that has been cut or has no bulb attached will not. This is where mtDNA can be helpful. As hair grows, the cells of the bulb multiply, undergo change where the nucleus is absorbed, and become incorporated into the growing hair. So though the hair shaft contains no nuclear DNA, it will contain mtDNA.

Let's say a couple of head hairs are found on a murder victim. The primary suspect says he doesn't know the victim and has never been in her house. He readily gives a DNA sample. Since the hairs found at the crime scene contained no bulbs, and thus no DNA, mtDNA from the hair and from the suspect's blood or buccal swab are tested and a match is found. What does this mean? It means that the hair must have come from either the suspect or a relative who shares his maternal lineage. The key is that we each share mtDNA with all of our maternal relatives. If the suspect has no brother, sister, maternal uncle, aunt, or cousin, or no other maternal relative who could have possibly been at the woman's house, the hair must have come from him. Though mtDNA is not as absolute as nuclear DNA, in a case such as this it might be enough to gain a conviction.

The first admittance of mtDNA evidence into a U.S. court occurred in *Tennessee v. Wade* in 1996. It also became important in the famous Boston Strangler case.

Who was the Boston Strangler? We all know that Albert DeSalvo was convicted of this series of rapes and murders, but was DeSalvo the real perpetrator? He confessed to many of the murders, but frequently got details wrong, raising suspicion that perhaps he did not commit all the crimes he took credit for. These types of false confessions are not uncommon with multiple murders. It seems that many of them want to "pad their resumes."

Recently, forensic science attempted to unravel this mystery beginning with the Strangler's final victim, Mary Sullivan. In October 2000, 36 years after her death, the exhumation of her body took place in Hyannis, Massachusetts. Investigators found a semen stain on her body. Tests for the presence of spermatozoa and for PSA were not possible due to degradation of the sample, but the material did contain mtDNA.

With DeSalvo dead and buried, blood was obtained from his brother Richard. Since the brothers should have identical mtDNA, matching the semen stain's mtDNA to Richard's would prove that Albert was indeed the killer. But no match was found, meaning that even though Albert DeSalvo confessed to killing Mary Sullivan, he did not. Or at least the stain found on her corpse did not come from Albert. Did he also falsely confess to other murders? Was he truly the Boston Strangler? We might never know for sure, but he was probably not Mary Sullivan's killer.

Y-chromosomal DNA analysis is a relatively new technique. The Y-chromosome is what makes males, males. It is found only in males, and a father passes on his Y-chromosome to any of his male offspring. So, similar to mtDNA coming down the maternal line, Y-chromosomal DNA is passed down the paternal lineage. By testing for STR repeats on the Y-chromosome (**Y-STR**) it is possible to show that two or more men share a common paternal ancestry. It has been shown that this technique can connect two males through their paternal genealogy across as many as 30 generations. The forensic usefulness of this technique is similar to that of mtDNA.

The CODIS System

As we will see with fingerprints (Chapter 13), in order to test the DNA of a crime scene sample against a suspect, a sample from the suspect must be available. What if there is no known suspect? Hopefully good old-fashioned investigative work will uncover a suspect or two, but if not, all is not lost. To get around this need for an identified suspect, large databases are often created so that testing a crime scene or suspect sample against the database can create the needed connection. With fingerprints it's the AFIS system, which we will look at in Chapter 13, but for DNA it is the CODIS system.

The **Combined DNA Index System (CODIS)** is a database of DNA fingerprints taken from felons and from biological fluids obtained at crime scenes such as assaults, homicides, and rapes. It began as a pilot project in 1990. In 1994, the **DNA Identification Act** authorized the FBI to set up the **National DNA Index System (NDIS)**, which became operational in 1998. This allows any CODIS-participating lab to compare DNA samples nationally.

To use the CODIS system, the DNA fingerprint of a crime scene or suspect sample is plugged into the CODIS database, where a computer will compare it against all the profiles in the system. If a match is made to a particular individual, fresh suspect samples will be taken and repeat testing in the crime lab will be done to confirm or refute the presumptive match.

Or the DNA could match DNA obtained from another crime scene and this would then serve to link the crimes. In this way evidence from two or more scenes can be considered together, and this alone might lead to the identity of the perpetrator. CODIS has already enjoyed many successes, exemplified by the Norman Jimmerman case.

In March 1989, Debbie Smith was forced from her home and into a nearby wooded area, where she was raped. Her attacker warned her that he knew where she lived and that she should not tell anyone or he would return and kill her. Debbie went to the police anyway. Blood from the prime suspect was tested against seminal DNA obtained from the victim's rape examination. No match. In 1994, Smith's neighborhood suffered a series of sexual assaults. Another suspect attracted the attention of police and again DNA analysis was undertaken. Again, no match.

Meanwhile, the state of Virginia, where Smith resided, began the process of developing a databank of DNA profiles taken from convicted felons. As new profiles were obtained, the Virginia Department of Forensic Services periodically matched these against unsolved crimes. One of these matches identified Norman Jimmerman as Debbie Smith's attacker. He was already serving time for robbery and abduction. His current sentence is 161 years.

Plant and Animal DNA

Humans aren't the only creatures that have DNA. In fact, DNA is essential for life, so all plants and animals contain DNA in the nuclei of their cells. And it is as individual in them as it is in humans. This can sometimes help solve cases.

Let's say a woman's body is found behind a building. Analysis of trace evidence from the victim and her clothing reveals a large amount of pine pollen. There are no pine trees within miles of the alley where the corpse was found. The prime suspect has a stand of pine tress on his property, leading investigators to suspect that that is the primary crime scene and the alley is a secondary dump site. The suspect denies any involvement, saying he doesn't know the victim, has never been around her, and besides pine trees are common throughout the city. A search warrant is granted and pollen samples are taken from the suspect's trees. DNA profiles are created on the various pollen samples and a match is made between the pollen found on the victim and that of a pine tree near the suspect's back patio. Not just a match to any pine tree but to this particular pine tree. This proves that the victim was near that tree at some time and most likely at the time of the murder.

This works in animal DNA, too, as in the landmark Snowball the Cat Case.

In 1994, Shirley Duguay of Prince Edward Island disappeared, her corpse turning up a few days later in a shallow grave. Also found was a leather jacket, which was soaked with her blood and dotted with white cat hairs. Her estranged husband, Douglas Beamish, owned a white cat named Snowball. DNA in blood taken from Snowball matched that of the cat hairs found at the burial site, proving that those hairs came from the Snowball and from no other white cat. Beamish was convicted, marking this case the first time that animal DNA was used to gain a conviction.

Other living things, such as bacteria and viruses, also possess unique DNA that can sometimes be used in the forensic arena. Proving that some criminals defy description and question your belief in humanity, the landmark case of Dr. Richard Schmidt marks the first time viral DNA analysis was used to gain a conviction.

In 1994, Dr. Richard Schmidt, under the guise of delivering healthcare, injected his girlfriend with blood taken from one of his HIV-infected patients. Six months later she was diagnosed with AIDS and went to the police. Sifting through Schmidt's records, investigators discovered that he had drawn blood from one of his AIDS patients on the same night that he had injected the victim. This was critical since the AIDS virus can survive only a few hours outside the human body.

The main problem facing investigators was that the HIV virus mutates often, so making a match between the virus taken from the unsuspecting source patient with that found in the victim could be problematic. Either could have mutated to the point that no conclusive match would be possible. Samples were then taken from 32 other HIV-infected individuals in the area. Testing revealed that the samples taken from the patient source and the victim's ex-girlfriend matched almost exactly, while the others did not, proving that no major HIV viral mutation had occurred in the immediate population. Schmidt was convicted of second-degree attempted murder and sentenced to 50 years.

Chapter 12

TOXICOLOGY

Toxicology is the science of drugs, poisons, and toxins. The forensic toxicologist is the scientist who deals with these substances and he, along with the toxicology laboratory, are critical components of every crime lab. Since drugs and poisons are often involved in accidental, suicidal, and homicidal deaths, this science is critical to many forensic investigations. The toxicologist is typically charged with analyzing unknown substances, evaluating drug involvement in abnormal behavior and responsibility for accidents, assessing the role of drugs or poisons in the cause and manner of death, and even testing employees in the workplace for illicit drugs.

You've no doubt heard the words *poison, toxin,* and *drug,* but what do these terms actually mean? Are they simply different ways of saying the same thing? Though you might think that a poison kills, a toxin harms, and a drug cures, these terms are indeed used almost interchangeably. The reason is that what can cure can harm, and what can harm can kill.

What Is a Poison?

If there are no real differences between a drug, a toxin, and a poison, what exactly is a poison? The basic definition of a poison is any substance that if taken in *sufficient quantities*, causes a harmful or deadly reaction. The key phrase here is "sufficient quantities," since anything and everything can be a poison.

The toxicity of any substance depends upon how much and over what time period it enters the body. Small amounts taken over a long period of time, though they can accumulate and become deadly, usually cause little harm, while a large dose taken all at once can prove deadly very quickly. For example, arsenic is a deadly poison that if taken in sufficient amounts can kill fairly quickly, but did you know that you likely have arsenic in your body right now? If you're a smoker, you have more than a little bit. The same goes for the deadly poisons mercury and cyanide. These substances are in the environment and can't be avoided, but they are in such small quantities that they cause little if any real harm.

Even water and oxygen can be poisonous. How can these two life essentials be deadly? If you drink too much water, it will severely dilute the sodium and potassium in the blood and tissues of the body, damage the kidneys, and lead to coma and death. In fact, there's a psychiatric syndrome, often associated with schizophrenia and other psychiatric disease, called **compulsive water drinking**, in which massive amounts of water are consumed and sometimes death follows. Pure oxygen, if breathed too long, will irreparably damage the lungs and will also lead to death.

The same is true for prescription medications. The heart drug **digitalis**, which comes from the foxglove plant and has been used for over a hundred years to treat heart failure and many types of abnormal heart rhythms, is a deadly poison. Too much can lead to nausea, vomiting, and death from dangerous changes in the rhythm of the heart. It's ironic that it can treat some abnormal heart rhythms while at the same time can cause other more deadly rhythms. It's all about the dose. The right dose is medication; the wrong dose is poison.

Historical Perspective

Toxicology is a relative new science even though its roots date back nearly 200 years. As with most medical and forensic scientific knowledge, the evolution from basic science to practical usefulness takes time, sometimes centuries. The typical pattern is that a new basic science discovery will enter the world of medicine and help resolve some medical problem and only then enter the forensic arena, where it is applied to criminal investigations. Arsenic is an excellent example, and the steps that led to a reliable test for arsenic are indicative of how many toxicological procedures developed.

For centuries arsenic was a common poison, but there was no way to prove it was the culprit in a suspicious death. Scientists first had to isolate and then identify **arsenic trioxide**, the most common toxic form of arsenic, in the human body and only then could arsenic poisoning become a provable cause of death. The milestones in this development were as follows:

- **1775**: Swedish chemist Carl Wilhelm Scheele isolated arsenic by employing chlorine, water, zinc, and heat to convert arsenic-containing substances into arsine gas. When this gas contacted a cold vessel, arsenic would collect on the vessel's surface.
- **1787**: Similarly, Johann Metzger showed that if an arsenic-containing substance was heated with charcoal, a shiny, black "arsenic mirror" would form on a cold plate held over the coals.
- **1806**: Valentine Rose first showed that arsenic could be uncovered in the human body when he treated the stomach contents of victims of arsenic poisoning with potassium carbonate, calcium oxide, and nitric acid, resulting in the production of arsenic trioxide. This could then be tested and confirmed by Metzger's test.
- **1813**: French chemist Mathieu Joseph Bonaventure Orfila developed a method for isolating arsenic from dog tissues, proving that ingested arsenic is distributed throughout the body. His book, *Treatise on General Toxicology*, is considered by many to be the first toxicological text and Orfila the "Father of Toxicology."
- **1821**: Sevillas used similar techniques to identify arsenic in the stomach and urine of poisoned individuals. This is marked as the beginning of the field of forensic toxicology.
- **1836**: James Marsh developed an easier and more sensitive version of Scheele's original test, in which the "arsenic mirror" was collected on a plate of glass or porcelain. The **Marsh test** became the standard and is the basis of the more modern method, the **Reinsch test**.

- **1851**: Following the lead of these earlier scientists, Jean Servais Stas, a Belgian chemistry professor, expanded the field of toxicology by developing methods for detecting opium, atropine, morphine, strychnine, quinine, and caffeine.

The work of these scientists propelled the field of forensic toxicology forward and culminated in the famous Marie Lafarge case.

Marie-Fortunée Lafarge (1816–1852) and her husband, Charles, had an unhappy and difficult arranged marriage. In 1840, Charles fell ill, and suspicions arose when it was discovered that Marie had ordered her servant and gardener to purchase a large amount of arsenic just months before Charles's illness. Marie said the arsenic was to kill rats, but several household servants said they had seen Marie mix a white powder into her husband's food. Charles died a painful death, his symptoms consistent with arsenic poisoning.

Testing of Charles's stomach contents and body tissues showed no arsenic, yet arsenic was found in the food Charles had eaten. This confusing situation stumped the experts. Then Mathieu Orfila entered the case. He retested all the materials and indeed found arsenic in Charles's body. He said the earlier tests had been improperly performed and that was why they showed no arsenic. Marie was convicted and given a life sentence.

In 1851, at least partially due to the public frenzy surrounding this case, Britain passed the **Arsenic Act**, which restricted the sale of arsenic-containing rat poisons to persons over 21 years of age.

The Modern Toxicologist

Modern toxicology deals with chemical substances and how these substances kill, harm, or alter the behavior of individuals. To this end, the forensic toxicologist is often asked to search for and analyze toxic substances in both the living and the dead and to offer his opinion as to the physiological, psychological, and behavioral effects of the toxin on the individual in question. For example, he might be asked to assess the state of inebriation of a vehicle operator who is involved in an accident or a hit-and-run, or whether an industrial accident victim was intoxicated on the job. Or he might be asked to determine if someone died from a particular drug or if the presence of a drug played a less direct role in the victim's death. This is often more difficult than it might seem.

When the toxicologist investigates a possible poisoning death, he must answer three basic questions:

- Was the death due to a poison?
- What was the poison used?
- Was the intake of the poison accidental, suicidal, or homicidal?

Not finding a drug might be just as important as finding one. Let's suppose that the toxicologist finds no drugs in someone exhibiting erratic or bizarre behavior. This might lead to a psychiatric evaluation and ultimately to a diagnosis and appropriate treatment. Or what if he finds that the driver in a vehicular accident had a low blood level of his anti-seizure medication? Could a seizure have led to the accident?

Biotransformation

Biotransformation is a big word meaning the conversion or transformation of a chemical into another chemical within the body. We also call this **metabolism** and the new product a **metabolite** or **breakdown product**. This process is simply the body destroying or breaking down chemicals and excreting them from the body. This is true of all chemicals that enter the body and is the reason most medications must be taken each day. The medication is designed to treat some medical problem but to the body it is also a foreign toxin and as such must be metabolized and excreted. So, you have to take another dose day after day to keep the blood level of the medication in the therapeutic range (see below).

For the toxicologist this means that in many cases he doesn't directly test for the drug in question but rather for one of its metabolites. Most often the metabolism of a drug or toxin deactivates it and prepares it for elimination from the body, usually by way of the kidneys. For example, many chemicals are not soluble in water, which means they aren't soluble in urine either. The body gets around this by converting (metabolizing) the chemical into a new chemical (metabolite) that is water-soluble, which can then be filtered through the kidney, into the urine, and out of the body.

Most metabolites are **inactive**, or inert, in that they possess no biological activity, while others are **active**. These active metabolites might possess biological properties that are weaker, stronger, or substantially different from the original compound. For example, cocaine is metabolized into three metabolites: norcocaine, which possesses active properties, and benzoylecgonine and methylecgonine, which are inert. Injected heroin, which is made from morphine, is immediately converted back into morphine, the chemical that gives the user the "high." Since both cocaine and heroin are metabolized to new compounds very quickly, testing for either would be useless. Instead, the toxicologist tests for their metabolites; finding them proves that the parent drug had been present.

Visible Signs of Poisoning

Poisoning has been a popular means for homicide for centuries. Socrates was given hemlock, Pope Clement VII death cap mushrooms, and Lucrezia Borgia supposedly employed arsenic and other poisons against her enemies, though this remains controversial. In France, arsenic was so popular that it became know as a *poudre de succession* (inheritance powder).

The main reason killers choose poisoning as their weapon of choice is that, unlike knives and arrows, poisons cause no visible changes in the body, either in the living person or at autopsy. In the days before toxicology testing existed, the poisoner "got away with it" more often than not. If the true cause of death could not be determined, how could anyone be held responsible?

But some toxins do leave behind visible signs. Corrosive chemicals such as acids and lye cause severe damage to the mouth, esophagus, and stomach when ingested. Poisonous mushrooms and chlorinated hydrocarbons such as carbon tetrachloride, which for years was used in carpet cleaning liquids, cause fatty degeneration of the liver, easily visible on microscopic examination of the liver tissues. Cyanide and carbon monoxide cause a cherry-red appearance to the blood and tissues and lead to pinkish lividity. Metallic poisons such as arsenic, mercury, and lead cause characteristic changes in the gastrointestinal tract and the liver.

But, most poisons work within the cells of the body, on a molecular level, and leave behind no visible evidence at autopsy. It is up to the forensic toxicologist to uncover the evidence.

Sample Collection

Since toxins rarely leave behind visible clues, the toxicologist must perform specialized tests on various body fluids and tissues. Which fluids and tissues are used depends on the particular drug in question and the situation under which it is tested. The goal of testing is to establish whether a particular drug is present and, if so, whether it was the cause of death, played a contributing role in the death, or was incidental and played no role at all.

The best places to obtain samples for testing are the locations where the chemicals entered the body, where they are concentrated within the body, and along their routes of elimination. Blood, stomach contents, and the tissues around injection sites might be entry points; liver, brain, and other tissues might be concentration areas; and urine might be where the drug and its metabolites are collected before final elimination. Testing these materials might reveal the poison.

For this reason, during an autopsy, blood, urine, stomach contents, bile, vitreous eye fluid, and tissue samples from the liver, kidneys, muscles, and brain are obtained. If an inhaled toxin is suspected, lung tissue will be taken. If a chronic heavy metal (such as arsenic or lead) poisoning is a consideration, hair samples are taken (more on this later).

It is important that the samples are collected prior to embalming, since this can interfere with subsequent testing. Furthermore, embalming fluids may contain methanol and other alcohols, which can make accurate alcohol testing difficult if not impossible after this procedure.

Blood is by far the toxicologist's most useful substance since most drugs and their major metabolites can be found in the blood. This would be expected since the distribution of the toxin from its entry point to the entire the body is accomplished through the circulation of the blood. Blood is easily sampled in the living with a simple venipuncture and at autopsy from the heart, the aorta (the main artery that carries blood from the heart to the body), or the femoral artery (in the groin area).

The toxicologist will not only determine if the toxin is present in the blood, but will also assess its level in the body. This is important since low levels might be of no consequence, higher doses might have toxic effects that contributed to the person's actions or played a role in his death, and even higher levels might have been the actual cause of death. Blood is the best substance for this assessment. Why is this?

To understand this, let's look into the concept of **bioavailability**. This means the amount of the drug that is available for biological activity. Since drugs work on the cellular level, bioavailability means the concentration of drug that reaches, or is available to, the cells of the body. For most chemicals, the blood level directly reflects the cellular level, and it is this level that determines the degree of toxicity of the drug in question.

For example, the level of alcohol in the blood correlates extremely well with a person's degree of intoxication, and the lethal blood alcohol level is well known. This knowledge allows the ME to accurately estimate a person's degree of intoxication in an automobile accident or whether the fraternity boy died from his binge drinking or from some other cause.

Or what of the individual who takes a handful of sedative (sleeping) pills in a suicide attempt? In order for the drug to "work" it must be dissolved by the stomach, absorbed into the blood stream, and carried to the cells of the brain, where the concentration of the drug in the brain cells determines the degree of "poisoning." Since the amount of the drug in the blood parallels the amount within the brain cells, testing the blood is like testing the cells.

Urine is sampled in the living with a cup and a trip to the restroom and at autopsy with a needle inserted into the bladder. Since the kidneys are one of the body's major toxin elimination routes, toxins are often found in greater concentrations in the urine than in the blood. However, unlike blood, the correlation between urine concentration and drug effects in the body is often poor at best. The urine level can indicate that the drug had been in the blood at some earlier time but it can't accurately determine the drug's effects on the individual at the time of its collection, or in the case of a corpse, the time of death.

Stomach contents, whether removed from a living person (maybe someone who attempted suicide or was unsuccessfully poisoned) with a gastric tube or removed from a corpse at autopsy, are tested for the presence of drugs or poisons. Finding the drug in the stomach does not correlate with its blood level and thus its effects on the person, but it does show that the drug had been ingested and in what quantity.

Liver tissue and the bile the liver produces and stores in the gall bladder can often reveal a drug or its metabolites. The reason is that the liver is the center of most drug and toxin metabolism. Many drugs, particularly opiates, concentrate in the liver and the bile and can often be found in these tissues when the blood shows no traces. Liver drug levels usually reflect the level of a drug during the hours before death, while the bile might indicate what drugs were in the system over the 3 to 4 days prior to death. Neither is very accurate, however.

Vitreous humor, the liquid within the eyeball, is water-like, so water-soluble toxins in the blood will also be found in the vitreous. The level of any toxin found in the vitreous lags behind that of the blood by about 1 to 2 hours. This means that testing the vitreous will reflect the concentration of the toxin in the blood 1 to 2 hours prior to death.

Hair "absorbs" certain heavy metal (arsenic, lead, and others) toxins and some other drugs. As we will see later, it also has the unique ability to give an intoxication timeline for many substances.

Insects are sometimes useful in situations where the body is severely decomposed and insects have been feeding on the corpse. Some insects concentrate certain drugs in their tissues so that even when the corpse is too decayed to be of toxicological benefit, testing the maggots might reveal that the drug had been present in the victim.

Toxicology and the Cause and Manner of Death

The ME, not the forensic toxicologist, is charged with assigning the manner of death, but he will often rely on the findings and opinions of the toxicologist in making this determination. To supply the ME with the needed information, the toxicologist must consider a number of factors.

The lethality of any drug is often expressed as its **LD50**, which stands for **median lethal dose** or **lethal dose 50 percent**. It is the amount that will kill 50 percent of those who take it, and varies greatly from drug to drug. In rats, the LD50 for diazepam (Valium) is approximately 1,200 milligrams per kilogram (mg/kg), while for cyanide it's around 6 mg/kg. This means that the average 70-kg male would need to ingest 84,000 mg of diazepam but only 420 mg of cyanide to have a 50 percent chance of dying from the drug. Diazepam taken alone is a fairly safe drug, while cyanide is deadly in very small amounts.

This, of course, varies greatly from person to person. Age, sex, body size and weight, the presence of other drugs or medications, the state of overall health, and the presence of other diseases impact any person's tolerance to some drugs. For example, a frequent and heavy drinker can tolerate a much higher blood alcohol level than could someone who never drinks. A heavy drinker might appear completely sober at a level that would render the normal person sloppily intoxicated—or even unconscious. Hardcore heroin addicts routinely inject doses of heroin and attain drug blood levels that would kill the average person in a matter of minutes.

Certain medical problems make some drugs more dangerous. Since amphetamines raise the blood pressure, rev up the heart, and in general tax the cardiovascular system, they pose a much greater risk for someone with heart disease or high blood pressure than they would for someone in good health. The same can be said for cocaine, which can also increase the likelihood of seizures in those with an otherwise controlled seizure disorder.

When the ME attempts to determine the cause and manner of death in the presence of drugs or toxins, he must consider all these factors and more. You will remember that the manners of death are natural, accidental, suicidal, homicidal, and the extra classification of undetermined. Drugs and poisons can be the direct cause or at least a contributing factor in any of these.

Natural: A person can die of natural causes even though drugs might be involved in the mechanism of death. What if a man with significant coronary artery disease (CAD) took an amphetamine or snorted a few lines of cocaine? Each of these raises the blood pressure, increases the heart rate, causes the coronary arteries to spasm (narrow), and adds a great workload to the pumping heart muscle. So they increase blood and oxygen demand while reducing supply, a situation that can lead to a heart attack (myocardial infarction, or MI) and/or a lethal change in heart rhythm (cardiac arrhythmia). Here the cause of death is a heart attack or a cardiac arrhythmia, events that he would be prone to due to his CAD, and the amphetamine or cocaine would be a contributory factor.

When the ME confronts such a situation, he must assess the extent of the victim's heart disease, the amount of the drug in the body, and the timing and circumstances of the death. If the amount of drug is low and the victim has severely diseased coronary arteries, the ME might conclude that the death was natural and that the drug played only a minor role. Or, if the victim's CAD was mild and the level of drug in his body was high, he might favor the drug as the culprit. In the former circumstance he might consider the death natural and in the latter accidental.

But, what if the victim intentionally took a large amount of cocaine or what if the amphetamines were given to him without his knowledge? The manner of death might then be suicidal or homicidal, respectively. Here the autopsy and lab results would be the same in either circumstance and the ME would need to rely on witness statements and on the results of the police investigation to sort this out. The picture might simply be too muddy for the ME to determine the manner of death, and he might then classify it as undetermined.

Accidental: Most accidental poisonings occur at home and often involve children ingesting prescription drugs, pesticides, household cleaners, paint thinners, weed killers, snail bait, you name it. In adults, accidental poisoning most often occurs because some product is mislabeled, usually because it has been placed in a container other than its original one. Maybe medications are dumped into another bottle, or some toxic liquid is placed in an empty liquor bottle, or the white powders cyanide or arsenic are stored in a container where they could be confused with sugar or salt.

Accidental poisoning deaths might also follow dosage miscalculations, such as the addict who accidentally injects too much heroin. Street drugs tend to have poor quality control, so the addict often doesn't know exactly what she bought or what she's taking. Similarly, some people believe that if one prescription is good, two must be better. This is a dangerous assumption, but it's not uncommon. Sometimes a patient who is taking the cardiac medication digitalis will decide on his own to double his dose. Maybe he's felt fatigued and hopes that increasing his "heart med" will give him more pep. All is well for a couple of weeks, but as the medicine accumulates within his body, he becomes ill and can die. Happens all the time.

Another factor in accidental drug deaths is the mixing of drugs, called **polypharmacy**. Alcohol taken with a sedative is notorious for causing death. Addicts often mix cocaine with amphetamines or heroin with tranquilizers or just about any combination imaginable, often with tragic results.

Suicidal: Sedatives (sleeping pills), narcotics, alcohol, and carbon monoxide (Chapter 9) are commonly used in suicide attempts. Often multiple drugs are involved, including "whatever is in the medicine cabinet."

This presents a difficult problem for the toxicologist. He must determine the level of each drug and assess its contribution to the victim's death. He might find that one particularly toxic drug was present in large amounts and that it was the cause of death or he might find that a certain combination of drugs was the cause. Of course, the mere finding of multiple drugs in the victim's system doesn't necessarily mean that he took them on purpose. It could have been an accidental overdose driven by the need for relief of physical or psychological pain, or the drugs could have been surreptitiously slipped into his food or drink by another, which would be a homicide.

Homicidal: As with accidental and suicidal poisonings, most homicidal poisonings occur at home where the killer has knowledge of the victim's habits and access to his food, drink, and medications. The police will of course focus on anyone who has this knowledge and access.

Undetermined: In some poisonings the ME can't determine the exact manner of death because the picture is unclear and the evidence not specific enough. This was illustrated in the case of the deceased heroin addict discussed in Chapter 7.

Toxicological Testing Procedures

The two biggest problems facing the toxicologist is that there are thousands of substances that are harmful, addictive, or lethal, and toxicological testing is time-consuming and expensive. Very few, if any, labs have a budget substantial enough to do this testing in every case where it might prove helpful. For this reason, the testing must be as focused as possible.

Often the circumstances of the death will point toward a particular drug. For example, a young girl found near an empty pill bottle would lead to one avenue of testing while a long-term addict found in an alley with fresh needle marks would follow another path. These and other crime scene clues can narrow the field of possibilities the toxicologist must consider.

The Two-Tiered System

Toxicological testing follows a two-tiered approach. **Screening** or **presumptive** tests are cheap, easy to perform, and, when negative, indicate that the drug (or class of drugs) in question is not present. No further testing is necessary. When positive, they indicate that a particular substance, or class of substances, is "possibly" present, and the toxicologist will move on to more focused **confirmatory** testing. These tests are more expensive and time-consuming but are designed to establish the identity of the exact drug present. This two-tiered approach saves time and money.

Let's say a corpse is found in an alleyway known for methamphetamine sales and use. If blood samples obtained at autopsy are negative for amphetamines, no further amphetamine testing is needed and the toxicologist will search for other classes of drugs. If the screening test is positive, confirmatory testing to identify the exact amphetamine present will follow.

Or the toxicologist might be asked to test a seized substance that is thought to be cocaine. If the screening tests are negative, cocaine is ruled out and the material must be tested for other drugs. If the presumptive test is positive, confirmatory testing would then be indicated. In most labs, testing for controlled and illegal drugs consumes 75 percent of the lab's time and resources.

Presumptive tests can be divided into color tests, immunoassays, thin layer chromatography, gas chromatography, and ultraviolet spectroscopy.

Color tests are those in which a reagent (any active chemical solution) is added to the questioned substance and a color change indicates that the chemical tested for is present. The color change results from a chemical reaction between the drug and the reagent, which produces a new compound that imparts a specific color to the mixture. These tests are cheap and easy and can quickly determine whether a specific chemical, or class of chemicals, is present. Common color tests include the following:

- **Trinder**: This test looks for salicylates (aspirin and similar compounds). The reagent contains ferric nitrate and mercuric chloride and turns a violet color if salicylates are present.
- **Marquis**: This method employs a reagent that contains formaldehyde and sulfuric acid and turns purple in the presence of most opiates (morphine, heroin, etc.) and brownish-orange if amphetamines are present.
- **Van Urk**: This is a test for LSD and other hallucinogenic drugs. The reagent is a mixture of dimethylaminobenzaldehyde, hydrochloric acid (HCl), and ethanol, and turns purple to indicate a positive reaction.

- **Dille-Koppanyi**: In this test for barbiturates, the sample is treated with cobalt acetate in methanol and isopropylamine in methanol and will turn violet-blue if positive.
- **Duquenois-Levine**: This three-step process tests for marijuana or other cannabinoids. The sample is treated with a mixture of vanillin and acetaldehyde in ethanol, then with HCl, and finally with chloroform. A deep purple color is a positive result.
- **Scott**: Also a three-step test, this method searches for cocaine by employing a mixture of cobalt thiocyanate and glycerin, followed by HCl, and then chloroform. Cocaine will turn blue after the thiocyanate is added, change to pink with the HCl, and then blue once again when chloroform is added.

Immunoassays are easy, sensitive, and useful for rapidly screening urine samples for certain drugs. However, the manufactured antibodies employed in these tests can also react with compounds that are similar to the sought-after drug, a lack of specificity that makes this a presumptive rather than a confirmatory test.

Thin layer chromatography (TLC) not only identifies many chemicals but is also useful for separating the components of a sample. Once TLC has tentatively identified a substance, its identity is confirmed with mass spectrometry (see below).

Gas chromatography (GC), like TLC, is primarily useful for making a presumptive identification and separating various compounds from one another. Positive result must be confirmed by mass spectrometry.

Ultraviolet (UV) spectroscopy takes advantage of the fact that different chemicals absorb UV light in varying amounts. Since it can't identify the exact compound, it is useful only for screening.

Drug screening protocols are used in hospitals as well as by the ME. If a patient entering the hospital is in a coma, appears intoxicated, or is exhibiting odd behavior, a drug screen will be ordered. In an hour or so the physician will know if any of several common classes of drugs are present. If so, she will follow one line of treatment; if not, she must search for other reasons for the coma, intoxication, or aberrant behavior. For the ME and the forensic toxicologist, drug screens quickly reveal whether any of the more common drugs are involved in a death or the abnormal behavior of a suspect.

Each lab has its own protocol for drug screening. What tests are used and in what order they are performed will depend upon the staff and equipment, budgetary restrictions, and the bias of the toxicologist in charge, but most standard screens include the following:

- **Alcohol**: Gas chromatography is used to isolate and identify alcohols and related compounds such as acetone.
- **Acid**: Urine immunoassays detect acidic compounds such as barbiturates and aspirin.
- **Alkali**: Gas chromatography screens for alkaline substances such as tranquilizers, synthetic narcotics, and antidepressants.
- **Narcotic**: Urine immunoassays reveal opiates, cocaine, and methadone.

By using these general screening procedures, the toxicologist can quickly exclude many commonly encountered drugs and narrow his search. Based on these results, further screening and confirmatory tests will be used to ultimately identify any unknown substance.

Confirmatory tests must possess **sensitivity** and **specificity**. This means they must recognize the chemical in question (sensitivity) and be able to identify it to the exclusion of all others (specificity). The most important confirmatory test used by the toxicologist is **mass spectrometry (MS)**. In MS, the sample is bombarded with electrons, which fragments the chemical into ionic fractions. This fragmentation pattern is called a mass spectrum, and it is different for each element and compound. So, MS gives a "chemical fingerprint" of the substance being tested and can identify virtually any compound. When the mass spectrum of an unknown substance is compared to known reference standards, such as the database maintained by the National Institute of Standards and Technology (NIST), the identity of the unknown sample is revealed.

In the forensic toxicology laboratory, MS is usually combined with gas chromatography (GC), a combination known as **gas chromatography/mass spectrometry (GC/MS)**. In GC/MS, GC is used to separate the test sample into components and MS is employed to identify each component.

Though used less often than MS, **infrared spectroscopy (IR)** can also reveal chemical fingerprints. Instead of electrons, the substance is exposed to infrared light. When any light strikes an object or substance, it is either transmitted (passed through), absorbed, or reflected. When exposed to infrared light, each compound transmits and absorbs the light in its own unique pattern and can thus identify the chemical substance tested. This test is also used in conjunction with gas chromatography, a combination termed **GC/IR**.

Heavy Metal Testing

Heavy metals and other metallic elements such as iron, mercury, lead, copper, arsenic, antimony, and selenium are potentially lethal and have led to accidental, suicidal, and homicidal deaths for many years. The most useful tests for detecting metals within the body's tissues are colorimetric assays, atomic absorption spectrophotometry, neutron activation analysis, and hair analysis.

Colorimetric assays are centuries old and easy to do. They depend on the fact that each metallic element (arsenic, lead, etc.) has a specific color when treated with certain reagents. The reagent is added to the test sample, which is then examined by a **photometer**, an instrument that accurately measures light and color. The major drawback of these tests is that they require a fairly large sample for testing. The most popular colorimetric test for heavy metals is the **Reinsch test**. In this procedure, the sample is dissolved in hydrochloric acid and a copper strip is placed into the solution. If a dark or silvery coat appears on the copper, one of the heavy metals is likely present.

Atomic absorption spectrophotometry (AAS) is a popular method for metal detection. The physics involved are complex, but this test is based on the fact that each metal reacts to a specific wavelength of light. A special detector examines a light beam before and after the sample is placed into the beam's path, and this reveals the sample's identity.

Neutron activation analysis (NAA) requires expensive and bulky equipment but is highly accurate. The test sample is exposed to low energy neutrons, after which it undergoes radioactive changes and releases x-rays and gamma rays. From these rays, the presence and concentration of the metals are determined.

Inductively coupled plasma-mass spectrometry (ICP-MS) is the best test for very small samples of metals, but it is expensive and not widely available. This test involves using an argon torch to heat the specimen to over 6000° Celsius, which forms an ionized gas of the substance. This gas is then passed through a mass detector that identifies the chemical by its mass and charge.

Hair analysis can not only reveal the presence of heavy metals and some other toxins but can also often give a timeline for the exposure (discussed later in this chapter).

Interpreting the Results

After testing has revealed the presence and concentration of a chemical substance, the toxicologist will attempt to interpret the results. He must determine the route of administration of each drug found and assess whether the concentrations played a role in the subject's behavior or death.

The route of entry might provide a clue as to whether the victim self-administered the drug or whether it was given by someone else. For example, if a drug was injected and the victim possessed no means to do so or if the injection site was in an area that made self-administration unlikely, homicide might be a stronger consideration. Furthermore, since the drug's concentration is usually greatest at the administration site, determining the route of entry aids in the search for the drug. Ingested toxins are usually found in the stomach, intestines, or liver; inhaled gases in the lungs; and if injected, the drug can often be isolated from the tissues around the injection site.

Drugs that are taken intravenously (IV) bypass the stomach and liver, directly enter the bloodstream, and are quickly distributed throughout the body. In this circumstance, the toxicologist might find high concentrations of the drug in the blood but little or none in the stomach and liver as would be seen with ingestion. This will help him determine the route of intake.

Earlier I discussed the concept of bioavailability and how the level of a drug in the blood closely correlates with the drug's actions and toxicity. This means that finding a large amount of a toxin in the victim's stomach does not necessarily mean that it was the cause of death. Drugs in the stomach will not kill until they are absorbed into the blood and distributed to the body. For example, if the toxicologist found a large amount of a tranquilizer in a victim's stomach, particularly if most of the pills were intact and had not been digested, and also found a low blood concentration of the drug, he would likely conclude that the pills were taken shortly before death and played little or no role in the victim's demise. On the other hand, if the pills had dissolved and the blood levels were high, he might conclude the opposite.

When the toxicologist determines the blood level of a certain drug, he might assign the level to one of four broad categories:

- **Normal**: This is the level expected in the general population under normal circumstances. We all have small amounts of lead, mercury, cyanide, and other nasty things in our systems. The key here is "small amounts." Finding these has no forensic utility.
- **Therapeutic**: This is the level your doctor strives for. If he gives you an antibiotic for infection, a medication for high blood pressure, or insulin for diabetes, he wants to achieve a blood level of the drug that will bring about the desired therapeutic effect. He might have to monitor the blood level of the drug and periodically adjust the dose. Too little will offer less benefit and too much can cause toxic side effects.
- **Toxic**: A toxic level increases the risk of side effects and can even lead to permanent harm or death. When a prescribed drug passes the therapeutic level and climbs into the toxic range, it has moved from being a medication to being a poison.
- **Lethal**: This is the level at which the drug could predictably lead to death. As discussed earlier, the LD50 of a drug is the blood concentration at which 50 percent of people would die.

It might seem logical that all the toxicologist has to do is measure the level of the drug and this alone will tell him whether it was the cause of death or a contributor to the death, or played no role at all. Unfortunately, it's not that simple. Each of us reacts to chemicals differently. What might be a therapeutic level for one person could cause toxic, even lethal, effects in another. Much, but not all, of this variance is related to age, sex, body size and weight, genetics, and nutritional and health status. But what about the person's habits? Alcoholics can tolerate more alcohol than can non-drinkers. Drug addicts commonly smoke or snort doses of cocaine or inject amounts of heroin that would kill the uninitiated in minutes. Lastly, some people can tolerate high levels of toxic drugs while other react to even very small amounts. It's mostly unpredictable. The toxicologist must consider these facts when assessing whether a given level of a drug is toxic or lethal or whether it contributed to the subject's behavior or death.

Acute Versus Chronic Poisoning

Sometimes the toxicologist is asked to determine whether a poisoning is **acute** or **chronic**. That is, was the death or toxic effects due to a single large dose or many smaller doses taken/given over a period of time? A good example is arsenic, which can kill in a single large dose or in repeated smaller doses administered over weeks or months. In either case, the blood level could be high. But the determination of whether the poisoning was acute or chronic is often extremely important. If acute, the suspect list might be long, since many people would have a one-time access to the victim or his food. If chronic, the suspect list would include only those who had long-term contact, such as a family member, a caretaker, or a family cook.

So, how does the toxicologist make this determination? In acute arsenic poisoning, the examiner would expect to find high levels of arsenic in the stomach and the blood as well as evidence of corrosion and bleeding in the stomach and intestines, signs commonly seen in acute arsenic ingestion. If he found little or no arsenic in the stomach and no evidence of acute injury in the gastrointestinal (GI) tract, but high arsenic levels in the blood and tissues, he might suspect that the poisoning was chronic in nature. Here, an analysis of the victim's hair can be invaluable.

Hair analysis for arsenic (and several other toxins) reveals not only exposure but also the timeline of the exposure. This is possible because arsenic is deposited in the cells of the hair follicles in direct proportion to the blood level of the arsenic at the time the cell was produced.

In hair growth, the cells of the hair follicles constantly reproduce and the older ones undergo change, lose their nuclei, and are incorporated into the growing hair shaft, a cycle that continues throughout life. Follicular cells produced while arsenic levels are high retain the poison as they are later incorporated into the hair shaft, while any that appeared while the arsenic levels were low contain little or no arsenic. Since hair grows about a half inch per month, the toxicologist can cut the hair into short segments, measure the arsenic level in each, and determine the timeline of the victim's arsenic exposure.

Let's suppose that a wife begins to add small amounts of arsenic to her husband's food in February and continues until his death in July. In May he is hospitalized with gastrointestinal complaints such as nausea, vomiting, and weight loss (all symptoms of arsenic poisoning). No diagnosis is made, but since he's doing better after several days, he is discharged home. Since this constellation of GI symptoms is common in many mild and self-limited GI problems, such as food poisoning and GI flu, physicians rarely consider arsenic as the problem so don't test for it. After returning home, the unfortunate husband once again falls ill and ultimately dies.

As part of the autopsy, the toxicologist might test the victim's hair for toxins and find the arsenic. If he then sections and tests the hair, he can determine the arsenic level essentially month by month. If the victim's hair is 3 inches long, the half-inch closest to the scalp will represent July, the next half inch June, the next May, and so on until the last half inch would reflect his exposure to arsenic in February, the month his poisoning began. Arsenic levels are expressed in parts per million (ppm). An analysis might reveal a pattern like that seen in Figure 12-1.

The toxicologist would look at this timeline of exposure and likely determine that the exposure occurred in the victim's home. The police would then open an investigation and would likely obtain a search warrant to look for arsenic within the home.

Common Drugs, Poisons, and Toxins

In the remote past, most poisoners favored easily available botanical products such as hemlock, oleander, deadly nightshade, foxglove, hellebore, monkshood, opium (from the innocent-appearing poppy), and many others. These are still employed, but more recently various other toxins must have been added to this list. The forensic toxicologist must know each drug's chemical makeup, physiological actions, symptoms and signs of intoxication, method of metabolism, toxic properties of each active metabolite, and how these chemicals affect a normal person, as well as those with various illnesses and addictions. This includes a working knowledge of street and recreational drugs, since these are often involved in injury and death.

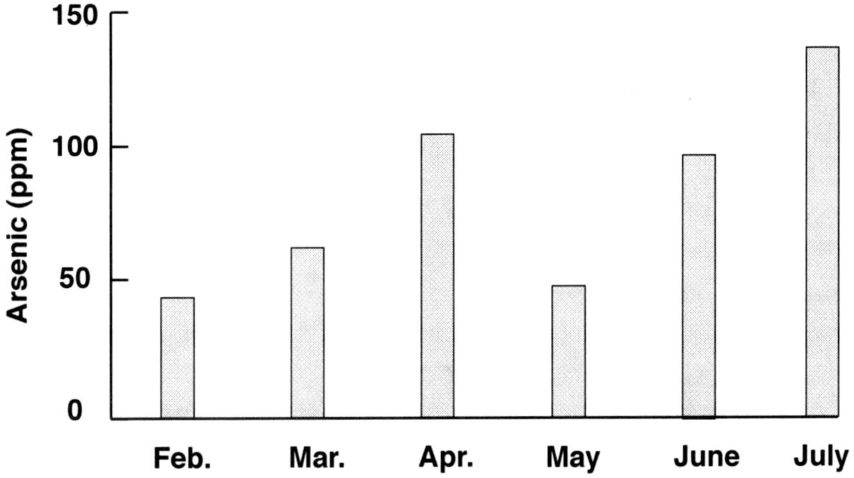

Figure 12-1

Timeline of chronic arsenic exposure. The arsenic exposure began in February and continued until May, when he was hospitalized. During this time the arsenic levels fell and he got better, but after he returned home and was again exposed to arsenic, the levels again rose until the time of his death in July.

Obviously, a discussion of every known chemical, drug, and poison is beyond the scope of this book, but we will look at those that most commonly confront the forensic toxicologist and consider how he and the ME assess their effects in deaths, injuries, behavior, or legal matters.

CNS Depressants (Downers)

The term **central nervous system (CNS)** basically means the brain and the brain stem (upper part of the spinal cord where the respiratory center resides). Drugs that depress the CNS cause sleepiness, poor coordination, slowed movements and reactions, distorted perceptions, and in large amounts coma, respiratory depression (slowing and weakening of breathing), and death from asphyxia.

Alcohols

Alcohol is derived from the fermentation of sugars and comes in a variety of types, with ethanol (ethyl or drinking alcohol), methanol (methyl or wood or denatured alcohol), and isopropanol (isopropyl or rubbing alcohol) being the most common. All are CNS depressants.

Ethanol is by far the most commonly abused drug. It is physically addictive and withdrawal can be an arduous and dangerous process. Without proper medical treatment, death rates from alcohol withdrawal syndromes such as **delirium tremens (DTs)** can be 20 percent or more.

When ingested, ethanol rapidly absorbs into the bloodstream and spreads through the body, including the brain, where its effects lead to giddiness, loss of coordination, slowed reflexes, altered judgment and perceptions, lethargy, coma, and death. Ninety-five percent of it is metabolized by the liver into water and carbon dioxide, and the remaining 5 percent is excreted unchanged through the kidneys and lungs, a fact that is critical to sobriety testing (see below).

To understand why alcohol is such a dangerous drug, let's look at the dynamics of its metabolism as compared to most other drugs. The body eliminates most toxins in what is called a **dose-dependent** fashion. The higher the dose taken, the more rapidly the toxin is metabolized. This occurs because if a small amount is taken, only some of the enzymes that break down the toxin are activated, whereas a larger amount will activate more enzymes in order to handle the increased load of toxin. In other words, the body activates only enough enzymes to get the job done. This is a very efficient system.

But, alcohol is metabolized in a **linear** fashion in that any amount of alcohol intake activates all the enzyme systems that destroy it. This means that from the first drink, the system operates at maximum capacity and there is little or no ability to increase it. The average rate of ethanol destruction in the body is roughly equivalent to one drink per hour. It can't handle more, and this is where the danger lies.

With rapid intake of alcohol, as is seen in binge drinking so common among college students, the body can't increase the metabolism of the alcohol since the system is already maxed out, and this excessive intake overruns the body's ability to deal with it. The result is that the concentration of alcohol in the blood will rise rapidly, leading to coma and death. You've no doubt read about such tragedies. The classic story is a college student becoming severely intoxicated, his friends putting him to bed to "sleep it off," and then finding him dead the next morning. As he lay there, his blood alcohol level continued to rise as alcohol from his stomach continued to enter the blood stream, overwhelming the metabolic system and causing respiratory depression and death from asphyxia.

Sobriety testing involves the assessment of the **blood alcohol content (BAC)**, which is expressed in grams percent, or grams (g) of alcohol in each 100 milliliters (mL) of blood. In most jurisdictions the legal limit for driving is 0.08 g/100 mL. Though there is individual variation, the correlation of the BAC to the signs and symptoms of intoxication is well established. Those who rarely drink tend to show signs of intoxication at lower BAC levels than do those who drink chronically and excessively. For the average person, the BAC level correlates with these symptoms and signs:

- BAC = 0.03: There will be little giddiness or impaired motor skills. (This is a single beer or one highball in most individuals.)
- BAC = 0.03–0.08: Coordination, reaction time, and judgment decline.
- BAC = 0.12: Nausea, vomiting, and severe loss of coordination can occur.
- BAC = 0.25: Coma is likely.
- BAC = 0.30: Deep coma is likely.
- BAC = 0.40+: Death is likely.

These facts come into play when a police officer conducts a **field sobriety test**. When he asks you to stand on one foot, stand steady with your eyes closed, repeatedly touch one finger to your nose, walk a straight line in the heel-to-toe manner, or some combination of these, he is testing your brain, particularly your cerebellar, function. The cerebellum is in the back of the brain and controls coordination and other motor skills. Alcohol primarily affects this area and your coordination and balance suffer, making each of these maneuvers clumsy or impossible. This is why you can't "fake" a field sobriety test. Physiology will conspire against you and you will stumble, waver, fall, or poke yourself in the eye.

If you fail the field test, he might ask you to take a **breathalyzer test**. In this test you breathe into a handheld device that measures the alcohol level in the exhaled breath. Recall that some of the alcohol in the bloodstream passes unchanged through the lungs. It goes directly from the bloodstream, into the air sacs of the lungs, and out with each breath. The amount of alcohol exhaled directly parallels the BAC so that the higher the BAC, the higher the concentration in your exhaled breath. This means that a breath test is a very accurate reflection of the BAC and, as with the field sobriety test, it can't be faked. A breath mint will not help.

If you fail either of these tests, blood for a BAC might be obtained to determine the exact level. This is particularly true if an accident, bodily harm, or death of another is involved.

In suspected alcohol-related deaths, the ME can measure the BAC in cadaver blood and determine whether the intoxication level was high enough to have caused or contributed to the death. However, there are problems with this determination. The blood alcohol level in some corpses will actually increase due to the action of bacteria, some of which produce alcohol.

To get around this, a determination of the alcohol level in the vitreous fluid of the eye will be done. Since the alcohol content of the vitreous reflects the blood alcohol level with a 1- to 2-hour lag, this can tell the ME what the blood level was 1 to 2 hours before death. He can then use this to estimate the likely level at the time of the accident. For example, if he found the vitreous alcohol content was 0.21 (over twice the legal limit), it would mean the victim had been very intoxicated two hours before his demise and very likely still over the limit at the time of the accident.

Embalming a body makes determination of the alcohol level at the time of death very difficult, if not impossible. During the embalming process, embalming fluid replaces most of the blood and leaves behind little for testing. It also contains alcohol, usually methanol not ethanol. The vitreous fluid is not affected by the embalming, so even in an embalmed corpse it might help the toxicologist estimate the level of intoxication at the time of death.

Methanol is a particularly nasty alcohol. Unlike ethanol, the liver converts methanol to **formic acid** and **formaldehyde**, compounds that can cause nausea, vomiting, pancreatic and other organ damage, confusion, loss of coordination, and brain damage that can lead to blindness, seizures, coma, and ultimately death from asphyxia.

Isopropanol (rubbing alcohol), if ingested, will be partially (20 percent) converted to **acetone**, which produces acidosis (excess acid in the body). This can in turn cause all the above-mentioned CNS signs and symptoms as well as hemorrhaging (bleeding) into the bronchial tubes (airways) and the chest cavity. One important point is that isopropanol also absorbs through the lungs and the skin, so that infants given water/alcohol sponge baths to treat a fever can experience isopropanol toxicity.

Opiates

The Greek word *narkotikos* means a "state of lethargy or sleepiness" and is the root of the word **narcotic**, a group of drugs that cause sleepiness, lethargy, and sluggishness. Narcotics are also termed **opiates** since some are derived from the opium poppy. Others are either synthesized from materials found in the poppy (semi-synthetic) or are made from scratch (synthetic). Unfortunately, the word *narcotic* has come to mean any powerful, illegal, abused drug. Such things as heroin and morphine, which are narcotics, are lumped with amphetamines and cocaine, which are not.

Opiates are alkaloid chemicals that come from the sap of the poppy. They were discovered by German chemist Friedrich Wilhelm Serturner when he extracted morphine from the plant in 1805. The opiates are divided into **natural**, **semi-synthetic**, and **synthetic**, depending upon their source and method of manufacture. All opiates are sedatives (sleep producing) and analgesics (pain relieving) that produce euphoria, lethargy, and, in larger doses, coma and death from respiratory depression and asphyxia, particularly if taken with alcohol.

Natural opiates come directly from the poppy, with **morphine** and **codeine** being the basic ones. Combining morphine with acetic anhydride or acetyl chloride produces **heroin** (di-acetylmorphine), the most commonly abused opiate.

The screening test for opiates is the Marquis test; if this reveals the presence of an opiate, testing for morphine and codeine is fairly straightforward. Heroin is a bit trickier since after injection it is almost immediately broken down into mono-acetylmorphine and then to morphine.

In the living person, testing for heroin will reveal nothing, while testing for morphine will show its presence. In heroin-related deaths, the results depend on timing. If the victim lived long enough after the heroin injection, the conversion process might be complete and only morphine would be found. But, if the victim died shortly after the injection, this process might be interrupted and the toxicologist might find both mono-acetylmorphine and morphine. If both of these substances are found, the victim used heroin, but if the toxicologist finds only morphine, it is not possible to say with certainty whether the victim used morphine, heroin, or both.

Again, the vitreous fluid might prove helpful. Even if the heroin in the blood has completely converted to morphine, the vitreous fluid might reveal mono-acetylmorphine, which will remain in the vitreous for a much longer period of time, proving that the victim did indeed use heroin.

Street heroin varies greatly in concentration and purity since it is often "cut" or expanded with talc or quinine. The actual amount of heroin varies from 3 percent to 65 percent or more. The typical user will melt the heroin powder in a spoon with a match or lighter, draw it into a syringe, and inject it intravenously. Sometimes a small piece of cotton will serve as filter to remove any particles as he draws the liquid into the syringe.

In heroin deaths, the autopsy findings include pulmonary edema (water in the lungs) and often talc crystals and cotton fibers in the lungs. The reason for the latter is that when the drug is injected, these crystals and fibers are carried through the right side of the heart and are filtered from the blood and trapped by the lungs.

Semi-synthetic opiates are molecular alterations of morphine and codeine and include many medical analgesics such as hydrocodone, oxymorphone, and oxycodone (OxyContin).

Synthetic opiates are constructed in a laboratory rather than being derived from either morphine or codeine. Methadone is the best known of this class, but others include meperidine (Demerol) and the various fentanyl drugs.

Barbiturates

Barbiturates are derived from **barbituric acid**, which was first synthesized in 1863 by German chemist Adolf von Bayer, who named his discovery after a female friend named Barbara. This class of drugs, known as hypnotics (sleeping pills), includes pentobarbital, amobarbital, secobarbital, butabarbital, and phenobarbital. Only phenobarbital, an excellent anticonvulsive (antiseizure) medication, is widely used today since the others have been replaced with newer and safer hypnotics. The Dille-Koppanyi color test is a common screening test for barbiturates.

CNS Stimulants (Uppers)

The most popular stimulants or "uppers" are the various types of amphetamine and cocaine. Each of these rev up the nervous system, increase the blood pressure and the heart rate, and can kill. They increase alertness, lessen fatigue, and suppress appetite but also cause irritability, anxiousness, aggressive behavior, paranoia, fatigue, and depression.

A major characteristic of these drugs is that chronic users develop **tachyphylaxis**. This means that the body "gets used to" them and their effects are lessened. The user must take ever-increasing amounts to get the same "kick." The physiology behind this phenomenon is that with chronic use the body gradually produces more and more of the enzymes that metabolize these drugs so that they are destroyed and eliminated at a faster rate, thus requiring larger and more frequent doses to get the desired effect.

Amphetamines

Amphetamines are in the phenethylamine class and are **sympathomimetics**, in that they "mimic," or act like, the sympathetic side of the autonomic nervous system. This is the fight or flight response. Amphetamines "rev up" the body for emergency action by increasing blood pressure, heart rate, and respiration (fight or flight), and impart a sense of high energy. With chronic use, fatigue, emotional lability, insomnia, irritability, and aggressive behaviors can occur.

Though usually taken in pill or capsule form, liquid amphetamines can be evaporated until only crystals, called "**crystal meth**" or "**ice**," remain. These are then smoked. This version is extremely powerful, dangerous, and addictive. Repeated use can lead to acute psychosis, paranoia, and erratic, aggressive behavior.

Amphetamines are widely available, easily manufactured in garage labs, and so commonly abused that testing for amphetamines is part of virtually every hospital and crime lab toxicology screen. For screening, UV spectroscopy can identify a substance as a member of the phenethylamine class but cannot distinguish one member from another. This class includes amphetamine, methamphetamine, ephedrine, pseudoephedrine, and phenylpropanolamine. Only amphetamine and methamphetamine are controlled substances, the others appearing in various legitimate medications, so that finding a member of the class in a person's blood is of little legal value. But, if confirmatory testing reveals amphetamines or methamphetamines, this can lead to use and possession charges.

Cocaine

Cocaine comes from the coca leaf and has probably been used by South American Indians since 2500 BC. It was first extracted from coca leaves in 1855 and by the 1870s was a popular ingredient in various elixirs and tonics. Like amphetamines, cocaine is a CNS stimulant that increases alertness, elevates blood pressure and heart rate, raises mood, and in higher amounts can cause seizures, strokes, heart attacks, and death. It is also subject to tachyphylaxis.

Typically, cocaine is snorted, where it rapidly absorbs through the nasal membranes and enters the bloodstream. If cocaine is mixed with baking soda and water and heated until all the liquid evaporates, the solid material remaining is "**free base**" or "**crack**" cocaine, which is then smoked. This form is absorbed through the lungs and into the bloodstream almost as quickly as if it had been given by IV injection and is extremely addictive. "Crack heads" often become involved in prostitution or commit crimes such as robbery and murder to get money to buy their fix.

In the bloodstream, cocaine is converted to methylecgonine and benzoylecgonine. Urine testing targets the latter of these two compounds and traces can be found up to 3 days after last use. Both immunoassay and the Scott color test are common screening tests.

Hallucinogenic Drugs

Hallucinogens alter perceptions and mood, lead to delusional thinking, and cause hallucinations.

Delusions are misperceptions of reality in that something or some situation in the real world is perceived to be something it's not. The person might believe that he is being watched by his boss, neighbor, or another family member. Maybe the buzzing on the phone line is some sinister organization monitoring him. Maybe a coworker is trying to harm him. Such beliefs can lead to inappropriate reactions, many of them criminal.

Hallucinations are sensory experiences that are not real. Unlike delusions, they are not a misinterpretation of some real event but rather the entire sensory experience is created within the person's mind. These creations might involve any or all of the senses: visual (sight), auditory (sound), olfactory (smell), taste, or tactile (touch). Sometimes these sensations are so real that the person can't separate the hallucination from reality, or worse the hallucination becomes the reality. Hallucinating individuals might see things that don't exist, hear soothing or threatening voices, smell flowers or rotten eggs, or feel the touch of silk or the creeping of bugs. Anything is possible.

Hallucinations are part of severe schizophrenia and other mental disorders, can occur in victims of strokes or senile dementia, and are often seen with use and withdrawal from alcohol and other drugs. And of course, hallucinogenic drugs are specifically designed to produce hallucinations. The most frequently encountered hallucinogens come from the plant world (marijuana, peyote, and mushrooms) or the chemistry laboratory (LSD, STP, PCP). Their identification depends upon both physical and chemical analyses.

Cannabinoids

Marijuana, the most commonly used hallucinogen, is derived from the Cannabis sativa plant. The active ingredient is **tetrahydrocannabinol (THC)** and it is found in marijuana at a concentration of 2 to 6 percent. **Hashish** is the oily extract of the plant and contains approximately 12 percent THC.

Marijuana is typically smoked, where it rapidly absorbs through the lungs, reaches peak blood levels in 15 to 20 minutes, and lasts about 2 hours. It produces euphoria, sedation, loss of memory, reduced coordination, and increases appetite. The latter effect is the rationale for its use as **medical marijuana** in cancer, chemotherapy, and HIV patients. It is also useful in the treatment of glaucoma because it lowers the pressure within the eyeballs, which is elevated in this disease.

The body breaks down THC into a series of compounds, the most important being **9-carboxy-tetrahydrocannabinol (9-carboxy-THC)**, which is the major urinary metabolite. Urine testing for this compound can remain positive for up to 2 months after last use. Presumptive testing typically uses the Duquenois-Levine test, which shows a purple color change in the presence of cannabinoids. This reaction will occur with all cannabinoids and not just THC, so it can't absolutely identify THC. Other presumptive tests include thin-layer chromatography (TLC) and gas chromatography (GC), and confirmatory testing is done by mass spectroscopy (MS).

Cacti and Mushrooms

Peyote is a small Mexican cactus that has enjoyed ceremonial use by many native tribes for centuries. Its surface is covered with small round bumps called **peyote buttons**, which are divided into sections like an orange, each section containing a cotton-like tuft inside. The active chemical is **mescaline**, a hallucinogen in the alkaloid family. Either thin-layer or gas chromatography can confirm the presence of the alkaloids.

The active ingredients in "magic mushrooms" are **psilocin** and **psilocybin**. Either Van Urk's reagent or Fast Blue B screens for these chemicals, which turn the former reagent purple and the latter red. Confirmatory testing is done by GC/MS or infrared spectroscopy.

LSD and Other Hallucinogenic Chemicals

The most common chemically produced hallucinogens are **lysergic acid diethylamide (LSD)** and **phencyclidine (PCP** or "**angel dust**").

LSD is very potent; as little as 25 micrograms can produce an "acid trip" that lasts for 12 hours. Though LSD is not directly fatal, its hallucinations are often vivid and have induced some users to harm themselves because of these altered perceptions. The primary screening test for LSD is the Van Urk color test.

PCP is easily manufactured in clandestine labs and is extremely powerful, producing unpredictable effects. It comes as a powder or in a capsule or pill. It can be swallowed or smoked, often after being sprinkled on a marijuana "joint." It causes visual and auditory hallucinations and can produce a **depersonalization syndrome**, where the user becomes detached and feels as if he is watching events unfold from a vantage point above the action. He might even see himself in the "scene" below. This drug can cause depression, irritability, and feelings of isolation and is notorious for producing psychosis, paranoia, and violent behavior. In a large enough dose, it can cause seizures and death. Urine immunoassay is used for PCP screening, and GC/MS provides confirmation.

Other chemical hallucinogens include **dimethoxymethylamphetamine (STP)**, **dimethyltryptamine (DMT)**, and **3,4-methylenedioxymethamphetamine (MDMA)**, also known as "**ecstasy**" (see below).

Date Rape Drugs

You've no doubt heard of "date rape drugs," often called "rave drugs." They are a collection of chemicals that share the ability to make the user relaxed, disoriented, and compliant. Some are pharmaceutically manufactured, while others are cooked up by people of unknown expertise, marginal experience, questionable drug habits, and a chemistry book. The major members of this group are **rohypnol** (flunitrazepam), **ecstasy** (3,4-methylenedioxymethamphetamine), **GHB** (gamma-hydroxybutyrate), and **ketamine** (ketamine hydrochloride).

Ecstasy, GHB, and ketamine are part of the "rave" culture and are staples at all-night dance parties called raves. Rohypnol, GHB, and ketamine are commonly used in "date" or "acquaintance" rapes, which is where the moniker comes from. They cause sedation, a degree of compliance, poor judgment, and, most sinisterly, amnesia for events that occur while under their influence. These properties make them "effective" in date rape situations.

A small amount of GHB or rohypnol can be slipped into the victim's drink or a bottle of innocuous-appearing water. She might appear and act normally, or might seem happy, excited, or mildly intoxicated. Neither the victim nor her friends recognize her true degree of impairment. She might leave with her would-be assailant because her judgment is impaired and euphoria enhanced. Only later will she realize that something happened, but her memory of events will be spotty or completely absent. This is exactly what happened with Andrew Luster's victims. Until they viewed the tapes, they had no memory of having sex with the man.

"That's exactly what I like in my room. A passed out beautiful girl." Andrew Luster, the great-grandson of cosmetics legend Max Factor, spoke those words into his home video camera right before having sex with his "passed out" victim, a woman he had surreptitiously given GHB. It wasn't the first time Andrew had employed such tactics. Police investigators turned up tapes of Luster having sex with several apparently unconscious women. He was arrested and charged with multiple counts of illegal drug possession, poisoning, and rape. His sensational trial took a bizarre turn when he fled to Mexico. His trial went forward without him and he was convicted and sentenced to 124 years in prison. Luster was finally captured by bounty hunter Duane "Dog" Chapman and returned to the United States to serve his sentence.

Luster's trial exposed the true danger of these drugs. Many of his victims testified that they had no memory of having sex with Luster, nor were they were aware he was video taping the act. Let's look at each of these drugs.

Rohypnol (street names: roofies, roaches, rope, Mexican Valium), a benzodiazepine sedative in the same family as diazepam (Valium) and alprazolam (Xanax), was originally developed to treat insomnia. Currently, it is neither manufactured nor approved for use in the United States but is available in Mexico and many other countries. It takes action 20 to 30 minutes after ingestion, peaks in about two hours, and its effects can persist for 8 to 12 hours.

Roofies typically cause sedation, confusion, euphoria, loss of identity, dizziness, blurred vision, slowed psychomotor performance, and amnesia. The victim has poor judgment, a feeling of sedated euphoria, and poor, if any, memory of events. Victims might suddenly "wake up" or "reenter reality" hours later with vague or no memory of what has happened.

Ecstasy (street names: E, X, XTC, MDMA, love, Adam) was first manufactured in 1912 and originally patented in 1914 as an appetite suppressant but was never marketed. It disappeared until the 1960s when it was "rediscovered" and became a drug of abuse. It has amphetamine (upper) as well as hallucinogenic effects. The user experiences enhanced sensations and feelings of empathy, increased energy, and occasionally profound spiritual experiences. It can cause increased blood pressure, teeth grinding (bruxia), sweating, nausea, anxiety, or panic attacks. In rare cases death from malignant **hyperthermia** (sudden and marked elevation of body temperature to 106° Fahrenheit or above, which basically "fries" the brain) can occur.

One problem for the user is that both ecstasy and GHB are sometimes referred to by the slang term ecstasy, though they are actually very different compounds. The street purchaser doesn't always know which he is getting.

GHB (street names: G, XTC, E, liquid ecstasy, liquid E, easy lay, goop, scoop, Georgia homeboy) was developed over 30 years ago as a "natural" food supplement and muscle builder. It comes as a white powder that easily dissolves in water, alcohol, and other liquids or as "liquid E," a colorless, odorless liquid. Its effects appear in 5 to 20 minutes and typically last for two to three hours. It causes loss of inhibitions, euphoria, drowsiness, and, when combined with alcohol, marijuana, cocaine, and many other drugs, increases the effects of these drugs. Many kids use it to enhance the effect of alcohol for a "cheap drunk." Users report that GHB makes them feel happy, sensual, and talkative. They might also experience enhanced sensuality, hallucinations, and amnesia.

Ketamine (street names: K, special K, kit-kat, purple, bump) is a rapid-acting intravenous or intramuscular anesthetic agent that causes sedation and amnesia. It was a common surgical anesthetic agent in the 1970s but fell from favor due to its unpredictable hallucinogenic and psychiatric side effects. It is still used medically in burn victims since it tends to "dissociate" the patient from the pain, making the intense discomfort of burns more bearable. In veterinary clinics it is used as an animal sedative, leading to another popular street name, "cat Valium." The ketamine that appears on the street is often stolen from animal hospitals and clinics.

Ketamine comes as a liquid that is often heated and evaporated to a white powder residue, which can be added to a liquid such as bottle of water, compacted into pills, or snorted, which is the preferred and most common method of usage. It takes effect almost immediately and is fairly short in its duration of action, typically 45 minutes to an hour or two.

Many of its effects are similar to those of ecstasy, but it also possesses "dissociative" effects, which means the person "dissociates" from reality in some fashion. The user might experience hallucinations, loss of time sense, and loss of self-identity. As with PCP, a depersonalization syndrome, where the person is part of the activities while at the same time is off to the side or hovering overhead watching the activity, including his/her own actions, can occur. Users call these effects "going into a K hole." Since ketamine is a sedative and general anesthetic, its potential for serious and lethal effects is real. If too much is taken, the victim may lose consciousness, stop breathing, and suffer brain damage or die.

Sniffing and Huffing

Huffing is the sniffing of volatile chemicals such as glue, gasoline, naphthalene (moth balls), toluene (paint thinners, fingernail polish, some paints), trichloroethylene (paint thinners, liquid typewriter correction fluid), aerosol propellants, some adhesives, and nitrates (amyl and butyl nitrate and nitrous oxide). Inhalation of these fumes can cause giddiness, euphoria, dizziness, slurred speech, headache, nausea, and vomiting, and with continued exposure, loss of consciousness, coma, and death. Permanent damage to the brain, liver, heart, and kidneys can occur.

Corrosive Chemicals

Corrosive chemicals are strong alkalis (lye) or acids (hydrochloric acid, sulfuric acid) that, when ingested, corrode or "burn" the tissues of the mouth, esophagus, and stomach, leading to severe bleeding, shock, and death. Rarely involved in homicides, most ingestions are accidental and involve children. A box of lye or a bottle of liquid or granular drain opener is often a tempting "snack" for a child. In rare cases adults will use a corrosive agent in a suicide attempt.

At autopsy, the ME has no trouble determining the cause and mechanism of death. The damage to the mouth, esophagus, and stomach is extensive and readily visible. Usually an open container near the victim will indicate the particular caustic substance used, but if not, samples will be taken from the mouth and stomach for analysis by the toxicologist.

Miscellaneous Toxins

Cyanide is one of the most lethal chemicals known and can enter the body by inhalation, ingestion, or directly through the skin. The most common forms are the white powders sodium and potassium cyanide (NaCN and KCN, respectively) and the gaseous hydrogen cyanide (HCN). Most poisonings are accidental, but suicidal and homicidal cyanide poisonings also occur. HCN is used in gas chamber executions. Here, KCN is dropped into a vessel containing hydrochloric acid (HCl), which reacts and produces the cyanide gas.

Cyanide is a metabolic poison, which means it damages the internal workings of the cells by attacking and neutralizing the enzyme **cyto-**

chrome oxidase in the cell's **mitochondria**, blocking its ability to use oxygen. Cellular death follows.

At autopsy, the ME might suspect cyanide poisoning from the bright, cherry-red color of the victim's blood and internal organs (see Chapter 9). This color is due to an excess amount of oxyhemoglobin and the presence of **cyanohemoglobin**, which is produced when cyanide combines with hemoglobin. If he sees this color change, the ME might then have the toxicologist measure the cyanide level in the victim's blood and tissues to confirm the presence of cyanide.

Strychnine comes from the seeds of the *Strychnos nux-vomica* plant and is a component of some rat and mole poisons. It is a neuromuscular toxin that causes powerful convulsive contractions of all the body's muscles, resulting in a posture known as **opisthotonos**, where the back is arched so that only the back of the head and the heels of the feet touch the floor. Death results from asphyxia, since breathing is impossible during such violent muscular contractions. At death, rigor mortis often occurs very quickly, since muscular ATP is consumed during these contractions (Chapter 6).

Mushrooms of the "magic" or psilocybin variety were discussed earlier under the section on hallucinogens. But more sinister are the mushrooms of the *Amanita* family, known by such names as **death cap** and **death angel** mushrooms. I'm sure you've read or heard about someone who collected a bunch of mushrooms, cooked them, ate them, and died. It happens all too frequently. These poisonous mushrooms have been implicated in accidental, suicidal, and homicidal deaths.

The death cap, so toxic that a single mushroom can kill, contains **amanitin**, which causes a drop in blood sugar (hypoglycemia), and **phalloidin**, which damages the kidneys, liver, and heart. The real treachery of these mushrooms lies in that fact that the symptoms, which are typically nausea, vomiting, diarrhea, and abdominal pain, are slow to onset, typically beginning 6 to 15 hours and sometimes as much as 48 hours after ingestion. In general, the later the onset of symptoms, the worse the chances for survival. This is because the toxins go to work on the liver and other organs almost immediately, but since symptoms are delayed for many hours, the victim doesn't know to seek medical help until it is too late. At autopsy, the ME would find severe damage to the liver and a low level of sugar in the blood. Toxicological testing would reveal the presence of the amantin and phalloidin toxins.

Ethylene glycol is the major ingredient in many antifreeze solutions. In the body, it breaks down into several compounds, the most important being **oxalic acid**. This acid causes the deposition of oxalate crystals in the brain and kidneys, which results in irreparable damage and death (see below). At autopsy, the ME will find the crystals in the tubules of the kidney. For some reason antifreeze is a favorite beverage of alcoholics when they can't get ethanol. When the ME is presented with the death of a homeless alcoholic, his search for the cause of death should include analysis for ethylene glycol.

Oxalic acid is also found in raw (not properly cooked) rhubarb, which can lead to accidental poisonings. It is rarely used for suicide or homicide. Ingestion of this plant causes harm in two basic ways. First, it is a powerful irritant to the GI tract and can cause mouth, throat, and esophageal pain and possibly bleeding. But its major toxic effects come from the chemical properties of the oxalic acid found in its leaves and stalks.

When oxalic acid is absorbed into the bloodstream, it reacts with calcium in the blood to form calcium oxalate. This reaction "consumes" the blood's calcium and the level of calcium falls to extremely low levels. Since calcium is necessary for the proper electrical function of the heart, these low levels can cause a cardiac arrest and death. In addition, the calcium oxalate in the blood is filtered through the kidneys, where it can "clog up" the microscopic tubules and severely damage the kidneys. Survivors often require dialysis or a kidney transplant. In lethal ingestions, the autopsy reveals burns of the mouth, esophagus, and stomach, low blood calcium levels, and calcium oxalate sludge in the kidneys.

Heavy metals are dangerous metallic elements such as arsenic, mercury, lead, bismuth, antimony, and thallium.

Arsenic was the major homicidal poison for hundreds of years, usually in the form of the white powder arsenic trioxide. Symptoms of acute poisoning begin half an hour after ingestion and include nausea, vomiting, abdominal pain, bloody diarrhea, a metallic taste in the mouth, and a slight garlicky odor to the breath. Arsenic severely damages the lining of the stomach and intestines and the ME will easily see this at autopsy in those who die. He will also find fatty deposits in the liver, kidneys, and heart.

Lead poisoning usually occurs in an industrial setting, but occasionally children will peel away and eat lead-containing wall paint. For decades, lead has been banned from interior paints, but some older buildings still have layers of old lead-based paint. This eating of non-food materials such as paint is called pica. Lead pica can cause anemia, nausea, vomiting, abdominal pain, weakness, numbness, and seizures.

To test for these metallic toxins, the toxicologist will employ the Reinsch test or one of the colorimetric tests for screening and atomic absorption spectrophotometry or neutron activation analysis for confirmation.

Insulin, a naturally occurring hormone that is essential for life, is also synthetically manufactured for use by diabetics. Not uncommonly, diabetics die from an accidental insulin overdose, but it has also been used for suicide and homicide. The injection of a large dose will dramatically drop the blood sugar level, and since the brain needs a continuous supply of nutrition, death can occur very quickly. For many years insulin was considered to be an almost perfect murder weapon since there was no way to trace it. Now, insulin levels can be determined by radioimmunoassay; if the level at autopsy is found to be very high the ME will search for an insulin-secreting tumor in the pancreas, which are rare and almost never cause a sudden and unexpected death. When he finds no tumor, he might suspect that insulin has been administered by another and launch a search for hidden injection sites on the corpse.

Succinyl choline, called **sux** for short, has also been considered a nearly perfect weapon of murder. It is an injectable drug that paralyzes every muscle of the body, preventing all movement, even breathing. Death is from asphyxia. It is difficult to detect, since it is very quickly metabolized by the body after injection, leaving behind little evidence of its presence. However, since the 1980s the GC/MS combination has allowed for detection of the drug's metabolites. If the ME suspects that this drug has been used, he will not only take blood samples, but will also excise the tissues around any suspected injection sites and send these materials to the toxicologist. Toxicological testing is directed toward finding metabolites such as **succinic acid**, which when found suggests that the drug was at one time present in the victim. This testing, which is fraught with problems and is controversial, is a direct result of the famous Carl Coppolino case.

Carl Coppolino and his wife, Carmela, were both physicians, who moved from New Jersey to Longboat Key, Florida. On the night of August 28, 1965, Carl called his friend Dr. Juliette Karow and told her he had found his wife dead of an apparent heart attack. Dr. Karow came to the Coppolino home, agreed with Carl's assessment, and ultimately signed Carmela's death certificate, stating that her death was due to a coronary thrombosis. The Sarasota County Medical Examiner agreed, so no autopsy was performed.

Shortly thereafter, Carl married wealthy socialite Mary Gibson, which angered his neighbor, Marjorie Farber. It seems that Marjorie and her husband had known the Coppolinos in New Jersey, where Marjorie and Carl had been having an affair. After the death of Marjorie's husband, William, and the Coppolinos' move to Florida, she followed the Coppolinos to the Sunshine State so she could continue her relationship with Carl.

Marjorie visited Dr. Karow and told her that Marjorie's husband's death back in New Jersey had not been the natural event everyone thought but that Carl, who was an anesthesiologist, had given her a syringe filled with a liquid and instructed her how to inject her husband with it. Her attempt failed. She managed to inject only a small amount of the drug, panicked, and called Carl who came over and finished off William by strangling him. Carl returned home and then Marjorie called the Coppolinos' home, saying that her husband had died of an apparent heart attack. Ironically, Carmela had gone to Marjorie's home and as a physician had pronounced William Farber dead and signed his death certificate, stating that his death was due to coronary thrombosis.

After Marjorie's revelations, an investigation into both deaths followed, with New York Chief Medical Examiner Dr. Milton Helpern performing an autopsy on each of the victims. Attorney F. Lee Bailey managed to gain an acquittal for Carl on the death of William Farber, but Helpern was well aware that Carl was an anesthesiologist and guessed that he might have access to many anesthetic drugs, including the muscle paralytic drug succinyl choline, which at that time was essentially impossible to find in a corpse. Dr. Helpern brought toxicologist Dr. Charles Umberger into the case. After months of research, Umberger finally managed to isolate some of the metabolites of succinyl choline such as succinic acid. He then found large quantities of this acid in the brain tissues of Carmela Coppolino. Carl was convicted of second-degree murder.

CHAPTER **13**

FINGERPRINTS

Take a close look at your fingertips and you will see very fine lines that curve and circle and arch. These lines are composed of narrow valleys called **grooves** and hills known as **friction ridges**. These ridges create friction, which allows you to pick up a glass or turn a doorknob. They are also the pattern you see when you view an inked fingerprint, and it is this that makes them so useful for criminal investigators.

When the world was poorly populated and people existed in small nomadic communities of thirty or forty individuals, everyone knew everyone else. If you wanted to know who Joe was, ask anyone and they could point him out. But, as populations grew, settled into ever-expanding cities, and developed systems of government, identifying others became more difficult. This fueled a search for a reliable method for identifying people. And since most people could not read, write, or sign their name, proving identity for legal matters was very difficult.

Fingerprints, along with DNA, are the most powerful methods for establishing identity. Though identical twins share the same DNA, even they have distinct fingerprints. Fingerprints are commonly left behind by criminals and in most cases are easily collected, which makes them ideal crime scene clues. They are easily stored and can be converted to digital data so that large databases can be created and shared across jurisdictions.

Though a well-accepted standard now, our recognition of the individuality of fingerprints didn't happen overnight.

The two most important characteristics of any method of identification are that it be absolutely individual and that it remains unchanged throughout the person's life. Fingerprints fit these requirements perfectly. But it took over 3,000 years and the astute observations of many scientists and criminal investigators before this tool became an accepted standard.

The History of Fingerprints

- **Prehistory**: Early pottery makers "signed" their works with an impressed finger or thumbprint.
- **1000 BC**: The Chinese used fingerprints to "sign" legal documents and criminal confessions. It is unclear whether this was a ceremonial practice or a method of personal identity.
- **Ca. 1000 AD**: The Roman attorney Quintilian exonerated a blind man accused of murdering his own mother by showing that a bloody palm print found at the scene had been placed by someone else in an attempt to frame the unfortunate man.
- **1685**: Marcello Malpighi, professor of anatomy at the University of Bologna, Italy, first recognized the "varying ridges and patterns" on human fingertips and used the terms "loops" and "whorls" to describe these patterns.
- **1823**: Johannes Purkinje of the University of Breslau, Poland, devised the first system for classifying fingerprints when he listed nine basic patterns and laid down rules for their individual classification. His work is the basis for today's classification systems.
- **1858**: In order to prevent fraud in contracts and pension distributions, Sir William Herschel, an English civil servant stationed in Bengal, India, required that the natives sign contracts with a hand imprint. He also kept records of his own prints and showed that they did not change over a 50-year period, a necessary discovery to the development of fingerprints as a forensic tool.
- **1880**: Henry Faulds, a physician and surgeon at Tsukiji Hospital in Tokyo, Japan, wrote that fingerprints could be used for personal identification and suggested that they might be useful for identify-

ing criminals. He also recognized that latent (invisible) prints could be exposed by dusting them with powder and used this method to exonerate a man accused of thievery.

- **1883**: Mark Twain apparently understood the discriminatory power of fingerprints and used the technique in his books, *Life on the Mississippi* and *Pudd'nhead Wilson.*
- **1892**: Sir Francis Galton published his classic textbook *Finger Prints*, the first book on the subject, in which he described three patterns that he called loops, arches, and whorls. More importantly, he provided evidence that no two prints were identical.
- **1892**: Juan Vucetich, a police official in La Plata, Argentina, convinced that fingerprints could identify criminals, devised a classification system that is still in use in most of South America. His methods resulted in the first use of fingerprints to solve a crime. On June 18, 1892, the illegitimate children of Francesca Rojas were murdered. She accused a man named Velasquez. Alvarez, a police investigator who trained under Vucetich, discovered that Rojas had a lover who had previously stated that he would marry her if she did not have children. A bloody fingerprint found at the scene matched Rojas's right thumb and she confessed.
- **1897**: Hermann Welcker compared his own prints with ones he had taken 41 years earlier and found they were unchanged, thus supporting the findings of William Herschel.
- **1899**: Sir Edward Henry devised a classification system based on five types of prints. His system is the basis for those used in Britain and America today.
- **1901**: Edward Richard Henry was appointed head of Scotland Yard and adopted a fingerprint identification system in place of anthropometry (see below).
- **1902**: Burglar Harry Jackson, who left his thumbprint at a crime scene, became the first person in England to be convicted by fingerprint evidence.
- **1903**: The New York State Prison system instituted the first systematic use of fingerprints for criminal identification in the United States.

- **1910**: Thomas Jennings became the first United States citizen convicted of a crime by use of fingerprints. Tried for murder in Chicago, Jennings was convicted and the verdict was upheld on appeal, making his case a landmark in the use of fingerprint evidence in court.

By the end of the 19th century, fingerprinting had not yet been established as the standard identification method but rather vied with **anthropometry** for that position in criminal investigations. The arguments continued until an odd and landmark confrontation between the two methods settled the issue.

Anthropometry and Bertillonage

Anthropometry (*anthrop* means human; *metry* means to measure) is the study of human body measurements for anthropological classification and comparison. Simply put, it is the making of body measurements in order to compare individuals with each other.

French police officer Alphonse Bertillon believed that the human skeleton did not change in size from about age 20 until death and that each person's measurements were unique. He also believed that people could be distinguished from one another by key measurements, such as height, seated height from head to seat, length and width of the head, right ear length, left little finger length, the width of the cheeks, and other measurements. He created a system of body measurements that became known as **bertillonage**. According to Bertillon, the odds of two people having the same **bertillonage measurements** were 286 million to one.

His greatest triumph came in February 1883, when he measured a thief named Dupont and compared his profile against his files of known criminals. He found that Dupont's measurements matched a man named Martin. Dupont ultimately confessed that he was indeed Martin.

For years, this system was accepted by many jurisdictions, but early in the 20th century flaws became apparent. Measurements were inexact and subject to observer variation due to the fact that measurements in two people who were of the same size, weight, and body type varied by only fractions of a centimeter. The measurement system wasn't exact enough to make such distinctions. The final blow to the bertillonage system occurred with the famous Will West case.

Though landmark in its importance, this case was more a comical coincidence. On May 1, 1903, Will West entered Kansas's Leavenworth Penitentiary, where the records clerk thought he looked familiar. West denied ever having been in the prison. As part of his intake examination, anthropometry was performed and officials were surprised to find that Will's measurements matched those of another inmate at Leavenworth named William West. The two men did look eerily similar, but each stated that they did not know each other and that they were not brothers. Fingerprints were then used to distinguish between the two Wills, after which Leavenworth immediately dumped anthropometry and switched to a fingerprint-based system for identifying prisoners. New York's Sing Sing Prison followed a month later.

Was the similarity between Will and William West simply a bizarre coincidence? Not really. A report in *The Journal of Police Science and Administration* in 1980 revealed that the two were likely identical twins. They possessed many fingerprint similarities, nearly identical ear configurations (unusual in any circumstance except with identical twins), and each of the men wrote letters to the same brother, same five sisters, and same Uncle George. So, even though the brothers denied it, it seemed that they were related after all.

Bertillon then reluctantly agreed to add fingerprints to his bertillonage profile. However, he added only those of the right hand, which proved to be a huge mistake.

On August 21, 1911, the Mona Lisa was stolen from the Louvre Museum in Paris. A thumbprint was found on the glass that protected Da Vinci's masterpiece. Alphonse Bertillon entered the investigation. Unfortunately, he had no classification system to streamline the search through his thousands of data cards, so he and his assistants had to spend several months digging through his files. They found no matches. Two years later, the police apprehended Vincenzo Peruggia and his prints matched the one found at the crime scene.

It turned out that Peruggia's prints were among those in Bertillon's possession all the time. Why no match? The print found at the scene was from Peruggia's left thumb, while Bertillon's files contained only that of the right. This unmasked yet another flaw in Bertillon's system and finally put it to rest.

Ridge Patterns

Fingerprints are actually friction ridge prints, since it is the ridge patterns that are the basis of printing and comparison. Their use for identification depends upon three principles:

- **Individuality**: No two people share the same fingerprints.
- **Stability**: Fingerprints remain unchanged throughout life, a fact confirmed by the work of William Herschel and Hermann Welcker.
- **Common patterns**: Fingerprints have general patterns that allow for a systematic method of classification, reducing the number of records that must be searched when looking for a match.

As mentioned earlier, Marcello Malphigi first recognized these ridge patterns and named them **loops** and **whorls**. The **arch** pattern followed more than 200 years later, when Sir Francis Galton identified it in 1892. Whorls, loops, and arches remain the basis for fingerprint identification and matching because, although everyone has them, how many and where they are located is unique. Not only do the patterns vary from person to person, but they also vary from finger to finger in any given individual. That is, we each have 10 unique prints, one on each of our digits.

Let's look at each of these basic patterns.

Arches rise in the center in a wave-like pattern. They are subgrouped into **plain** (Figure 13–1) and **tented** (Figure 13–2) varieties. Tented arches

Figure 13–1
Plain arch. This arch has a low central rise.

Figure 13–2
Tented arch. This type of arch rises more sharply than does a standard arch.

possess a sharper central rise than do plain arches. Only 5 percent of all pattern types are arches.

Loops, which make up 60 percent of all patterns, have one or more ridges that double back, or loop, on themselves. They come in either **single** (Figure 13–3) or **double** (Figure 13–4) varieties. Single loops are further divided into two types depending upon the direction the ridges flow in relation to the **radius** and the **ulna**, the two bones of the forearm. The radius is the larger of the two and is on the thumb side, so **radial loops** flow

Figure 13–3
Single loop. A single loop occurs when one or more ridges double back on themselves.

Figure 13–4
Double loop. A double loop is two loops nested against one another.

downward and toward the thumb side. The ulna, the smaller forearm bone, lies on the little finger side, so ulnar loops flow in that direction.

Whorls resemble whirlpools and comprise 35 percent of all patterns seen. These are subgrouped into several types. **Plain whorls** are concentric circles like a target (Figure 13–5); **spirals** (Figure 13–6) look like a wound spring; **central pocket loop whorls** (Figure 13–7) resemble a loop with a whorl at its end; **double loop whorls** are two loops that collide to produce an S-shaped pattern; and **accidental loop whorls** (Figure 13–8) are similar to central pocket loop whorls but with subtle differences.

Figure 13–5
Target whorl. Resembles a bull's eye.

Figure 13–6

Spiral whorl. Looks like clock springs.

Figure 13–7

Central pocket loop whorl. Resembles a loop with a whorl at its end.

Figure 13–8

Accidental loop whorl. Similar to a central pocket loop whorl.

Fingerprint Classification Systems

Once it was proven that fingerprints are individual and remain unchanged for life, a system for effectively using this knowledge became imperative. Sorting through and comparing thousands, and eventually millions, of print cards simply wasn't practical, so some system for narrowing the search became necessary.

The purpose of any classification system is to add order to chaos by finding common traits among the individual items. For example, bookstores organize books by subject matter or genre and most libraries use either the Dewey Decimal System or the Library of Congress Classification System. Department, grocery, and hardware stores have their own unique organization systems.

The same is true for fingerprint files. They are useful only if they can be stored in great numbers and quickly searched. The Federal Bureau of Investigation (FBI) stores approximately five hundred million fingerprint files, so organizing them into groups makes the matching process much easier. The system used by the FBI and other U.S. jurisdictions is based on the Henry System devised in 1899 by Sir Edward Henry.

The Henry System

Sir Henry's system is too complicated to explain in its entirety here, but a brief look will expose how it works. At its heart is the presence or absence of whorl patterns on the various fingers of a 10-finger print set. Scores are assigned based on which fingers have whorls, with some fingers getting higher scores than others.

First, Henry paired the fingers in a numerator/denominator scheme:

$$\frac{\text{R. Index}}{\text{R. Thumb}} \quad \frac{\text{R. Ring}}{\text{R. Middle}} \quad \frac{\text{L. Thumb}}{\text{R. Little}} \quad \frac{\text{L. Middle}}{\text{L. Index}} \quad \frac{\text{L. Little}}{\text{L. Ring}}$$

If a whorl pattern is seen on either of the first pair (right index and right thumb), it is assigned a value of 16 points, on the second pair (right ring and right middle) 8 points, the third 4 points, the fourth 2 points, and the fifth 0 points. Any finger having an arch or a loop pattern is given a value of 0. Finally, 1 is added to both the numerator and denominator.

Let's say that a whorl appeared on both the right index finger and the right thumb. According to the scheme, each of these would receive 16 points and would be indicated by placing a 16 in both the numerator and denominator at the first position of the sequence. If neither had a whorl, both numerator and denominator would have a 0. Further, if a whorl appeared on the right thumb but not the right index, then the numerator would be assigned a 0 and the denominator a 16. In these situations, the first position in Henry's chart would, respectively, look like this:

$$\frac{16}{16} \quad \frac{0}{0} \quad \frac{0}{16}$$

So, a set that showed whorls on only the right index finger, the left middle and ring fingers, and both little fingers would have this score:

$$\frac{16}{0} + \frac{0}{0} + \frac{0}{4} + \frac{2}{0} + \frac{0}{0} + \frac{1}{1} = \frac{19}{5}$$

By using Henry's scoring system, files can be separated into 1,024 groups. The final match is made by hand, but only those prints with the same overall score as the print in question are examined, which greatly focuses the search. So the system does not make the match but rather reduces the number of files agents must wade through.

One major drawback to Henry's system was that it requires a complete 10-finger set of prints. Otherwise the overall score can't be calculated. Unfortunately, criminals rarely leave behind a full set of prints. Maybe one or two fingers, maybe only a single partial print. This proved to be major obstacle until computers and the **Automated Fingerprint Identification System (AFIS)** entered the arena.

AFIS was established in 1977 through a collaboration between the FBI and the National Bureau of Standards (now the National Institute of Standards and Technologies, or NIST). With the growing numbers of print sets in the FBI's database, some method for storing, retrieving, and matching became a necessity. Imagine hundreds of agents sitting at hundreds of desks looking through thousands of print cards, searching for a match to the partial print left behind by a serial killer. Not very efficient.

The AFIS computer scans, digitally encodes, and stores fingerprints, after which it can search thousands of these files each second. If a "hit" (match) occurs, a fingerprint examiner will hand-check the prints so that even in the computer age, a trained human eye makes the final match.

An example of the power of such rapid searches is illustrated by the famous Nightstalker case.

Between June 1984 and August 1985, a series of brutal rapes and murders occurred throughout Southern California and the Bay Area, putting the entire state on edge. The killer became known as the Nightstalker because he entered his victims' homes at night through unlocked doors, often after he had cut the phone line. He would shoot any adult males present and then rape his female victims, often in the bed next to her dead or dying spouse. Sometimes he would then kill his female victim and other times not. He made some of his victims swear an oath to Satan and at one scene scrawled a satanic pentagram on the wall and on the woman's thigh.

His final victim was a Mission Viejo woman whom he raped in the bed next to her boyfriend who had been shot in the head. Both survived the attack.

Earlier, a teenager, working on his motorcycle in his parents' garage, saw an orange station wagon enter and then leave the neighborhood. He wrote down the license plate number and the next morning called police and gave it to them. The stolen car was found abandoned two days later. It had been wiped clean but a single partial fingerprint was found.

The print was sent to Sacramento, where it was entered into the newly installed AFIS system and within hours a match was made. It was estimated that to perform a by-hand match of the print against the 1.7 million print cards in the Los Angeles area alone would have taken an agent 67 years.

The print revealed that the Nightstalker was Richard Ramirez, a 25-year-old drifter from El Paso, Texas. Once his likeness went out over the media, residents of East Los Angeles recognized him and overpowered him as he attempted to steal a car. The police arrived in time to save him from an angry mob. On November 7, 1989, he received a death sentence.

Locating and Collecting Fingerprints

Before print matching can be utilized, the prints must be located and collected. Sometimes the prints are readily visible, while at other times they require a diligent search. A print left in grease, paint, or blood on a wall will be much easier to find than one left on a trash bag by a hand not contaminated with any visible substance. Yet, each can be critical to solving the crime.

Fingerprints are of three basic types:

- **Patent prints** are visible to the naked eye. They occur when the perpetrator gets a substance such as blood, ink, paint, dirt, or grease on his fingers and leaves behind a visible print.
- **Plastic prints** are three-dimensional and occur when the perpetrator impresses a print into a soft substance such as wax, putty, caulk, soap, moist paint, or even cold butter.
- **Latent prints** are invisible and can't be seen without special lighting or processing.

How patent and plastic prints are laid down should be obvious, but what about latent prints? During normal daily activities, the friction ridges of the fingers, palms, and foot soles pick up oils, salts, and grime. Then whenever one of these body parts, say a finger pad, contacts another surface, this residue is deposited. So, latent prints come from "dirty" fingers. Freshly washed hands will leave fainter latent prints than will fingers that are contaminated with sweat and grime. It is the job of the crime scene technicians and police to locate, expose, and collect these hidden prints.

The best surfaces to search for latent prints are any place the perpetrator might have touched such as the murder weapon, any tools or objects left behind, opened drawers or out of place furniture, and entry and exit points.

Patent and plastic prints are visible and can be easily photographed, and the photo can be used for matching. An angled light might increase contrast, but little else is needed to make these prints photographable. On the other hand, latent prints require special handling, and the criminalist has several methods for exposing and collecting them.

Often the simplest approach is best. An angled light source, with or without the aid of a magnifying glass, might expose the print. Also, since the oils of the print will fluoresce (glow) when exposed to some laser and ultraviolet lights, these might snap it into view so it can be photographed. At other times, fingerprint powders are necessary.

Fingerprint powders adhere to the moisture and oils of the latent print residue and expose the pattern of the friction ridges. They come in a variety of colors; the color chosen should offer the greatest contrast with the background surface. Black (made from carbon black or charcoal) and gray (made from aluminum or titanium powder) are used most often, but white or another light color should be used when the background is dark.

Magnetically sensitive powders also come in varying colors. These powders are used with a special magnetic "brush," which doesn't require contact with the print, so it is less likely to damage or smear it. Passing the device over the print deposits the powder, making the print visible. Other specialized powders are **fluorescent**, which will cause the print to fluoresce under a laser light.

Once the print has been exposed by one of these methods, it is photographed and then "lifted." **Lifting** is done by gently laying the sticky surface of a strip of transparent tape over the print. The print pattern sticks to the tape, which is then peeled away and placed on a card for later examination and matching.

All these techniques work very well if the print has been deposited on a smooth, firm surface. Latent prints on more porous surfaces must be treated with chemicals, which reveal print patterns by reacting with some component of the print residue. The reaction creates another compound that is more clearly visible. Common chemicals used for exposing prints include cyanoacrylate, iodine, ninhydrin, and silver nitrate.

Cyanoacrylate is a component of Super Glue. When heated, its vapors will bind to the amino acids in print residues, revealing the latent print in white. This is often done in a **fuming chamber**, which is simply an airtight box that will prevent the gaseous glue from escaping. A few drops of the glue are put into a pan, which is placed over a heating element, and after a few minutes vapors will fill the chamber and begin to react with the print. Once the print has been exposed with cyanoacrylate, it can be photographed as is, powdered like other prints, or exposed to a fluorescent dye.

Rather than setting up a fuming box at the crime scene, police now frequently use a **handheld wand** that heats a small cartridge of Super Glue mixed with a fluorescent dye. The released fumes are then directed at the latent print. In this way, the cyanoacrylate "fixing" and the fluorescent dying of the print occur at the same time.

As you might expect with Super Glue, the fumed print is quite hard and stable. It will actually fix the print to the surface it is on so that it can later be presented in court exactly as found. For example, if the print was found on a knife handle, the knife can be shown in court so that the jury sees not only the print but also its exact location on the weapon.

Iodine fuming also employs a fuming chamber. In this case solid crystal iodine releases iodine vapors, which combine with the oils in the latent print to produce a brownish print. The print is very short-lived and fades quickly, so it must be photographed quickly. Or the print can be "fixed" by spraying it with a solution of starch in water, which will preserve the print for several weeks or months.

Ninhydrin (triketohydrindene hydrate) has been a staple of law enforcement for many years and is very useful for exposing prints on paper products. The object is either dipped in or sprayed with a ninhydrin solution, which reacts with the print's oils, producing a purple-blue print. One drawback is that this reaction is extremely slow and can take several hours before the print becomes visible. Heating the object to 80 to 100 degrees will hasten the reaction.

Silver nitrate is a component of photographic film. When a latent print is exposed to silver nitrate, the chloride of the salt (sodium chloride) molecules in the print residue reacts with the silver to form silver chloride, a colorless compound that turns black or reddish-brown when exposed to ultraviolet light.

Bloody Prints

Bloody fingerprints are most often patent, but sometimes they are too faint to photograph, and the usual powders might not expose them well enough. A laser light might prove helpful, but even if not, the criminalist can use Luminol or Amido Black.

Luminol will be discussed in detail in Chapter 14 since it is better suited for larger pattern impressions such as shoe prints, but it can occasionally help with fingerprint exposure. It reacts with the blood's hemoglobin, causing it to fluoresce when viewed in dark conditions. The glow doesn't last long, so once the print is exposed it must be photographed fairly quickly. A big advantage of Luminol is that reacts with extremely small traces of blood—down to parts per billion. It can find blood where none seems to exist, even in scenes that are many years old or have been cleaned or painted over.

Amido Black, also called **naphthalene blue-black**, reacts with blood proteins and turns the bloody print a blue-black color. The print is then photographed for later comparisons.

Digitally Enhancing Prints

Often a print is unclear and its minute details fuzzy and difficult to see well. If so, the print can be scanned into a computer and manipulated by one of several programs that enhance, improve, and clean it up. Changing the light, contrast, clarity, and background patterns can make a previously obscure print jump into view.

Fingerprints and DNA

An exciting new discovery is what has been termed **touch DNA**. This is DNA deposited simply by touching an object. As we saw in Chapter 11, the PCR-STR DNA analysis technique requires only very small amounts of DNA, and theoretically only a single nucleated cell. Since print residues contain not only oils and grime but also cellular debris from the person's finger, DNA can often be extracted from a fingerprint.

Altered Fingerprints

For many years, criminals have attempted to alter or remove their fingerprints with heat or cutting edges, but unless the damage is deep within the tissues, as with a third-degree burn, the prints will reappear as soon as the skin repairs itself. Completely obliterating a print is difficult, and any scars left behind will actually create new individual characteristics an examiner can use for making a match. Not only are no two prints identical, but also no two finger pads are damaged in exactly the same way. Even Public Enemy Number One tried this ploy.

John Dillinger is a name known to virtually every American. He was one of our most notorious criminals, attaining the moniker of Public Enemy Number One. In an effort to evade the cops, he underwent facial plastic surgery and tried to remove his fingerprints with acid. After his betrayal by the famous "lady in red," Dillinger was shot dead outside Chicago's Biograph Theater. Prints taken at the morgue proved that the dead man was indeed Dillinger. The acid had damaged only a portion of his finger pads, leaving enough ridge detail for matching with his prints on file with the police.

Glove Prints

Some criminals wear gloves to prevent leaving behind prints. Thin latex surgical-type gloves are sometimes so thin that the friction ridges still protrude, and their pattern might be left on a smooth surface if the glove is contaminated with blood, grease, paint, or some similar substance. In addition, there have been cases where the perpetrator tossed aside these gloves near the crime scene and his fingerprints were obtained from inside the glove's fingertips.

Even using leather or cloth gloves is no guarantee. Though fingerprints will not be left, the pattern of the glove fingertips or palm might be. If the glove has defects, such as snags in cloth gloves or creases and scars on the surface of leather ones, these can leave a distinctive patterned print at the scene. If the gloves are located and the examiner is able to match the print to defects in the gloves, this can be strong evidence that the gloves in question were used during the commission of the crime. This and other patterned evidence will be examined in Chapter 15.

CHAPTER 14

BLOODSTAINS

Violent crimes often involve the shedding of blood. From a forensic point of view, blood provides the ME with a wealth of information. Bloodstains can often indicate exactly what happened at the crime scene and in what sequence. The analysis of bloodstain patterns is both science and art. Science tells us how blood behaves, but understanding the messages hidden within its patterns requires knowledge, experience, and common sense.

The analysis of blood can be divided along **biological** and **physical** lines. Biological analyses provide evidence of diseases, such as AIDS or diabetes, which can be possible indications of a natural cause of death. Toxicological examinations (Chapter 12) reveal the presence of alcohol or drugs, which could have caused or contributed to the death. ABO typing (Chapter 10) and DNA analysis (Chapter 11) can help identify a victim or suspect.

But, in this chapter we will address blood's physical properties, or how it behaves as a liquid. The bloodstain pattern at the crime scene can be used to determine the cause and manner of death and to reconstruct the crime scene.

It is unknown exactly when bloodstain patterns were first used in a criminal investigation, but it was mentioned in an English court proceeding as early as 1514. It wasn't until 1895 that Polish scientist Dr. Eduard

Piotrowski published the first work on bloodstain pattern recognition in which he cataloged the results of his extensive studies of blood spatters. The famous case of the *State of Ohio v. Samuel Sheppard* was landmark in the use of bloodstains in United States courtrooms.

This famous case inspired the popular television series and major motion picture *The Fugitive*. The real case began on the night of July 4, 1954, when Dr. Samuel Sheppard's wife, Marilyn, was brutally murdered in their home. Sheppard said an intruder attacked and bludgeoned his wife to death. He had attempted to protect her but was knocked unconscious. When he awoke, he examined his wife for signs of life, including checking the pulse in her neck, and then called for help.

The home appeared to have been ransacked as if the attacks were part of a home invasion robbery. But police found inconsistencies in the crime scene bloodstain pattern. For example, Sheppard had no blood on his hands, body, or clothing. Such stains would have been expected had he been the one to bludgeon his wife, and their absence would seem to exonerate Sheppard. But this complete lack of blood on him and his clothing raised many questions. Because of the brutal nature of the attack, the killer would have been covered with blood, and some of that blood should have been transferred to Sheppard during their struggle. In addition, Sheppard had no blood on his hands, which would be likely if he had checked for a pulse in his wife's blood-covered neck.

Sheppard said that his watch, wallet, ring, and keys were missing, and he believed that the killer had taken them and, indeed, the police found a green bag with the missing items not far from the house. Again, the bag and wallet had no blood on them as would be expected if the killer had handled them with his bloody hands. And wouldn't Sheppard's pants, wrists, and hands have blood transfers as the killer removed the wallet, keys, watch, and rings? No such stains were found, which meant that whoever took those items and placed them into the bag did so with clean hands.

Several very fine blood spatters, produced by flying blood droplets, were found on the face of Sheppard's watch, indicating that the watch had been near the victim at the time she was struck. Had they come from contact with the victim's neck as Sheppard felt for a pulse, the stains would have been in the form of transfer smears and not spatter droplets.

Police determined that most likely Sheppard bludgeoned his wife to death, cleaned the blood from his hands and body, trashed the house to make it look as though a burglary had occurred, placed his watch and the other items in the green bag, and tossed the bag where police would find it. He had obviously overlooked the spatters on his watch. Based on the blood, or lack of blood, evidence as well as other evidence, Sheppard was convicted of murder. The case didn't end there, and over the decades the family of Dr. Sheppard have returned to court to clear the doctor's name in what is viewed by many to be a wrongful conviction. Dr. Sheppard was posthumously declared innocent, but his story remains controversial to this day.

As seen in the Sheppard case, an analysis of bloodstain patterns, called **blood spatter patterns**, can often allow the ME to determine the origin of the bloodstains, the type of weapon used, the direction from which an object struck the victim, the relative positions of the victim and the assailant or assailants, the locations and movements of the victim and assailant during the attack, the number of blows or gunshots delivered to the victim, and the truthfulness of any suspects and witnesses.

Characteristics of Blood

Blood is a complex substance, consisting of liquid (plasma) and solid (cellular) components. It shares many physical properties with other liquids in that it moves and flows as gravity dictates, tends to pool in "low-lying" areas, and spreads to cover a surface or to conform to the shape of any container. It possesses **viscosity**, a measure of its "thickness," and **surface tension**, which is an elastic-like property that results from the attraction of a liquid's molecules for each other. It is the force that holds a liquid together and that pulls a falling drop into a spherical shape.

Blood is more viscous (thicker) than water, and unlike water and other liquids, it clots. Within its liquid plasma are cellular elements such as red blood cells, white blood cells, and platelets, and various proteins, many of which are involved in the clotting process. When blood clots, it separates into a solid dark-red clot and a clear yellow liquid we call **serum**. Blood will remain a liquid as long as it's inside the body's vascular system and is moving. When it leaves the body it will clot in a few minutes, and at death it clots within the blood vessels almost as quickly.

Any unchecked blood loss will ultimately lead to death from **exsanguination** (bleeding to death). This blood loss can be in the form of a drip, ooze, flow, gush, or spurt, and each of these leaves a distinctive bloodstain pattern. As blood flows from the body, it begins to pool and clot, a process that normally takes from 3 to 15 minutes. This timeline is variable and can be affected by diseases, such as hemophilia and leukemia, as well as blood-thinning medications like heparin and warfarin.

When blood begins to clot, it first forms a dark, shiny, jelly-like mass. With time, this clot will begin to contract and separate from the serum, leaving a dark central clot haloed by the yellowish serum. Investigators can use this to make a rough estimate of the time lag since the blood left the victim's body. If still liquid, the bleeding occurred only a few minutes before; if a shiny and gelatinous pool, the bleeding likely occurred 30 minutes or more earlier; and if separated into clot and serum, it is probable that one to several hours have passed.

At death, the heart stops, the blood ceases to circulate, and bleeding stops. Within minutes, the blood begins to clot within the vessels and tissues of the body. This means that corpses do not bleed, so any bloodstains resulting from spurting or gushing of blood must have occurred before death. Impact spatters, on the other hand, can occur after death if the assailant continues striking the victim. Or transfer patterns can occur if the assailant steps in a blood pool and tracks it through the scene.

Blood Spatter Patterns

The mechanisms by which blood leaves the body can be divided into two categories: passive and projected. **Passive** mechanisms depend on the action of gravity alone, while **projected** blood results when some force other than gravity is applied. Drips and oozes are passive, while arterial spurts, cast-off blood, and impact spatters are projected. Each of these mechanisms creates unique stain patterns that are called **bloodstain patterns** or **blood spatters**.

Passive Bloodstain Patterns

Passive stains are due to the effects of gravity and are not ejected or forced from the body by some other force. Blood that oozes or drips from the body will "go downhill," collecting in the lowest areas near the injured or deceased person. Stairs, ramps, floor drains, or any steeply angled floor might carry the blood a considerable distance before it clots. Obviously, gushing or fast-flowing blood will create larger pools and be able to travel farther from the body than would oozing blood, which will clot before moving too far from the body.

Blood might drip from an injured person's wounds, a blood-covered weapon, the assailant's hands, a tabletop, or any elevated object that is coated with blood. If a person is shot or stabbed in the shoulder, blood might run down his arm and drip from his fingers. An assailant fleeing with a bloody knife or bludgeon will drip blood in his wake.

Typically, a drop is formed when a small amount of blood breaks away from a larger blood source. Because of the drop's surface tension, it will be spherical and remain so until it strikes some surface or is itself struck by some object. Blood drops don't fracture into smaller drops simply by falling through the air, but if the drop strikes a table edge or is struck by a swinging arm or weapon, it can shatter into smaller droplets. Otherwise, it will fall as a sphere until it reaches the floor or some other surface.

When a falling blood drop strikes a flat surface, it will splash in all directions, creating a circular spatter around the point of impact. The diameter and shape of this spatter pattern depends upon the size and speed of the drop, the angle of impact, and the nature of the surface it strikes. A blood drop, like any other falling object, will gather speed as it falls until it reaches **terminal velocity**, its maximum free-fall speed, which is approximately 25 feet per second.

The drop's spatter pattern will increase in size as it falls from a distance of an inch up to about 7 feet, where it produces a circle of nearly an inch in diameter. Above that height, no significant increase in spatter diameter is seen. If the drop approaches at a right angle (90 degrees) to the surface, the spatter pattern will be a symmetrical circle around the point of impact and its diameter will depend on the distance traveled (Figure 14–1). If it strikes from a more acute angle, the spatter will be an elongated elliptical pattern, with the narrow or pointed end aiming in the direction of the drop's travel (Figure 14–2).

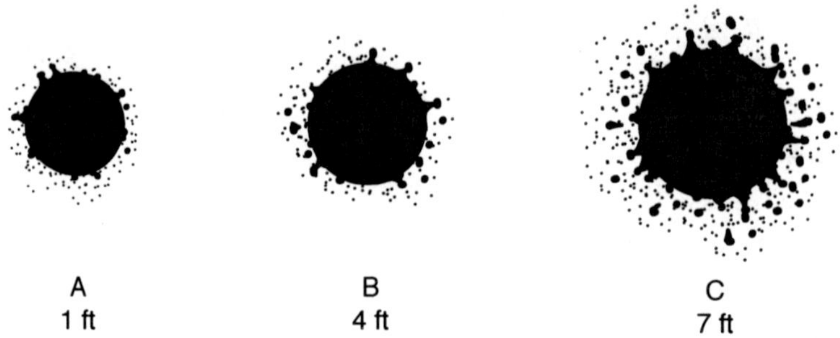

Figure 14–1

Vertical blood drop. The diameter of the bloodstain produced by a vertically falling drop of blood onto a smooth surface increases with the distance traveled: 1 foot (A), 4 feet (B), or 7 feet (C).

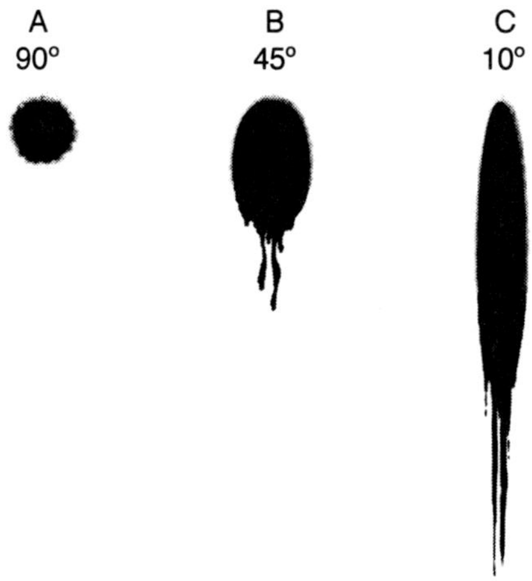

Figure 14–2

Angled blood drop. The shape of the stain pattern depends upon the angle of impact. The circular pattern seen in a 90-degree approach angle (A) progressively elongates as the angle becomes more acute, as is seen in impact angles of 45 degrees (B) and 10 degrees (C).

Using trigonometric functions, it is possible to calculate the angle of impact by measuring the dimensions of the stain (Figure 14–3), a determination that is critical for accurate crime scene reconstruction. The formula uses the width (W) and length (L) of the stain:

$$\text{Angle of impact} = \arcsin W/L$$

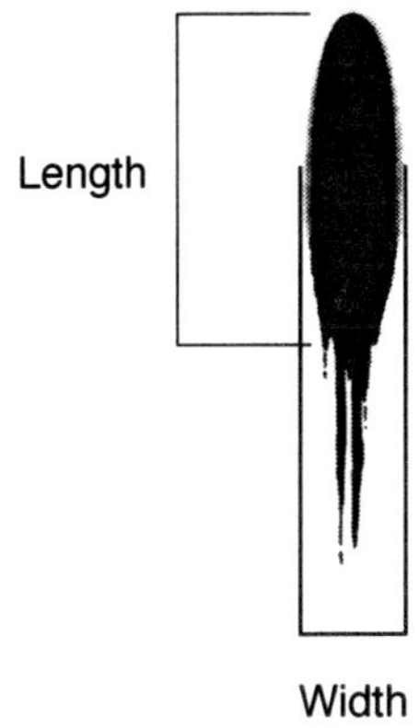

Figure 14–3
Angle of impact calculation. A blood drop's angle of impact can be calculated by measuring its width and length.

Some **secondary** or **satellite** spatters can create confusion. If a large drop of blood falls onto a hard surface, small secondary droplets might splash away and surround the original circular stain. Since these have directionality, they are elongated, but as opposed to the angled drop described above, the elongated "tails" of these satellite droplets tend to point toward the direction from which they came and not the direction they were traveling. The examiner must be aware of this or he might conclude that the drops came from the exact opposite direction, and this could greatly alter his understanding of what happened during the assault.

The nature of the surface impacted will also significantly alter the size and character of the spatter (Figure 14–4). Hard, smooth surfaces such as glass, glazed tile, or polished marble will create much smaller spatters than will rough, irregular surfaces such as unfinished wood or concrete.

As mentioned earlier, the dead don't bleed—under most circumstances, that is. There are situations where a body might continue to shed blood for a few minutes after death. This is called the **peri-mortem period**—the time around the time of death.

Take the example of someone killed by a throat slash. She falls dead fairly quickly and her heart stops, but the major arteries and veins of her neck, which hold a considerable volume of blood, might continue oozing blood until they have emptied or until the blood clots. This can take several

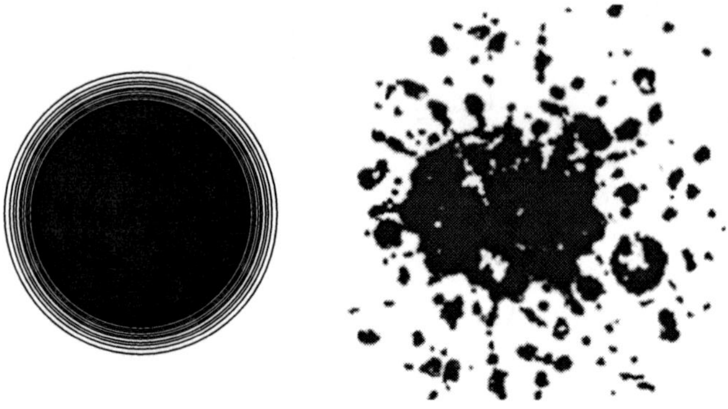

Figure 14–4

Target surface and spatter shape. The character of the struck surface alters the spatter pattern of a blood drop. A smooth surface (A) will create a small, round spatter, while a rough surface (B) causes a very irregular spatter.

minutes, so that a pool of blood might collect near the victim's neck even after death has occurred.

Projected Blood Spatters

Projected blood spatters are created by some force other than gravity. These include internal forces such as the heartbeat and breathing (arterial bleeding and expirated blood) or external forces such as a gunshots, knife wounds, and blunt-force trauma. As we will see later in this chapter, the disseminated bloodstains vary in size and shape, depending on the mechanism of their creation. This knowledge is extremely helpful in crime scene reconstruction since skilled spatter pattern analysis can reveal the blood source, the source's location at the crime scene, and the mechanism that produced the spatters.

A single gunshot can produce a spatter pattern, but a single blow with a blunt object typically does not. Why? A bullet that enters and exits the body causes immediate bleeding and carries blood and tissue with it through the exit wound. This produces a characteristic spatter pattern on any object "downwind" from the exit point. In a victim repeatedly struck in the head, the first blow will strike only skin and hair and thus will not cause a spattering of blood. It will however cause damage and bleeding so that the bloody scalp becomes a **blood source**. A blood source is defined as any collection of blood, in this case on and within the scalp. Subsequent blows to the same area will cause spattering. So, the initial blow produces the blood source and subsequent blows produce the spattering.

Locating the blood source within the crime scene is accomplished by determining the **point of convergence** and the **point of origin** of the spatter. The former employs simple plain geometry, the latter three-dimensional solid geometry. It's not as difficult as it might sound.

Just as we saw with blood drops, the individual droplets that make up the spatter strike nearby surfaces with varying **angles of impact** and **directionality**. The impact angle is the angle of approach relative to the surface struck, while the directionality is the direction from which it approached. The directionality of each stain is used to locate the point of convergence (Figure 14–5). It is a two-dimensional location that is determined by the convergence of imaginary lines drawn through the long axis of two or more spatters.

At the crime scene, strings are stretched along the long axis of each stain. The strings intersect at the point of convergence. If the angle of

Figure 14–5

Point of convergence. Lines drawn through the long axis of each bloodstain will intersect at the point of convergence, which indicates the location of the blood source.

impact of each stain is added to this measurement, the point of origin is revealed (Figure 14–6). This is done by using a protractor to angle each of the imaginary lines or strings to correspond with each stain's angle of impact. Today, laser lights are sometimes used instead of strings, and computer programs are available to help with the calculations. The point of origin is the point in space where the lines intersect and indicates the three-dimensional location of the blood source.

Let's say the blood spatter analyst examines a crime scene and finds spatter patterns on the floor, wall, and sofa and determines that the point of origin was approximately five feet from the wall, three feet from the sofa, and six feet above the floor. This would indicate that the victim was standing near the wall and the sofa at the time of the attack. If he found that the proximity to the wall and sofa were as above, but the distance to the floor was only 1 to 2 feet, the victim was likely lying on the floor when struck. This creates two entirely different scenes: In the former, the victim could easily have been threatening his attacker and a self-defense plea might be reasonable, while in the latter that scenario would be unlikely.

A **void pattern** also helps with crime scene reconstruction. A void pattern is an absence of blood spatters in an area where you would expect to

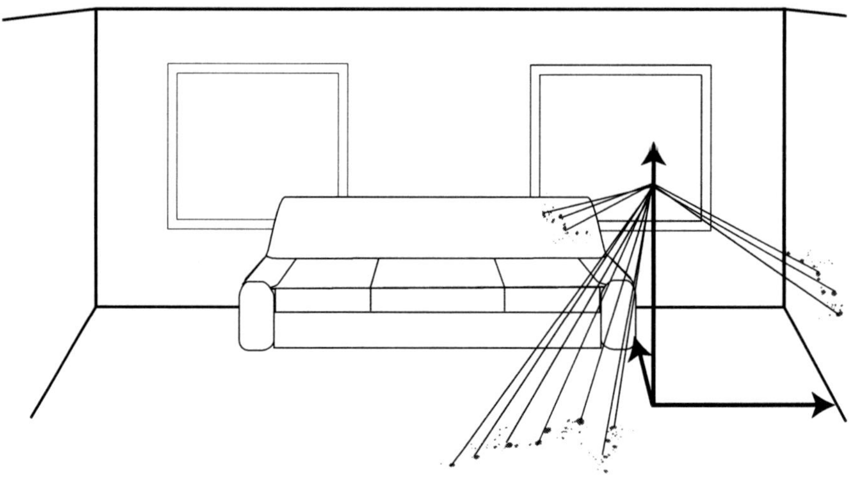

Figure 14–6

Point of origin. By using both directionality and angle of impact of each stain, the point of origin of the stains is revealed.

see them, and this might indicate where the attacker was standing. For example, if someone is severely beaten and blood spatters are found on the walls, floor, and furniture in every direction except to one side of the victim, it is likely that the attacker stood at that position during the attack and intercepted the spattered blood. Here the blood droplets would be on the attacker and not on the floor or other objects.

Similarly, if a spatter pattern is found on a suspect's body or clothing, it means he was present at the time of the attack. Spattering of blood can occur only during the impacts that produce them, so if the suspect had spatters on his clothes, arms, or face, he must have been in close proximity to the victim at the time of the attack. Someone who came along later and accidentally got blood on his clothing would not show a spatter pattern but rather blotches or smears. These stains are called **transfer patterns** (see below). This information can help investigators confirm or refute a suspect's statement regarding whether he was at the scene during the attack or not. An example is supplied by the Sam Sheppard case presented earlier in this chapter. The spatter on Dr. Sheppard's watch must have occurred during the attack and not later as he said.

So, the analysis of blood spatter patterns can reveal the blood source and the source's location at the crime scene. It can also provide clues as to the mechanism that produced the spatters.

Spatter Classification

Classifying spatter patterns helps determine what produced them. Was the blood shed as a result of a gunshot, a blow to the head, or a severed artery? The two methods for classifying projected blood spatters are the **mechanism** that produced them and the **velocity** with which the blood was shed. Using these, the ME can usually determine how the spatter was produced, which can help reconstruct the events of the crime and test the veracity of suspect and witness statements.

Spatter Mechanisms: Impact, Projection, and Combination

This system uses the mechanism that produced the stains and divides them into three major types: impact, projection, or combination spatters.

Impact spatters typically occur with beatings, stabbings, gunshots, or any other circumstance where the victim is "impacted" by a foreign object.

Projection spatters result from arterial bleeding, castoff blood, and expirated blood. Arterial bleeding occurs whenever an artery is torn or punctured and blood is pumped through the defect by the beating heart. Castoff stains occur whenever a blood-soaked object, such as a bat or pipe, is swung. The swinging action "casts off" droplets of blood, which might be found on the floor, walls, ceiling, or any nearby object. Expirated blood results when the victim's lungs or airways contain blood and the victim is breathing. Each expiration sprays blood from the victim's mouth and nose. These are common after gunshot or stab wounds to the chest where one of the lungs is injured.

Often the spatters found at a crime scene are a **combination** of these. For example, a victim who is stabbed in the chest or neck might leave a combination of impact spatters from the force of the attack, castoff spatters from the arc of the knife, arterial projection spatters if a major artery is damaged, and expirated blood from the injured and bleeding lungs or trachea.

Spatter Velocity: Low, Medium, and High

The other classification method uses the force with which the impacting object strikes and the resulting velocity of the blood as it leaves the blood source. This system divides spatters into low-, medium-, and high-velocity spatters, which indicate the object and the mechanism that created the spatter.

Low-velocity spatters are created by an object moving less than 5 feet per second, which results in spatters that are typically 4 millimeters or greater in diameter. Examples of these types of spatters would be dripping blood from a hand or weapon, arterial bleeding, and castoff blood.

As we saw above, if the dripping source is standing still, the drops fall vertically and create circular stains. But if the source is moving, such as from a fleeing injured victim or an escaping assailant who is carrying a blood-covered weapon, the drops will strike the floor at an angle, producing elongated stains with projections extending in the direction of movement. Such information is vital to crime scene reconstruction.

Let's suppose that an assailant with blood on his hands stands near the body of his victim. He will drip blood onto the floor, leaving a round bloodstain pattern for each drop. If he begins to move around in the house, the drops that leave his hands will have a forward motion, or directionality, resulting in stains that are oval with an elongated tail pointing in the direction of travel. They would appear similar to the angled impacts shown in Figure 14–2. This can indicate the assailant's movements within the crime scene and perhaps lead to his escape route, where following his trail might uncover a discarded murder weapon or other evidence.

Arterial bleeding is also considered low-velocity. If an artery is damaged during an assault, suicide attempt, or accident, the blood loss might be in the form of gushes or spurts, depending upon the size of the artery, the extent of the damage, and whether clothing or some other object covers the injury. A freely spurting artery results in a spatter pattern that is linear and cascading in nature (Figure 14–7). Its distance from the wound,

Figure 14–7

Arterial blood spatters. Arterial bleeding occurs in rhythmic spurts. If the blood strikes a vertical surface, it will produce long, linear or arcing stains that "bleed" downward under the influence of gravity.

length, and volume will decline steadily as the blood loss increases and the victim's blood volume and blood pressure declines.

Castoff blood, also a low-velocity spatter pattern, is blood that is cast off or flung from a bloody object due to centrifugal force. An example would be the arcing blows delivered by an assailant who continually struck a victim with a baseball bat or similar object. With each swing, blood collected on the weapon is "cast off" and peppers the walls, ceiling, and any other nearby objects. Castoff patterns are typically fairly uniform trails of droplets that reflect the arc of travel of the weapon (Figure 14–8). Determining the point of convergence and the angle of impact of these castoff stains will reveal the assailant's position at the time he swung the weapon. In some cases, it is possible to estimate the perpetrator's height and even his handiness, or at least which hand struck the blows.

Figure 14–8

Castoff blood spatters. Blood cast off from a moving weapon typically forms a linear bloodstain pattern.

In some cases, the number of these castoff patterns found will indicate the minimum number of blows to the victim. Because every swing of the weapon might not produce castoff stains, there might have been more blows delivered, but there can't be fewer.

Medium-velocity spatters come from objects moving between 5 and 100 feet per second and are typically smaller than stains from low-velocity droplets, typically between 1 and 4 millimeters in diameter. Medium-velocity spatters come from impacts with blunt or sharp objects and from expirated blood.

Spatters from impacts with a blunt object are distributed in all directions in a radial pattern. Analysis of the directionality and impact angle of the stains can help locate the point of origin, and a void pattern can indicate the position of the attacker.

If the wounds are to the face, throat, or lungs, blood will mix with the exhaled air, creating a fine spray and producing a mist spatter pattern. This misty pattern might be found on and around the victim as well as on the attacker, and would indicate that the victim lived for a while after delivery of the blows.

High-velocity spatters result when an object strikes at a speed above 100 feet per second. These spatters tend to be very small, usually less than 1 millimeter in diameter, and often appear as mist-like stains. Gunshots and high-speed machinery injuries often produce such high-velocity spatters.

Transfer Patterns

Transfer patterns occur when a blood-soaked object contacts an unstained object. Bloody fingerprints and footprints are common examples. A perpetrator who brushes against or kneels in a bloodstain, or wipes the weapon or his hands on his shirt, transfers the victim's blood to his clothing. Matching the blood from such a transfer stain to the victim's blood will show that the suspect and the victim were in contact with one another during or after the blood-shedding event.

Sometimes, a blood-soaked fabric can leave behind a recognizable pattern. For example a victim's blood might soak into the perpetrator's shirt. If he then leans on a countertop or other smooth object he might transfer the blood to that surface, and this stain might reveal the weave pattern of his shirt. If this pattern is unique, it might prove to be useful evidence.

Blood Spatters and Crime Scene Reconstruction

The ME will use passive, spatter, transfer, and void patterns to reconstruct the crime scene and to determine the sequence of events that led to the victim's injury or death. This in turn might reveal whether a suspect or witness is being truthful about the circumstances of the crime. This analysis might also indicate that the body was moved or that someone attempted to clean up the scene. Long smears might reveal the path of a dragged body and faint smears and streaks on a freshly cleaned floor could indicate an attempt to clean up the scene.

Some bloodstains might be latent (invisible to the naked eye); if so, Luminol is frequently used to expose these hidden stains. Even in well-scrubbed scenes, Luminol can often reveal bloody tracks, drag marks, and even mop marks left behind by the attempted clean up. Luminol is so sensitive it can even reveal blood on surfaces that have been repainted. The fresh paint picks up some of the blood remaining on the surface, such as a wall that has been wiped clean, and this blood becomes incorporated within the new paint. Luminol, which can detect blood in parts per billion, will often expose the blood within the fresh paint.

Blood spatter patterns are often critical to crime scene reconstruction, which is part art, part science. This is a complex subject and can't be completely covered here, but let's look at a sample case, which will give you a feel for how all this works together.

Let's say a husband says he came home and found his wife had been bludgeoned to death. He checked to make sure she was dead, walked to the kitchen, and called the police, and then waited on the porch for their arrival. A reasonable and believable sequence of events. But, what if the victim is stretched out on the living room floor and the amount of blood around the body seems meager in view of the violence of the attack? What if no spatter patterns are found on the floor, wall, or furniture near the body? Such evidence would suggest that the victim had not been attacked where she lay. What if an examination of the kitchen revealed that the floors had been freshly cleaned? What if one leg of the husband's pants showed a very fine spatter and several tiny drops of the victim's blood were found on the carpet between the kitchen and the location of the body?

This evidence would refute the husband's story in many ways and would elevate him to the top of the suspect list. The spatter analysis would suggest an entirely different scenario, beginning with the fact that the victim was likely killed in the kitchen and moved to the living room, probably in an effort to deflect the investigator's attention away from the true crime scene. The kitchen was then cleaned, but the drops on the carpet that fell while moving the body went unnoticed by the husband. Luminol might reveal drag stains where the body was moved, mop strokes where the kitchen floor was cleaned, and wipe marks from where he cleaned the cabinets or kitchen table. Even worse news for the husband would be the spatter pattern on his pant leg, which would indicate that he had at least been present at the time of the attack. Again, like Dr. Sheppard's watch.

Let's look at a second example.

John comes home from work two hours early one day and finds that the back door to his house has been pried open. As he enters, he hears someone moving around upstairs, so he goes to his den where he keeps a handgun locked in a drawer. Taking the weapon, he climbs the stairs and enters his bedroom, where he surprises a burglar, standing near a chest of drawers and rummaging through his wife's jewelry case. The burglar charges him and John manages to get off a single shot, which hits the intruder in the upper arm. But the thief strikes John in the side of the head twice with a metal pipe. The gun falls to the floor and John retreats into the hallway, his attacker in pursuit. John heads toward the bathroom in the hopes of locking himself inside, but doesn't make it. He is clubbed to the floor, rolls to his back, and attempts to defect the blows. He is struck in the head several times before he loses consciousness. The attacker strikes him three more times, killing John. He then returns to the bedroom, takes the jewelry box and rushes down the stairs and out the back door.

Using fingerprints and the AFIS system (Chapter 13), the police quickly identify the perpetrator and arrest him at his home. He admits to the robbery but says that the killing was in self-defense. Will the blood spatter patterns at the scene expose his lie?

In the bedroom: The bullet that entered the thief's arm would produce high-velocity spatter over the carpet, the chest of drawers, and perhaps the bed or any other nearby furniture. There would also be medium-velocity spatter on the floor and doorway from the blows to John's head. DNA analysis could easily determine whose blood was where, and firearms examination (Chapter 17) would reveal that the victim's gun was the weapon that fired the bullet through the thief's arm. Also, using gunshot residue techniques and perhaps fingerprints, it would be shown that indeed John had pulled the trigger. So far, the perpetrator's story holds up.

In the hallway: Blood drops from both men would be found on the hardwood floor of the hall and the shape of these drops would indicate that both were moving toward the bathroom at the end of the hall. Bloody shoe prints might also help in this regard. Near the bathroom, blood spatter analysis would show that several blows were delivered to the now unarmed John, and defensive wounds on his hands and arms would indicate that he defended himself. Spatters from the killing blows would cover the floor, wall, and perhaps the door leading into the bathroom. The point of origin of these spatters would indicate that John had been on the floor when the killing blows were delivered.

Based on the bloodstain evidence, the criminalist should be able to reconstruct the scene and determine the exact sequence of events. The fact that John was unarmed, on the floor, and in a defensive posture would refute the killer's claim that he had killed John in self-defense. The perpetrator might not face only burglary charges but also murder charges. He could easily have fled with John injured and down, but he chose to continue his attack, ultimately killing John.

CHAPTER **15**

IMPRESSIONS: SHOES, TIRES, AND TOOLS

Pattern evidence is evidence that is useful for identification, comparison, and matching based on its "pattern." Fingerprints, palm prints, footprints (Chapter 13), blood spatters (Chapter 14), and even the braid pattern of rope ligatures stamped in bruises on a strangulation victim's neck (Chapter 8) are examples of pattern evidence that can be useful in criminal investigations. Other pattern evidence, which is the subject of this chapter, include shoe and tire impressions and tool marks. In most cases, these yield only class evidence, but by examining wear, tear, and damage marks, the criminalist might be able to individualize the evidence.

For example, the tread pattern of a shoe or a tire might identify the size, the model, and the manufacturer of the product, and these details alone will narrow the search by focusing investigative efforts on the sellers and buyers of that particular product. But even if this leads to a particular suspect, wearing shoes of the same size and brand or driving a car with the same brand and style of tires does not mean that his shoes or his tires left the impressions at the crime scene. It simply means that he could have and, along with anyone else who wears similar shoes or who drives a car with similar tires, does not exclude him from the suspect list. But, if the wear pattern or areas of damage to a suspect shoe or tire exactly match that of the impression found at the crime scene, this would individualize the evidence and point the figure more directly at the suspect.

Shoe Impression Evidence

Shoe manufacturers typically produce many styles, shapes, and sizes of their products. Some possess plain, simple leather soles with few distinguishing features while others, particularly athletic shoes, have intricate, easily recognizable tread patterns. As we go about our daily activities, the soles of our shoes contact a wide array of surfaces such as hardwood or tile floors, carpets, soft soil, rain-soaked sidewalks, mud, grass, snow, sand, and the list goes on. The soles tend to pick up dirt, oil, grease, moisture, and debris from one surface and deposit these substances on other surfaces, leaving behind shoe prints.

Like fingerprints, shoe impressions can be **patent** (visible), **latent** (invisible), or **plastic** (three-dimensional). Patent prints often consist of dirt, grease, paint, blood, or some other easily visible substance, while latent prints result from the transfer of the thin layer of accumulated grime on the sole of the shoe to hard surfaces such as polished wood or tile floors, glass, pieces of paper, or cardboard. Plastic prints can be laid down in soft, malleable substrates such as mud or snow.

These impressions can associate a suspect with the crime scene, aid crime scene reconstruction, link several scenes together, indicate the minimum number of participants in the crime, and many other things.

Scene and suspect association: The most important function of shoe impressions is to associate a particular person with the crime scene, and often this alone is enough to focus investigative attention toward the individual. For example, if a shoe print is found at the crime scene and the print is matched to shoes that belong to someone who had no legitimate reason to be there, the simple finding of the print is strong evidence against the person. Why else would his shoe print be at the scene?

Or, even if the person has a plausible reason for his shoe prints to be found at the scene, the prints might still be useful in confirming or rebutting his alibi or story. Let's say his shoe print was found at a homicide scene. In blood. This would suggest that he participated in or was at least present during or shortly after the commission of the crime. He might say he was never there, but his prints in the victim's blood would say otherwise. Remember O. J. Simpson's "ugly ass" Bruno Magli shoes? The finding of this uncommon and expensive sole pattern at the Nicole Brown and Ron Goldman murder scene and the photos of O. J. wearing the exact same model and size were crucial in the civil judgment against Simpson.

The FBI maintains a database of thousands of footwear sole patterns that can help reveal the manufacturer, size, and style of the shoe that left the crime scene print. This determination can be used to include or exclude a suspect as the possible perpetrator. If the suspect owns, or it can be proven that he has owned, an identical size and style of shoe, he cannot be eliminated as a suspect, but if he neither possesses nor has ever possessed such a shoe, he might be excluded from consideration.

Crime scene reconstruction: A suspect whose shoe prints are found at the scene might say he stumbled into the scene but had nothing to do with the crime. If so, finding his prints in areas he says he never entered could be crucial to refuting his story. For example, a neighbor says he walked next door to borrow a cup of sugar and saw the woman who lived there lying on the kitchen floor, bludgeoned to death. He says the door was unlocked, so he checked her for a pulse, called 911, and waited for the police. He went nowhere else in the house. If the police then discover his shoe print in the woman's bedroom near where her empty jewelry box is found, his story immediately becomes suspect.

Prints often indicate the points of entry and exit. Plastic shoe prints in the soft soil of a flower garden beneath a pried-open window and matching dirt and grime prints on the floor inside the home would indicate the point of entry. The same could be said for prints found on pieces of glass from a shattered window. Prints left on tile or wooden floors, stairs, countertops, windowsills, ladders, and even chair seats reveal the perpetrator's movements within the crime scene. Prints found near an open rear door might indicate the exit route, and a search for evidence along that path might turn up a discarded weapon or articles of clothing such as a mask or gloves. Perpetrators often leave evidence in their wake as they rush from the scene.

Scene linkage: A shoe print can link several crimes. If an identical print is found at several different crime scenes, it indicates that the same perpetrator is involved in each. This linkage can be crucial since each scene might have other evidence that taken alone is of little help, but when considered together could be significant. Let's say that identical prints are deposited at several murder scenes. At one scene a blonde hair is also found, at another gray carpet fibers from a Toyota, at another red wool clothing fibers, and at yet another blood spatter patterns that suggested the killer was left-handed and approximately 6 feet tall. Viewed piecemeal, this evidence would tell the investigators little, but with the shoe prints linking the crimes, a clearer picture emerges. The focus is now on a 6-foot, left-handed male who drives a Toyota with gray carpets and wears a red wool shirt or jacket. This of course does not supply conclusive identification, but it does construct a better profile of the perpetrator and helps investigators focus their search and narrow their suspect list.

Minimum number of participants: Multiple shoe prints indicate that more than one person was involved. Three distinct types of prints would suggest that a minimum three persons were involved. There could have been more, with some of the perpetrators failing to leave behind shoe impressions, but there couldn't be fewer.

Class and Individual Shoe Print Evidence

Shoe impressions are most often **class** evidence but are occasionally distinctive enough to be **individualizing**. Each person wears out their shoe soles a little differently from everyone else. These wear patterns are more prominent in some areas than in others, since some people walk more on the outside of their feet, others favor the heel, and still others shuffle along on the balls of their feet. How a person's foot strikes the ground determines how the shoe sole will wear.

The surfaces a person frequently walks on can alter the wear and damage pattern. The wear pattern of an office worker would vary greatly from that of a construction worker or a coal miner. A shoe that mostly walks over carpets and wooden floors will suffer much less damage than would one that frequently travels over gravel or rough concrete.

Matching a crime scene impression to shoes of the same size and manufacturer would supply class evidence, while matching the impression to the exact wear pattern, whether minimal (Figure 15–1) or more extensive (Figure 15–2), will supply individualizing evidence. It's the wear pattern that makes the print individual evidence.

Figure 15–1

Minimal shoe tread wear pattern. This tread shows minimal wear and damage to the sole.

Figure 15–2

Extensive shoe tread wear pattern. This sole shows more extensive wear.

Individualizing evidence is not simply confined to the wear pattern since other damage and foreign materials, such as cuts, nicks, scratches, and gouges or a stone trapped in the tread, can make the shoe print very distinctive. If a print revealing a gouge or a small, embedded rock is found at the crime scene and a suspect's shoe possesses the exact same gouge or rock pattern, the print positively identifies that shoe as the one that left the print. Of course, if weeks or months have gone by before the shoes are located and examined, any gouges or cuts might have been altered, new ones might have appeared, and the embedded rock might have come loose so that the individualizing characteristics are lost and a positive match cannot be made.

Gathering and Analyzing Shoe Impression Evidence

Patent and latent shoe prints are two-dimensional; plastic ones three-dimensional. The crime scene handling of these prints employs different techniques.

Patent prints are often made by mud, grease, paint, blood, or some other transferable material. When a person steps into blood or paint, the liquid coats the sole of the shoe, so that when he walks on another surface, the liquid is transferred to the new surface in a pattern that reflects the shoe's sole pattern. These prints are by definition visible and can simply be photographed.

Latent prints are not readily visible to the naked eye and are deposited by shoes that are relatively clean. "Relatively" is the operative word here since shoe soles constantly pick up debris, most often in the form of oils, dust, and fine dirt, and when they then contact a clean surface, a faint print is left. Searching for and handling these latent shoe prints is similar to what we saw with fingerprints (Chapter 13). Latent shoe prints can be dusted with fingerprint powder and then either photographed or lifted with special adhesive tape. For latent dust or fine dirt prints, an **electrostatic lifting device** might prove useful. This device uses high-voltage electricity to create an electrostatic charge, which transfers the print to a lifting film specifically designed for this purpose.

Latent blood prints can often be exposed with Luminol. Let's say the perpetrator in a robbery-homicide kills the victim in the living room of her home and then walks up the stairs and takes jewelry from her bedroom. As he walks on the bloody carpet near his victim, his shoe soles will pick up blood, and then as he walks across the room and up the stairs, his bloody shoe prints will be transferred to the flooring. Though easily visible at first, these tend to fade as the blood is wiped from his shoe soles with each step, and will eventually disappear. Luminol can expose these latent prints and reveal the perpetrator's movements within the house.

Plastic prints are those made in soft materials such as mud or snow. Before the impression is manipulated or casted, it should be photographed. Angled light often helps bring out depth and detail. Impressions in snow and sand, where contrast is poor, can be lightly sprayed with dark paint before photographing.

Once photographed, a cast, which is a three-dimensional model of the shoe sole, can be made and matched against the shoes of any suspects. Though plaster of paris was used in the past, **dental stone**, which is a hard, durable plaster, is most often used today. Dental stone comes as a powder, which is dissolved in water. A metal or wooden frame is placed around the impression, and the dental stone mixture is carefully poured into the shoe impression and allowed to set. This can take from 20 minutes to a couple of hours, depending upon ambient temperature and humidity.

In soft mud and sand, the weight of the dental stone can deform or alter the impression and damage the evidence. In this situation, it is useful to spray the impression with shellac or an acrylic lacquer, which will "harden" and support the impression, making the casting process more fruitful. Dental stone and plaster are of little use in impressions left in snow since these are easily deformed, and snow of course melts. In this circumstance, snow print wax, a product that stabilizes snow impressions, can be applied before a cast is made.

A special form of three-dimensional shoe impression occurs when someone steps on a carpet, leaving behind faint indentions in the pile. The indention will fade with time due to **depression hysteresis**. *Hysteresis* is a Greek word that means "to lag or be delayed"; in this situation it means that the impression remains or lags behind the footstep. Sometimes an angled light will reveal these impressed footprints. Or **interference holography**, a technique that makes use of a split laser beam to create a holographic image of the print, can be employed. Though great detail is not revealed, the size and overall structure of the shoe can be determined.

The crime scene (unknown) shoe print, whether photographed, lifted, or casted, is then compared to prints obtained from a suspect (known) shoe. The sole of the suspect shoe is coated with ink and its sole pattern is transferred to a sheet of paper or acetate. A visual inspection will quickly determine whether the two possess the same tread and general wear patterns. If so, a magnifying glass, or in some cases a low-power microscope, might reveal individualizing cuts and scars. After completing his examination, the examiner can say one of three things: The impressions match, they do not match, or the results are inclusive, meaning that neither a match nor the exclusion of the unknown print is possible.

Tire Impression Evidence

As with shoe prints, tire impressions can be patent if laid down in mud, oil, paint, road grime, or blood; latent if due to less evident street grime and oil; and plastic if impressed in mud, snow, or on soft road shoulders. Also, as we saw with shoe prints, tire tracks are class evidence that indicate a particular manufacturer and tire size, but individualizing this evidence depends on finding unique wear and damage patterns.

Tires possess several design features that help with classification and identification (Figure 15–3). The tread is wrapped around the tire's circum-

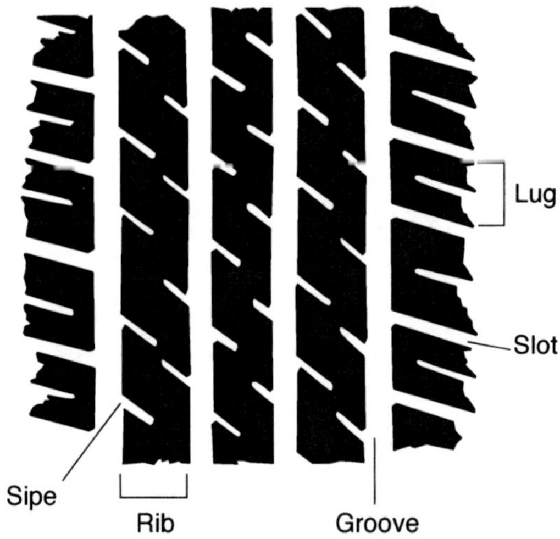

Figure 15–3
Tire tread pattern. An example of a tread pattern, showing the most common design features.

ference in alternating **ribs** (high points or ridges) and **grooves** (depressions). Transverse grooves, called **slots**, run at a 90-degree angle to the circumferential treads. This cross-hatching effect breaks up the ribs into square-shaped islands called **lugs**, whose surface is covered with small grooves called **sipes**. These features are fairly standard and appear on most tires.

Two other important elements are also useful in identification. **Tread wear bars** (also called wear indicators) are bars of rubber that are placed in the grooves at scattered points around the tire. Raised above the floors of the grooves about 1/16 inch, which is much lower in height than the tread ribs and lugs, they reveal the degree of tread wear; when fully exposed they indicate that the tire should be replaced. Obviously, a tire would have to be significantly worn before these bars would appear in a two-dimensional impression, but they might be clearly visible in a three-dimensional one.

Noise treatments are minor variations in the sizes of each design element, which are designed to improve traction and reduce road noise. A close inspection of any tire tread will show that it is not simply a monotonous repetition of the pattern but rather that the lugs are of three to nine (on more expensive tires) different sizes. The purpose of this variation is to reduce the sonic vibration that occurs at high speeds. If the tread design is completely uniform, this vibration will increase due to the development of harmonic waves, while a slight variation in design pattern prevents this harmonic buildup.

The importance of these design elements to the forensic investigator lies in the fact that each of these varies from manufacturer to manufacturer and can aid in determining the maker and the type of tire in question. Several databases of tread designs, including an extensive one maintained by the FBI, are available to facilitate this process.

Tire track evidence can also reveal information about the car itself. Track width, or **stance**, can be measured from the center on one tire to the center of the tire opposite it. If the tracks reveal that the vehicle was turning, it is at times possible to determine the **wheelbase** (distance between the center of the front wheel hubs and the center of the rear wheel hubs) and the **turning radius**. These characteristics vary among vehicle models and might help narrow the field of search. For example, a large sedan or SUV will have a wider stance, longer wheelbase, and wider turning radius than will a "smart car."

Tires are continually subjected to wear and to road hazards, which produce defects that make the tire unique and distinguishable from others of the same model and size. These wear patterns vary not only from car to car but also from tire to tire on a particular car. Cuts, tears, gouges, accumulated debris such as rocks and nails, and "flat spots," islands of excess wear, add a unique quality to the tread impression.

At times, impressions from two, three, or all four tires can be recovered at the scene. It is important to collect each and to determine their relative locations on the vehicle. A new car, with new tires, will have the same brand at all four positions, but older cars might have one or more replacement tires from different manufacturers. This can be critical evidence. For example, if impressions obtained from a crime scene reveal that the vehicle possessed a different brand of tire at each position and a suspect vehicle is identified that has the same four brands in exactly the same positions, that is very strong evidence that that particular vehicle left the impression. What are the odds that two people with the same car would replace the tires with the same types of tires at all four positions? Couple this with matching wear patterns and defects on each of the tires and the match becomes extremely conclusive.

Gathering and Analyzing Tire Impression Evidence

Like shoe impressions, tire impressions might be patent, latent, or plastic.

Patent impressions are typically photographed. It is important that the photo is at a 90-degree angle to prevent distortion and that a ruler is placed near the track for later size determination.

Latent impressions are typically found on firm surfaces such as paved roads or cardboard pieces or similar debris found on or near roadways. These invisible prints come not only from collected road grime and oils but also from the extender oils used during manufacturing to make the tires more pliable. The amount of these extender oils present in a given tire varies from manufacturer to manufacturer and with the age of the tire. These oils fluoresce under ultraviolet light, exposing the tread pattern, which is then photographed. Since tar also fluoresces under ultraviolet light, this technique is not useful on tar-covered roads.

Plastic impressions are photographed, usually employing angled light to add detail and depth, and then casted using dental stone. These castings are usually better than photographs for comparisons since they possess more detail, accurately reflect depth and design element contour, and expose any unevenness in the tire tread pattern.

To compare crime scene (unknown) impressions with those of the suspect (known) vehicle, tread patterns are obtained by "inking" the suspect tire and rolling it down a long piece of white paper. It is important to capture the entire tread since the noise reduction patterns and any and all individualizing defects are the keys to making an individual match. Obtaining only a foot or so of the pattern might miss this critical information.

Tool Mark Evidence

Criminals often use "tools" such as screwdrivers, crowbars, chisels, shears, cutters, and presses. Tool marks are the impressions or marks left by these implements. The principle behind tool mark analysis is that no two tools are identical and thus that each tool leaves behind a unique mark. Some of these unique variations occur during the manufacturing process, where even mass-produced products have minor flaws that distinguish them from one another. Also, with use, the tip, sides, and cutting edges of each tool develops nicks, scrapes, striations, and other minor defects, which, even though many are microscopic, allow for individual characteristics to be identified when the tool is used.

Tool marks fall into three classifications: indented, sliding, and cutting.

Indented marks result when a tool is pressed into a soft material such as putty, caulking, or thick paint. A screwdriver used to pry open a window will often leave behind an indented mark in the paint or the window's soft caulking. Class characteristics such as width and thickness might help determine the size of the screwdriver used, but these indentions are rarely distinct enough to make a conclusive match to a particular screwdriver.

Sliding marks occur when a tool moves across a stationary surface. Chisels, screwdrivers, and crowbars often produce these marks when wedged into a doorjamb or window seal, leaving behind a pattern of lines or striations in the wood and paint. These striations might vary from tool to tool and reveal both manufacturing and use defects, which if sufficiently distinct, can yield a conclusive match with a suspect tool.

Cutting marks come from tools such as wire or bolt cutters, which can leave behind lines and striations on the cut edge of the severed object.

Since many of these cutting tools are hand ground, the striation pattern is unique to the particular tool used and might allow the examiner to state that the pattern is sufficiently unique that it could have been produced only by the particular tool in question. The best cut surfaces for comparison are those made in soft metals such as copper and lead, which tend to retain the microscopic detail of the tool's blade.

At the crime scene, the best place to look for indented and sliding tool marks is at points of entry, such as windows, doors, cabinets, and safes. Cutting marks are typically found on chains and lock hasps. Once located, the marks are photographed and, if possible, removed to the lab for further processing. A door, windowsill, lock, or chain might be taken in its entirety to the lab, but if this is not practical, a cast should be made of any indented marks that cannot be moved. Several casting materials are available, but the most versatile seems to be rubberized silicon since it can maintain the minute detail of the impression and not damage the indented object.

An important caveat: The suspect tool should never be placed in contact with the impression in an effort to see if it "fits." This could alter the impression and make it inadmissible in court.

The comparison microscope, which places two images side by side, is the most useful tool for making tool mark comparisons since microscopic lines, grooves, and striations are readily seen. For this comparison, the examiner will make a "known" cut by using the suspect implement to cut into some soft material such as lead, which will retain the striations and defects of the blade, while its softness will not damage or alter the blade. This is critical since the blade is the evidence, and any alteration of it might make it inadmissible in court. The crime scene (unknown) cut surface is then compared to the lab-produced (known) cut surface under the comparison microscope (Figure 15–4).

Sometimes making a comparison cut through soft lead is not adequate for making an accurate comparison. In this circumstance, the examiner might recreate the crime scene cut as closely as possible by attempting to cut the same material in the same manner. For example, if a bolt cutter was used to cut a lock hasp and the lab possesses both the cut lock and a suspect bolt cutter, the examiner will use the cutter to cut a similar lock hasp. He will attempt to use the same angle and pressure as was used by the perpe-

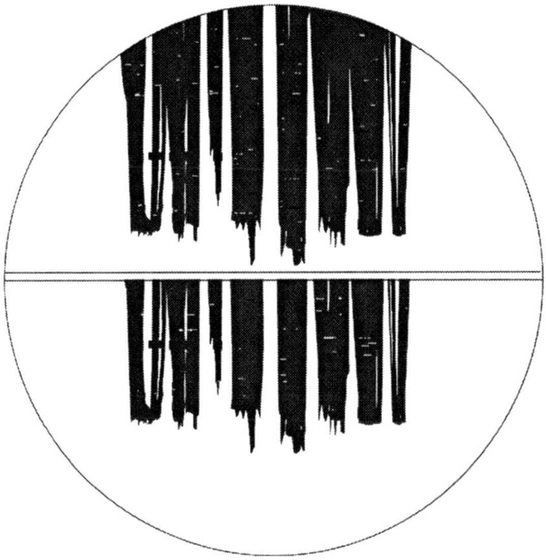

Figure 15–4

Tool mark striations. Marks obtained at the crime scene (unknown) and those made in the lab by the suspect tool (known) as seen through the comparison microscope.

trator and will then examine the crime scene cut and the lab-produced cut with the comparison microscope.

It's not quite that simple, though, since the severed bolt or lock hasp is typically smaller than the device's cutting edge. If an accurate comparison is to be made, the lab-produced cuts must be created by the same portion of the cutting blade that produced the cut at the crime scene. The examiner could make several cuts using different areas of the blade, but this would be time consuming and could damage the blade, making further comparisons impossible. Fortunately, there are chemical tests that will reveal traces of the cut object on the tool's cutting edge. For example, many locks possess zinc coatings and, if so, testing the blade for zinc might reveal the exact portion of the blade that made the cut. This allows the examiner to make a similar cut at the same place and thus make a more accurate comparison.

Other types of tool marks include indentions produced by hammers, the edges of holes produced by drill bits, and even marks produced by mechanical pill presses. Many illegal drug labs compress their product into tablets, and this process will often leave behind distinguishing marks on the surface of the pill. Microscopic examination of the press and the suspect pills might lead to a match.

Fabric Impressions

Fabrics, leathers, and other materials can also leave behind impressions, the most common from gloves (Chapter 13). Like fingertips, gloves pick up grease, dirt, grime, and blood and can deposit either patent or latent prints on surfaces. Sometimes the deposited patterns can be used for comparison with a suspect glove.

Leather gloves tend to crease, wrinkle, and crack with use, and the pattern of these defects might be sufficiently individual to allow a match to a specific glove. Gloves made from cotton and other fabrics might leave behind an imprint of their weave pattern as well as pulls, snags, tears, and other imperfections, which might make the print individual enough for conclusive matching. Glove prints are handled in a manner similar to fingerprints in that patent prints can be photographed and latent prints can be dusted with fingerprint powder and then photographed and lifted.

Other fabrics might also leave impressions. Blood, oil, grease, or dirt on clothing can be transferred to a wall or other object by contact. A killer who kneels next to his bleeding victim might later transfer a bloody fabric pattern to the floor, or a wall or door. Fabric impressions from the clothing of hit-and-run victims have been found in the dirt and grease on car fenders and bumpers. A perpetrator might sit on an uncovered chair, countertop, or car fender and transfer a unique pocket-stitching pattern to the surface. Leaning on a tabletop might leave behind the weave pattern of a sleeve or jacket. The possibilities are almost endless.

CHAPTER 16

TRACE EVIDENCE

The Locard Exchange Principle, introduced and discussed in Chapter 3, states that whenever two objects contact each other, a transfer of materials occurs. Nowhere is this principle more clearly demonstrated than in the location, collection, and analysis of trace evidence. Trace evidence can best be defined as any small bit of evidence that the perpetrator doesn't see and doesn't realize he is leaving behind or carrying away. It clings to clothing, latches onto shoe soles, nestles into hair, and settles into nooks and crannies. It is often very durable and survives for months or years.

This transferability is the main reason that crime scenes must be secured and access must be controlled. Each person who enters the scene will add and/or take away trace materials, and this contamination might render some evidence items useless. Obviously, if the first officers on the scene do not yet know a crime has occurred or if they must disarm and apprehend a suspect or assist a victim, some contamination will occur. The same is true for medical and rescue personnel who must help the injured and firemen who must extinguish a blaze. Such contaminations make the criminalists' job much more difficult.

The major use of trace evidence is to create an **association** or **link** between suspects, places, and objects. In many situations, it is the only evidence that makes this critical connection.

Trace evidence is predominantly **class** rather than **individualizing** evidence (Chapter 3). It can exclude a suspect but can rarely absolutely implicate him. For example, if a blonde hair is found at a crime scene and the suspect has black hair, he is eliminated as the source of the hair and the police must develop another suspect. But, if the suspect's hair matches that found at the crime scene, he remains a suspect. The hair might be his or it might be from someone else with similar hair.

Types of Trace Evidence

The bulk of trace evidence investigation involves hair, fibers, glass, paint, soil, and plant materials. Each of these can be brought to or carried away from the crime scene by the perpetrator without his knowledge and can serve to connect him to the scene.

Hair

Hair is small and easily shed, clings to clothing and other materials, and goes unnoticed. It is hardy and survives for a long period of time, even many years after a body has undergone putrefaction. Nuclear DNA is found in hair that has attached bulbs (follicles) and mitochondrial DNA is present in the hair shaft (Chapter 11). Many toxins, particularly heavy metals such as arsenic, can be found in hair (Chapter 12).

Hairs, both human and animal, are frequently found at crime scenes. In analyzing hair evidence, the ME's first task is to determine whether the hair is from the victim, the perpetrator, the family dog, or from some unknown source. After this is completed, hair analysis predominantly deals with its structure and chemical characteristics, which the examiner will use to match hairs from known (the suspect) and unknown (the crime scene) sources. It is essential to note that hair varies not only from person to person but also from one area of an individual's body and another. A person's head, pubic, and axillary (armpit) hair are often very different. Not in DNA or toxicological terms, but in structure.

The forensic use of hair analysis is one of the earliest forensic techniques, with the first paper on its use published in France in 1857. By the turn of the century the microscopic examination of hair was widely used and in 1931 Professor John Glaister (1856–1932) published his landmark book on the subject, *Hairs of the Mammalia from the Medico-legal Aspect.*

It is now a common forensic technique that has been used to solve many cases, including the famous Atlanta Child Murders case (Chapter 3).

To understand how the criminalist uses hair as evidence, let's look into the nature of hair itself.

Structure of Hair

Hair, like fingernails, is a skin appendage that grows from a pocket of specialized cells called a **follicle**. The shaft of the hair possesses three parts (Figure 16–1). The central core is called the **medulla**, the surrounding portion the **cortex**, and the thin outer coating the **cuticle**. Each of these areas is used by the examiner in his comparisons.

Medulla: The width of the medulla relative to the overall width of the hair is useful in distinguishing human hair from animal hair and also serves as a point of comparison when attempting to match two human hairs. This measurement is called the **medullary index**. In most animals, this index is greater than 0.5, which means that the medulla is more than half the thickness of the hair, making it more or less hollow and very

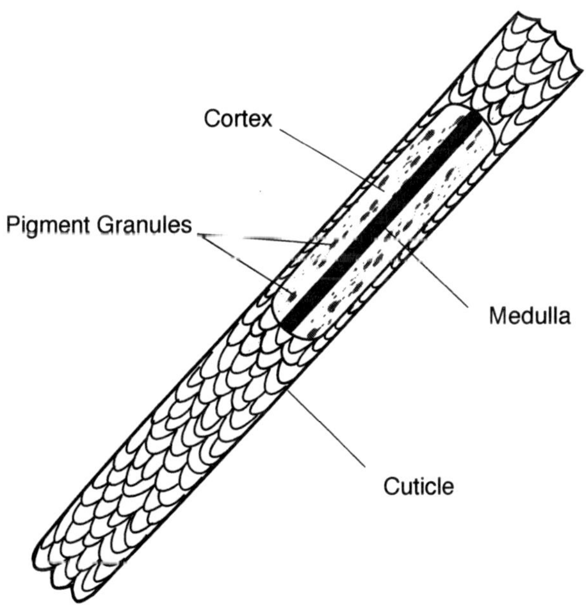

Figure 16–1

Hair shaft structure. The hair shaft consists of a central medulla, a pigment-containing cortex, and a scaly cuticle.

effective for insulation. In humans, the medulla is narrower, with an index of approximately 0.3, or about one-third the width of the shaft. The material within the medulla might appear to be solid and continuous, interrupted, or fragmented (Figure 16–2).

Not all hairs have a medulla. Human head hairs possess either no medulla or one that is fragmented. A notable exception is seen in those of Mongoloid racial background, where the medulla is typically continuous. In animals, the medulla material might appear fragmented or disjointed or might contain cells arranged in various patterns. For example, the medulla of cat hair resembles a string of pearls. The criminalist will often refer to databases of hair types from various animals to help him determine the species of origin.

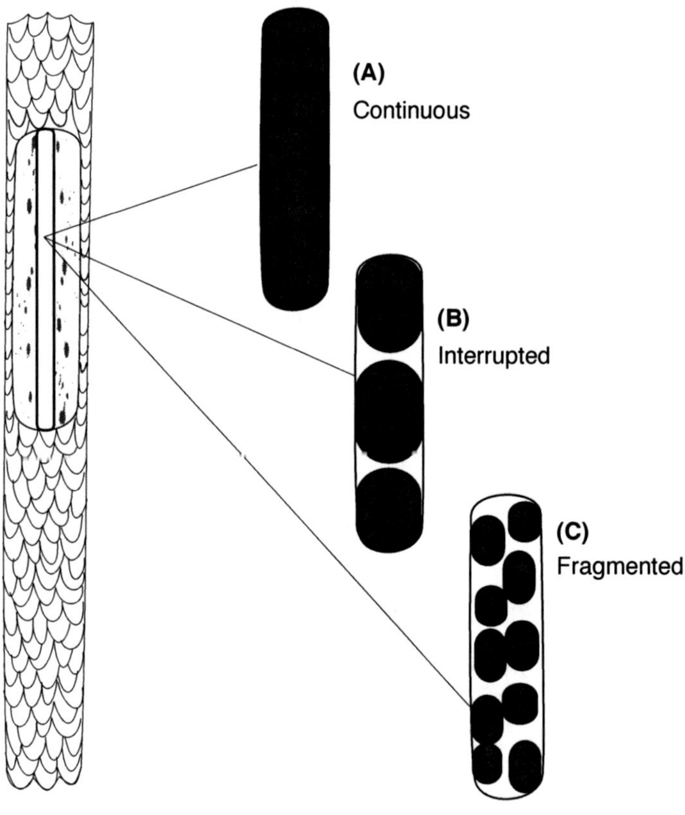

Figure 16–2

Hair medullary patterns. Some hairs have no medulla but those that do are either continuous (A), interrupted (B), or fragmented (C).

So this medullary pattern varies greatly from species to species and from person to person, a fact that makes it extremely useful when comparing two hairs. If the medulla of two hairs (crime scene and suspect's) possess the same medullary index, share the same color, and possess the same medullary pattern, then they could have shared a common origin, namely the suspect. If not, the suspect did not shed that particular hair at the scene.

Cortex: In human hair, the cortex is the largest portion of the shaft and is the area where the hair pigment is located. The pigment particles vary greatly in color, shape, and distribution patterns. In addition, the cortex contains tiny air pockets called **cortical fusi** and other structures such as **ovoid bodies**. The patterns of each these elements vary from person to person, which helps with matching. If two hairs share the same color and distribution pattern of pigment, fusi, and ovoid bodies, then the examiner can say that they likely shared a common origin.

Cuticle: The cuticle is the layer of cells that covers the shaft's surface. They look like fish scales or roofing tiles, overlap, and always point up the shaft and away from the bulb. The three basic types vary by species. **Coronal** (crown-like) scales give the hair a mosaic surface appearance and are rarely seen in humans but are common among rodents. **Spinous** (petal-like) scales tend to be somewhat triangular in shape and are not found in humans but are typical of cats. **Imbricate** (flattened) scales are found in humans and many other animals. The examiner can use the scale pattern to determine the species as well as for matching one hair to another.

Hair Analysis

To make a comparison, the examiner needs an unknown (crime scene) hair sample and known hair samples from the victim and any suspects. The known hair samples should be taken from various areas of the victim's and the suspect's body, since hair characteristics vary by location. The examiner will then use a comparison microscope to view the two hairs side by side. He will first compare their color and width. If these do not match, they did not come from the same source and further analysis is not necessary. If these characteristics do match, he will then examine the medulla and the cuticle to determine if the two hairs might have shared a common origin.

One of the first questions the examiner must answer is where on the body the unknown hair likely came from. Since hair varies depending on its location, the examiner will want to match the crime scene hair with hair taken from the same location of any suspect. In general, hair taken from different body areas tend to have different cross-sectional geometry. Head, eyebrow, and eyelash hairs are more likely round, axillary hairs oval, and beard hairs triangular.

Another important characteristic is the hair color. This can present problems since our perception of color is very subjective. What some people see as red someone else might see as red-orange. The examiner will circumvent this bias by using infrared **microspectrophotometry**. This device is free from bias since it analyzes color by detecting its actual wavelength, which reveals its "true" color. Not only will this help with matching but it might also help him determine if the hair has been dyed, bleached, or treated and, if he has a complete strand, how long ago the last treatment was. Since hair grows approximately a half-inch a month, a one-inch segment of undyed or unbleached hair near the root would suggest that the last treatment was two months earlier. This might serve as another point of comparison.

It would be helpful if the criminalist could accurately determine the race, sex, and age of the person who shed a particular crime scene hair as this would significantly narrow the suspect pool. In some cases this is possible, but these determinations are neither easy nor absolute. Caucasians tend to have straight or wavy hair with a round or oval cross-sectional shape and a finer and more evenly distributed cortical pigment pattern. Those of Negroid ancestry have curly hair that is cross-sectionally flat to oval and the cortical pigment is denser and unevenly distributed. Unfortunately, these characteristics are not completely reliable. Neither age nor sex can be determined with any degree of accuracy, though with an attached follicle, DNA analysis can easily determine sex.

Similarity among all these characteristics is essential for a match, but even a match is not absolute proof that a particular individual shed the hair in question. Yet, it is still important evidence. A study performed by the Royal Canadian Mounted Police showed that if a crime scene head hair matches a suspect's head hair in all the above respects, the odds that the crime scene hair came from someone other than the suspect is 4,500 to 1. With pubic hairs, the probability falls to about 800 to 1.

Another question the examiner might address is whether the crime scene hair was shed naturally, yanked out, or cut. This can help with reconstruction of the crime scene. Since yanking hair from the scalp often rips out follicular tissues also, the finding of follicular tissue suggests that the hair was forcibly removed rather than falling out naturally. Obviously a cut edge would indicate that some sharp instrument was employed to remove the hair.

Analyzing hair chemistry can also be helpful. Many of the chemicals within your body can also be found in your hair. By using techniques such as neutron activation analysis (NAA), which can detect over a dozen different chemicals, the chemical content of hair can be determined. Since it is rare for two people to have the exact same chemicals in their hair, comparing the types and amounts of these substances might allow the forensic examiner to determine whether two hairs likely came from the same person or not. This technique was employed in the murder conviction of John Vollman.

In 1958, 16-year-old Gaetane Bouchard of Edmundston, Canada, disappeared until her body, with multiple chest stab wounds, turned up in a gravel pit. Near the pit police found tire tracks and two chips of green paint, which appeared as if they had been chipped from an automobile by flying gravel as the car drove away. Witnesses stated they had seen Gaetane in a light green car with John Vollman, a 20-year-old musician from across the border in Madawaska, Maine.

Vollman owned a light-green 1952 Pontiac with chipped paint. One of the crime scene chips matched one of these defects. A single hair was found clutched in the victim's hand. This hair, as well as hair from Vollman, were subjected to neutron activation analysis, a new technique at that time. The two hairs proved to be very similar in chemical content. Based on these findings, Vollman changed his plea from not guilty to guilty of manslaughter. This was the first murder case in which "atomic evidence," as it was called in 1958, led to a conviction.

Though hair evidence is predominantly class evidence, there are circumstances in which it can supply DNA, which is highly individualizing (Chapter 11). Hair production and growth occur when follicular cells die, lose their nuclei (and DNA), and are incorporated into the hair shaft. This means that the hair shaft is composed of cellular debris and possesses no nuclear DNA. The follicle (bulb) is composed of living cells, which do possess DNA. If during their struggles hair is pulled from the assailant, the follicular tissue often remains attached and can serve as a source of DNA, which can be used for fingerprinting and matching.

But even with no follicular material, DNA in the form of mitochondrial DNA (mtDNA) in the hair shaft can still prove useful. Though not as individualizing as nuclear DNA, mtDNA can be powerful evidence and is often sufficient to level charges and gain a conviction. For example, if the mtDNA of a hair found at a crime scene matches that from hair taken from the suspect's siblings or other maternal-line relative (mother, grandmother, maternal aunt, etc.) it proves that the person shedding the hair at the scene shared a maternal lineage with the suspect's relatives. This means that either he was there or one of his relatives was. And if no other close relative could have committed the crime, the suspect has some explaining to do.

Fibers

Fibers are everywhere. They are found in clothing, carpet, car mats, bedding, towels, and a long list of other things we contact on a daily basis. Because they are common, come in such a wide variety of types, and, like hair, are easily shed, transferred, and transported unnoticed by the criminal, they are extremely useful types of trace evidence.

Time is critical in collecting fiber evidence since studies have shown that this evidence is quickly lost. After four hours 80 percent of fibers clinging to clothing have fallen away, and by 24 hours that jumps to 95 percent. For this reason, a search for trace evidence on the clothing of the victim and of any suspects should be done as soon as possible.

Fibers are classified into three basic types: natural, manufactured, or synthetic.

Natural fibers come from animals, plants, and minerals and are often easily identified and compared by microscopic inspection alone. **Animal hair** is considered a fiber, rather than a shed animal hair, when it is woven or used to manufacture clothing and other household items. Examples would be wool, mohair, cashmere, and silk. **Plant fibers** include cotton, by far the most common, hemp, flax, and jute. Because cotton, which has an easily recognizable "twisted-ribbon" pattern, is so common, un-dyed white cotton is most often of little evidentiary value. **Mineral fibers** are things such as asbestos.

Manufactured fibers, also called **regenerated** fibers, are produced when raw cotton or wood pulp is dissolved and the cellulose extracted. The cellulose is then "regenerated" into fibers such as rayon, acetate, and triacetate.

Synthetic fibers come from **polymers**, which are substances made up of a series of single molecules (**monomers**) strung together in long molecules that can be thousands of monomers in length. The molecule looks like a long chain, each link representing a monomer. The properties of the polymer depend upon the chemical structure of the repeating monomer.

Polymer fibers are made by melting a polymeric material and then extruding it through the very fine holes of a **spinnerette**. The extruded fiber quickly hardens and can then be woven into fabrics. Nylon and polyester are synthetic fibers.

Fiber Identification and Comparison

The fiber analyst is often asked to determine the likely source of a fiber. Is it a carpet fiber and, if so, who manufactured it? Or he might be presented with several fibers and asked to assess whether they came from a common source. Does the fiber on the victim's clothing match fibers taken from the floor mats of the suspect's car? In order to make these determinations, he will evaluate the fiber's **physical**, **optical**, and **chemical** properties.

To assess the fiber's physical properties, the analyst will examine the unknown fiber under a **stereomicroscope**, which reveals its three-dimensional structure, and gauge its diameter, shape, color, shine, and any curls and crimps. When matching two fibers, he will use a **comparison microscope** so that he can compare the two fibers side by side. He will view the cross-section of the fiber to determine if it is single-stranded, multi-stranded, or tri-lobed, where it will appear as if three strands were melted together into one. If the fiber or piece of fabric has been damaged, a **scanning electron microscope (SEM)** will reveal fine structural and surface details that might help determine whether the fabric was torn, cut, or ripped by a bullet.

Optical analysis begins with **microspectrophotometry**, which will determine the fiber's true color without the problem of observer variance (see above). When **polarized light** is added, the **reflective index**, a measure of how the fiber reflects light of various types, can be estimated, and this in turn can help determine its makeup. Different materials reflect visible, UV, and infrared light in varied and characteristic ways, and this can help identify the fiber type as well as determine whether two fibers are similar or not. Similarly, the examiner will determine the fiber's **refractive index (RI)**. When light passes from one medium to another, it is refracted (bent). You've seen this many times. A stick dipped into a bowl of water will appear to be bent even though it is actually straight. The cause of this phenomenon is that light moves at different speeds in different mediums, faster through air and slower through water, causing the light to bend so that the stick appears that it too is bent. The degree of this bending is called the refractive index, and since different fibers possess different RIs, this can serve as a basis for identity and comparison.

Another similar property is called **birefringence**. When light passes through some synthetic fibers, it is refracted twice, once on entering the fiber and again as it exits back into the air. The light emerges as two different waves of polarized light, each with its own refractive characteristics. This birefringence is another useful tool for identification and comparison.

If the compared fibers vary in any of the above characteristics, they do not match and could not have come from the same material. No other testing is indicated. If they are similar in all these physical and optical properties, the examiner might then move forward with testing the fiber's chemical makeup.

Two commonly used procedures for the chemical analysis of fibers are the combination of a **scanning electron microscopy (SEM)** with **energy dispersive x-ray spectrometry (SEM/EDS)** and the combination of **gas chromatography** and **mass spectrometry (GC/MS)**. Each of these techniques reveals the chemical composition of the fiber and of any pigments or treatments that might have been added to it, either during the manufacturing process or as a later alteration. In fact, GC/MS can separate and identify each chemical found in the fiber or any of its treatments. For example, the presence of tin and bromide might indicate treatment with a fire retardant, while titanium oxide reveals the presence of a de-lustering product (which lessens the fiber's luster or shine). These chemical determinations can often indicate the manufacturer of the fiber or might serve to more strongly match one fiber to another.

After the examiner analyzes the physical, optical, and chemical properties of any known and unknown fibers, he might be able to say that the two likely came from the same source, or if they differ in any of their characteristics, he would conclude the opposite.

Glass

Glass products are a large part of our daily lives since they are found everywhere—windows, cups, plates, and drinking glasses, as well as car headlamps and plate glass doors. Glass comes in many sizes, shapes, types, and colors, and varies greatly in its chemical composition. It easily breaks, typically scattering fragments when it does, and at crime scenes these slivers and chips will attach to weapons, shoes, clothing, and even settle on the perpetrator's skin and in his hair.

Glass analysis, with the exception of fracture patterns (discussed below), is rarely individualizing evidence, but rather class evidence. Usually the best the examiner can do is state that two pieces of glass are similar and might have come from a common source.

Glass is produced by heating a mixture of sand (silica or silicon dioxide), limestone (calcium carbonate), and soda (sodium carbonate). It possesses a hard, smooth surface, and is an ideal substrate for fingerprints and shoe prints. For example, an intruder might touch a window or other glass object or might step on a piece of glass from a shattered window, leaving his finger and shoe prints, respectively. Broken glass can also injure the perpetrator, resulting in the deposition of his blood, and thus his DNA, at the crime scene.

As we saw with fibers, the analysis of glass involves examining its physical, optical, and chemical properties with an eye toward **identification** and **comparison**. The examiner is often given a fragment of glass and is asked to identify its source (drinking glass, window pane, car headlamp) and hopefully identify the likely manufacturer. Since different glass manufacturers use different manufacturing components, processes, and techniques, analyzing the fragment's properties will often indicate who made it and when. For example, a shard of glass from a car headlamp, shattered during a hit-and-run, might reveal the make, model, and year of manufacture of the car.

The examiner is also frequently asked to compare two glass fragments to determine whether they share a common origin. Did the chip of glass found on the suspect's clothing come from the shattered window at the crime scene?

Physical Properties

The first step in glass analysis is to assess its physical properties: color, thickness, shape, pattern, and opacity. Often these characteristics alone provide a clue to the source and reveal whether two pieces could have come from the same source or not. Glass fragments from a window, a crystal cocktail glass, an eyeglass lens, and an automobile windshield have very different physical properties.

But sometimes this isn't enough. Let's say the examiner is comparing pieces of a broken drinking glass found at the crime scene (known) with a piece found in a suspect's pant cuff (unknown). The two samples might have the same color, shape, and thickness, but that doesn't necessarily mean they were once part of the same glass. Here the examiner would test the **density** of the two fragments. Density is a measure of weight to size. A one-inch-square of dense glass weighs more than does an identical-sized piece from less dense glass.

Comparing densities requires a cylindrical container filled with liquids of different densities. The liquids most often used are **bromoform** and **bromobenzene**. They are mixed together, the piece of glass is added, and then one or the other of the liquids is added until the glass is suspended, neither rising nor sinking. At this point, the glass and the liquid mixture possess the same density. Since the densities of the liquids are known, the density of the mixture, and thus of the glass, can be easily calculated. If the known piece of glass has been suspended in this way, the unknown piece can be added. If it too remains suspended, the densities of the two are identical. If the unknown fragment either sinks or floats, the two pieces do not share the same density and thus could not have come from the same source.

But, even if the physical characteristics and density match, the fragments still could have come from different sources. The examiner will then turn to analyzing the fragments' optical properties.

Optical Properties

Various glass products **transmit**, **reflect**, and **refract** light in different ways. Transmitted light passes through the glass, reflected light bounces off it, and refracted light passes through but its path is refracted (bent). One problem with matching two pieces of colored glass is that each of us perceives color differently. In order to remove this observer variation, optical examination is automated and employs special optical and computer equipment that can evaluate the true color, transparency, and reflectivity of a glass object.

As we saw with fiber analysis, the degree of refraction is called the **refractive index (RI)**. With glass, this property is tested by submerging the fragment in a liquid, such as **silicon oil**, that changes its refractive index according to its temperature. The oil is then slowly heated. At the point where the piece of glass seems to disappear, the RIs of the glass and the oil are equal. Since the RI of the silicon oil at any given temperature is known, measuring the temperature will yield the RI of the glass.

If the two samples vary in any of these properties, they do not share a common source and further comparison testing is not needed. But if they do match in all the above characteristics, the examiner will turn to the fragment's chemical makeup.

Chemical Properties

During the manufacturing process, various substances are added to glass to change its color, transparency, texture, and strength. Cookware and glassware need to be relatively heat and shock resistant so **boron** is often added. Less sturdy glass, such as windows, have a high **sodium** and **calcium** content due to the addition of **soda lime**. Bottle glass often contains **aluminum oxide** and colored glass contains various **pigments**. Lead is added to make crystal sparkle and **magnesium oxide** adds strength to plate glass. The forensic chemist will test for these additives and any impurities in the glass with an eye toward matching the chemical makeup of any known and unknown samples.

It bears reiteration that if at any step in the testing process the two samples differ in any of their physical, optical, or chemical properties, the examiner can state with confidence that they did not come from the same source and further testing is unnecessary. If they are identical in every respect, that is strong evidence that they shared a common source but it is not absolutely conclusive. Thus, the evidence can be **exclusionary**, but not necessarily proof positive. The notable exception is the matching of lines of fracture.

Glass Fracture Patterns

The underlying principle of **fracture line analysis** is that no two objects fracture in exactly the same way. This can be broken plastic, ripped paper, tape torn from a roll, or shattered glass. The line of fracture in each of these, and many other circumstances, are as individual as fingerprints. For example, let's say that a piece of car headlamp is found attached to the clothing of a hit-and-run victim. If a suspect car with a broken headlamp is found and the glass bit exactly fits into the gap in a jigsaw manner, the examiner would feel confident that the piece came from that exact headlamp.

The examiner might also be asked to determine how and why a glass object, such as a window, fractured. The window's fracture pattern often yields clues as to the speed and direction of the impact, and this in turn might indicate what object caused the break. Was the object moving at a low velocity, such as a rock or fist, or at a higher rate, such as a bullet or explosive shrapnel?

Cracks in windows and other flat plates of glass tend to be **radial** and **concentric**. Radial cracks spread outward from the point of impact like spokes. Concentric cracks are a series of progressively larger circles around the point of impact. Overall, the cracked window can resemble a spider web.

Determining the direction of the impact can be critical to crime scene reconstruction. Did the bullet penetrate the window from outside in or was it fired from within the house? Did a perpetrator break the window and enter or did someone within the house break the window in an attempt to "stage" the scene and make a domestic homicide look like a breaking and entering murder?

Stress-fracture lines known as **conchoidal lines**, which radiate away from the impact site (Figure 16–3), can help with this determination. Viewed through the thickness of the glass, these lines tend to curve out and away from the point of impact. Looking more closely at these conchoidal fractures, smaller lines called **hackle marks** radiate in a perpendicular direction from edges that face away from the impact site.

When a bullet penetrates a window without completely shattering it, it will leave a hole, often with surrounding fracture lines. On the side of approach, the bullet creates a clean hole, while on the opposite side, a small cone-shaped plug of glass is forced out. Simple visual inspection of the impact site will reveal the bullet's direction of travel. If multiple bullets

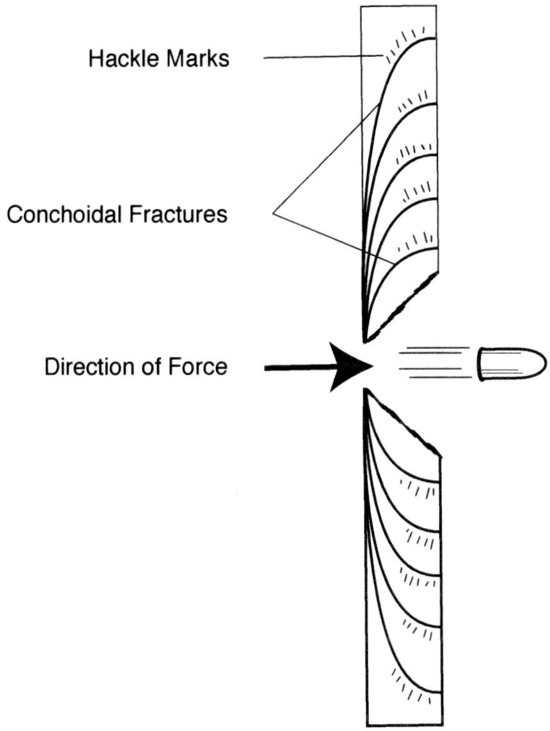

Figure 16–3

Conchoidal fracture lines. Conchoidal fracture lines tend to curve out and away from the point of impact. Hackle marks also reveal the direction from which the force was applied.

fracture the glass, it is often possible to determine the order in which they struck. Typically, the radial fractures caused by the second bullet will not cross those of the first but rather will end when they encounter glass that is already fractured (Figure 16–4).

These findings can be extremely important in corroborating or refuting suspect and witness statements, in reconstructing the events of the crime, and in assigning culpability. Let's say two gang members do a drive-by shooting of a rival gang member while he is sitting in his car. The driver fires through the victim's car window and begins to drive away. His accomplice then takes the gun and fires again. Both bullets pass through the window and strike the victim, one in the shoulder, and the other in the head, killing him. Since both bullets came from the same gun and both men have gunshot residue on their hands (Chapter 17), which of the shooters was the

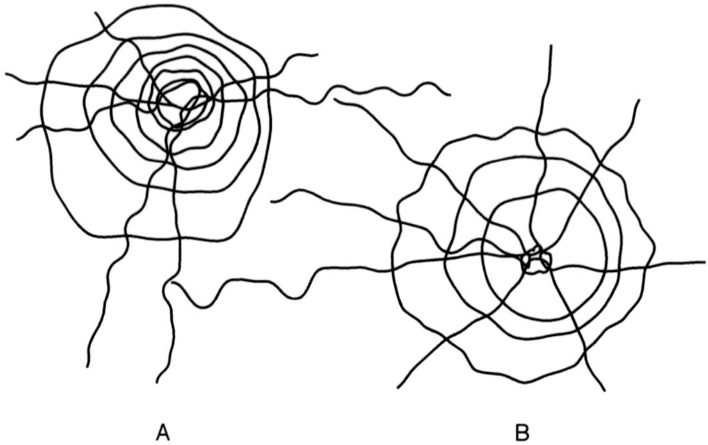

Figure 16–4
Intersecting fracture lines. Impact radial fracture lines end abruptly at those produced by a previous impact. In this case, fracture B followed fracture A.

actual killer? Was it the first bullet (the driver) or the second (the passenger)? The dilemma is resolved when analysis of the fracture lines in the victim's car window reveal that the second bullet was the killing shot.

Paint

Like glass, paint is everywhere. Walls, doors, cars, various decorative items, and many other objects are covered with paint. For this reason, paint chips and smears are often transferred from one painted surface to another or to a victim or perpetrator, during the commission of a crime. A perpetrator might walk across a freshly painted floor or brush against a freshly painted wall. He might then transfer this to his car, home, or belongings. Or he might get paint on the tools he uses to break into a home or office. Or paint chips might settle in his hair or clothing if a painted object is shattered or damaged.

For most crime labs, automobile paint constitutes the most common samples submitted for evaluation, and the examiner is often asked to determine the origin and manufacturer of the paint or to compare two samples to determine whether they share a common origin. To do this he will analyze the paint sample's physical, optical, and chemical properties as well as any fracture patterns, and in repainted vehicles, the order and thickness of the layers.

Paint is a complex liquid with four basic parts: binders, pigments, extenders, and modifiers. **Binders** are typically natural or synthetic resins to which the pigments are added. **Pigments** add color and might be organic (most blues and greens) or inorganic (most reds, yellows, and whites) in nature. Common chemical pigments include titanium oxide, which is white, and iron oxide, which is a component of many red pigments. **Extenders** add solid bulk, which increases the covering capacity of the paint. **Modifiers** change the gloss, flexibility, hardness, and durability of the paint. An example is lead oxide, which toughens paint and makes it resistant to weather. The type and proportion of each of these varies greatly from paint to paint, and they are the basis for analyzing paint in the crime lab.

The painting of an automobile is a multi-step process that results in laying down several layers of paint products. Common layers are as follows:

- **Electroplated primer**: An epoxy resin electroplated to the car's metal to provide corrosion and rust protection.
- **Primers**: Smooth out imperfections and provide a base for the base (color) coat.
- **Base coat**: The layer that gives the car its color.
- **Clear coat**: Clear acrylic or polyurethane that adds shine, depth, and protection for the base coat.

Since each manufacturer has its individual methods for producing each of these products, an analysis of these coats, together or individually, can often reveal the manufacturer, make, model, and production year of the vehicle. Each can also serve as a point of comparison between two paint samples. Often color alone will make this distinction, particularly with automotive paints, since some colors are unique to a particular automaker. To aid the examiner, there are several comprehensive databases of home and automobile paint.

To analyze the paint's physical and optical properties, such as color and luster, **microspectrophotometry** is used to determine its true color without the problems of observer bias. Often **infrared microspectrophotometry** is favored over the one employing visible light.

Next, layers or coats are examined for the thickness and sequence of colors if several have been used. In a car that has been repeatedly repainted, this can be extremely important evidence. Let's say a paint chip is recovered from the clothing of a hit-and-run victim, and this chip shows that the car had been repainted several times. Maybe the original color was red, but the vehicle was repainted in the order of black, a different shade of red, and finally yellow. If a suspect vehicle is located and a sample is taken for comparison and this sample shows the exact same colors in the exact same sequence and thickness of layers, what are the odds that another vehicle could have been serially repainted in this fashion? And if the chemical analysis of each layer of the crime scene sample matches those of the suspect vehicle, this is highly individualizing evidence.

As we saw with other chemical analyses, paint analysis will employ the combination of gas chromatography and mass spectroscopy (GC/MS), but with a slight twist. Since the paint chip is a solid, a process called **pyrolysis gas chromatography (pyrolysis GC)** is used. Pyrolysis is the conversion of a solid into a gas with high heat. In pyrolysis GC, the chip is vaporized and the resulting gas passes through the GC column and is separated into its various chemical components. It then undergoes mass spectroscopy, which reveals the "chemical fingerprint" of the components of the paint and allows for an accurate comparison of the paint samples. Other analytic methods would include **scanning electron microscopy (SEM)** and **energy dispersive x-ray spectrometry (EDS)**, a combination termed **SEM/EDS**; **infrared spectrophotometry** (often used in conjunction with gas chromatography); **x-ray diffraction (XRD)**; and **analytic electron microscopy (AEM)**. The finding that a known and an unknown sample are chemically identical strongly suggests, but does not absolutely prove, that the two samples came from the same source.

As with glass analysis, the most individualizing evidence in paint analysis is a physical match of the edges of a paint chip. If the edges of a known and unknown paint chip can be shown to perfectly mesh in an exact jigsaw fashion, this is fairly conclusive evidence that the two are from the same source. Again, no things fracture in exactly the same way.

Soils and Plants

Soil and plant materials are often left behind or carried away from crime scenes and can provide a link between a suspect and the crime. Soil from crime scenes, or from a suspect's shoes, clothing, or car tires, or from tools such as shovels, often find their way into the crime lab.

Soil is a complex mixture of minerals, plant, and animal matter together with tiny particles of manmade products such as glass, paint, asphalt, concrete, and other materials. It varies greatly from region to region and from locale to locale in a given area. For example, the soil near the beach in California is much different from the red clay of Alabama. And the soil in a California beachfront community will differ greatly from the soil in a downtown Los Angeles park.

Soil analysis begins with a visual and microscopic inspection and progresses to the determination of color, consistency, pH (a measure of soil acidity), and mineral content. If each of these characteristics matches, chemical analysis with GC/MS and/or x-ray diffraction will follow.

Another technique known as **differential thermal analysis** is based on the fact that soils absorb and release heat at differing rates. In this test, a sample is placed into a specially designed furnace and heated. The point at which it breaks down, melts, or boils is determined. This point can be compared with other soils and their thermal properties can be said to match or not.

Plant materials have great forensic significance. They might be part of a soil sample or perhaps be found on corpses, clothing, flooring, car mats, tools, and any number of places. Leaves, stems, pine needles, bark, flower petals, seeds, and pollen might be submitted for analysis.

Since various plants are native to different areas, the identification of a plant product might help determine the place of origin of the soil sample. For example, if pine needles are found on the floor near a homicide victim and there are no pine trees near the residence, it is likely that the killer brought them with him on his clothing or shoes. A determination of the particular species of the pine tree might narrow the area of search for the suspect.

Pollen, which comes from flowering plants, can be extremely useful to the forensics examiner. Pollen grains are tiny and rarely noticed, yet they are highly distinctive for their plant of origin. They cling to clothing, the victim's or suspect's hair, and even in envelopes that contain threatening letters or ransom notes. Microscopic identification of pollen found on a suspect might reveal that he had been in an area where the particular plant was in bloom, and this might serve to link him to a nearby crime scene. There are several pollen reference databases that help with species identification.

Finally, DNA (Chapter 11) might play a role because, like humans, plants have their own unique DNA. Let's say a corpse is found along a roadside and on examination pine pollen is found in the victim's hair. The nearest pine trees are a mile away, and as the police search that area they find a vagrant sleeping beneath one of the trees. Pine pollen taken from his clothing, sleeping bag, and the nearby ground are similar to those found on the victim. Yet, the vagrant denies that he has ever seen the victim. If the DNA of the pollen obtained from the victim matches that from the pollen found on the vagrant it would conclusively prove that the pollen found on the victim didn't come from just any pine tree, but rather came from the specific tree under which the vagrant was found. Not good news for him.

CHAPTER 17

FIREARMS EXAMINATION

This area of forensic investigation is popularly called **ballistics**, an incorrect term but one that is well-ingrained and difficult to shake. Ballistics is actually the science of projectile motion, or how a bullet, artillery shell, rocket, or other hurled object travels through air. How firearms work and how guns and ammunition are identified and compared is the job of the **forensic firearms examiner**.

In Chapter 8 we looked at what bullets do to the human body and how the coroner evaluates such injuries. In this chapter we will look at guns and ammunition and how their identification and comparison can solve crimes involving guns. The duties of the forensic firearms examiner require that he be familiar with all types of firearms and ammunition and understand the inner workings and ballistic characteristics of each.

He might be presented with bullets, bullet fragments, shell casings, or weapons and be charged with the following:

- Determining the caliber, the type, and the manufacturer of the weapon and/or ammunition used in a crime

- Assessing the distance between the victim and the weapon at the time the weapon discharged
- Matching a bullet or shell casing to a particular weapon
- Comparing bullets or shell casings from different crime scenes to hopefully link the crimes to one another
- Employing firearms evidence in the reconstruction of crime scenes
- Testing for gunshot residue
- Restoring damaged or removed weapon serial numbers

Weapon and Ammunition Components

Guns are typically classified as **rifles**, **shotguns**, or **handguns**, the latter being further subdivided into **revolvers**, **semiautomatic pistols**, and **machine pistols**. A handgun can be held and fired in one hand, while rifles and shotguns are typically held against the shoulder and fired from that position. Shotgun barrels are smooth-bored, meaning the inner surface of the barrel is smooth, while rifles and handguns are **rifled**, meaning they have **grooves** cut into the inside of the barrel. The areas between these grooves are called **lands**, so that the lands are the high points and the grooves the valleys between them. These grooves spiral down the barrel and impart spin to the bullet as it passes through. This spin greatly increases the fired bullet's range and accuracy.

Rifle and handgun **cartridges** are composed of the **bullet** (the actual projectile) and a **shell casing**, which is filled with smokeless powder. The bullet fits into the casing and when the powder inside explodes, the bullet is propelled down the barrel of the gun. The shell casing remains in the cylinder of a revolver until manually removed, while in most automatic weapons it is ejected.

After firing, the **shell casing** usually retains several marks that are highly individual to the particular gun that fired the cartridge. Both the **firing pin** and the **breechblock** (the rear of the firing chamber against which the casing recoils during firing) will imprint impressions on the back of the casing. In addition, with automatic and semiautomatic weapons, the casings typically show **extractor** and **ejector** marks, which result from the mechanism that ejects the spent cartridge and seats a new one in the firing chamber.

Except for self-loaded ammunition, true gunpowder is rarely seen today. It has been replaced by **smokeless powder**. Depending upon their chemical composition, these smokeless powders are termed single, double, or triple based. Single-base powders contain **nitrocellulose** as the only explosive component. Double-base powders contain nitrocellulose and **nitroglycerin**, while triple-base ones also contain **nitroguanidine**. Powders also contain **stabilizers** such as **diphenylamine** and **ethyl centralite**. Other additives include **plasticizers** (to reduce the absorption of moisture by the powders) and **flash suppressants**. The chemical makeup of the powder and the type and amount of each of these additives varies among manufacturers, and this fact serves as a method for chemical identity and comparison.

Most cartridges are of the **center-fire** variety, meaning that the cartridge's base (bottom) possesses a centrally located cup of primer. When the shooter pulls the trigger, the gun's firing pin strikes the primer cup, igniting the primer and, in turn, the powder. The explosion of the powder produces a large volume of gas, predominantly composed of carbon monoxide, carbon dioxide, and nitrogen oxide, which forces the bullet from the shell casing and down the barrel. Other cartridges, termed **rim-fire** weapons, do not have a primer cup, but rather have the primer around the rim of the shell. The firing pin in these weapons, typically .22 or other small-caliber weapons, strikes the rim of the shell and not the central area.

Bullet and Shell Casing Examination

The field of firearm examination is not new and its history is long and fascinating.

- **1784**: In Lancashire, England, Edward Culshaw was killed with a muzzle-loading flintlock pistol. A surgeon removed a small piece of the paper wadding, used to pack the powder in the gun, from Culshaw's wound. The paper scrap jigsaw matched paper found in the pocket of the chief suspect, John Toms, who was convicted of the crime. So the first "ballistics" case actually dealt with the paper wadding and not the gun or the bullet.
- **1835**: When confronted with a case of a burglary in which a servant suffered a gunshot wound, Henry Goddard, one of Scotland

Yard's Bow Street Runners, noticed an odd "bump" on the fired bullet, which he had dug from the headboard of the servant's bed. An examination of the servant's own bullet mold revealed that the mold had a defect that matched the mark on the bullet. He concluded that the servant had himself made the bullet and shot himself to cover his theft, and that no outsider had been involved.

- **1863**: The bullet that killed Confederate General Stonewall Jackson was found to be a .67 caliber ball, the size used by Confederate forces. Since the Union troops used a .58 caliber ball, the killing bullet must have been fired by one of Jackson's own men.
- **1864**: Union General John Sedgwick fell to a Confederate sniper, who fired from a distance of 800 yards. The caliber and the hexagonal shape of the bullet indicated that it had come from an English-made Whitworth rifle, imported by the Confederacy for use by snipers.
- **1889**: Alexandre Lacassagne discovered that marks found on bullets recovered from shooting victims could be matched to a particular gun barrel by simply counting the number of grooves.
- **1898**: German chemist Paul Jeserich used a microscope to compare the striations on two bullets fired by the same gun.
- **1913**: French professor Victor Balthazard stated in his paper Archives of Criminal Anthropology and Legal Medicine that each fired bullet retains its own unique marks.
- **1920**: Physicist John Fisher invented the helixometer, a probe fitted with a light and magnifying glass, which allowed a detailed examination of the inside of a gun barrel.
- **1920**: The Sacco and Vanzetti case brought firearms examinations to the public attention (see below).
- **1923**: In New York City, Charles Waite, Philip Gravelle, Calvin Goddard, and John H. Fisher established the Bureau of Forensic Ballistics to offer firearm identification services throughout the United States.
- **1925**: Gravelle and Goddard invented the comparison microscope, which revolutionized firearm examinations.

The Sacco and Vanzetti Case

On April 15, 1920, security guards Alessandro Berardelli and Frederick Parmenter were shot dead by two men who stole more than $15,000 of payroll money. At the scene, investigators found several .32 caliber shell casings, which were manufactured by three firms: Remington, Winchester, and Peters. Two days later the getaway car was found and traced to an earlier robbery, which ultimately led police to Nicola Sacco and Bartolomeo Vanzetti. Sacco had a .32 caliber handgun and a total of 29 bullets manufactured by Remington, Winchester, or Peters. The two were arrested and charged with double murder.

Since the two men belonged to an anarchist movement that advocated violent political change, the case became America's first "Red Scare." The defense team put together an alliance of anarchist, communist, and union leaders called the Sacco-Vanzetti Defense Committee, which labeled the trial a "witch hunt."

The case hinged on proving that the killing bullets came from Sacco's gun. A match was made and Sacco and Vanzetti were convicted and sentenced to death. But, the story did not end there.

Continued protests by anarchists led to the formation of a committee in June 1927 to look into the case, and America's leading ballistic expert, Calvin Goddard of the Bureau of Forensic Ballistics in New York, was asked to examine the evidence with his two new forensic tools: the comparison microscope and the helixometer. He found the match was conclusive and that Sacco's gun had indeed fired the bullets. On August 23, 1927, the two killers died in the electric chair.

Yet the controversy persisted. In 1961 and again in 1983 the case was reexamined and on each occasion Goddard's findings were confirmed.

The modern forensic firearms examiner is charged with weapon type identification, bullet and shell casing identification and matching, crime scene analysis, gunshot residue testing, and serial number restoration. Let's look at each of these.

Weapon Type

A gun found at a crime scene or confiscated from a suspect can provide a great deal of evidence. It might be matched to the killing bullet or to bullets from other crime scenes, thus linking several scenes together. It can serve as a substrate for fingerprints and trace evidence such as blood, hair, and fibers that can be traced to the perpetrator. **Blowback** of blood and tissues from the victim in close-range shootings can cling to the gun and link the weapon to the victim in cases where no bullet is recovered.

But what if only a bullet is found? Maybe found at the scene or removed from the victim at autopsy? With no gun to compare it to, how can the examiner use this evidence?

He will first attempt to identify the caliber and type of bullet. If the bullet is mostly intact, the caliber can be determined by simply measuring it. If it is severely deformed, it can be weighed, which will not give the exact caliber but will eliminate some calibers. For example, the weight of .22 caliber and .44 caliber bullets are very different, so a heavy bullet would suggest that a .44 or .45 caliber weapon was likely the gun of origin as opposed to a .22 or .25 caliber weapon.

The type of jacketing, if any, is easily determined and often helps identify the type of weapon used. A **jacketed bullet** is one that is covered, or jacketed, with a metal, Teflon, or some other hardy material. The purpose of this is to lessen the deformity seen with simple lead and to increase the penetrating power of the bullet. The so-called "cop killer" bullets that can penetrate body armor and vehicles are examples. A fully jacketed bullet is typically fired from a rifle, while a simple lead bullet indicates that a small-caliber handgun was the likely weapon.

Different manufacturers produce barrels with different numbers and widths of lands and grooves and with different directions and degrees of twisting. The examiner can use these rifling characteristics when confronted with an unknown bullet to place the weapon into one of several categories:

- **Colt type**: Six broad grooves, narrow lands, and a left-hand twist.
- **Browning type**: Six broad grooves, narrow lands, and a right-hand twist.
- **Smith & Wesson type**: Five lands and grooves of equal width and a right-hand twist.
- **Webley type**: Seven broad grooves, narrow lands, and a right-hand twist.

- **Marlin type**: Marlin rifles use a technique known as **microgrooving**, which leaves between 8 and 24 narrow grooves inside the barrel.

If the examiner is given a .32 caliber bullet recovered from the scene or at autopsy and he finds ballistic striations consistent with the bullet having traveled down a barrel with 5 lands and a right twist, he can say that the weapon was likely a Smith & Wesson. Investigators can then focus on .32 caliber Smith & Wesson handguns.

Bullet Examination

The lands and grooves inside a rifled barrel not only impart spin to the bullet but they also cut into its side, leaving behind marks called **striations**. These marks are linear, parallel to the long axis of the bullet, and are more prominent on soft lead bullets than on metal or Teflon jacketed ones. In fact, sometimes they are absent on such jacketed bullets.

Each rifled barrel is minutely distinct. The manufacturer's rifling tool cuts through each metallic barrel a little differently, and with repeated use the rifling tool itself is worn and damaged so that rifling patterns vary from barrel to barrel even when produced by the same tool. This means that bullets fired from the same gun will share the same striation patterns, while those fired from different guns will not. But rifle barrels aren't static, so with repeated firing the grooves and lands undergo wear and damage. This adds even more individual characteristics to the barrel but can also create problems for the examiner. If the gun that fired a crime scene bullet is not located and tested for a considerable period of time and if the gun has been fired hundreds of times in the interim, the grooves could be so altered that a match is no longer possible.

With an intact bullet, striation comparison is usually easy, but unfortunately the examiner rarely receives an undamaged bullet. More often the bullets have been damaged or fragmented by bones or walls or other solid objects. Still, if it is not severely deformed, a microscopic examination will reveal the striation pattern imprinted on at least some of its surfaces.

These individualizing striations are useful in many situations. Multiple bullets found at a crime scene can be compared to see if they came from one gun. If not, more than one weapon was used. If bullets collected from two different crime scenes match, this will serve to link the two crimes. Most importantly, a bullet removed from a homicide victim can be compared against a suspect weapon. A match identifies the murder weapon and this might be the key to identifying the killer. If a victim is shot by two assailants, matching the killing bullet to one of the guns would indicate which shooter would face the more serious charges.

The first step in this comparison process is to obtain an intact bullet fired by the suspect weapon. The examiner, using ammunition similar to that found at the crime scene, will fire the weapon into a test-firing chamber (bullet trap or water trap), which captures the bullet without damaging it. The lab-fired bullet (known) can then be compared with the crime scene bullet (unknown) by using a **comparison microscope**, which places images of the two bullets side by side. If the microscopic striations match, the crime scene bullet came from that weapon; if not, the investigators must continue their search for the murder weapon.

The bullet might also retain important trace evidence. Paint, fibers, bits of glass, and other materials can cling to the bullet as it passes through or ricochets off walls, doors, bricks, and windows. Small bits of flesh and blood might also be found. These microscopic bits and biological materials can on occasion be the key to solving a case and help reconstruct the crime scene. For example, a husband might say that his wife ran away from home. Family and friends insist she would not do that. During their investigation, the police find a bullet embedded in a basement wall, and the crime lab discovers that it holds a speck of blood, which is then matched to DNA (Chapter 11) obtained from the missing woman's toothbrush, hairbrush, or mailed letters. Even without a body, such evidence could lead to an indictment.

Shotguns do not have rifled barrels, and they fire a wad of round pellets (shot) rather than a single bullet, so striation comparisons are not part of the examination of shotgun ammunition. Shot extracted from walls, furniture, or from victims, either in surgery or at autopsy, will not determine the gauge of the shotgun but will give information about the ammunition used. The various sizes of shot are numbered, with the lower the number the larger the pellets within the shotgun shell. A Number 8 shot is smaller than a Number 4. Shot varies in diameter from 0.05 inch for Number 12 shot to 0.33 inch for OO shot, also called Double O Buckshot. The examiner can use these measurements to estimate what size shot was used.

Shell Casing Examination

At some crime scenes, bullets are not found and the only ballistic evidence available is one or more shell casings. These casings often possess several types of marks that are of interest to the ballistics examiner. As with bullets, the comparison of multiple casings found at one scene, casings found at different scenes, or casings from a test-fired suspect weapon might provide important information.

Revolvers retain the shell casings within the revolving cylinder and aren't found at crime scenes unless they are manually removed and discarded. Automatic and semiautomatic weapons eject the casings as each bullet is fired and a new one is seated into the firing chamber.

Useful shell case markings include the following:

- **Firing pin impressions**: Whether the casing is center-fire or rimfire, the firing pin impression, where the pin strikes the base of the cartridge, is usually unique enough to make a match.
- **Breechblock markings**: The breechblock is the back wall of the firing chamber. When the powder in the casing detonates and pushes the bullet down the barrel, Newtonian physics dictates that the casing is forced back against the breechblock. This leaves an impression on the base of the casing.
- **Extractor and ejector markings**: Automatic and semiautomatic weapons have mechanisms that remove the spent shell from the chamber and eject it from the weapon (ejector) and that extract the next bullet from the clip and seat it in the firing chamber (extractor). These extracting and ejecting mechanisms leave their own unique scratches and marks on the sides of the shell casings.

Each of these unique shell casing marks can be viewed and compared with a comparison microscope and are usually distinctive enough to individualize the casing to a particular weapon. The power of such evidence was first brought to the public's attention after the famous St. Valentine's Day Massacre and reinforced by many other cases such as the odd Branion murder case.

During the Roaring '20s, Prohibition made alcohol a profitable commodity, which led to warfare among crime families for control of this product. Nowhere was this more evident than in Chicago where Al "Scarface" Capone squared off with George "Bugs" Moran.

On the evening of February 14, 1929, seven of Moran's men waited in a Clark Street warehouse for a shipment of hijacked liquor. Moran himself was late arriving, which ultimately saved his life. As he approached, he saw five police officers enter the warehouse, so he retreated. The "police officers" were actually Capone's men, who lined Moran's men up and massacred them with Thomson submachine guns.

The real police arrived shortly after and ultimately recovered 70 shell casings from the scene and later several bullets from the victims. Because of the high-profile nature of the case, firearms expert and cardiologist Dr. Calvin Goddard, who became famous during the Sacco and Vanzetti Case (see above), was called in. He determined that the shell casings were from Thomson submachine guns and, using his comparison microscope, that none of the Thomsons owned by the Chicago Police Department were the murder weapons. This meant that the killers had impersonated police officers and Capone immediately became the primary suspect. Police raided the home of one of Capone's hit men and found two Thomsons, which Goddard identified as two of the murder weapons.

Two businessmen in Chicago were so impressed with Goddard's work that they helped fund the Scientific Crime Detection Laboratory (SCDL), the first independent crime lab, at Northwestern University in 1929. Following this model the FBI set up its own crime lab in 1932.

On December 22, 1967, Dr. John Branion left a hospital in south Chicago, passed by his home, picked up his son from nursery school, and then went to pick up a friend for lunch. The friend couldn't make lunch so Dr. Branion went home, arriving just before noon. He found his wife in the floor of a utility room dead from four gunshot wounds. He called the police.

Firearms expert Burt Nielson examined the shell casings recovered at the scene and the bullets removed from the victim and determined that the weapon was a .38 caliber. He also noted that the casings bore ejector markings that could only have come from a Walther PPK. Branion, a gun collector, said that he did not own a Walther. A warranted search of Branion's home turned up a Walther PPK brochure, an extra ammunition clip, and a Walther branded target, all of which bore the serial number 188274. Police also found two boxes of .38 caliber ammunition, one full and the other missing four cartridges.

The importers of Walther handguns in New York revealed that the Walther PPK bearing the serial number 188274 had been shipped to James Hooks, a friend of Dr. Branion's. Branion was convicted and sentenced to a long prison term. He was released on bond while he undertook an appeal of his conviction. By 1971, with his appeal going nowhere and facing a return to prison, he fled to Uganda, where he enjoyed the protection of the dictator Idi Amin. He even served as Amin's personal physician. Unfortunately for Dr. Branion, Amin was eventually toppled and Branion was extradited back to the United States to serve his sentence.

Gunshot Residues

When a gun is fired, the primer and the powder within the cartridge explode, forcing the bullet down the barrel, followed by most of the explosive gases and particulate matter produced by the explosion. However, some of these materials escape through the breach and other openings in the weapon. This is particularly true of revolvers, which tend to "leak" more gases than other types of weapons. The chemical and particulate components of these gases, called **gunshot residue (GSR)**, cling to the shooter's hand, arm, clothing, face, and hair. They also settle on nearby walls, furniture, and other objects as well as on the victim's skin and clothing in close-range gunshots.

On light-colored clothing, the GSR pattern might be visible as smudges or smears, while on dark, multicolored, or blood stained clothing, the pattern might be invisible. **Infrared photography**, as well as the **Griess test**, will often reveal these patterns. In the Griess test a sheet of photographic paper or a sheet of acetic acid-dampened filter paper is pressed over the area and then immersed in Griess reagent, which reacts with the inorganic nitrites in the GSR, revealing the pattern.

The ultimate goal of GSR analysis is to place the gun "in the suspect's hand." Unfortunately, simply being near the gun when it was discharged or handling the gun afterward can leave GSR on anyone, not just the person that fired the weapon. A major problem is that GSR fades rapidly, usually dissipating after a couple of hours, and can also be wiped or washed away. For this reason, testing should be accomplished as soon after the gun is fired as possible.

The suspect's hands, face, and clothing should be inspected and samples obtained. The old "paraffin test," where melted paraffin was used to pick up the residue, is rarely used anymore, and sampling is done by swabbing the suspect's hands, arms, and clothing with a moist swab or filter paper. The samples are then subjected to chemical testing designed to detect the byproducts of primer and gunpowder combustion, which are predominantly the metals lead, barium, and antimony.

The screening test is to treat the swab or filter paper with **diphenylamine**, which turns blue when positive. Unfortunately, other substances such as fertilizer, tobacco, cosmetics, and urine can yield false positive results. The presence of GSR must be confirmed by more specific confirmatory tests such as **neutron activation analysis** and **atomic absorption spectrometry**, which reveal elevated levels of barium and antimony when positive.

Sometimes GSR is found not on the shooter's hands, but on his clothing or in his hair. A **scanning electron microscope (SEM)** can often locate these tiny GSR particles and when paired with **energy dispersive x-ray spectroscopy (EDS)**, gives a "chemical fingerprint" of the substance tested. Using SEM/EDS, the finding of lead, barium, and antimony in such small particles is highly suggestive that the particle is indeed GSR.

Restoring Serial Numbers

The serial number of a weapon found at a crime scene or one proven to be a murder weapon by bullet or shell casing examination can lead to the registered owner. But that doesn't mean that the owner is the one who used it and left it at the scene. The owner might have sold or given the gun to someone or it might have been stolen and the two cases (the murder and the gun theft) can be linked. Comparing the evidence in the two cases would move the investigators closer to identifying the perpetrator.

But, sometimes criminals attempt to grind or file away the gun's serial number in the hopes that the weapon can't be traced. If so, the examiner might employ tests such as magnaflux, chemical and electrochemical etching, or ultrasonic cavitation to restore the damaged numbers. Each of these techniques relies on the changes in the structure of the gun's metal that follows the serial number stamping process. When the metal is pressure stamped, not only is the metal indented with the numbers, but also the metal beneath the numbers is stressed and undergoes structural changes.

Magnaflux is useful only if the weapon is composed of iron-containing metals. The gun is placed in a strong electromagnetic field or beneath a strong magnet, which magnetizes the weapon. The lines of magnetic force in a magnetized object usually run parallel to each other, but the disordered metal beneath the stamped numbers disrupts this order. If after magnetization, the gun is sprayed with a special oil that contains iron-like particles, the particles will collect in the areas of disordered metal, thus revealing the hidden number. The major advantage of this process is that it is nondestructive and doesn't alter the weapon, which is the evidence in this circumstance.

Chemical and electrochemical etching are destructive processes, which limit their use. In these tests an etching solution is spread over the damaged area. The solution "eats" the disordered metal faster than the surrounding metal, bringing the numbers into view. Adding an electric current (electrochemical etching) hastens the process. Either of these must be done carefully, since over-etching will destroy the evidence forever.

Ultrasonic cavitation is also a destructive process. The gun is placed in a special ultrasonic bath and exposed to very high frequency vibrations, which causes **cavitation**—a process in which tiny bubbles form along the surface of the metal. With continued exposure, the cavitation begins to eat away the metal. The process proceeds fastest in the areas of disorder and, as with chemical etching, the serial number is revealed.

National Ballistic Database Systems

What if the ballistics examiner is given only a single bullet or shell casing and no suspect weapon for comparison? As mentioned earlier, he can often determine the type and manufacturer of the weapon that fired the bullet, but that's as far as he can go. But there are several databases that he can use to compare the ballistic markings with those taken from weapons used in other crimes.

DRUGFIRE, a ballistic identification system developed by the FBI in the 1990s, has been replaced by the **Integrated Bullet Identification System (IBIS)** maintained by the **Federal Bureau of Alcohol, Tobacco, Firearms, and Explosives** (**BATF**, or **ATF** as it is commonly called). This computer-based system stores digital photos of fired bullets and shell casings. The **National Integrated Ballistic Information Network (NIBIN)** is a joint venture between the FBI and the ATF that uses the IBIS system to compare ballistic markings.

These databases remain incomplete, but if images of a crime scene or test-fired bullet or shell casing are entered into the IBIS system and if a matching bullet or casing is in the database, a match, which is then confirmed by an experienced firearms examiner, can be made. This will then serve to connect two scenes and help in the solution of both crimes.

CHAPTER 18

ARSON INVESTIGATION

Arson investigations are difficult and become even trickier when explosions are involved. The main reason is that the crime scene and the evidence are typically severely damaged if not completely destroyed. The arson investigator uses both physical and chemical evidence to determine whether the fire was natural (lightning), accidental (faulty wiring, unattended open flame, etc.), or intentional. In cases where homicide is involved, he will call in the ME to determine the cause and manner of death.

Before we explore how arson scenes are investigated, let's look at the nature of fire itself.

Fires and Explosions

Fire is a chemical reaction in which fuel materials and oxygen are consumed and heat and light are produced. From a chemistry perspective this is called **oxidation**, which is when a substance combines with oxygen, or some other **oxidant**, to produce another substance. Fires and explosions are also termed **exothermic**, meaning that they produce energy and heat.

It might surprise you that the process of **rust formation** is also an oxidative process, so to the chemist rust is simply a very slow fire. In this case, iron (Fe) combines with oxygen (O_2) to produce iron oxide (Fe_2O_3), or rust.

This process might take months or years, and since it is so slow, no detectable heat or light is produced.

Fire results when a fuel source combines with oxygen, but simply bringing together O_2 and a flammable fuel, such as paper or gasoline, will not produce fire. Heat is needed. This triad—fuel, oxygen, and heat—must be present for a fire to begin. The removal or suppression of any of these will prevent a fire from starting and, if already burning, will extinguish or slow it, while the addition of one or more will accelerate it. Spraying water on a fire will extinguish it because it lowers the temperature, blocks oxygen from reaching the fuel, and in some circumstances dilutes the fuel. On the other hand, adding gasoline or oxygen will increase the fire's intensity.

If the initiation of a fire requires heat, exactly how much is needed? It depends on the fuel. The temperature at which fire will break out is called the **ignition temperature** and it varies widely from substance to substance. The ignition temperature for gasoline is quite different from that of wood. However, once combustion occurs, the fire will continue because the fire itself, like all exothermic reactions, produces enough heat to continue the burning process.

The fuel consumed in a fire can be solid (wood, drapes, carpets, furniture, roofing materials), liquid (gasoline, paint thinners, alcohol), or gas (natural gas), but in order for any of these fuels to ignite, they must first be in a gaseous state. Put another way, flammable gases will ignite, but before solids or liquids can burn they must be converted to a gas.

With a liquid fuel, the applied heat must be sufficient to vaporize (turn into gas) the fuel. This temperature is called the **flash point**, which is the lowest temperature that will vaporize a liquid fuel. It varies from liquid to liquid. Gasoline possesses its characteristic odor because it is an extremely **volatile** liquid, which means it is constantly releasing gas vapors. When gasoline catches fire, it is these vapors that are burning and not the liquid gasoline. The heat from the fire continually vaporizes the gasoline, thus producing a continuous supply of gaseous fuel.

Solids will burn only when enough heat is applied to convert the solid to gas by a process called **pyrolysis**. In the case of wood or paper, the heat turns the surface of these solids to a gas, which then can mix with O_2 and ignite. When you see wood burning, what you are actually seeing is the burning of a very thin layer of "wood gas" over the surface of the wood. If the temperature is too low for pyrolysis to take place, the solid might still burn, but we call this **smoldering**, a slow, flameless burn. But add heat or oxygen and the smoldering burn might generate enough heat for the pyrolytic reaction to occur and the fuel will burst into flames. Blowing, fanning, or using a bellows to direct air at a fire will cause a smoldering log to burst into flames, thus the term "fanning the flames."

Spontaneous combustion, basically a self-starting fire, rarely occurs because the conditions required are uncommon. A collection of rags soaked with certain oils and placed in a poorly ventilated container can combust spontaneously. In this circumstance, heat from the slow oxidation of the oils raises the temperature to the ignition temperature of the oils, and fire results.

Explosives are fuels that are capable of undergoing very rapid oxidation, reactions that are so rapid that the oxygen in the air is not sufficient. Explosives get around this by containing their own oxygen in the form of **oxidants** or **oxidizing agents**. For example, black powder is composed of sulfur, carbon, and potassium nitrate. Since potassium nitrate contains oxygen, it serves as the oxidizing agent.

Motives for Arson

Why do people intentionally set fires? The reasons are many and varied, but arson invariably has a payoff. Common ones include the following:

- **Financial gain**: Insurance fraud is at the heart of many arson cases. Perhaps quick money is needed and the insurance on the home or warehouse is greater than the property's value. A torched home might have contained money or insured valuables, which were of course removed before the fire was started. This way the perpetrator not only has the insurance money, but also the insured items.
- **Cover another crime**: Arson is often used to cover another crime, such as theft. Maybe an employee has embezzled from the company or has stolen goods from a company warehouse and attempts to cover his crime by destroying the warehouse and/or any financial records in a fire.
- **Revenge or terror**: A grudge or deep-seated hatred for another might lead the arsonist to set fire to home or business. Or an

individual or a group might burn a structure in order to create fear or make a political statement.

- **Suicide and murder**: Fire is rarely used for suicide or murder because it is simply too painful for the former and too unpredictable for the latter. However, it is often used in an attempt to disguise or cover a murder. The killer's hope is that the corpse will be so damaged that the true cause of death is impossible to determine. Unfortunately for the killer, a structure fire is rarely hot enough, nor does it burn long enough, to completely destroy a body. Even bodies that are significantly charred will often be remarkably well preserved internally, allowing the ME to uncover signs of trauma, poisons, and other causes of death.
- **Psychopathology**: A fascination with fire is almost universal among humans. What is more pleasant than a crackling fire on a cold winter day? But some individuals possess a pathological love for fire, and starting them feeds some deep psychological need. This is the drive behind many serial arsonists.

Arson Investigation

The investigation of a suspected arson revolves around the answer to two questions: (1) Where was the fire's point of origin? and (2) What was the cause of the fire?

Point of Origin

All fires have a **point of origin**, and locating this is the cornerstone of any arson investigation. Materials found in this area help the investigator determine whether the fire was accidental or intentional and whether any **igniters** (the heat source that ignited the fire) or **accelerants** (substances that facilitate the start and spread of the fire) were used. For example, a point of origin near an overloaded wall outlet would favor an accidental fire, while finding one in a corner of a warehouse, far removed from any electrical source yet near a charred gasoline can, rags, paper, remnants of matches, or other combustible materials would suggest arson. Much to the dismay of many arsonists, these types of materials often survive even very destructive fires.

For the arson investigator, time is the enemy, since many of the volatile substances that cause or accelerate a fire rapidly dissipate. He will often begin his investigation by interviewing witnesses who might have seen the fire in its earliest stages, and this helps with locating the point or points of origin. In addition, the color of the flames and smoke might be helpful since many accelerants and combustible materials produce characteristic flame and smoke colors. For example, gasoline produces yellow flames and white smoke, wood produces red and yellow flames and gray or brown smoke, and rubber and some petroleum products produce red-orange flames and black smoke.

Locating the fire's point of origin requires an understanding of how fire moves through a structure. Fire typically spreads laterally and vertically so that once the point of origin has been located, the investigator can often follow the path of the fire as it spreads through the structure. This is often possible in even heavily damaged structures. Conversely, backtracking along the fire's route of spread might lead to the origin point. The investigator will search for a "V pattern," since fire tends to rise and spread in a V-shaped pattern on a wall or other vertical surface. The point of origin is typically at the foot of the V. But sometimes the structure is so severely damaged that this is not possible. Here the astute and experienced investigator knows that typically the greatest degree of damage is near the point of origin, so he will search for that area. Unfortunately, many things obscure and confuse the issue.

Wind, drafts from open windows, the airflow pattern of the particular structure, stairs, elevators, and many other things can alter the way the fire spreads and where it burns the hottest. Materials used in construction and decoration, such as plastics, paints, insulating or sound-retarding materials, synthetic carpeting, and wall coverings can create confusing "hot spots" and patterns of spread. Stored fuels and other flammable liquids not only interfere with the location of the true point of origin but might also make the search for accelerants difficult, since they themselves are accelerants. The arsonist might have started multiple fires within the building or might have sloshed a path of gasoline or other accelerant throughout or around the structure. In this case the fire might have multiple points of origin. Obviously, a fire with multiple points of origin is virtually always arson.

The intensity of the fire at any particular location can be estimated by assessing its effect on structural materials. Steel beams might buckle if the fire is extremely intense. Glass tends to melt at around 1500° F. Cracking and flaking of walls and floors (spalling) indicate an area of high heat. Wooden beams, floors, and walls can char, leaving an alligator-skin-like pattern. If so, the smaller "scales" tend to be near the hottest point of the fire. If the building is equipped with a system of smoke detectors, the timing with which they alarmed helps determine the path the fire took through the structure.

Liquid fuels present special problems for the investigator since liquids spread and conform to the shape of their container. If gasoline is poured on a floor, it will spread across the room, run down the stairs, and seep into the baseboards, and the fire will follow this path. Gaseous fuels, such as natural gas, are even more problematic since they diffuse in all directions and fill a room or the entire structure. When an ignition source is added, they typically explode rather than burn, and finding an exact point of origin might be impossible.

Cause of the Fire

Once the point of origin is determined, a search for potential causes follows. This requires an examination of the circumstances and factors that brought the fire and the fuel into contact in this place at this time. A search near the point of origin might reveal igniters and accelerants.

Potential ignition sources include such things as electrical wiring, oil lamps, candles, cigarettes, fireplaces, and timing devices, which can be very complex or as simple as a match. Often the arsonist will light the fire and toss the match aside, believing that the resulting fire will completely destroy it. However, match heads contain **diatoms**, which are single-celled organisms found in the diatomaceous earth used in match production. These tiny creatures, which were discussed in Chapter 9 as a tool in determining the cause of death in drownings, possess silica-containing shells, which are very tough and survive fires. Interestingly, match manufacturers use different materials that contain different diatom species, which can be distinguished from one another by their shell structure, and in some cases these can not only indicate that a match was used but can identify the brand.

Another low-tech device is a candle placed on a pile of paper. When the candle burns down, it ignites the paper and the fire takes off. A cigarette laid across an open book of matches is equally as simple. Or the ignition source might be a complex electrical timing device. Sometimes the igniter and an accelerant are combined as in a "Molotov cocktail." This is typically a glass container filled with a flammable liquid. A cloth "fuse" is stuffed into a hole in the jar's lid or the bottle's neck. The cloth is lit, the device is tossed into the building, the glass shatters, and the fire is off and running. A thorough search might reveal candle residue, a cigarette butt, the remains of the electrical device, or the neck of the bottle with cloth remnants inside.

Accelerants

Accelerants, which are almost always used by arsonists to make sure the fire "takes hold," are any substances that promote or accelerate the intensity and the progress of the fire. They can be solids (paper, black powder, kindling wood), liquids (gasoline, kerosene, alcohols, paint thinners), or gases (natural gas, propane). Liquid accelerants, particularly gasoline and kerosene, are by far the most common. Even if the structure is severely damaged, traces of these accelerants usually remain. They soak into carpets and brickwork, seep into baseboards and crevices, and settle into areas beneath the fire.

To locate remnants of the accelerants, the arson investigator might employ specially trained dogs that "sniff out" traces of accelerants or perhaps a detector such as a **vapor trace analyzer (VTA)**. This "artificial nose," which is actually a specialized gas chromatograph, is extremely sensitive and tests for flammable hydrocarbon residues in the air around sites of accelerant residue. The VTA has a nozzle, a heating element, and a temperature gauge. A sample of the air, and any accelerant vapors it might contain, is drawn in through the nozzle and passed over a heating element. If the sample burns it will raise the temperature within the device, causing a bump in the temperature gauge, which is presumptive evidence that a flammable residue is present. Samples of charred wood, carpet, or other debris that might hold accelerant residue will then be collected and taken to the lab for more thorough analysis. Since most accelerants are volatile petroleum-based hydrocarbons, their vapors dissipate rapidly, so to prevent loss of this crucial evidence, the gathered materials should be placed in nonporous containers such as sealed cans or glass jars.

Once in the lab, the first step in the analysis is to extract any accelerant chemicals from the debris. The most common methods used for this are as follows:

- **Steam distillation**: The charred material is heated and the steam is collected and condensed. The resulting liquid will contain any volatile hydrocarbons.
- **Solvent extraction**: The sample is placed in a container with a solvent such as chloroform, carbon tetrachloride, methyline chloride, or carbon disulfide, which leaches any accelerant hydrocarbons from the material. These are then separated from the solvent.
- **Head space vapor extraction**: The natural volatility of the hydrocarbons creates a vapor-rich gas above the material in the closed container's "head space," which can then be removed.
- **Vapor concentration**: The sample is heated in a closed container that contains charcoal. Volatile hydrocarbons leave the sample and absorb into the charcoal. The hydrocarbons are then extracted from the charcoal by employing a solvent.

Once any volatile hydrocarbons have been extracted, they are analyzed using a **gas chromatograph (GC)**, which will separate them into their components. These are then compared to known standards, and the identity of the substance is revealed. Usually GC is all that is needed for identification, but if further delineation of the sample is needed, GC can be combined with **mass spectroscopy (GC/MS)** or with **infrared spectroscopy (GC/IR)**, either of which will give a molecular "fingerprint" of the substance. Once the actual accelerant used is uncovered, investigators can then focus on anyone who purchased, owned, or had access to that type of product.

Gasoline, the most common accelerant, is ubiquitous, so knowing that gasoline was used is usually not very helpful. But each batch of gasoline produced varies slightly in its chemical makeup and additive content. Though it is not possible to determine the exact manufacturer of a given sample, a comparative analysis between the unknown (crime scene) sample and those taken from nearby or suspect service stations might suggest that the gasoline came from a particular station. Though this is not completely reliable, an investigation into who purchased gasoline at that location during a particular time period might lead investigators to a suspect.

Homicidal Fires

When a body is discovered among the fire debris, the coroner and homicide investigators are called in to identify the corpse and determine the cause and manner of death. Identifying an unknown corpse was discussed in detail in Chapter 5, but in general and depending upon the condition of the body, the ME will use physical characteristics such as stature, age, sex, tattoos, birthmarks, and surgical scars as he attempts to uncover the identity of the deceased. Surgical appliances such as artificial hips and pacemakers usually survive fires and can be helpful.

Fingerprints, dental matching, and DNA might also be useful. Fingerprints might not be obtainable and the corpse could be so severely damaged that no usable DNA survived the fire, but even in severely burned bodies, the teeth survive. In some cases, the internal organs survive and usable DNA can be obtained from these organs, from the bone marrow, or from the dental pulp.

The ME will also search for evidence as to the cause and manner of death, which was covered in great detail in Chapter 7. One question the ME must answer is whether the victim was alive at the time the fire started or not. If so, an accident is possible; if not, homicide becomes a more likely manner of death. To help with this, the ME looks at things such as the position of the body, the blood and tissue carbon monoxide (CO) level, the presence or absence of soot in the lungs and airways, and the nature of the burns.

The position of the body can be telling. For example, if the corpse is found on a bed, the cause of death is determined to be smoke inhalation, and the fire's origin is found to be a cigarette in contact with bedding, the death would likely be accidental. But what if the victim is a nonsmoker? Could the cigarette be the arsonist's chosen igniter and the death actually be homicidal? The ME can often measure the nicotine level in the victim's urine, where a high level would indicate that he was indeed a smoker and a low level would suggest just the opposite. On the other hand, what if the corpse is found bound and gagged in the basement with a gunshot or stab wound or significant blunt trauma that fractured the skull? Of course, this would suggest homicide.

A common misconception is that if a body is found curled into a fetal position the victim was alive at the time the fire started. This is simply untrue. A burning corpse will often assume a "pugilistic position" or a boxer's posture. The legs and arms are flexed and the fists are tucked beneath the chin. This posture is due to contraction of the body's muscles as the fire "cooks" and dehydrates them.

Most deaths in fires are due to asphyxia (Chapter 9) from the inhalation of smoke and carbon monoxide (CO), a byproduct of the combustion of organic materials such as wood. The ME will test the victim's blood and tissues for CO. A normal level is less than 10 percent, though in smokers it might be slightly higher. In victims of CO asphyxiation the level ranges from about 45 to 90 percent. The finding of a high level suggests that the victim died from smoke and CO inhalation, while a low level favors the victim being dead at the time the fire started.

Another autopsy finding in victims of CO poisoning is a high level of **carboxyhemoglobin**, the combination of CO and the blood's hemoglobin. Carboxyhemoglobin imparts a bright, cherry-red color to the blood, muscles, and organs of the victim. When the ME sees this he will suspect that CO inhalation played a role in the death and will then proceed to prove this by assessing the CO level in the blood and tissues.

The finding of **soot** in the mouth, throat, lungs, and airways suggests that the victim was alive and breathing as the fire burned.

When a living person suffers a burn, the body will immediately begin the repair process by diverting extra blood flow to the area. This causes the surrounding tissues to become **hyperemic**, meaning that the tissues are filled with blood, which brings in white blood cells (WBCs) to begin the repair process. If the ME performs microscopic examinations of the burned tissues and sees increased blood and WBCs in the surrounding areas, the victim was alive at the time the tissues burned. If the victim was already dead, no reaction could occur since the heart is not beating and no blood could flow into the area.

An examination of any blisters on the skin might also help. The fluid that collects inside blisters that occur during life tend to be rich in protein, while those that occur after death are not. The ME can often test the protein level and determine whether the blistering occurred pre- or postmortem.

So, burns with surrounding hyperemia and many WBCs and blisters filled with protein-rich fluids would indicate that the victim was alive at the time of the fire. If the opposite is the case, the victim was likely dead before the fire reached him.

Explosions

An explosion is an extremely rapid oxidative reaction that releases a large volume of expanding gas, which compresses the surrounding air in a concussive wave. This wave travels at high speed and does severe and sudden damage to anything in its path. This creates numerous problems for the investigator, since the explosive device and any surrounding structures are heavily damaged if not completely destroyed. Unless a secondary fire occurs, determining the point of origin is usually easy, but finding fragments of the device or any igniters or timers might be more difficult.

Explosives are deemed high or low by the speed of the pressure wave they produce. **Low explosives** typically move at rates of 1,000 meters per second or less, while **high explosives** may reach up to 8,500 meters per second. The most commonly used low explosives are black powder and smokeless gunpowder. High explosives are subdivided into **initiating** or **non-initiating**, depending upon their sensitivity to heat, friction, or mechanical shock.

Initiating explosives are very sensitive, which means that they have a great potential for unexpected detonation. For this reason they are rarely used in home-manufactured bombs but are found in primers and blasting caps, where they are used to initiate other less sensitive, non-initiating explosive materials. Mercury fulminate and lead azide are commonly used in this fashion.

Non-initiating explosives are more stable, are less likely to be accidentally detonated, require a fuse or some type of initiating device to set them off, and are the most commonly used materials in commercial and military applications. Examples would be **dynamite**, **TNT** (trinitrotoluene), **PETN** (pentaerythritol tetranitrate), and **RDX** (cyclotrimethylenetrinitramine). Though dynamite is still available, it and other nitroglycerine-based explosives have largely been replaced by ammonium nitrate-based explosives. **ANFO**, an easily made explosive material, is a mixture of ammonium nitrate and fuel oil. Ammonium nitrate, found in fertilizers, is an oxygen-rich oxidant. Bombs produced from this substance were involved in the 1995 Oklahoma City and the 1993 World Trade Center bombings.

Searching the scene of a bombing requires great attention to detail. The finding of fragments from the explosive device, the igniter, and any timer might be crucial to determining the type of explosive used and ultimately the person responsible. Besides locating these fragments, the search is directed toward the collection of debris to test for unexploded residue, which is almost always present.

Microscopic examination of the debris might reveal black powder and gunpowder, which are easily recognizable by the color and shape of their particles. After this inspection, the debris is rinsed with a solvent such as acetone, in which most explosives are soluble. The resulting solution is then analyzed, using thin-layer or gas chromatography as well as mass spectroscopy and infrared spectroscopy, and the explosive used is identified. Once this is known, investigators can focus on the sellers and buyers of that particular product.

Serial bombers are similar to **serial arsonists** in that they typically have deep-seated anger toward someone or an institution such as a company or the government. At times the bombings are meant to deliver a political message or cause terror. But, as with most serial offenders (see Chapter 20), serial bombers develop habits. They repeatedly use the same types of explosives and timing or triggering devices. An analysis of the explosive material and of any devices associated with the bomb can often link several bombings together and ultimately lead to the perpetrator.

CHAPTER 19

QUESTIONED DOCUMENTS

Documents often come into play in criminal and civil cases. An embezzler might alter ledgers to cover his theft. Kidnappers send ransom notes. An altered check, a back-dated insurance policy, a forged will, and even a lottery ticket can divert a large amount of money into the wrong hands. In these and other situations a **forensic document examiner** might be asked to analyze various documents with an eye toward authenticity and to look for alterations and forgeries.

Document examination dates to 1609, when François Demelle published the first scientific treatise on the subject in France. In 1810 in Germany, chemical testing of the ink dye used in a document known as *Konigin Hanschritt* is believed to be the first use of document analysis in a legal setting.

The modern document examiner can expect to deal with complete or fragmentary documents that are handwritten, typed, or photocopied. The documents might be letters, checks, wills, lottery or claim tickets, receipts, ledgers, ransom or hold-up notes, harassing letters, driver's licenses, contracts, deeds, and counterfeited currency or stamps, not to mention writings and symbols scrawled on walls, doors, or any other object.

The term **questioned document** is applied to any document whose source or authenticity is in question. When criminal investigators come across such documents, the forensic document examiner will be asked to do the following:

- Determine whether a document is authentic and was produced by the person and at the time it was purported to be.
- Determine whether the document has been altered.
- Expose damaged or obliterated writing.
- Compare handwriting, signatures, and typewritten or photocopied documents.
- Determine the age and source of papers and inks.

One very important point: A forensic document expert examines the physical characteristics of the writing and sometimes its content but he does not attempt to determine the writer's personality type. This is the job of a **graphologist**, and **graphology** is a controversial subject that has yet to gain widespread legal acceptance.

To perform his job, the examiner will employ several microscopic, photographic, and chemical techniques, but mostly he will use his skill and experience. This is an exacting art that can't be completely discussed in this book, but let's look at some of the situations in which the forensic document examiner might play a role.

Handwriting

Each person's writing style is personal and unique and results from unconscious, automatic actions. Furthermore, people never write the same way twice since our handwriting is affected by our mood, position, writing surface, and by whether we use a pen, pencil, or crayon.

As we age, our writing style changes, not always dramatically, but enough to recognize. This is important when comparing older documents, since new samples of the author's handwriting might differ from how she wrote decades earlier. Illnesses such as stroke or Parkinson's disease significantly alter handwriting as can fatigue, stress, impaired vision, hand or arm injuries, and intoxication with drugs or alcohol. The document examiner must take each of these variables into consideration when he is comparing handwriting samples.

When comparing two documents or signatures to determine their authenticity, the examiner must have examples (called **exemplars** or **standards**) of the person's writing that he knows are authentic. And since a person's writing style varies a little each time he writes, the more examples the examiner has, the better. To begin his comparison, he will look for points of similarity and points of difference between the known standards and the questioned document. He will assess several things:

- **Overall form** includes the size, shape, slant (right, left, or vertical), proportion (relative height), and the beginning and ending strokes of the letters. Does the writing slant one way or the other or employ angles, loops, or curves to make various letters? How do the individual letters begin and end?
- **Line features** deal with writing speed and fluidity, the amount of pen pressure applied, the spacing of the letters and words, and how the letters are connected. Does the writing flow or is it broken and hesitant? Is it written firmly or lightly? Are the letters and words crowded or spread out? Are the words written in a single smooth line or was the pen lifted in the middle of certain words?
- **Margins and format** is the overall layout of the writing. Are the page margins wide or narrow? Are the written lines parallel or do they slant up or down?
- **Content** deals with grammar, punctuation, and word choice. Are there consistent mistakes in spelling and punctuation? Do certain phrases repeat? Does the writing reveal the author's ethnicity or educational level?

If the examiner has enough standards he can usually determine whether the questioned document and the standard share the same authorship or not. If he has only a few examples to work with, he might not be able to get a "feel" for the person's writing style. Another complicating factor is that the standards might have been written by a different instrument and under different circumstances. For example, comparing a letter written on quality stationery with a fountain pen with crayon scribbles on a wall or a quickly scratched-out ransom note is often difficult if not impossible.

What if the examiner has no usable known standards available? How can a comparison be made? In this situation, the examiner might request that the person writes something on similar paper and with a similar instrument. This brings up the concept of requested and non-requested standards. **Requested standards** are writings or signatures that a person produces at the request of the examiner. **Non-requested standards** are documents or signatures that are of known authorship.

Let's say the examiner is asked to determine whether a check has been forged. He will need a copy of the real account holder's signature, which can usually be gotten from old checks stored by the bank. These would be non-requested standards, which he could then compare to the signature on the questioned check. The examiner will also ask the suspected forger to write his signature (actually the signature on the check, which he claims is his) several times. These would be requested standards and should be written on the same type of paper and with a similar writing instrument as those used on the check in question. With the questioned check and these requested and non-requested standards, the examiner should be able to determine whether the check is legitimate or has been forged.

Non-requested writings have several advantages. They are more likely than requested standards to reveal the writer's true writing habits and might also contain words and phrases that the writer repeatedly uses. Such phrases and words can be strong evidence against him. For example, old letters or notes might contain phrases that are identical to those used in a ransom note.

Non-requested standards also have several major disadvantages. These standards must themselves be authenticated, and if they can't be, they are of little value to the examiner. This was a major concern in the famous Hitler Diaries forgeries (see below). Another problem is that, as discussed above, handwriting changes over time due to aging, illness, etc. For this reason, the examiner should attempt to obtain documents written by the suspected author around the same time as the questioned document. For example, if he is asked to determine whether a 20-year-old handwritten will was indeed written by the purported author, he would search for documents written 20 years earlier. These would reflect his style at the time the will was prepared much better than would more recently written documents.

Requested writings also have advantages. Their authenticity is unquestioned since the examiner can actually watch the person write. Furthermore, the examiner can dictate exactly what he wants written, such as words or phrases from the questioned document, which allows him to compare the writing word for word.

A major disadvantage of requested writings is that this situation makes some people nervous or causes them to concentrate too much on the writing process, which can lead to changes in their "normal" signature. Or the person might attempt to purposefully disguise his writing style. For example, the suspected author of a ransom note will not want his handwriting to match the note and will attempt to disguise his handwriting. One way around this is to have the suspect write several pages of material. The more he writes the more his natural style will come through. Another trick is to dictate the same material to the writer several times. If he is attempting to disguise his handwriting style, he will likely use different devices with each attempt. Basically, he forgets what he did in the last draft so must make up changes "on the fly." A good examiner can then find the hidden style elements and the devices used to disguise them.

What if a suspected forger refuses to give a sample of his writing, pleading that it violates his Fifth Amendment right not to incriminate or testify against himself? Can he be forced to supply the samples? The short answer is yes. The Supreme Court decided in *Gilbert v. California* that handwriting was part of identifying physical characteristics and was not protected by the Fifth Amendment. Further, in the case of the *United States v. Mara*, the court also decided that this did not violate the Fourth Amendment protection against unreasonable search and seizure.

The Examination Process

The process of examining questioned documents follows a logical path. The examiner will first look for gross likenesses or differences—things such as slant, letter and word formation, angles, loops, flourishes, spacing, and other physical characteristics of the writing. If he finds significant differences, the comparison can end and he can state that the two documents were not written by the same person. If these gross characteristics are similar, he will examine things such as pen pressure, writing speed and fluidity, pen lifts, and line slant, characteristics that are ingrained and repetitive and are difficult to disguise.

Sometimes a misspelled word is important. If the standard exemplars and the questioned document have the same misspellings, this can be useful evidence. This played a role in the infamous 1969 Charles Manson Family Tate-LaBianca murders. The words "Healter Skelter," a misspelling of the title of a Beatles song on their famous *White Album,* were written in blood on a refrigerator door at the home of Leno and Rosemary LaBianca. The same incorrect spelling was found at the Manson Family's hideout at Spahn Ranch, an old deserted movie set. This similarity was used in the trial of Manson and his followers, who were convicted of the murders.

No single feature, but rather a combination of features, will allow the examiner to determine whether the writings came from the same person or not. This is by nature a very subjective judgment, but ultimately, the examiner might be able to say that the documents absolutely match, match with a high probability, probably match, do not match, or his evaluation is inclusive and he can't say one way or the other.

As we saw with fingerprints, ballistic patterns, and DNA databases, several handwriting databases also exist. The FBI maintains the **National Fraudulent Check File**, the **Bank Robbery Note File**, the **Anonymous Letter File**, and the **Forensic Information System for Handwriting (FISH)**, which contains scanned and digitized documents. A questioned document can be compared with these reference files and if a match is made, it will then be visually confirmed by a forensic document examiner.

Forgery

As mentioned in Chapter 8, *rape* is a legal term and not a medical diagnosis. The physician can determine whether penetration has likely occurred, whether trauma is present, and whether semen is found in or on the victim, but the courts must decide the "intent." That is, was this rape or consensual? The same is true of forgery. It is legal terminology and not a forensic determination. Forgery is defined as the writing or the alteration of a document with the "intent to defraud." The document examiner can determine whether a document was written by someone other than the stated author or whether the document has been altered, but the "intent to defraud" is decided by a judge and jury.

Criminal investigations often involve forged documents or signatures on checks, wills, contracts, and other documents. Since forged writing is not natural, even the most careful and gifted forger leaves behind evidence of his efforts.

The two most common methods of forgery are **freehand simulation** and **tracing**. Freehand methods simply copy the signature, while tracing involves placing the document over the original signature and tracing its lines. Either technique leaves clues:

- **Prior drawing** is when the forger lightly traces a signature in pencil and then writes over it with ink.
- **Forger's tremor** is a fine "shakiness" to the writing from the forger's attempts to make an exact copy.
- **Uneven speed and pressure** results because careful writing and tracing are not smooth and flowing like natural writing, so the forger uses varying speeds and pen pressures as he carefully creates each letter.
- **Hesitations** result from the writer's starting and stopping frequently in his efforts to be exact.
- **Unusual pen lifts** occur because copying and tracing are tedious, causing the forger to frequently lift the pen to check his work.
- **Patching and retouching** are common because the forger must continually add, remove, and repair marks.
- **Blunt beginnings and ends** occur because beginning and ending strokes of natural writing are very difficult to duplicate, so forged words are often relatively blunt on each end.

To identify some of these defects, the examiner might use a magnifying glass or even a low-power microscope. In the case of prior drawing, microscopic examination often reveals both the pencil and the ink lines. In addition, infrared light will make some inks appear transparent, exposing the underlying graphite from the pencil.

Disguised writing is a special form of forgery. Here the suspect attempts to change or disguise his own writing. Ransom notes and threatening letters are often written this way so that the author can deny ownership at a later date. Or a suspect might attempt to disguise his writing when confronted with an incriminating letter that he wrote in his natural handwriting. He might change the size, slant, and form of some letters, but still his own writing style will usually slip through, and an experienced document examiner will recognize those features.

Altered Documents

Forgers often attempt to remove, add, or change portions of a written document for financial gain, the creation of an alibi, and many other reasons. These modifications might be a simple date change, the reconstruction of a portion of a document, or a signature or dollar amount alteration on a contract or check. These changes fall into three broad categories: erasures, obliterations, and alterations.

Erasures are often easily accomplished with a rubber eraser, knifepoint or other sharp instrument, sandpaper, or even a fingernail. Exposing such changes are important, even if the original words or marks can't be visualized, because they are proof that the document was altered, and this alone might be a crime or might render many legal documents null and void.

Most of these alterations are visible with the naked eye, perhaps requiring oblique (angled) light to reveal the imperfections left on the paper or the indented remnants of erased writing. Sometimes a magnifying glass or microscope is required. Rubber erasers leave behind tiny fragments of the eraser and the ink that, even though they nestle into the fibers of the paper, fluoresce (glow) when exposed to ultraviolet or infrared light. Dusting the page with **lycopodium powder**, which clings to and exposes the tiny rubber particles, can also help.

Obliterations are the destruction or damage of the paper that holds the words or signature. Fire is the most common obliteration technique. The criminal erroneously believes that once the paper is burned, the writing is lost forever. But if the paper is charred but intact, reflecting light at various angles off its surface can often expose the contrast between the ink and the charred paper background, revealing the writing. The page can then be photographed.

Charred pages are extremely fragile and easily crumble, so they must be handled carefully. Spraying the page with a solution of **polyvinyl ace-**

tate in acetone stiffens it and makes handling it safer and easier. The page can then be floated on a solution of alcohol, chloral hydrate, and glycerin and photographed, sometimes using infrared light. **Autoradiography** can also be used. In this technique the pages are sandwiched between two photographic plates and placed in a dark room for two weeks. The writing is essentially "photographed" by the plates; when they are developed, the writing is revealed.

Sometimes the forger will use chemicals such as bleach to remove the writing. These chemicals react with ink to produce a colorless compound and the writing disappears, but under a microscope the examiner can see remnants of the ink as well as discoloration of the paper in the area of treatment.

Lasers are a more modern method of obliterating writing. The laser not only vaporizes the ink but also burns the paper fibers, and these changes can be seen under a microscope.

Alterations are the changing or adding of words. Sometimes simply erasing or obliterating words or numbers isn't enough and the forger needs to replace these with others. Maybe changing the amount of a check or the date on a contract or will. If the writing is obliterated before other writing is added, the examiner will see the above-mentioned changes in the underlying paper and will then analyze the new writing and compare it to the old for differences in technique.

The examiner will use a magnifying glass or a low-power microscope to seek subtle changes in ink color, line thickness, double lines, and pen pressure. If a ballpoint or roller ball pen was used, defects in the ball of either are often visible. The original pen might have had a very smooth, flawless ball, while the forger's pen, which might be identical in all other respects, might have an uneven or defective ball that leaves behind gaps and imperfections in the written line. The same is true for pencil leads and fountain pen nibs.

Overwriting, another form of alteration, is where the forger adds to or overwrites a portion of a document. Maybe changing a 3 to an 8 or adding a zero or two to a check amount. If the forger uses the same ink as the original writer these types of changes can be extremely difficult to uncover, but most often the forger does not have access to the pen or the ink used for the original writing and must make do with one of similar color. A careful examination of the inks used will reveal the areas of alteration.

Though the two inks might appear identical under normal light, they are usually very different when exposed to ultraviolet (UV) or infrared light. Depending upon the chemical makeup of the inks, UV light might cause them to fluoresce, fade from view, or appear unchanged. Each will react differently so that one ink might fluoresce and the other fade from view, thus revealing that two different inks were used. Infrared light is invisible to the unaided eye, so it is usually coupled with photography to capture the image of the writing. **Infrared photography**, which is basically photographing the page under a blue-green light with infrared-sensitive film, will often distinguish the two inks very clearly. If these light techniques don't help, the examiner might resort to testing the chemical contents of the inks to reveal their differences (see below).

Indented Writing

Whenever something is written on a pad and the written page is removed, the remaining second page is **indented** by the path of the pen over the removed page. This indented writing is also called **second page writing**. I'm sure you are aware that if the side of a pencil lead is rubbed back and forth over the surface of the indented page, the "invisible" writing appears. Of course, the forensic document examiners would never use this method, since this would destroy, damage, or alter the page, which is the evidence. Instead, he will use a simple angled light to expose indented writing, which will then be photographed. A more sensitive method is the use of an **electrostatic detection apparatus (ESDA)**, which was developed by Freeman and Foster in 1978. It can on occasion uncover indented writing several pages below the original. No one knows exactly how ESDA works, only that it does.

In ESDA, the page is covered with a Mylar sheet, placed on a porous metal plate, and a vacuum is applied, which pulls the Mylar tightly against the page. Static electricity in the Mylar sheet-page combination is produced by passing an electric wand over them. This process charges the entire surface of the Mylar, but the charge is greatest in the indentions. Black copy machine toner is then poured or sprayed over the Mylar. The toner attaches to the surface in proportion to the degree of charge, which means that the indentions retain the greatest concentration of the toner and the indented writing is revealed and photographed. The original page (the real evidence) has not been damaged or altered in any way.

Paper and Ink

The chemical analysis of papers and inks falls to the forensic document examiner and the forensic chemist. As mentioned above, sometimes the examiner must chemically analyze the inks used on a forged or altered document to reveal that two different inks are present, suggesting that the document has indeed been altered. At other times he is asked to determine whether a document has had pages added or whether it was actually created at a certain time. If the pages of a document are of differing types of paper, it might mean that pages have been added or exchanged, and if the paper or the ink had not been manufactured until after the purported date of the document, something is amiss.

Most paper is made of wood and/or cotton to which chemical additives that affect its opacity, color, brightness, strength, and durability have been added. The manufacturing process also includes the addition of various coatings, fillers, and sizings. **Coatings** improve the appearance and surface properties of the paper, some making the paper better for copiers or printers, others better for writing. **Fillers**, such as titanium oxide and calcium carbonate, add color, strength, and surface texture. **Sizings** make the surface less porous to ink, so writing and printing will be sharp and clear. The types and amounts of each of these vary among manufacturers and paper types, and chemical testing can distinguish one type and manufacturer from another. By analyzing each page's chemical content, the examiner can determine whether they are all the same type and from the same manufacturer, and might even be able to distinguish among various lots of paper produced by the same manufacturer.

Watermarks, translucent designs that can be seen by holding the page up to a light, are very helpful since they usually indicate the manufacturer, the date of its production, and sometimes for whom the paper was made. Forging a watermark is difficult and easy to spot since a true watermark has fewer fibers than the rest of the page. This is what makes it visible when held up to a light. Forged marks are added images, and thus have an underlying fiber density equal to the rest of the page.

Paper analysis played a key role in revealing that the diaries purported to have been written by Adolph Hitler were modern forgeries.

On February 18, 1981, Gerd Heidemann, an employee of German publisher Gruner + Jahr, claimed to have found some lost diaries of Adolph

Hitler. He said he had received the documents, handwritten in almost illegible German script, from a wealthy collector whose brother was an East German general. Heidemann's boss, Manfred Fischer, agreed to purchase the 27-volume diary along with a previously unknown third volume of *Mein Kampf* for 200,000 marks.

Fischer sent portions of the documents, along with samples of Hitler's handwriting, to Dr. Max Frei-Sulzer of the Zurich police forensic department and to Ordway Hilton, a world-renowned document examiner in Landrum, South Carolina, for authentication. Unfortunately, neither Dr. Frei-Sulzer nor Hilton were aware that the handwriting samples purported to be Hitler's came from the same source as the diaries themselves, so both men determined that the writings were from the same hand and therefore that the documents were authentic. Bantam Books, Newsweek, and publisher Rupert Murdock entered into a publication rights' bidding war, which was ultimately won by *Newsweek* for $3.75 million.

Fortunately, at the request of Gruner + Jahr, the West German police forensic department conducted their own examination and discovered that the paper on which the diaries were written contained **blankophor**, a whitener that did not exist until 1954. Also, the bindings contained threads of viscose and polyester, neither of which existed in the 1940s. In addition, none of the inks used were widely available during World War II, and, finally, a measurement of chlorine evaporation from the ink revealed that the documents were less than a year old.

Sometimes the key to determining authenticity lies in the ink used. Inks that appear the same physically can vary greatly with chemical analysis. As seen above in the Hitler Diaries case, this can also reveal whether a particular ink existed at the time the document was supposedly prepared. Another simple example is that the ballpoint pen was first publicly marketed in 1945, so a document prepared with this type of instrument could not be older than that.

As we saw in Chapter 16, **microspectrophotometry** allows the examiner to accurately determine whether the colors of two inks match without the interference of observer bias. If the colors perfectly match, it is likely they came from the same batch. In addition, **thin layer chromotography (TLC)**, which can test very small samples of the inked paper punched from the written lines with a thin hollow needle, can determine whether two inks are identical. This can help with the examination of forged or altered documents.

Several ink reference databases, such as the **Ink Library**, which is part of the U.S. Secret Service Forensic Services Division's Questioned Document Branch, are helpful. In addition, the U.S. Treasury Department maintains an extensive database of the TLC patterns of commercial inks. More recently, many manufacturers have begun adding fluorescent dye "tags" to their products so that they can be more easily identified. Since the tags change annually, the year of manufacture can be readily determined.

Even with all these sophisticated techniques available, some forgery cases are very difficult to unravel as illustrated by the famous Mormon Forgeries, a case that involved many different forensic science techniques, including document examination.

On October 15, 1985, in Salt Lake City, Utah, two pipe bombs exploded, one killing businessman and Mormon bishop Steven Christensen and the other grandmother Kathy Sheets. The package that killed Sheets had been addressed to her husband, Gary, also a bishop in the Mormon Church. The next day a third bomb exploded in the car of Mark Hofmann, a young man who dealt with historical documents. Hofmann survived and told police that he had seen a strange package sitting on the passenger's seat of his car and when he reached for it, it exploded. Bomb investigators examined the scene and knew immediately that Hofmann was lying since the evidence indicated that he had been kneeling in the driver's seat, working with the bomb when it detonated rather than standing outside the car reaching in. Hofmann became the lead suspect in the other bombings, since it was felt that he was likely preparing a third bomb for delivery when it accidentally went off.

Police learned that Hofmann was somewhat of a whiz at locating ancient documents and, in fact, had recently discovered not one but two copies of the *Oath of a Freeman*, a 17th-century work that was the first document ever printed in America. Prior to Hofmann's "discoveries," no copies were known to exist. He had also found what became known as the "White Salamander Letter," a document that undermined the very tenets of Mormonism and greatly embarrassed the church. The police soon uncovered evidence that many of the "historical documents" Hofmann had sold to the Mormon Church were forgeries. Did Hofmann plant the bombs in an attempt to cover his forgeries?

The case was long and complex but ultimately ended when Hofmann was confronted with evidence that proved that he had forged his "discoveries." Hofmann confessed to the bombings and the forgeries in exchange for a life sentence rather than face a possible death sentence in court. He then told investigators how he pulled off the forgeries, which were so realistic that many experts had deemed them authentic.

The original *Oath of a Freeman* had been printed by Stephen Days, who also printed the *Bay Psalm Book*. Hofmann purchased a cheap copy of this book, cut out the letters, and rearranged them into the *Oath of the Freeman*. He then used this model to create a printing plate, which he used to print the two copies of the *Oath*. He added wear patterns to the letters to simulate the changes that would be seen with repeated use in a real printing press, by grinding down portions of some letters and rubbing the entire plate with steel wool. This gave the printed document realistic printing defects.

But for the documents to stand up to the rigorous scrutiny that he knew would follow, he needed to "age" the paper and the ink he used. For the paper, he pilfered blank flyleaf pages from other 17th-century books in the Brigham Young University Library. This way the paper would be authentic to the time period and pass any carbon-14 dating done on it. In a very clever move, he burned one of these pages to produce the carbon black he needed to make the "ancient" printing ink he needed. Again, C-14 dating of the ink would pass muster. He mixed the "ancient" carbon black with linseed oil, beeswax, and tannic acid, which he obtained by boiling a 17th-century leather book binding in distilled water. Through this process he produced "old" ink. But, ink oxidizes with age and turns from dark black to a rusty hue. To simulate this effect, Hofmann used a combination of peroxide (an oxidizing agent) and a hand iron, which added heat and sped up the process. All these precautions meant that if the ink were visually and chemically tested, it would appear as if it had been prepared in the 17th century.

Prosecutors brought in forensics document examiners George J. Throckmorton and William Flynn, who, after examining the documents, discovered several things wrong. Letters with "tails" such as *y* and *j* seemed to overlap with taller letters such as *l* and *t* when the former appeared in the line above the latter. This overlapping was a product of Hofmann's pasting together of the letters when he made the template for his press and would not be possible with the handset type used in the 17th century. In handset type each letter is a raised figure on a small cube and the cubes are lined up on a page-sized holder in the proper order to produce the words and sentences, line by line, down the page. This means that each letter is "within" the area of its cube and overlapping is not possible.

They also noted evidence of scorching of the paper and ink from the hand iron and what is called the "alligator effect," the cracking and breaking of the ink from the use of chemical oxidants to artificially "age" the ink. Natural aging doesn't produce such changes. They found many other problems with the documents, so the very clever Hofmann failed to deceive the even more clever document examiners.

Typewriters and Photocopiers

Typewriters are frequently used to write threatening letters and ransom and extortion notes, since criminals erroneously believe this will make the letter untraceable. Not so. When a typewriter is involved, the two most common questions asked of the document examiner are (1) What make and model typewriter produced the document? and (2) Was the document prepared using this particular suspect typewriter?

The answer to the first question relies on **class** characteristics, while the answer to the latter requires identifying **individual** characteristics. To identify the make and model, the examiner will consult available databases of typefaces used in various models, both old and new. Most manufacturers use either pica or elite typefaces, but the size, shape, and style of the letters vary so that a particular manufacturer can be identified. This alone narrows the search for the exact machine that produced the document.

When a suspect machine is identified, the examiner will search for individual characteristics such as misaligned or damaged letters, abnormal spacing before or after certain letters, and variations in the pressure applied to the page by some letters. For example, a certain letter might have nicks or spurs, or a letter could lean to one side or be slightly higher or lower than the others, or one letter might be loose or depressed slightly and strike the page with less force. These defects can be compared to a suspect typewriter and offer powerful individualizing characteristics.

This type of comparison was a critical part of the famous Leopold and Loeb case of 1924.

Nathan Leopold and Richard Loeb were new kinds of killers, earning the moniker "Thrill Killers." On May 21, 1924, 19-year-old Leopold and 18-year-old Loeb murdered classmate Bobby Franks with a chisel to see what it felt like to kill someone and to see if they could get away with it. Even though Franks was dead, they sent a ransom note as part of their attempts to deflect the investigation. Unfortunately for them, Leopold left his glasses at the crime scene. The spectacles had an unusual hinge, which allowed police to trace them to a Chicago optometrist who said he had written only three similar prescriptions, one to Nathan Leopold. The investigation ultimately led to a match between the ransom note and a typewriter Leopold used in his law study group. Despite the efforts of famous defense attorney Clarence Darrow, the two boys were convicted and sentenced to life in prison.

One problem with typewriter comparison arises with the old IBM Selectric typewriter, which possesses an interchangeable type-head sphere. This means that the typewriter must have the same sphere that was used to prepare the document in place at the time of the examination and if it has been replaced, no match can be made.

The ink ribbons of old typewriters retain the typed message, which can simply be read from the ribbon. Even if the ribbon has been used in several passes, portions of the message might still be retrievable—if the ribbon hasn't been changed, that is.

Today typewriters have given way to computers, which connect to printers that might use daisy wheel, dot matrix, ink jet, or laser technologies. These vary very little so that the examiner can't often distinguish one from another. Still, if the suspect printer is available, the examiner might find subtle changes in how it jets and lasers certain letters. This is more difficult and less often possible than matching a typewriter to a document.

Photocopied documents can sometimes be matched to a particular copy machine. A copy machine takes an image on a page and duplicates it onto another by a complex series of events. First, a lens focuses the page's image onto a drum, which has been charged with static electricity and coated with selenium or another light-sensitive substance. The drum retains the image as it is bathed with a toner that attaches to the surface of the drum in proportion to the strength of the electrostatic charge. This toner image is transferred to the blank page, which is then exposed to a "fixing" agent.

The mechanisms within the machine that pull the paper onto and remove it from the copy surface can leave marks on the page, or the cover glass, camera lens, or drum might have scratches or defects that mark each page produced. Occasionally, these marks can be identified and matched to the machine that produced the page in question.

Art Forgery

Some examiners specialize in forged works of art, the examination of which has many things in common with document examination. These examinations include physical, optical, and chemical techniques.

Art forgers tend to be smart, meticulous, and talented since they must accurately copy the works of well-known masters. The creation of *Christ with the Adultress*, purported to have been done by Dutch painter Johannes Vermeer in the 1600s, is an example of just how clever art forgers can be.

Prior to and throughout WWII, the Nazis purchased and stole art from all over Europe and Russia, secreting many of the works in bunkers, caves, and mines. After the war, a cache of such paintings was uncovered in an Austrian salt mine. Among them was a work titled *Christ with the Adultress*, which appeared to be a previously unknown work by Johannes Vermeer. An investigation traced the painting to Han van Meegeren, another Dutch painter. Since he had sold the piece to the Nazis, he was arrested as a collaborator.

Meegeren confessed that the work was a forgery, but authorities didn't believe him until, while under house arrest, he produced other astonishing forgeries. He said that his original intention was to create fakes, trick art experts, and then expose their ignorance. He apparently had created many such forgeries during the run-up to WWII. He deviated from his original plan when he found he could sell the works to the Nazis.

So, how did he create fakes that fooled the experts? For his 17th-century canvases, the period in which Vermeer painted, he purchased lesser works of that time period and, using pumice, removed most of the original art. He then ground his own pigments, much as did Vermeer, and added them to a synthetic phenolformaldehyde resin (known as Albertol or Ambertol). To "age" his paintings, he dried them in an oven at 105° for an hour, added a coat of varnish, and rolled them over a drum to "crack" the paint. Ink was then spread over the painting and allowed to seep into the cracks, and finally a second coat of varnish was applied. The painting was then ready for sale.

Examiners analyzed many of the paintings Meegeren had produced over the years to ascertain if he was truthful about his methods. Chemical analysis showed that phenolformaldehyde resin was indeed present and that a blue pigment used in some of the paintings was not available until the 19th century. X-rays revealed remnants of the original underlying paintings on the canvases he had used. The *Christ with the Adultress* was indeed a 1930s forgery.

CHAPTER 20

CRIMINAL PSYCHOLOGY

The study and analysis of the psychology behind criminal activity falls to the **forensic psychologist** and **psychiatrist**. These titles are often used interchangeably but in reality are quite different. A doctor of psychology possesses a PhD; a psychiatrist a medical degree that, as with every other physician, is earned after four years of medical school. He would then complete a residency in psychiatry.

As we saw with clinical and forensic pathologists, the duties and capabilities of the clinical psychologist/psychiatrist and the forensic psychologist/psychiatrist are very different. Clinical psychologists are trained to test and interview patients in order to determine their mental state, competence, and sanity and to offer counseling. A clinical psychiatrist does all this but in addition, his medical degree allows him to perform psychotherapy and prescribe medications. In the forensic arena each attempts to dissect the criminal mind to search for motives, competency, and sanity in criminal and civic cases.

Society has long searched for a method to identify the "bad guys," the rationale being that if criminals can be identified and put away, the public is safe and, if not, the public is at risk. This fear is fueled by such seemingly "normal" serial killers like Ted Bundy, John Wayne Gacy, and Dennis Rader, the BTK Killer. These predators looked and acted, at least in public, like everyone else. This is discomforting to most people.

The search for methods to identify the "criminal type" has a long and sordid history. Though this chapter will deal with more modern methods, a look at a couple of the more famous, yet completely erroneous, methods developed by Franz Joseph Gall and Cesare Lombroso will underline how far we've come.

Franz Joseph Gall, a German physician, developed the field of **phrenology** around 1800. He believed that criminals could be identified by reading the "bumps" on a their head. The concept was that the criminal's abnormal brain would alter the shape and contour of the overlying skull bone and feeling for these changes could identify the criminal personality.

Cesare Lombroso, a professor of psychiatry in Pesaro, Italy, published his book *The Criminal Man* in 1876. In it he stated that criminals could be identified and classified by physical characteristics such as cleft palates, poor teeth, long arms, an asymmetric head shape, prominent jaw or cheekbones, large ears, a hawk nose, fleshy lips, extra fingers or toes, and other physical "defects." In his 1895 publication, *Criminal Anthropology*, he further suggested that some characteristics indicated the type of crime the person would likely commit. According to Lombroso, assassins had prominent jaws and pale faces; ravishers possessed short hands, narrow foreheads, and light hair; and pickpockets possessed long fingers (which actually makes sense) and black hair.

These theories, and many others, are ridiculously naive and have long since fallen by the wayside, but the search for the "criminal mind" continues. Profiling, which will be discussed later in this chapter, is one example. In addition, current research into such high-tech devices as CT scans, MRIs, and PET scans hopes to develop methods for evaluating the brain function of criminals. The goal is to develop techniques as wide ranging as a better lie detector to identifying those with brain disorders that could lead to aberrant behavior.

The Forensic Psychiatric Professional

Modern forensic psychiatrists and psychologists take a more reasoned and scientific approach to evaluating suspects and criminals than did their predecessors. Their duties include the following:

- Testing suspects for mental illness.
- Assessing a perpetrator's sanity.
- Establishing a perpetrator's mental state at the time the crime occurred.
- Determining competency to stand trial, offer testimony, sign contracts, and perform other actions.
- Evaluating suspects for signs of deception and malingering.
- Profiling perpetrators and victims.

The forensic psychiatric professional is often involved in both criminal and civil matters and might be brought to the case by the prosecution, the defense, or the judge. Criminal cases might involve homicides, robberies, or kidnappings, as well as cases of assault, battery, and sexual misconduct. He might be asked to assess the role of alcohol and drugs in the defendant's conduct or to determine sanity or competency to stand trial. He might be asked to assess the subject's understanding of reality and responsibility and offer a judgment as to the suspect's state of mind at the time of the crime. He might also offer investigators information for use in witness and suspect interrogations.

In civil cases, he might be asked to determine competency to sign wills and contracts, manage personal affairs, vote, offer testimony, or stand trial. He might become involved in spousal and child abuse cases, disputes involving child custody, sexual harassment, disability, or emotional suffering.

In cases of apparent suicide, the psychiatrist might perform a **psychological autopsy** to determine whether the victim likely took his own life or not. Interviews with family, friends, and coworkers can often reveal the victim's behavior during the period before the tragedy and determine whether drugs and alcohol, financial problems, or social difficulties could have led to suicide.

To perform these duties he will use various medical records, examinations, and tests, psychiatric tests and interviews, police and witness reports, and crime scene evidence. The evaluations employed by these professionals are too complex to cover in this book, but a glimpse at a few of them should give you a feel for what these evaluations involve.

Psychiatric Testing

The first step in these evaluations is a complete medical and neurological examination in order to make certain that no illnesses or treatments that might interfere with the psychiatric evaluation are present. Strokes, certain liver or kidney diseases, and head trauma can alter the subject's ability to think, understand, and reason. Many prescription and illicit drugs alter brain function. Medications for seizure disorders, diabetes, heart disease, insomnia, and weight loss, as well as essentially every known sedative and mood elevator can affect psychiatric testing.

Once this testing is completed, a psychiatric evaluation will follow. This testing falls into several categories: personality inventories, projective tests, and intellectual and cognitive assessments.

Personality inventories, designed to determine the subject's basic personality type, are highly standardized and reliable. Common ones are the **Minnesota Multiphasic Personality Inventory (MMPI)**, the **Millon Clinical Multiaxial Inventory (MCMI)**, and the **California Psychological Inventory (CPI)**.

Projective testing evaluates personality and thought processes. These tests are less standardized and more subjective than the inventories and include the **Rorschach test**, **projective drawing**, and the **Thematic Apperception Test (TAT)**.

In the **Rorschach test** (inkblot examination), the subject is shown a series of abstract inkblots and is asked to describe what she sees. Her descriptions might reveal aspects of her personality, thought processes, and connection to reality, and offer clues to her inner fantasies.

In **projective drawing**, instead of looking at inkblots, the subject produces the drawings, which are then analyzed. He might be asked to draw a house, a tree, a member of the opposite sex, or a frightening scene or situation. His drawings might reveal his inner thought processes and fantasies. For example, if the house he draws is on fire, the woman has been stabbed, or the tree is leafless and with broken branches, these constructs might provide a look into his inner world.

In the **Thematic Apperception Test (TAT)**, the person is shown pictures of common situations and asked to make up a story to go with them, the goal being to garner a glimpse into her inner thoughts and fantasies. For example, after viewing a photo of a man and a woman talking, she might say that the two are planning their wedding or that they are arguing over money or that they are saying negative things about her. Each of these answers would indicate a different psychiatric state.

Intellectual and cognitive tests are designed to assess the subject's intelligence, mental competency, thought processes, and ability to understand his behavior. The most common intelligence test is the **Wechsler Adult Intelligence Scale (WAIS)**, which assesses **intelligence quotient (IQ)**.

After these tests are completed and evaluated, the forensic psychiatrist will interview the subject and probe deeper into any exposed areas of concern. This is where his training and experience come into play. A complete discussion of this complex subject is beyond the scope of this text, but two interviewing techniques deserve mention: hypnosis and the use of drugs during the interview process.

Hypnosis is used to help suspects and witnesses recall certain events and details. But since it is fairly easy to fake hypnosis, any information obtained in this process must be corroborated. Moreover, hypnotized individuals are often highly suggestible, so the mere asking of questions can alter their memory for certain events. It is possible that these "new memories" will become part of their real memory and render the validity of any future interviews and court testimony suspect. Some courts allow testimony from previously hypnotized witnesses, while others do not.

There is no "truth serum," but certain drugs such as sodium pentothal can lower inhibitions and defenses. Pentothal is a narcotic that makes the recipient drowsy, euphoric, and talkative. As with hypnosis, any information gleaned in this fashion is suspect and would likely be challenged in court.

Competence and Sanity

In determining competence and sanity, the forensic psychiatrist might be involved in all three phases of the criminal justice process: pre-trial, trial, and post-trial.

During the pre-trial phase he could be asked to determine the suspect's competency to stand trial. This competency involves the defendant's ability to understand the charges against him, the possible consequences of the charges, his rights under the law, the workings of the courtroom, and the roles of the judge and the attorneys. If he has no understanding of these matters, he can't be fairly tried. For example, if he truly believes that the judge is his grandfather or that the judge and the attorneys are involved in a conspiracy "to get him," his ability to participate in his own defense is compromised. A competency examination can also determine whether the subject is competent enough to confess, testify, waive his Miranda rights, accept or refuse an insanity defense, and even to be executed.

During the trial, the forensic psychiatrist might offer opinions regarding the suspect's mental state at the time of the crime. If the person was mentally ill, temporarily or permanently, at the time he committed the crime, he might present a defense based on insanity.

In the post-trial sentencing phase, the psychiatrist might address the defendant's need for admission to a treatment facility as opposed to a prison, or to offer his opinion regarding the defendant's level of "dangerousness" or the likelihood of future criminal activities. In death penalty cases, he might be asked to comment on the person's competency to be executed.

As we saw with rape (Chapter 8), **insanity** is a legal term, not a medical term. A psychiatrist can't "diagnose" insanity. Only a judge or jury can make that determination. Psychiatrists can diagnose mental disorders and advise the court as to their findings, but the final say comes from the law and not from medicine.

Legal insanity is a poorly defined term that varies among jurisdictions, but for most the yardstick is the **McNaughten Rule**, which dates to 19th-century England. It basically deals with whether the defendant suffers from any mental disorder that prevents him from understanding the nature and the consequences of his actions. In other words, at the time of the crime's commission, did he know that his actions were illegal or was he in some way incapable of altering his illegal behavior? In 1984, Congress passed the **Omnibus Crime Code for Insanity**, which states that a person can be found not guilty by reason of insanity if they did not *appreciate* the illegality of their behavior. The term *appreciate* is vastly different from the word *know* in that it implies a higher degree of understanding than simple knowledge.

Both the McNaughten Rule and the Omnibus Code address the fact that a crime has two parts. One is the criminal activity, termed the *actus reus*, while the second part is the *mens rea*, the criminal intent.

Diminished capacity is a special form of "insanity" and, like true insanity, its definition varies among jurisdictions. Diminished capacity is the belief that certain conditions present during the commission of the crime can reduce the person's ability to alter her actions or to distinguish between right and wrong. In other words, the perpetrator was not capable of forming a specific criminal intent or could not act in a purposeful manner. For example, if the defendant suffers from paranoid delusions due to chronic cocaine or methamphetamine abuse, she might not have been capable of planning a murder, and this might change her degree of liability—say, from first- to second-degree murder.

Lies and Deceptions

Criminals lie. Always have and always will, for self-protection if nothing else. Whether it's forgery, establishing a false alibi, staging a crime scene, or lying in court, the criminal will alter, distort, and manufacture the truth to his own ends. Such distortions, exaggerations, and deceptions present problems for the forensic psychiatrist, who, even though trained and experienced in detecting deception, occasionally falls prey to a clever suspect. The case of Hillside Strangler Kenneth Bianchi is one famous example.

During the 1970s, a series of brutal rapes and murders occurred across Los Angeles. The victims' bodies were dumped in plain sight on hillsides throughout LA County, earning the killers the moniker the Hillside Stranglers. Through a long and complex investigation, the police finally arrested Angelo Buono in Los Angeles and his cousin, Kenneth Bianchi, in Bellingham, Washington.

Using knowledge that he got from college psychology classes and from the movies *Three Faces of Eve* and *Sybil*, Bianchi concocted an insanity defense by alleging that he suffered from multiple personality disorder (MPD). In his story, Steve, an evil alter ego, forced Bianchi to kill the young women, so he was no more than an innocent pawn. He was so good that he fooled several psychiatric professionals.

Finally, Dr. Martin Orne, an expert in hypnosis, evaluated Bianchi and managed to bring out Steve. Though initially convincing, Bianchi made several mistakes. While he was Steve he referred to Steve as "he" rather than "I" on several occasions. If he were truly Steve at that time he would not use the third-person pronoun "he." Also, when "introduced" to an imaginary someone whom Kenneth knew but Steve didn't, he acted out a handshake with the nonexistent person. "Seeing" this imaginary person, much less shaking hands with him, would mean that he was hallucinating (seeing something or someone that was not really there) and this is not part of MPD. Finally, Dr. Orne told Bianchi that it was very unusual for an MPD victim to have only one other personality and that most had several. Almost immediately, "Billy" was born, giving Bianchi three separate personalities. After his ruse was exposed, Bianchi confessed and agreed to testify against his cousin Angelo in exchange for favorable treatment by the court.

In the case of **malingering**, a special form of deception, the subject will attempt to make any physical or mental defects appear worse, or in some cases less severe, than they are, or will manufacture them completely. Fortunately, the MMPI and several other tests include scales that often indicate such deceptions.

Other forms of deception, though not intentional, are erroneous eyewitness accounts and false confessions.

Eyewitness accounts are notoriously unreliable, and numerous studies such as R. Buckhout's 1974 *Scientific American* article "Eyewitness Testimony" have attested to this fact. The article revealed the results of an experiment in which 52 people witnessed a purse-snatching, yet only 7 were able to identify the thief. This is typical of the many other studies done in this area.

Though this might seem counterintuitive, memory is neither simple nor reliable. Creating, storing, and recalling memories is a complex process, involving communication among several areas of the brain. Our ability to recall event details fades with time, and the natural tendency is to fill in any blanks with what we believe should have happened, an unconscious effort colored by our beliefs, prejudices, motives, and expectations. Add to this the stress of witnessing a frightening or threatening event, and false or altered memories seem almost inevitable.

False confessions are more common than most people realize and occur for several reasons. Sometimes a friend or family member confesses to a crime to protect the real culprit, or a false confession might serve to deflect police attention from another crime. For example, a suspect might confess to stealing a car or robbing a store but say that he knows nothing of the murder that occurred at the same time in another location. If he is guilty of the robbery, he could not possibly be the killer.

But, what of the people who confess for no apparent reason? Here, psychological factors such as low self-esteem, fear of the police, a need for fame, or the need to please the authorities or another person might play a role. Some people have deeply hidden feelings of guilt, real or imagined, and believe that a confession will lead to a deserved punishment. The use of alcohol or drugs can cloud judgment and lead to confusion, false memories, and fabrications, resulting in a false confession. Certain police interrogation tactics might also lead to false confessions. Isolation and fatigue break down resolve. The "good cop/bad cop" routine is sometimes employed to trick the suspect into confessing to the good cop, thinking that he will protect him from the bad cop.

In Chapter 3, we discussed the difference between direct and circumstantial evidence. Confessions and eyewitness accounts are direct evidence, while things like DNA, fingerprints, toxicological testing, trace evidence analysis, firearm examinations, and virtually everything done by the ME and the crime lab are circumstantial in nature. This simply means that "circumstantial cases" are often much stronger than are those based on direct evidence.

Serial and Multiple Offenders

Serial offenders have always created special problems for law enforcement. Whether serial rapists, bombers, arsonists, or killers, the episodic nature of their crimes and their apparent lack of connection to their victims have forced law enforcement officials to develop new techniques for dealing with these types of offenders.

Most murders have readily visible motives (financial gain, revenge, to cover another crime) and occur between two people who know each other or at least have some connection. For these reasons, the earliest stages of any homicide investigation focus on people who know the victim and could profit from the victim's death. The formula investigators use is: How + Why = Who? The *how* is everything the perpetrator used to commit the crime and cover his trail, and the *why* is the motive. Of these, the *why* is often the most important.

But with serial predators the motives tend to be more personal and not readily apparent. More often than not, even when the motive is discovered, it seems irrational. *But it isn't to the killer.* And that's critical to understanding offender profiling (discussed below).

Multiple Murderer Classification

Multiple murderers are those who have killed more than one person. They are classified according to the location and sequence of the killings into **mass**, **spree**, and **serial** types.

Mass murderers kill more than four people in one place at one time. These killers often have a clear agenda and want to send a message. This is the killer that walks into his workplace, shoots several people, and then takes his own life or goes out in a "blaze of glory" with the police killing him in an exchange of gunfire. The motive for mass murderers is often some perceived wrong or some deep-seated anger at someone or some group or organization. Examples would be the University of Texas Tower shooter Charles Whitman, Columbine killers Eric Harris and Dylan Klebold, and Virginia Tech mass murderer Seung-Hui Cho.

On August 1, 1966, a bright, sunny day in Austin, Texas, ex-Marine Charles Whitman became one of America's most notorious mass murderers. After killing his wife and mother, he climbed the 27-story tower on the campus of the University of Texas, armed with an array of rifles and handguns. He opened fire on everyone in sight, striking people as far away as 500 yards and even hit a plane that carried a police sniper. Before he was himself gunned down by police officer Ramiro Martinez, Whitman managed to kill 16 and wound 31 people. His motives were never truly known, but he did apparently abuse amphetamines and his journal suggested that he wanted to die dramatically and did not want his wife or mother to suffer the humiliation that would certainly follow his actions. He also stated that the money from his life insurance policy should be used to pay his debts and to "donate the rest anonymously to a mental health foundation" so that research could "prevent further tragedies of this type." He also requested an autopsy, which revealed that he had a glioblastoma (brain tumor) that might or might not have contributed to his behavior.

At 11:30 a.m. on April 20, 1999, 18-year-old Eric Harris and 17-year-old Dylan Klebold, wearing trench coats, military fatigues, and ski masks, entered Columbine High School in Littleton, Colorado, armed with rifles, automatic weapons, shotguns, and homemade pipe bombs. Their rampage began in the cafeteria, where fellow students were taking their lunch break, and ended in the library, where the two killers took their own lives. In between, they killed 1 teacher and 12 students and wounded 2 dozen others. Diaries and a videotape, made by the boys the morning of the massacre, revealed a deep-seated hatred of many of their classmates.

On April 16, 2007, Virginia Tech student Seung-Hui Cho went on a killing spree that made him the deadliest mass murderer in modern U.S. history. At approximately 7:15 a.m., Cho fatally shot 2 people in a dorm and then changed clothes, grabbed more weapons and ammunition, and went to the post office, where he mailed a package of papers and a video to NBC News. His rampage then continued. He ultimately fired 174 rounds, killing another 30 people and wounding many others, before turning his weapon on himself. The materials sent to NBC were Cho's written and videoed manifesto in which he railed against "rich kids" who he believed participated in "debauchery" and were "deceitful charlatans."

Spree killers kill several people at two or more locations with the killings linked by motive and with no "cooling off" period (see below) between. The spree killer goes on a rage-fueled rampage, moving from place to place, city to city, even state to state, leaving bodies in his wake. Once he begins, he doesn't stop or deviate from his goal, and, as with mass murders, his spree often ends in suicide or a confrontation with law enforcement. Andrew Cunanan is a classic example of a spree killer.

Andrew Cunanan was often described as a "high-class male prostitute" who catered to wealthy older men. He lived and played in a hedonistic world until late 1996, when he began to feel his world unraveling. In mid-April 1997, he threw himself a going-away party in San Diego, telling some people that he was moving to San Francisco and others that he was going to Minnesota to "settle some business." He flew to Minneapolis, where on the night of April 27, 1997, he used a hammer to beat 28-year-old Jeffrey Trail to death in the Minneapolis apartment of Cunanan's lover David Madson. Five days later, at a lake 50 miles away, he shot Madson in the head and fled in Jeffrey Trail's red Jeep.

He drove to Chicago, where he met 72-year-old real-estate mogul Lee Miglin, whom he tortured and killed with pruning shears and a garden saw. Cunanan then headed east in Miglin's Lexus. On May 9, he shot and killed William Reese in Pennsville, New Jersey, stole the dead man's red

Chevrolet pick-up, and headed south. Cunanan was now on the FBI's Ten Most Wanted list.

He ended up in Miami, Florida, where on the morning of July 14, he shot Gianni Versace twice in the head in front of Versace's residence, Casa Casuarina. On July 25, caretaker Fernando Carreira summoned police to a boathouse where Cunanan was hiding. Cunanan took his own life before police could apprehend him.

His motives for killing Versace were vague at best, but some believe that Cunanan felt that Versace, whom Cunanan had met before, either slighted him in some way or merely represented the world of privilege that no longer welcomed Cunanan.

Serial killers kill three or more people at different times and locations with a "cooling off" period (see below) between the killings. The catalog of serial killers includes some very famous names: Bundy, Gacy, Lucas, Ridgeway, Dahmer, Kraft, Rader, and many others.

The Psychopathology of Serial Offenders

Obviously a huge and controversial subject, there are many theories about what generates these offenders and what triggers their aberrant behavior. Even the terms used to define their psychopathology are controversial. Terms like **psychopath**, **sociopath**, and **borderline personality disorder** have been applied to these offenders, with some preferring one term over the other and arguing that one term is more correct than the others. I'm not going to enter that fray but rather will examine some, but certainly not all, of the more accepted theories regarding what drives these criminals.

There are subtypes of serial killers, and even these subclassifications are controversial. Some people believe there are three types, and others as many as seven or more. Some commonly described subtypes are as follows:

- **Visionary killers** are psychotic and believe that they are directed by some demon or god to commit murder. David Berkowitz, the so-called Son of Sam, who claimed he was directed to kill by a neighbor's dog named Sam, is an example.
- **Mission-oriented killers** believe they are ridding the world of certain types of people. This is their mission. Gary Ridgeway, the Green River Killer, killed street prostitutes for this reason.

- **Lust** or **sexually sadistic killers** are motivated by sexual gratification and fantasy. These are the types most people think of when they hear the term "serial killer." Ted Bundy fit this definition.
- **Hedonistic** and **thrill killers** derive pleasure from killing.
- **Profit-motivated killers** are driven by material gains. Examples would be the many "black widow" killers who serially kill their husbands, or the nice lady who runs a boarding house and kills her tenants after taking out insurance on them or so she can continue cashing and pocketing their welfare checks.
- **Power and control killers** gain satisfaction from controlling and often torturing their victims.

The problem with such classifications is that serial killers are many and varied and defy easy classification. Bundy could be deemed sexually sadistic, hedonistic, or power and control. In fact, he was all of these.

Society has always had difficulty understanding and dealing with serial offenders since their behaviors seem so far removed from the rest of society. These individuals tend to be self-centered (egocentric and narcissistic), manipulative, emotionally shallow, and devoid of empathy and remorse. They can often lie with impunity, fool even the cleverest interrogator, and occasionally pass a polygraph examination.

Serial rapists and serial killers have a great deal in common and to many are exactly the same, merely at different stages in their psychopathological derangement. Many serial killers begin as serial rapists and progress to murder to cover the crime or to increase their enjoyment.

The current thinking that these individuals cannot be reliably rehabilitated is not a new concept. In the 1930s, laws that mandated that sexual offenders be evaluated and treated by medical professionals appeared, and by the 1960s such programs existed in virtually every state. It soon became clear to those charged with treating these predators that these offenders didn't fit into the usual diagnostic categories and did not respond to the usual treatment regimens. By the 1990s, many states closed these specialized treatment centers and longer prison sentences became the norm.

What makes these types of offenders resistant to treatment?

It appears that the psychosexual pathology that drives many of these predators becomes ingrained early in life and strengthens as the individual matures through puberty and into adult life. Many, but not all, come from backgrounds of physical, psychological, and sexual abuse and attempt to insulate themselves from this abuse by creating a protective world rich in fantasy. In some, these fantasies take on sexual and violent characteristics and can simmer for years or decades before the offender begins to act them out.

There is little doubt that **fantasy** plays a powerful role in some serial offenders. Early on, his fantasies might be amorphous and benign, but as he mentally plays it out, over and over, year after year, it becomes more refined, and often sexual and violent themes commingle until they are inseparable. When the offender seeks victims, he is in fact seeking a character in his fantasy play. He looks for a certain type of person or one with a specific look. Ted Bundy sought women with dark hair, parted in the middle. This was the character he needed for his fantasy.

This points out the important fact that these fantasies tend to be very specific. The killer has spent many years creating and refining his fantasy script and knows exactly what type of person and what scenario he needs to create to fulfill his desires. These specific details are what make it possible to develop a profile of the killer. Since the fantasy is specific and repetitive, certain elements of the criminal act will be specific and repetitive. This is manifested in the killer's **signature** (see below).

I earlier mentioned the **cooling off period**. It is part of the serial killer's world but not the spree or mass murderer. The latter two types are driven by rage, and the rage continues unabated throughout their killing spree. The fantasy-driven serial killer is seeking some level of gratification and once he has completed the killing and attained gratification, he is "satisfied" for a time period. This "down time" is the cooling-off period, which might last days, weeks, months, and even years. But the fantasy continues, the desire returns, and the killer again trolls for victims.

Serial Offender Profiling

Simply stated, **offender profiling**, more an art than a science, examines the evidence and makes a best guess as to the type of individual that would commit the crime in question. The profiler will look at the crime scene, the autopsy data, the victim, and the likely pre- and post-crime behavior of the killer to make this assessment. How did the killer gain access to the victim? What did he do to the victim? Did he try to cover his tracks, and if so, how? What is it about this victim that attracted the killer? What motive or fantasy drove the killer to harm this person in this manner at this time in this location?

The offender is often termed the **unknown subject**, or **unsub** for short. It is important to note that profiling will not point to an exact individual, but rather will create a picture of the type of person who would have committed the crime. To do this, the forensic psychiatrist will assess the unsub's physical and psychological makeup, the area where he lives and/or works, and what behaviors he might have exhibited before and after the crime, and evaluate his **modus operandi (MO)** and his **signature** (both discussed later). If done properly, profiling can often help the police narrow the focus of their investigation.

Besides the usual investigative techniques, law enforcement officials have increasingly turned to criminal profiling to help track serial offenders. Since these are often "stranger" killings, the usual connections between the killer and the victim are not present. But, there is always a connection of some type. Something in the killer's psyche drives him to attack a particular victim at a particular place and at a particular time.

Criminal profiling evolved from studies done by the **FBI's Behavioral Science Unit (BSU)**, which was established in 1972. The studies included a series of jailhouse interviews with convicted serial killers and were designed to gain insight into violent criminals, and indeed certain commonalities among these types of offenders were found.

One of the basic tenets of profiling is that behavior reflects personality. How a person acts derives directly from his personality and psychological needs and fears, meaning that at a crime scene the perpetrator not only leaves behind physical evidence but also behavioral and psychiatric evidence. As John Douglas, one of the originators of profiling, says, "In order to understand an artist, you must look at the artwork." In profiling, to understand the offender (the artist) you must look at the crime scene (the artwork).

Understanding this behavioral evidence is the key to finding the perpetrator, since it often adds the critical "why" to the "how" that crime investigators have traditionally used. Analyzing the evidence offers insight into the killer's motives, his level of intelligence and sophistication, and his reasons for selecting this particular victim, which allows the profiler to estimate "what type of person" would commit this particular crime in this particular manner.

For example, serial killers often "pose" their victims. This posturing could be to shock whoever finds the body or it could be a recreation of his fantasy mental image. The pose might be degrading, angelic, or anything in between, but it typically reveals how the perpetrator feels about the victim. If he harbors a hatred for the victim or the person the victim is representing (his mother, prostitutes, or all women), the posing will reflect this and in turn will suggest the "why" of the crime.

The first major success of criminal profiling, in a mid-20th-century case known as the Mad Bomber, came long before the art of profiling came into existence.

On November 16, 1940, an unexploded bomb was found on a window ledge at the Manhattan office of Consolidated Edison, the power company known as Con Ed. An attached hand-printed note said, "Con Edison Crooks—This is for you." A year later, in September 1941, a second unexploded bomb was found. Three months later, after the Pearl Harbor attack, the bomber sent a letter to police in which he stated that out of his sense of patriotism he would send no more bombs until the war was over. Though he sent many letters over the years, no further bombs turned up until April 24, 1950, when another unexploded bomb appeared in a phone booth at the New York Public Library. Between 1951 and 1955 over a dozen bombs were set, many of which exploded, and letters from the bomber, expressing anger at Con Ed, repeatedly arrived. On December 2, 1956, a very powerful bomb exploded in Brooklyn's Paramount Theater, injuring several people. This prompted police to bring in psychiatrist Dr. James Brussel, who was known for his uncanny ability to analyze crimes and to speculate as to what type of individual could be the culprit.

After reviewing the evidence, Brussel concluded that the person responsible was a middle-aged male, who was paranoid, introverted, and held a grudge against Con Edison. He told police that the man had likely had issues with and might have been fired from the company. He was well educated, probably of Slavic decent, lived with an older female relative, and was extremely neat and meticulous in his work. He would be good with tools and when captured would be neatly dressed, likely in a double-breasted suit, buttoned.

In one letter the bomber had given the date of September 5, 1931, for an incident that had particularly enraged him. Checking Con Ed's records, police discovered that a boiler explosion at Con Ed on that date had injured George Metesky, who had subsequently written a letter of complaint to the company. When this was checked against letters from the Mad Bomber, many similar phrases appeared. When police arrested Metesky at his home, they found he was 54, of Polish extraction, unmarried, and living with two older sisters. He was also wearing a double-breasted suit, buttoned.

If actions speak to personality, then looking at the characteristics of the crime scene should offer clues to the perpetrator's mental state. One method for categorizing offenders from crime scene evidence divides them into organized, disorganized, or mixed offenders.

Organized offenders are more sophisticated and more patient, show evidence of planning, tend to be of average or better intelligence, are employed, and have social relationships such as spouses and families. Even though they are driven by their fantasies, they maintain enough control to avoid being impulsive. They prepare and even rehearse. They target specific victims, or types of victims, and use control measures such as restraints to maintain victim compliance. They bring the tools they need to gain access to and control of the victim and avoid leaving behind evidence. They hide or dispose of the body and most likely will have a "dump site" already selected.

Disorganized offenders, on the other hand, usually live alone or with a relative, possess lower than average intelligence, are unemployed or work at menial jobs, and often have mental illnesses. They have little control over their fantasies and often act impulsively. They rarely use ruses to gain the victim's confidence, but rather attack with sudden violence and overwhelm the victim. The crime scene is often messy and chaotic and shows no evidence of previous planning. They do not bring tools, but rather use whatever is handy. The body is often left at the scene and there is little attempt to avoid leaving behind evidence.

Mixed offenders possess characteristics of both types and leave behind a mixed scene. They often show evidence of planning and a sophisticated MO, but the assault itself might be frenzied or messy, indicating at least some control over deep-seated and violent fantasies.

To help standardize the profiling process, profilers developed categories of **descriptors**, which "describe" the type of individual that would perpetrate the crime. Some of these descriptors are as follows:

- **Age**: Most serial killers are in their 20s or 30s, with organized offenders tending to be older and more mature than disorganized ones.
- **Sex**: Almost all are male. Sexually sadistic serial killers are driven by fantasies, which in turn are driven by testosterone, the male sex hormone. A mixture of sexual and violent impulses is at the heart of these types of killings.
- **Race**: Most don't cross racial lines, so white offenders kill whites and black offenders kill blacks. Though not universal, this trend speaks to the specificity of the perpetrator's fantasies. He will seek out victims of a certain age, sex, and ethnicity as dictated by his personal and specific fantasies.
- **Residency**: Organized offenders might be married, have a family, and be well liked by their friends. Disorganized offenders, because of their mental instability and immaturity, tend to live alone or with a family member. Proximity of the perpetrator's home to the crime scene is also important. Disorganized offenders, because of their mental instability, tend to kill close to home because the immediate area is a comfort zone and movement out of this zone is stressful. On the other hand, organized offenders are more mobile and have a broader range. Though their first few victims might be close to home, with experience their comfort zone expands and they increase their predatory boundaries.
- **Social skills**: Those that use a ruse to ensnare their victims, as did Ted Bundy, typically possess good social skills (organized), whereas those that use a blitz-style attack are less comfortable with conversation (disorganized).
- **Work and military history**: Organized offenders often have a stable work history and are more likely to have left any military service with an honorable discharge. Disorganized offenders often have difficulty holding a job or completing military service.

- **Educational level**: Organized offenders tend to have more schooling than their disorganized counterparts, since the discipline and pressure of school is not handled well by a disorganized person.

Using these descriptors, the profiler can create a "picture" of the type of person that likely committed the crime, and this helps investigators hone in on specific suspects. Profiling also plays an important role in the interrogation of suspects since it can help investigators design questions that apply psychological pressure and hopefully unravel lies or even produce a confession.

In addition, profiling might help determine whether a crime scene has been "staged." Staging means changing the appearance of the scene so that it will look as if the murder took place in a different manner and for a different reason. For example, a husband who kills his wife in a fit of anger might empty drawers and closets, knock over furniture, and break a door lock or window to make it appear as though a burglar committed the crime. When the investigators discover that the wife was severely bludgeoned and stabbed 20 times, suspicion falls on the husband. A burglar would not engage in such overkill but rather would kill and run. Overkill is usually personal, and anger is a common underlying drive.

Trophies and Souvenirs

Criminals often take valuable objects such as money, jewels, and electronic equipment, as well as incriminating evidence, such as the murder weapon or a used condom, from the crime scene. But serial offenders tend to take objects that have no monetary or evidentiary value, but rather hold some personal meaning to them. The so-called **trophies** or **souvenirs** might be clothing, jewelry, hair, photos, and even body parts from the victim.

The terms *trophy* and *souvenir* have been used interchangeably, but differences between the two exist. The distinction lies in how the offender feels about the victim. If he views the victim as a conquest, he will view the taken object as a trophy of his triumph. When he later handles it, it will remind him of his domination of the victim. If he sees the victim as a cherished member of his fantasy, it would be a souvenir, and he will use it to relive the experience and make it part of his masturbatory fantasies.

MO Versus Signature

Modus operandi (MO) includes all the things necessary to commit the crime and get away with it. Did the perpetrator drive or walk to the scene? Did he bring weapons and tools with him or simply use what was available? Did he break a window, pry open a door, or use a ruse to gain entry or overpower the victim? Did he take things of value from the scene? Did he restrain or harm the victim? Each of these reveals his method of doing things.

It is important to point out that MO can evolve over time. As the unsub learns better ways to commit his crimes and to avoid detection, he might change his mode of entry, his ruse, his disguise, the time of his attacks, the weapon used, and any other aspect of his MO.

A **signature**, which has nothing to do with completing the crime or with getting away with it, consists of acts that are important to the offender in some very personal way. Torturing or overkill of the victim, postmortem mutilation or posing, and the taking of souvenirs or trophies are signatures. These are actions driven by the killer's psychological needs and fantasies. Unlike MO, the signature never changes. The perpetrator may refine it, but the basic signature remains unchanged. For example, if a serial killer poses his victims in a religious manner, such as praying or in a crucifixion posture, he might later add details such as candles, crucifixes, and other ceremonial objects. The details of the signature have changed, but its basic form and theme remains the same.

The stability of the signature lies in its driving force: the unsub's fantasies. These fantasies develop early in life and become refined into an obsession over years of mental reenactment. The victim is merely an actor in the play the unsub has rehearsed in his head thousands of times. His signature actions arise from this personal fantasy, and since this fantasy never changes, the signature remains intact. In the above example, the religious posing and paraphernalia are an important aspect of the killer's fantasy, the reason he committed the act in the first place, so each of his victim's will receive similar treatment.

This "signature" stability helps the profiler. Religious posing might indicate some issue with religion, church, or a priest, and this would be incorporated into his profile and help shorten the suspect list. The signature might also help link a series of crimes. If several victims are found posed, bound, mutilated, or killed in a similar manner, the investigator would search for other linking clues, since linking crime scenes is often crucial in tracking the killer, as we will see in the next case.

In 1979, the body of 26-year-old teacher Francine Elveson was found on the roof of her apartment building. She was nude and had been object-raped with a pen and an umbrella and mutilated. Her body was placed in a position that reflected the shape of the *chai* (the Jewish symbol of good luck). She was known to wear a *chai* pendant, which was missing from the scene.

The FBI profile suggested that the killer was disorganized, since there seemed to be little planning and the scene suggested a fantasy-driven murder, which meant that the killer was likely a white male, 20 to 35 years old, and unemployed. He must have also known the victim's habits and that the apartment house's roof would be private enough for him to complete his assault, murder, and escape. The ritualistic and sadistic nature of the murder and the fact that he did not rape the victim himself, but rather used objects, suggested that he was sexually inadequate and had no stable relationships with women. He likely had some form of mental illness and probably had been in a psychiatric hospital at some time.

This profile caused police to focus on Carmine Calabro, a 30-year-old, unmarried, unemployed male who often visited his father, who lived in the victim's apartment building. He was undergoing treatment at a psychiatric hospital and had been absent without permission at the time of the murder. He was convicted when his dental anatomy matched bite marks on the victim's body.

Victimology

Victims are also profiled since knowing the victim can add to the offender's profile. This is called **victimology** and is basically an assessment of the person's risk of becoming a victim as a result of her personal, professional, and social life. A detailed understanding of the victim's lifestyle and habits provides clues as to why this particular victim was selected at this location and time. Victimology divides victims into high, medium, and low risk.

- **High-risk victims** are frequently in high-risk situations. Prostitutes, particularly those that "walk the streets," typically work at night, interact with strangers on a regular basis, willingly get into cars with strangers, and, in short, are easy targets. Other high-risk behaviors include drug use, a promiscuous lifestyle, night-time employment, and associating with people who possess criminal personalities.

- **Low-risk victims** are those that stay close to work and home, don't visit areas unfamiliar to them, have a steady job and many friends, don't use drugs, and lock their doors at night.
- **Medium-risk victims** fall between these two.

Why the offender selects a particular victim is determined by both the perpetrator's fantasy needs and the victim's vulnerability. Some victims are taken because they fit a role in the perpetrator's fantasy. The offender might spend days or weeks "cruising" for the victim that most closely matches his fantasy. He will ignore other potentially easy victims because they are not "right." Here, either high- or low-risk victims can simply be in the wrong place at the wrong time, but high-risk victims place themselves in vulnerable positions much more often than do low-risk victims and so are more likely to be victims of opportunity.

Geographic Profiling

Another type of profiling is called **geographic profiling**. This is an analysis of the pattern of the perpetrator's assaults and is based on the premise that serial offenders have a certain "comfort zone" within which they feel free to carry out their crimes. The geographic profiler would like to know where the victim was abducted, where the actual assault or murder took place, and where the body was dumped. If several assaults have occurred, the profiler will have several such locations to work with. He can then locate these points on a map and define the killer's domain.

This might show that the murders are clustered in a small area, which would indicate that the killer is not very mobile and might not possess a car or have a job. Or the range might be broad, indicating that the perpetrator is highly mobile and probably possesses a vehicle with high mileage that he uses to troll for victims. Whether the range is narrow or broad, the perpetrator will likely reside or work within or near this "comfort zone."

It is also important to determine which victim was killed first. This is often straightforward, but sometimes months or years pass before dumped bodies are found, so the order of the killings is more difficult to determine.

Why is this important? The comfort zone for most serial killers usually begins small and grows over time. This means that the first victim was probably abducted close to the killer's home or workplace, and this knowledge can be crucial to identifying the killer.

Linking Criminals and Crime Scenes

Linking several crime scenes can link evidence (Chapter 3), which in turn might narrow the suspect pool. For example, if a crime scene in Phoenix is linked by signature to similar scenes in Los Angeles and Las Vegas, the evidence uncovered at each scene can be grouped. Let's say a witness in Phoenix saw a tall man leave the area in a blue van, a shoe print in Los Angeles revealed that the killer wore a certain size and model of athletic shoe, and hair found at the scene in Vegas suggested that the killer dyed his blonde hair black. Linking this evidence presents the police with a suspect who is tall, dyes his hair black, wears athletic shoes, and drives a blue van. But, how does this linkage happen?

As with the **Automated Fingerprint Identification System (AFIS)**, which allows the matching of fingerprints from various crime scenes and suspects (Chapter 13), the FBI also created other databases to deal with serial offenders. The first was the **National Center for the Analysis of Violent Crime (NCAVC)**, which serves as a repository for violent crime data throughout the country. This led to the development of the **Violent Criminal Apprehension Program (VICAP)** and **PROFILER**, which maintain profiles on serial murderers.

When an investigator is confronted with a murder or a series of murders, he can create a profile of the scene in question, enter it into the VICAP and PROFILER databases, and compare it with others from around the country. If enough similarities are found, the scenes might be the work of one killer, and the evidence from each scene can now be viewed in a different light. This linkage might the key to solving all of the crimes.

A FEW FINAL WORDS

I hope that your journey through this book was informative and fascinating and that you learned many new things and achieved a better understanding of what forensic science can and cannot do. I hope you will use these materials as a springboard to rummage through other books and around the cyber world and more fully explore the topics that struck a chord or piqued an interest in you. Most importantly, I hope you had fun. While researching and writing it, I surely did.

Visit my website at www.dplylemd.com and you'll find articles and questions from writers about all kinds of forensic topics. And if you feel so moved, drop me a note and let me know what you thought of this book.

D. P. Lyle, MD

APPENDIX: FORENSIC SCIENCE TIMELINE

Prehistory: Early cave artists and pot makers "signed" their works with a paint or impressed finger or thumbprint.

3500 BC: Mesopotamians performed animal autopsies in order to communicate with divine forces

1000 BC: Chinese used fingerprints to "sign" legal documents.

3rd Century BC: Erasistratus and Herophilus performed the first autopsies in Alexandria.

1st Century AD: Emperor Claudius identified the severed head of his mistress by recognizing her distinctive discolored tooth.

2nd Century AD: Galen, physician to Roman gladiators, dissected both animal and humans to search for the causes of disease.

Ca. 1000: Roman attorney Quintilian showed that a bloody handprint was intended to frame a blind man for his mother's murder.

1200s: First forensic autopsies done at the University of Bologna.

1247: Sung T'zu published *The Washing Away of Sins,* the first forensic text.

1276: De Officia Coronatoris, which described the coroner's duties, was published in England.

1348–1350: Pope Clement orders autopsies on victims of the Black Death to hopefully find a cause for the plague.

Late 1400s: Medical schools were established in Padua and Bologna.

1500s: Ambrose Paré wrote extensively on the anatomy of war and homicidal wounds.

1591: Hans and Zacharias Jansen designed the first crude microscope.

1604: First autopsies in North America were done by French settlers on St. Croix Island.

1609: François Demelle published the first treatise on document examination in France.

1642: University of Leipzig offered first courses in forensic medicine.

1683: Antony Van Leeuwenhoek employed a microscope to first see living bacteria, which he called animalcules.

Late 1600s: Marcello Malpighi first correlated autopsy findings to various diseases.

1685: Marcello Malpighi first recognized fingerprint patterns and used the terms “loops” and “whorls.”

1775: Paul Revere recognized dentures he had made for his friend Dr. Joseph Warren and thus identified the doctor’s body in a mass grave at Bunker Hill.

1775: Carl Wilhelm Scheele developed the first test for arsenic.

1784: In what was perhaps the first ballistic comparison, John Toms was convicted of murder based on a matching of paper wadding removed from the victim’s wound with paper found in Toms’s pocket.

1787: Johann Metzger developed a method for isolating arsenic.

1798: François-Emmanuel Fodéré published *Traité de Médecine Légale.*

1801: Andrew Duncan began lecturing on legal medicine at Edinburgh University.

1805: Friedrich Wilhelm Serturner isolates Morphine from the poppy.

1806: Valentine Rose recovered arsenic from a human body.

1810: The first use of document examination in a criminal investigation involved the analysis of ink dye on a document known as *Konigin Hanschritt* in Germany.

1813: James S. Stringham became first professor of Medical Jurisprudence in the United States.

1813: Mathieu Joseph Bonaventure Orfila published *Treatise on Poison,* the first toxicology textbook.

1821: Sevillas isolated arsenic form human stomach contents and urine, giving birth to the filed of forensic toxicology.

1823: Johannes Purkinje devised the first crude fingerprint classification system.

1835: Henry Goddard matched two bullets to show they came from the same bullet mold.

1836: Alfred Swaine Taylor developed first test for arsenic in human tissue.

1836: James Marsh developed a sensitive test for arsenic.

1850: Johann Ludwig Casper published the first color forensic pathological lithographs.

1851: Jean Servais Stas identifies vegetable poisons in corpses.

1855: Cocaine was first isolated from coca leaves.

1857: First paper on hair analysis was published in France.

1858: In Bengal, India, Sir William Herschel required natives sign contracts with a hand imprint and showed that fingerprints did not change over a 50-year period.

1862: Izaak Van Deen developed the guaiac test for blood.

1863: Schonbein developed the hydrogen peroxide test for blood.

1863: Adolf von Bayer synthesized barbituric acid.

1863: The bullet that killed General Stonewall Jackson was shown to have come from one of his own troops.

1868: Swiss biologist Friedrich Miescher discovered DNA.

1875: Wilhelm Konrad Rontgen discovered x-rays.

1875: Richard Caton proved that animal brains possessed electrical activity.

1876: Cesare Lombroso published *The Criminal Man,* which stated that criminals could be identified and classified by their physical characteristics.

1877: Medical examiner system established in Massachusetts.

1880: Henry Faulds showed that powder dusting would expose latent fingerprints.

1882: Alphonse Bertillon developed his anthropometric identification system.

1883: Mark Twain employed fingerprint identification in his books *Life on the Mississippi* and *Pudd'nhead Wilson.*

1887: England passes the Coroner's Act, which establishes the position of coroner.

1889: Alexandre Lacassagne showed that marks on bullets could be matched to those within a rifled gun barrel.

1892: Sir Francis Galton published his classic textbook, *Finger Prints.*

1892: In Argentina, Juan Vucetich devised a usable fingerprint classification system.

1892: In Argentina, Francesca Rojas became the first person charged with a crime on fingerprint evidence.

1893: Hans Gross published *Criminal Investigation* and coined the term "criminalistics."

1895: Dr. Eduard Piotrowski published his text on bloodstain pattern recognition.

1897: Herman Welcker showed his own fingerprints taken in 1897 matched those taken in 1856, thus supporting the findings of William Herschel.

1897: Paul Brouardel laid out the autopsy findings in victims of strangulation in his book *La pendaison, la strangulation, la suffocation, la submersion.*

1898: Paul Jeserich used a microscope for ballistic comparison.

1899: Sir Edward Henry devised a fingerprint classification system that is the basis for those used in Britain and America today.

1901: Karl Landsteiner delineated the ABO blood typing system.

1901: Paul Uhlenhuth devised a method to distinguish between human and animal blood.

1901: Edward Richard Henry became head of Scotland Yard and adopted a fingerprint identification system in place of anthropometry.

1902: Harry Jackson became the first person in England to be convicted by fingerprint evidence.

1903: The first systematic use of fingerprints for criminal identification in the United States began in the New York State Prison system.

1904: Oskar and Rudolf Adlar developed the benzidine test for blood.

1905: President Theodore Roosevelt established the FBI.

1910: Edmund Locard opened first forensic laboratory in Lyon, France.

1910: Thomas Jennings became the first United States citizen convicted of a crime by use of fingerprints.

1910: Hans Gross published *Criminal Psychology.*

1912: Masaeo Takayama developed a microcrystalline test for blood hemoglobin.

1912: Ecstasy was first manufactured.

1913: Victor Balthazard published his belief that each fired bullet carried unique marks.

1915: Leone Lattes develops method for ABO typing dried bloodstains.

1915: State of New York adopted medical examiner system.

1920: Physicist John Fisher invented the helixometer.

1920: The Sacco and Vanzetti case brought ballistics to the public's attention.

1923: Los Angeles Police Chief August Vollmer established the first forensic laboratory.

1923: The Bureau of Forensic Ballistics was established in New York City.

1923: *Frye v. United States* set standards for the admission of scientific evidence into U.S. courtrooms.

1924: Willem Einthoven invented the electrocardiogram (EKG).

1924: Hans Berger invented the electroencephalograph (EEG), the first objective test of human brain activity.

1925: Philip Gravelle and Calvin Goddard developed the comparison microscope.

1926: The Sacco and Vanzetti Case highlighted the value of the newly developed comparison microscope.

1929: The ballistic analyses used to solve the famous St. Valentine's Day Massacre in Chicago lead to the establishment of the Scientific Crime Detection Laboratory (SCDL), the first independent crime lab, at Northwestern University.

1931: John Glaister published his landmark book on hair analysis.

1932: FBI's forensic laboratory established.

1939: The FBI Bulletin published W. H. Krogman's seminal article on examining skeletal remains, bringing the field of anthropology to the world of forensic Investigation.

1943: Avery, Macleod, and McCarty discovered that DNA carried genetic information.

1953: Watson, Crick, and Wilkins identified DNA's double-helical structure.

1954: Indiana State Police Captain R. F. Borkenstein developed the Breathalyzer.

1954: Human bite mark evidence first entered a United States courtroom in *Doyle v. Texas.*

1971: William Bass established The Body Farm at the University of Tennessee in Knoxville.

1972: The American Academy of Forensic Sciences established the Physical Anthropology Section.

1974: Detection of Gunshot residue by SEM/EDS developed.

1977: FBI instituted the Automated Fingerprint Identification System (AFIS).

1978: ESDA developed by Freeman and Foster.

1984: Sir Alec Jeffreys developed the DNA "fingerprint" technique.

1987: In England, Colin Pitchfork became the first criminal identified by the use of DNA.

1987: First U.S. use of DNA for a conviction in the Florida case of Tommy Lee Andrews.

1990: Congress established the Federal Medical examiner's Office in the Armed Forces Institute of Pathology.

1990: The Combined DNA Index System (CODIS) was established.

1992: The Polymerase Chain Reaction (PCR) technique was introduced.

1993: *Daubert v. Merrell Dow* established new rules for the admission of scientific evidence into the courtroom and altered the Frye Rules set in 1923.

1994: The analysis of short tandem repeats (STRs) was introduced.

1996: Mitochondrial DNA first admitted into a U.S. court in *Tennessee v. Ware.*

1998: The National DNA Index System (NDIS) became operational.

INDEX

Note: page numbers followed by *f* indicate figures.

B

C

D

E

F

H

I

M

P

T

U

V

ABOUT THE AUTHOR

D. P. Lyle, MD is the Macavity Award winning and Edgar? Award nominated author of many non-fiction books (*Murder & Mayhem; Forensics for Dummies; Forensics & Fiction; More Forensics and Fiction; and Howdunnit: Forensics*) as well as numerous works of fiction, including the Samantha Cody thriller series (*Devil's Playground* and *Double Blind*); the Dub Walker Thriller series (*Stress Fracture; Hot Lights, Cold Steel,* and *Run to Ground*); and the Royal Pains media tie-in novels (*Royal Pains: First, Do No Harm* and *Royal Pains: Sick Rich*). His essay on Jules Verne's *The Mysterious Island* appears in *Thrillers: 100 Must-Reads* and his short story "Even Steven" will appear in ITW's anthology *Thriller 3: Love is Murder.*

He has worked with many novelists and with the writers of popular television shows such as Law & Order, CSI: Miami, Diagnosis Murder, Monk, Judging Amy, Peacemakers, Cold Case, House, Medium, Women's Murder Club, 1-800-Missing, The Glades, and Pretty Little Liars.

He was born and raised in Huntsville, Alabama, where his childhood interests revolved around football, baseball, and building rockets in his backyard. The latter pursuit was common in Huntsville during the 1950s and 60s due to the nearby NASA/Marshall Space Flight Center.

After leaving Huntsville, he attended college, medical school, and served an internship at the University of Alabama; followed by a residency in Internal Medicine at the University of Texas at Houston; then a Fellowship in Cardiology at The Texas Heart Institute, also in Houston. For the past 30 years, he has practiced Cardiology in Orange County, California.

Website: http://www.dplylemd.com/
Blog: http://writersforensicsblog.wordpress.com/